The Necromantic State

The Necromantic State

Spectral Remains in
the Afterglow of Venezuela's
Bolivarian Revolution

IRINA R. TROCONIS

DUKE UNIVERSITY PRESS
Durham and London
2025

© 2025 DUKE UNIVERSITY PRESS
All rights reserved
Project Editor: Ihsan Taylor
Designed by A. Mattson Gallagher
Typeset in Minion Pro and Source Sans 3
by Westchester Publishing Services

Library of Congress Cataloging-in-Publication Data
Names: Troconis, Irina R., [date] author.
Title: The necromantic state : spectral remains in the afterglow of
Venezuela's Bolivarian revolution / Irina R. Troconis.
Description: Durham : Duke University Press, 2025. | Includes
bibliographical references and index.
Identifiers: LCCN 2024026376 (print)
LCCN 2024026377 (ebook)
ISBN 9781478031079 (paperback)
ISBN 9781478026822 (hardcover)
ISBN 9781478060055 (ebook)
Subjects: LCSH: Chávez Frías, Hugo—Influence. | Ghosts in popular
culture—Venezuela. | Politics and culture—Venezuela. | Political
culture—Venezuela. | Collective memory—Political aspects—
Venezuela. | Venezuela—Politics and government—1999- | BISAC:
SOCIAL SCIENCE / Ethnic Studies / Caribbean & Latin American
Studies |SOCIAL SCIENCE / Anthropology / Cultural & Social
Classification: LCC F2329 .T76 2025 (print) | LCC F2329 (ebook) |
DDC 306.20987—dc23/eng/20241216
LC record available at https://lccn.loc.gov/2024026376
LC ebook record available at https://lccn.loc.gov/2024026377

Cover art: Remnants of campaign posters of Venezuelan
president Hugo Chávez on a wall in Caracas, January 7, 2013.
REUTERS / Jorge Silva.

Unless otherwise noted, the photographs in this book were taken by
the author.

PUBLICATION OF THIS BOOK HAS BEEN AIDED BY A
GRANT FROM THE HULL MEMORIAL PUBLICATION FUND
OF CORNELL UNIVERSITY.

A los míos

CONTENTS

ACKNOWLEDGMENTS

In the many years of working on this project, I have been scared, plagued with self-doubt, and ready to throw away, in an instant, every word I ever wrote. I have also been excited, amused, and deeply moved. More importantly, I have never been alone. You, all of you whose generosity will always make these acknowledgments fall short: you are the reason this book exists. Because of you, I found the strength and the courage to write about ghosts, and to do so with my mind and with my heart. I will forever be happily haunted by the immense debt of gratitude I owe you.

I extend my thanks to Diana Taylor, not only for her invaluable advice, but also for opening my eyes to the infinite and wonderful possibilities of performance. To Jo Labanyi for her excitement, her mentorship, and for teaching me that perfectionism is just another word for cowardice. To Gabriel Giorgi for his guidance and the many laughs we have shared throughout the years. To Gabriela Basterra and Laura Torres-Rodríguez for believing in this project when it was just a paragraph on a page, and for still believing in it now, three hundred pages later. To Luis Duno-Gottberg for his kindness and for helping me see this project with new eyes.

To Tess Rankin for her incredible job editing my messy sentences and translating all the quotes, and for the gift of her friendship. You have been with me every step of the way, in the highs and in the lows, reading every word of this manuscript—more than five times (!)—with care and love. I hope that you are proud of what we have accomplished.

To Gisela Fosado, Alejandra Mejía, Ihsan Taylor, and the entire editorial and production teams at Duke University Press, for their trust, their support, and their guidance. You have made this journey a truly enjoyable experience. My thanks go out as well to the anonymous reviewers for their enthusiastic feedback, which helped me significantly improve this manuscript.

To Andrew Ascherl, for making sense of everything and turning it into such an elegant index.

To Zeb Tortorici, colleague, mentor, and friend, for believing in what I do and how I do it. You know that this would not have been possible without everything you have taught me.

To Deborah Castillo for giving me access to her wonderful world, and for encouraging me to write about it. To Violette Bule, Ana Alenso, and Adriana Rondón-Rivero for the gift of their art and the hope it carries.

To Erwin Vásquez for the many risks he took while driving me around Caracas.

To Moisés Troconis and Lisbeth Troconis for hunting ghosts with me.

To Diómedes Cordero, Germán Carrera Damas, Tulio Hernández, Wagner Barreto, and Alfredo Angulo for their feedback and for the many books I carried back with me to New York that summer of 2016.

To everyone in Venezuela who took time out of their lives to chat with me, argue with me, travel with me, show me new things, and who, in doing all of that, helped me feel less of a stranger in my own country.

An outstanding group of colleagues and friends read parts of this manuscript and offered many helpful comments and suggestions. Thank you Osdany Morales, Francisco Marguch, Rafael Cesar, Cristina Colmena, and Michel Otayek, for being my first readers and the best cohort anyone could ever ask for. Thank you to Paul Fleming and to the "Afterlives" fellows at Cornell's Society for the Humanities for their brilliant insights and for being an endless source of inspiration. Thank you Ioana Luca and Claudia Sadowski-Smith for the opportunity to collaborate with you and for helping me figure out what this book was really about: you are extraordinary editors. Thank you, Raj Murali, for reminding me why I do what I do.

I was able to articulate the ideas that ground this book and the methodology that frames it because I had two role models whose work has inspired my own since the early years of my career. Thank you to Alicia Ríos for *Nacionalismos banales*, and to Javier Guerrero for *Tecnologías del cuerpo*.

Thank you both for your friendship, your infinite patience, and your always honest and careful reading.

Rafael Sánchez: you left us too soon, and I will never stop missing you and hoping to have one more conversation with you. Thank you for your brilliance and your kindness. Your work made everything make sense and will continue to inspire generations of Venezuelan scholars.

Writing about Venezuela, my home, has never been easy. To do it, I have relied on the friendship of other Venezuelans and Venezuelanists who have always been there, first row, cheering me on. Thank you Manuel Silva-Ferrer, Magdalena López, Vicente Lecuna, Juan Pablo Lupi, Alejandro Castro, Rebeca Pineda-Burgos, Elena Cardona, Víctor García Ramírez, Miguel Vásquez, Alejandro Velasco, Eleonora Cróquer Pedrón, Katie Brown, Robert Samet, Beatriz González-Stephan, Waleska Solórzano, Nicole Fung, Gabriel Muñoz, Raquel Rivas Rojas, Gina Saraceni, Gustavo Guerrero, Santiago Acosta, Elizabeth Barrios, Carlos Colmenares Gil, Noraedén Mora Méndez, Juan Cristóbal Castro, Víctor Rivas, Johann Kirchenbauer, Lorena Velásquez, Omar Osorio-Amoretti, and María Teresa Veras Rojas. Thank you for sharing the burden and the joy.

Cornell University has given me many things, but nothing as precious as the support of my colleagues in the Department of Romance Studies. My thanks go to all of you, for endorsing the crazy projects and initiatives that have fed this book in the last five years. A special shout-out goes to Edmundo Paz-Soldán, for believing in me from the very beginning. Liliana Colanzi and Patricia Keller, for the love of ghosts that always brings us together. Simone Pinet, for asking the best questions. Julia Chang, for her generosity and care. Carolyn Fornoff and Vanessa Gubbins, for so many therapy sessions with fries and wine. Imane Tehrmina, for her infinite support in the shape of cat memes and coffee runs. Karen Pinkus, for being a truly caring mentor. Debra Castillo, for her brilliance and her guidance. Laurent Dubreuil and Laurent Ferri, for always making me laugh. Cecelia Lawless, for *estar pendiente*. Mary K. Redmond, Thierry Torea, Silvia Amigo-Silvestre, Ewa Bachminska, Tomás and Mónica Beviá, Irene Eibenstein-Alvisi, Denise Osborne, Brisa Teutli, Alice McAdams, Itziar Rodríguez de Rivera, Emilia Illana Mahiques, and Macarena Tejada López for so much kindness. To Carolyn Keller, Mary Beth Martini-Lyons, Rob van Brunt, Katy Kempf, Marcus May, Alicia Rhodes, Callean Hile, Dorothy Lovelace, and Haley Evanoski, for making magic happen every day.

I have had the immense privilege of teaching a kind and brilliant group of students throughout my career who have been, often without knowing, my source of inspiration. I extend my thanks to the graduate students in the Department of Romance Studies for so many illuminating conversations, for their dedication, and for *tanto cariño*. I want to recognize, in particular, the support of André Nascimento and Stephanie López, who started with me at Cornell, and who now are off to begin their own careers as professors. I also want to recognize the students who had to endure my first hybrid graduate seminar on memory and who have been my anchor ever since: Isabel Calderón Reyes, Roberto Ibáñez Ricouz, Federico Giordano Perla, Lu Han, Ashley Edlund-Chescheir, Lilly Schaber, and Arturo Ruiz Mautino. A special shout-out also goes to Waleska Solórzano, Gina Goico, Tabaré Azcona, Rosamaría Durán, Lena Sow, and Montse Chenyun Li.

Every course I have taught at Cornell has informed, in one way or the other, the ideas in this book. However, my deepest debt of gratitude goes to the students in my "Oil, Ghosts, and Beauty Queens" course, and in my "Specters of Latin America" course. I hope you know that, when I wrote this, it was you I was talking to all along.

To my Ithaca family: Amal El-Ghazaly, Leila Wilmers, Andrew Musser, Cindy Kao, Bo-Jhang Ho, Janet Loebach, Andrew Campana, Ivanna Yi, Cristina Florea, Erik Born, David Bateman, Jonathan Branfman, Katie Mann, and Marten van Schijndel. To my brilliant and supportive interlocutors: Eunjung Kim, Nagore Sedano, and María Edurne Zuazu Bermejo. To Begüm Adalet: I keep running out of ways to thank you for so, so much.

To the incomparable professors who taught me to think the way I do, and the incomparable friends who supported me throughout that first journey into academia: Ilan Stavans, Paul Rockwell, Rosalina de la Carrera, Lawrence Douglas, Martha Umphrey, Nasser Hussain, Anjali Anand, Ian Mellis, Jean Santos, Sadie Casamenti, and Ambika Kammath. I also extend my thanks to Amherst College for the John Woodruff Simpson Fellowship for the study of Latin America, which allowed me to travel to Venezuela and conduct the research for this project.

My family is my world, and no words could ever express how thankful I am for them. But I keep trying. Thank you, Mary Barboza de González, my beloved ghost. I miss you always, and I hope I have made you proud. Moisés Troconis, Iris González de Troconis, Eileen Troconis, Justin Goot, Apollo, Eclipse, and Panda: thank you for being the reason behind everything good and everything worthy that I do. Thank you for a love that knows no bounds, and for being, each of you in your own way, my heroes.

Dorian Miron: I simply would not be here without you. You have been, for what now feels like a lifetime, my rock, my light, my north, the force that has gotten me through my worst moments, and the love that makes every joy a hundred times more joyful. I feel so lucky that I get to spend the rest of my days thinking of new ways to tell you how much I love you. For now, I will just simply say: this is for you.

Last, but certainly not least, thank you, reader, for giving this book a home. Whether I know you or not, I am thrilled and honored to share this ghost h(a)unting journey with you.

And so it begins.

Tess Rankin did all the translations included in this book, with financial support from the Humanities Research Grant awarded by the Society for the Humanities at Cornell University in 2023.

Introduction

The Necromantic State

If he loves justice at least, the "scholar" of the future, the "intellectual" of tomorrow should learn it in and from the ghost. He should learn to live by learning not how to make conversation with the ghost but how to talk with him, with her, how to let them speak or how to give them back speech, even if it is in oneself, in the other, in the other in oneself: they are always there, specters, even if they do not exist, even if they are no longer, even if they are not yet. They give us to rethink the "there" as soon as we open our mouths.

Jacques Derrida, *Specters of Marx*

Similarly, in the city, everything that has happened in some lane, in some piazza, in some street, on some sidewalk along a canal, in some back alley is suddenly condensed and crystallized into a figure that is at once labile and exigent, mute and winking, resentful and distant. Such figure is the specter or genius of the place.

Giorgio Agamben, "On the Uses and
Disadvantages of Living among Specters"

Dead Man Walking

On the night of December 8, 2016, a ghost walked among the residents of the central and western areas of Caracas (figure I.1). Tall, ethereal, and luminous, he walked with determination, accompanied by the pulse of an upbeat song that made his haunting entertaining rather than frightening. From the streets, he jumped on top of the Panteón Nacional, the building holding the sacred remains of the heroes of the nation, and moved to the Liberator's Mausoleum, home to Simón Bolívar's remains. There, his ghostly body disappeared, leaving behind only the magnified features of his face: the all-too-familiar face of Hugo Chávez, popularly known as "the colossus, giant, light, supreme, guiding, unique, immense, saintly, undefeated, superior, eternal, immortal, celestial, universal, galactic leader" (Barrera Tyszka 2015, 195) of the Bolivarian Revolution. Challenging the finitude of his death, he addressed his people once again: fragments of the last speech he gave in December 2012 played as the soundtrack to a sequence of photographs that showed him alongside his successor, Nicolás Maduro. Those who missed the "live" spectacle of Chávez's ghostly return could witness it online by following the hashtag #PlenoComoLaLunaLlena created by Ernesto Villegas, then the country's minister of popular power for communication and information, who proudly announced on Twitter that a "luminous" Chávez was walking around Caracas.[1]

Chávez's specter was in fact a hologram made with video mapping. Unlike highly sophisticated holograms that hover above the ground seemingly disconnected from the technology that created them, Chávez's hologram was shamelessly rustic: no effort was made to conceal the vehicle that projected it from the street, and his movements were repetitive and simple. As a result, no one seemed shocked or scared at the sight of it. This was not an uncanny apparition unexpectedly showing up to demand a wrong be righted, but the latest iteration of a familiar encounter with a familiar figure. Perhaps

I.1   Chávez's hologram in Caracas. Taken from Colombeia TV 2016.

the most noteworthy emotional reaction to this encounter—other than that of Villegas, who excitedly narrated the ghost's journey on Twitter—was the anger of those who saw this as just another example of the government wasting resources that could be used to alleviate the country's dire economic crisis. Beyond the content of this critique, what is most interesting is what it implies about Chávez's ghost: that it was an expense, a production, a haunting staged and narrated by a state unafraid of taking magic at face value, confident in its belief in ghosts because, well, it could actually *make* them.

This literal, in-your-face, state-manufactured ghost complicates a critical understanding of the ghostly that, in the context of Latin America and particularly since the 1990s, has seen apparitions, ghosts, and specters as uncanny and subversive forces that make us aware of contemporary society's blind spots and of injustices from recent and distant pasts, and that threaten to unsettle the status quo in the name of better, more just futures. Chávez's ghost does not return from oblivion with vengeful determination to unsettle the status quo. If anything, it seems to do the opposite: ensure that things stay, at least in appearance, exactly as they are and as they were when he was alive, and remind everyone who encounters him that he is still there, too animated and too visible to be actually, fully dead.

His spectral presence is evidence of a temporal reality that does not fit so easily into narratives of temporal breaks that have taken place on a continent that has lived through numerous dictatorships, armed conflicts, and revolutions. Transitions, postdictatorship periods, and, more generally, the recognition that a break, however messy, happened and something new or seemingly new began, reflect ways of understanding time that do not accurately capture the state Venezuela found itself in after Chávez's death. This state is an affectively charged atmosphere—an "afterglow"—of temporal overlaps, political irresolution, and social tensions marked by the stubborn lingering of a past that is at times barely noticeable and at times overwhelmingly present, and that draws our attention and anchors our body and our gaze to the haunted ground where Chávez's specter materializes as a hologram and, as we will see in the following chapters, as things as diverse as a doll, a tattoo, and an omnipresent pair of watchful eyes.

Rather than thinking of that ground—the "there" that Jacques Derrida mentions in the epigraph—as a decontextualized, strictly metaphorical space, Chávez's specter demands that we think of it as a material space where the specter is a presence imbued with political authority, affective purchase, and social dynamism. It also demands that, as scholars, we consider what it means to, in Derrida's terms, "talk to the ghost and let the ghost talk back" when the ghost is not a rhetorical figure, but something—an object, an image—that occupies the same space that we do at the same time. In other words, something that haunts us as we attempt to write about haunting; something that makes it impossible to write about ghosts without writing with them.

The Necromantic State: Spectral Remains in the Afterglow of Venezuela's Bolivarian Revolution is about writing about and with ghosts as much as it is about Chávez's spectral afterlife. My analysis of this afterlife is set in a Venezuela caught in a present that began in 2013 with Chávez's death and that has yet to see a definite ending, for Chávez's haunting, like all hauntings, is ongoing. This period—ten years and counting—has seen the consolidation of an economic, political, and humanitarian crisis unprecedented in the country's modern history.[2] It has also seen an accumulation of objects, images, and performances, which I refer to as Chávez's spectral remains, that infuse the presence of the "Comandante Eterno" (Bastidasa 2022) in public, private, and virtual spaces with dynamism and an ordinary yet powerful sort of magic.

At its core, this book is, in Kathleen Stewart's words, "an experiment, not a judgement" (2007, 1). It is not a judgment in that it does not offer a final verdict on the achievements and failures of the Bolivarian Revolution or of Chávez himself. Many books do, grounded in the authors' expertise in economics, political science, anthropology, sociology, and history—all fields in which groundbreaking work on contemporary Venezuela has been done in the last two decades.[3] This book is instead an experiment in what I propose to call "ghost h(a)unting": a methodological approach grounded in interdisciplinary constellations that juxtapose and merge affect theory, performance studies, memory studies, cultural studies, and media studies; that treats the ghost as a material, social, and political figure rather than as a metaphor; that captures the simultaneous experience of hunting down ghosts and being haunted by them; and that allows us to critically engage with that which remains unresolved and is happening "in the now."

It is also an experiment in conceptualizing the state as a performer, identifying and analyzing how a state might perform its power, ground its legitimacy, and perpetuate its authority through neither violence nor bureaucracy but through ordinary, affective, and often intimate acts of creativity, imagination, and—in the specific case of contemporary Venezuela—necromancy.[4] These acts are not awe-inspiring spectacles staged for a passive people to respond with applause or paralysis. They are staged *with* people in a process of cocreation that turns conjuring up ghosts into a collective endeavor that can be empowering but can also circumscribe political imagination, neutralize popular resistance, and limit the vocabularies available to articulate alternative understandings of authority, subjectivity, the power of the past, and the urgency of the future.

With this approach, *The Necromantic State* departs significantly from two scholarly trends that have shaped the academic analysis of the Bolivarian Revolution: the state- and/or Chávez-centered approach, and the history-from-below approach. The former includes works focused on Chávez himself, underscoring his populist, authoritarian, charismatic, and heroic characteristics; and scholarship centered on the operations of the Bolivarian state, most recently in connection with Maduro's regime.[5] The latter includes works that center the people in the social movements, community organizing, political activism, alternative economic practices, and cultural production emerging in the barrios, where various popular groups have shifting relationships with state institutions, defined neither by unquestioning obedience nor pure confrontation.[6] These "histories from below" reveal the contours of a revolution that was in the making long before Chávez arrived in power and that promised to continue without him if necessary (Ciccariello-Maher 2013, 21). Taken together, these works create a picture of Venezuela during the Bolivarian Revolution riddled with tensions, with the state and the people often at odds.

This book does not follow these paths. It is not a book about Chávez; it is about Chávez's *specter*. It is not a book about the achievements and shortcomings of the Bolivarian state; it is about the creative, theatrical, and playful operations that allow a state to conjure the dead and mobilize spectral power when the state's authority and legitimacy are in crisis. And it is not a book about the people, an anthropological account of how popular groups choose to remember Chávez. It is instead a book about the spectral remains that populate the space the people routinely traverse and occupy—spectral stuff that demands and shapes behaviors and forms of creative labor, that gives material weight and visibility to certain political vocabularies, making them omnipresent and compelling in ways that, I argue, run the risk of placing invisible yet sturdy confines on popular imaginative acts that rehearse alternative political and social futures and alternative forms of relationality. Focusing on this stuff means renouncing an attempt to identify exactly where the state ends and where civil society begins, and letting the binaries state/people, power/resistance, and even *chavismo/oposición* combust—if only for a little while—so we can explore public participation in the perpetuation of state power, and examine the work the people and the state do together that creates norms of worldly existence that are internalized as common sense.

Critically engaging with Chávez's specter allows us to consider the relationship between stately matters and ghostly matters, magic and new technologies, and haunting and political imagination, both in the broader context of the modern state—a state that, Michael Taussig notes, is always "lusting in its spirited magnificence, hungry for soulstuff" (Levi Strauss and Taussig 2005)—and in the specific context of contemporary Venezuela, where the state is "hungry for soulstuff" *and also* trapped in an unprecedented sociopolitical crisis of national and continental implications. This oscillation between the abstract and the concrete, the speculative and the factual, demands a renewal of the vocabularies we have developed to talk about specters, and to classify the everyday nature of our relationship with the male salvific heroes we stubbornly yearn for in Venezuela and elsewhere. Thus, this introduction presents the terms that will be fundamental throughout the book to understand the operations of Chávez's specter and the magical state (and the magical people) that conjures it, and the methodology I have developed to analyze those operations: necromancy, spectral remains, afterglow, and ghost h(a)unting. These terms are inspired by the vast scholarship on the cult of Bolívar developed by numerous Venezuelan historians (Germán Carrera Damas, Luis Castro Leiva, Ana Teresa Torres, Alicia Ríos, Elías Pino Iturrieta, and Rafael Sánchez), Michael Taussig's theorization of the magic of the state, Jacques Derrida's conceptualization of specters, and Avery Gordon's groundbreaking sociological study of ghostly matters. However, I take this vocabulary of specters, magic, haunting, and the state in new theoretical directions not so much in an effort to identify a new problem but rather to see an old problem in a new way, a task that became urgent the night that Venezuela's most notable dead, tired of the cold stillness of monuments and graves, got up and started walking. *Literally.*

Bolívar, Reloaded

In the early hours of July 16, 2010, Chávez announced on Twitter that Bolívar's remains had been exhumed as part of an investigation that had been initiated, at his request, into whether Bolívar had died of tuberculosis—as historians had asserted throughout the years—or had in fact been poisoned. His tweets read: "Hello, my friends! What amazing moments we've experienced tonight!! We've seen the remains of the great Bolívar! With Neruda, I said: Our Father who art in the earth, in the water, and in the air, you awaken every one hundred years when the pueblo awakens," and then, "I admit that we've cried, we've sworn. I tell you: that glorious skeleton must be Bolívar, you can feel the flame burning in him" (López 2010).

The commission in charge of the exhumation was led by the then vice president Elías Jaua. It took over nineteen hours for Bolívar's coffin to be opened. The numerous cameras recording the event for national and international media outlets showed a group of forensic experts dressed in white sterile suits working ceremoniously to finally reveal the Liberator's body to the sound of the national anthem playing on a continuous loop.[7] It was an uncanny, jarring spectacle: an odd overlap of nationalism and forensics, of religious fervor and scientific rigor, of military rituals and archeological work, of new sterile suits and old dusty bones, of death and life. This last overlap—dead Bolívar and living Bolívar—framed Chávez's tweets and the speech he gave when the exhumation was televised to the Venezuelan people: "Let us not see him as dead, no. Bolívar returned when our people awoke, to paraphrase Pablo Neruda. Let us see these hollows in the skull as eyes that watch us and that from the beyond or from here . . . Bolívar is alive, let us not see him as a dead man, let us not see him as a skeleton, he is like a bolt of lightning, like a sacred flame" (Apolinar Rea 2010).

"Bolívar is alive. Let us not see him as dead, as a skeleton." A difficult command given that, thanks to the exhumation, Bolívar's bones were *right there*, displayed for everyone to see, and yet one that is remarkably easy to comply with in a country where national identity, cultural values, and political practice have historically been anchored in what Germán Carrera Damas called "the cult of Bolívar." In his groundbreaking book *El culto a Bolívar*, Carrera Damas explains how this cult permeates every aspect of Venezuelan identity, and how it has become an instrument of both political legitimation and political manipulation. He defines it as "the complex historical-ideological formation that has allowed values derived from the figure of the hero to be projected on all aspects of the life of a people" (Carrera Damas [1969] 1973, 21) and ties the need for its emergence and endurance to its having been transformed "[into] an aspect of national unity, in defense of the principle of order; into an aspect of government, as a guiding force behind political inspiration; and into an aspect of national advancement, as the religion of the moral and civic perfection of a people"(43). The cult has led Bolívar to become the ultimate national hero: his qualities, enhanced by the religious admiration his figure awakens, represent the very best of the Venezuelan people, and his accomplishments on the political stage and on the battlefield have set the tone and the goals for every political project and every political leader since his death.[8]

Carrera Damas's work was the first to offer a critical reflection on the Venezuelan nation and people's relationship with the figure of Bolívar, a relationship that, from then on, would be studied in those terms, as a cult.[9] This framing illuminated not only the relationship's religious undertones— which in turn emphasized its peculiar excess—but also its manipulative nature: how politicians had transformed a cult that had originally come *from* the people into a cult *for* the people to generate support for their political agendas. This distinction was further developed by anthropologist Yolanda Salas de Lecuna in *Bolívar y la historia en la conciencia popular* (1987), where she discusses how the hero's life and deeds are narrated in popular history and oral tradition. Salas de Lecuna shows how in the streets, in the countryside, and on Sorte Mountain, Bolívar is sometimes the son of a Black woman, sometimes the reincarnation of Indigenous leader Guaicaipuro, and sometimes as powerful as Jesus Christ; he is almost always endowed with magical powers that come alive in places like Sorte, where practitioners of the cult of María Lionza communicate with his spirit and seek his advice and help.[10]

The spiritual invocation of Bolívar in these peripheral spaces has an equally powerful state-organized counterpart in public spaces like plazas, schools, municipal buildings, and public offices. There, Bolívar is not just present; he is *omnipresent*, a fact that Michael Taussig masterfully captures in *The Magic of the State*:

His image is everywhere, a controlled frenzy of kitsch across the cultured landscape, the bridges, the bus stops, the money, cigar wrappers . . . not to mention his statue centering every hamlet, village, town and city nailing it to the earth just as his horse spreads its wings skywards. . . . There can be no better form of expression of the culture of the official than the blank nothingness of the eyes looking out at the populace in a conspiracy of silence that it's all a game, a stupid, necessary, terrible, and unholy game. One day he'll wink. The day after we're dead. (Taussig 1997, 112)

This habitual exposure to Bolívar influences how past, present, and future are understood and narrated. As Alicia Ríos points out, "the material and symbolic monument that is erected around the father of the nation capitalizes on social forces and is constructed at the heart of not only the nation's origin story but, above all, of stories about the nation's future" (2013, 35). Bolívar becomes, as she argues, not only somebody who once existed and continues to exist but also someone who is always "about to arrive" (35). Another consequence of this exposure is that Bolívar becomes a unifying force capable of neutralizing, at least in principle, conflicts and differences among the people/his children. As Rafael Sánchez notes:

The ongoing goal is the saturation of Venezuela's public spaces with as many Bolívar-mirrors—busts, equestrian monuments, oversized portraits—as possible, so that, whenever the need arises, the nation's heterogeneous majorities may be wrested from their dangerous wanderings and, through reflection, made to coalesce in front of those mirrors as a mobilized Bolivarian "people." (Sánchez 2016, 294)

However, Bolívar's power as a unifying figure short-circuited following the night of June 16, 2010, when the exhumation of his remains led to the creation of a new portrait of the Liberator. In 2012, a digital portrait of Bolívar was released to celebrate his 229th birthday with a few but noticeable modifications to the traditional image that had been reproduced in paintings and on the country's currency. The new Bolívar—the "true" one, according to Chávez—was not shockingly different from the old one. His hair seemed curlier, his skin darker, his cheekbones fuller, and his eyes smaller, but, overall, the most unsettling effect came from seeing him as a digital creation, almost too humanlike, too "fleshy," when compared with his likeness that for over a century was based on oil paintings and nineteenth-century portraits. Nevertheless, the fact that, from then on, Chávez would often appear next to the new portrait—which came to be known as "Chávez's Bolívar"—led to a sort of blurring of features that made it impossible not to start seeing similarities between the two men: not to wonder whether, in fact, Bolívar (reloaded) was supposed to look like Chávez. If so, the portrait would be the climactic culmination of the intimate relationship Chávez had built with Bolívar, one that until then had been rhetorical and performative and that included acts such as Chávez mimicking Bolívar's "Juramento del Monte Sacro" in his "Juramento del Samán de Güere," leaving an empty chair for Bolívar's spirit to oversee the meetings of the members of the MBR–200, repeatedly delivering public addresses to the nation with a portrait of Bolívar near him, and appearing in rudimentary collages that combined his face and Bolívar's body.[11] This time, it was not an overlap but a *fusion* of the two: a continuity performed in the flesh that brought them together as one, that tied Bolívar inextricably to the Bolivarian Revolution so there was no Bolívar left outside it, and that thus further deepened the antagonism of an opposition that was left Bolívar-less.[12]

To be left like that, without Bolívar, was of course unacceptable, and the opposition responded to Chávez's Bolívar with their own Bolívar, which recuperated his likeness from the traditional portrait. What followed was a battle of Bolívars that unfolded most evidently in public buildings—their political affiliation represented by which of the two portraits was displayed—and that carried on after Chávez's death in 2013. At the inauguration of the opposition-led Asamblea Nacional in January 2016, for example, Henry Ramos Allup ordered workers to remove the portraits of Chávez's Bolívar (and of Chávez himself) that adorned the building and replace them with the old ones. Five years later, as the majority in the assembly became once again *chavista*, the discarded portraits were marched back into the building in a procession that was part of a public ceremony in Caracas's Plaza Bolívar and that included a man dressed like Bolívar passionately reciting one of his speeches (figure I.2).

As we watch the video of this procession and notice the deputies of the assembly gathering behind political figures like Diosdado Cabello (former president of the assembly) and Maduro's wife Cilia Flores (first lady) as they hold the framed portraits of Chávez and (the new) Bolívar, who look like they too are moving, gently swaying from side to side, we cannot help but think of Ana Teresa Torres's reflection on the animated and lively nature

INICIA NUEVA ERA POLÍTICA EN VENEZUELA

I.2   Portraits of Chávez and Bolívar returning to the building of the Asamblea Nacional. Taken from LBRV 2021.

of Venezuela's male salvific heroes, so stubborn in their determination to stay undead:

> But Venezuelan heroes do not rest in the National Pantheon; instead, they roam free. They leap from their canvases and land on the asphalt, dodging cars, they introduce themselves into the internet, they are the protagonists of the press and television, and they threaten us with their omnipresence. . . . "We won't die," they seem to say. "It doesn't matter what you do to make us disappear, or how much time has passed; we will resist." (Torres 2009, 11–12)

Torres's words capture the sort of animation that characterizes the ghost and the omnipresence that turns the occasional apparition of the ghost into an ongoing state of haunting. They also underscore something else: the importance of technology, particularly of new technologies and the internet, in facilitating this animation, in making the omnipresence of the ghost feel lively in a way that departs from the monumental, stable, and stale omnipresence of statues and busts. The ghost here is often an e-ghost: a ghost that is not only animated by the use of technology but that goes viral, blurring the lines between private and public, seeming current in a way no monument could, seeming alive in a way that the cult of Bolívar—outside peripheral spaces—could not conceive of.

This technological force is one element that made Chávez's relationship with Bolívar stand out in a long history where every president before him was also, in one way or another, Bolivarian. As Ríos argues, "Chávez relies considerably on the media to promote his ideas and outlook, he uses the most advanced marketing campaigns to 'sell' his revolution, in addition to having initially benefitted from the so-called anti-politics" (2013, 88–89). It was then not the fact that Chávez talked to Bolívar, unearthed his remains, and strived to resemble him (all of which had happened before) that made his relationship uncannily peculiar. It was the fact that, thanks to technologies old and new, Bolívar seemed to *talk back*, to acquire an agency that surpassed the historical conceptualization of the cult—so focused on the stillness of monuments, statues, busts, and plaques—and that invites us to consider the nation as haunted and to take the ghost at face value.

We could argue then that, with Chávez, there was a new (old) ghost in town. A stately, familiar, techno-magical ghost that sits uncomfortably amid crowds of Venezuelan and Latin American ghosts demanding justice and challenging the state when it insists on erasing or selectively remembering the past and its violence. There sits Bolívar reloaded, his digital portrait a sign that the magic once kept to the shadows of the state's public domain has flooded into the light, with conjuring, invocation, and spiritual possession now part of the state's repertoire of memory practices. And there sits (and walks and talks) Chávez now too, and we cannot *not* see him, not only because he is everywhere, but because, thanks to the relationship he developed with Bolívar while he was alive, seeing and talking to ghosts is neither spooky nor unusual, neither a metaphor nor a delusion.

Maduro's public conversations with birds and butterflies, which he claims embody Chávez's spirit, are proof of this, as discussed in chapter 4. Hearing Maduro "translate" birdsong for his audience, we cannot help but wonder if the literalness of the president's communication with the dead has changed something in the magic of the state that Taussig so brilliantly theorized. After all, the spirit queen Taussig encountered, with her magic mountain and her lively ghosts, is no longer hidden in the shadows of a periphery accessible only through pilgrimage, set apart from the state's officialdom. She is *right here*: she has become the state (and the state has become her). And we, amid birds and butterflies, animated portraits and walking holograms, have been granted front-row seats to the performance of a state that has ceased to be secretly and metaphorically possessed and is now unabashedly in conversation with the dead.

The Necromantic State

In *The Magic of the State,* Taussig shows how the magical power of the dead—and, particularly, of Bolívar—is invoked and mobilized both by the practitioners of the María Lionza cult on Venezuela's Sorte Mountain and by the modern state. Unlike the literal acts of spirit invocation that take place at night on Sorte, the state's invocation of the dead occurs in daylight and in public spaces saturated with the state's "artwork": murals, monuments, statues, and slogans that reproduce the image of the Liberator to the point where "the untiring ubiquity of it all" forces the populace to seek out "his empty gaze in a pursuit doomed to eternity" (Taussig 1997, 110–11). In Taussig's analysis, these reproductions both reveal and hide the magic within the state; they are what he calls "*hiddenness performed*" (120; original emphasis), an intermittently exposed public secret that points to the fiction of and within the state, and the dismissal of that fiction for the purposes of maintaining the illusion that the state's authority is built on the cold rationality of officialdom rather than on rituals that allow the dead to literally exist among the living.

Looking at the state's iconography alongside the acts of spirit possession taking place in the state's periphery through Taussig's narrative—a hybrid of fiction and fact that draws attention to "the continuous work of make-believe in art no less than in politics and everyday life" (Levi Strauss and Taussig 2005)—means acknowledging the magical underpinnings of state authority. It also means recognizing the fictional yet powerful boundary that prevents the state from fully merging with the spirit mountain, and the people from fully embodying the dead that the state invokes and embellishes. Taussig hints at this boundary—even as he reveals its make-believe nature—when he mentions how, when the president invokes the spirit of the Liberator on public occasions, "we might, on reflection, want to understand this as figurative, rhetorical, poetic, turn of speech. He doesn't really mean it" (Taussig 1997, 186). He also argues that, while the magic might be in the state, "there's no denying that from there it's just a short step to where people get into the act willingly and are able to make magic from it, allowing their very bodies to blur with the spiritual power of the state in horrendous displays of mimetic excess" (188).

Figurative language and a short step: the gap between Sorte's magical Bolívar and the state's "magical" Bolívar is small—and it is imagined—but it is there nonetheless. The illusion of separation ensures that the rituals on the magic mountain and those staged in the state's theater of self-praise and self-legitimation do not suddenly merge. The two entities—the state and the magic mountain, the president and the spirit queen—remain separate but in a mode of ongoing exchange where images and "effervescent shocks" circulate between them: "The President deftly follows Ofelia in this, and she follows her President. This is the magic circle" (Taussig 1997, 107).

Enter Chávez.

In *The Magic of the State*, Chávez appears only once, in a photograph showing him in the military uniform he was wearing when he publicly surrendered after the 1992 coup he and the members of the MBR–200 had orchestrated against the then president, Carlos Andrés Pérez. Though the coup failed and Chávez was imprisoned, the event turned him into an iconic figure that fueled growing popular discontent with the establishment. Chávez's revolutionary fervor inspired a prayer that Taussig includes in his text and that modifies the wording of the Lord's Prayer to make it about "*Our Chávez who art in prison*" (1997, 108; original emphasis). The prayer was printed on cards that circulated in Caracas in the early 1990s and again in 2014, when a revised version became popular among *chavistas* who wanted to commemorate Chávez after his death.

Taussig returns to Chávez in a 2005 interview with David Levi Strauss, where he argues that "people today gain magical power not from the dead, but from the state's embellishment of them. And the state, authoritarian and spooky, is as much possessed by the dead as is any individual pilgrim. The current president of Venezuela, Hugo Chávez, is the embodiment of this" (Levi Strauss and Taussig 2005). By 2005, many magical things had taken place between Chávez and Bolívar that prove Taussig right, but none of them as spectacular and shamelessly literal as the public opening of the Liberator's coffin in 2010, which turned Chávez into a sorcerer, a necromancer, and the recipient of the newly risen spirit of Bolívar. Chávez had not yet become ill with cancer, which led, as we will see in chapter 1, to healing ceremonies staged publicly in the presidential palace, rumors about curses and rituals performed to save his life, and a still-growing body of works in different disciplines intent on uncovering Chávez's "black magic" side. In 2005, there were no sets of ghostly eyes looking at people from buildings and T-shirts, no hologram of a dead man wandering around Caracas, no presidents actually talking to magical birds. There was no severe economic and humanitarian crisis, no unprecedented wave of Venezuelans leaving the country; *chavistas* and *opositores* did not love each other but also did not kill each other back then, and radically new futures still seemed possible.

I highlight these differences because they are the reason why I have chosen to refer to the state that appears in the following chapters as a "necromantic state." This term does not represent a conceptual break with Taussig's theorization of the magical state: the fact that the modern state draws its power from the dead—as Taussig argued—is, if anything, rendered even more explicit in the staging of Chávez's afterlife in contemporary Venezuela. However, the term does allow me to highlight a radicalization in the magic of the state, one that responds to and is shaped by the specific historical context that frames my analysis in this book. This context includes the popularization of new technologies and their use by the state, the political and social crisis that marked the transition from Chávez to Maduro, the still indisputable centrality of Chávez in the rhetoric of the Bolivarian Revolution, Maduro's lack of popular support, the inability of oil—the state's other source of magic—to save the country from the economic crisis that followed Chávez's death, the opposition's failure to provide a viable political alternative, and the confrontations among members of Chávez's political party.[13]

The cumulative effect of these factors on the country required that Chávez stay as alive as possible. First, because he was the only one who could smooth out contradictions in the state's rhetoric and performance and also inspire the sort of loyalty that could keep a failing political project alive. Second, because he represented and continues to represent one of the last things all Venezuelans have in common: the extreme political polarization that has marked the country since his arrival in power having become, paradoxically, the last vestige of a shared political and social language. All modern states have always needed to bring the dead back to life, as Taussig shows; however, the conditions that define the decade following Chávez's death have made this act of resuscitation urgent in Venezuela. So urgent, in fact, that it was not enough for the rituals of spirit possession and the conversation with the dead to be not quite real: the dead had to *actually* walk among the living. Chávez had already proved that this was possible when, in front of cameras and a national audience, he made Bolívar's bones talk, thus demonstrating that a state did not need to outsource the actual magical work to the periphery of the magic mountain and the spirit queen anymore: if the circumstances truly required it, the state could also practice necromancy.

The term "necromancy" rarely appears in contemporary works of political theory, performance, or cultural studies.[14] The overwhelming majority of studies on the topic focus on the practice of necromancy itself—often referred to as "black magic"—and provide detailed instructions on how to communicate with the dead and inhabit the world of the occult. These studies, along with various dictionary entries that define the term, note that necromancy has traditionally been performed in graveyards and that it sees the corpse that results from a premature or violent death as retaining "some measure of unused vitality," which leads necromancers to use parts of corpses as ingredients and charms while performing their rituals of invocation.[15] The dead are brought back to life for use either as weapons or as tools of divination because they are thought to have knowledge of the future.

Understood in this way, the practice of necromancy reflects, with uncanny accuracy, the state's conjuring of the dead during Chávez's and Maduro's presidencies. So much so in fact that, as I note in chapter 1, the term "black magic" was used to talk about the popular and stately rituals performed to save Chávez's life after he was diagnosed with cancer. The power necromancers attribute to the parts of the corpse mirrors the power the state attributed to Chávez's eyes, signature, and miniatures of his body, while the belief that the dead can tell the future grounds Maduro's frequent invoking of Chávez's words as foreshadowing the success of the ongoing revolutionary process. I read these resonances not as coincidence but as evidence that necromancy has become part of the state's magical repertoire of mnemonic practices. If that is true, then the dead that have returned cannot be dismissed as figments of the imagination or understood as metaphors. Thanks to the state taking its role as necromancer seriously, the ghost is now a material, political, and social figure, one that does not metaphorically hover above the present but actually inhabits it alongside the living.

In the context of the Bolivarian Revolution then, the magic of the state acquires a necromantic hue that populates public space not only with more monuments, slogans, and statues, but also with remains that, in necromantic terms, "retain some measure of unused vitality," which allows them to walk (in the case of the hologram), to observe (in the case of Chávez's eyes), to talk (in the case of Maduro's birds and butterflies), to play (in the case of Chávez-themed toys), and to become familial (in the case of the collectible phone cards and Chávez's signature). This animation is not only the work of the state. In the following chapters, we will see how Maduro's invocation of Chávez and the production and circulation of Chávez-themed objects and images take place through a process of cocreation and co-performance where both the people and the state participate in and sustain the operations that allow Chávez to linger as a specter. This joint participation is inevitable partly because of the official rhetoric of the Bolivarian Revolution, which since its conception under Chávez's leadership has advocated for the development of mechanisms for popular participation that would enable people to shape the operations of state institutions, and which also created a chain of equivalence between the people, Chávez, and the state.[16] Thus, whatever the Bolivarian state did—in terms of social and economic policies but also in terms of creating visual and political vocabularies for the nation—it did for and, most importantly, with the people, in theory if not always in practice.

However, that the people and the state work together to stage Chávez's haunting publicly and often privately does not mean that the state's necromantic performance does not form people's identities, vocabularies, habits, and ways of imagining themselves, political authority, and the state. Quite the contrary. As Diana Taylor reminds us, public spectacles provide a site for individual and state formation, which occurs in part through a complicated exchange of gazes: "looking, being looked at, identification, recognition, mimicry" (1997, 30). Although, as she later argues, not everything that intervenes in individual and state formation is always visible; performative hauntings and specters, she notes, shape what and how we see what is around us. Furthermore, as Achille Mbembe argues, the state's "mastercode"—the "world of meanings" it creates and attempts to institutionalize (2006, 382)—becomes part of people's common sense, thus challenging "binary categories used in standard interpretations of domination (resistance/passivity, subjection/autonomy, state/civil society, hegemony/counterhegemony, totalization/detotalization)" (382). Throughout this book, I argue that being haunted, too, becomes common sense. Thus, I do not use "necromantic state" only to refer to a state that performs necromancy. It also refers to the state in which haunted people live: one where, everywhere you go, you find yourself comfortably trapped in a conversation—at times loud, at times quiet—with the dead.

Of Ghosts, Specters, and Spectral Remains

Throughout this introduction, I have referred to Chávez both as a ghost and as a specter, as if they meant the same thing. However, in this section (and from now on), I will settle on "specter" to talk about Chávez's lingering in the political and social landscape of contemporary Venezuela. The question then becomes: What does it mean to call Chávez a specter? More generally, what exactly is a specter and how can we—why should we—differentiate it from a ghost?

Considering the vast scholarship written on the subject of spectrality, a straightforward definition of the specter should not be too difficult to find.

And yet it is. It seems that the determination to define the specter runs counter to the specter itself, counter to the power it has to unsettle what we take for granted and, in the process, "set heads spinning" (Blanco and Peeren 2013, 1). Let us look, for example, at the following definitions of the specter introduced by Julian Wolfreys and Jacques Derrida:

> Thus, to reiterate the point, the question of spectres is a question of that which presents itself or touches upon itself at and in excess of the limits of definition. . . . Names, conventionally applied, fix the limits of an identity. Yet this "strange name"—*spectre*—names nothing as such, and nothing which can be named as such, while also naming something which is neither something nor nothing; it names something which is neither nothing nor not nothing. (Wolfreys 2013, 71)

> Here is—or rather, there is, over there, an unnameable or almost unnameable thing: something, between something and someone, anyone or anything, some thing, "this thing," but this thing and not any other, this thing that looks at us, that concerns us [*qui nous regarde*], comes to defy semantics as much as ontology, psychoanalysis as much as philosophy. (Derrida 1993, 5)

Something which is neither nothing nor not nothing. Something, between something and someone, anyone or anything. For Wolfreys, the specter is what appears at the very limit of interpretation; as a thing, as "something," it stands beyond binary oppositions, erasing the division between pairings like life and death without attempting to redraw the lines that separate and define them. For Derrida, the specter is not about the supernatural; it is, rather, what María del Pilar Blanco and Esther Peeren call "a conceptual metaphor" (2013, 1), a system of producing knowledge that engages the scholar of today and tomorrow, placing upon them an ethical demand that requires embracing uncertainty, heterogeneity, and multiplicity, and feeling the weight of a gaze that concerns them. This gaze is key to Derrida's conceptualization of the specter and to the very choice to speak of specters rather than of apparitions, phantoms, or ghosts. As Blanco and Peeren point out, "specter" and "spectrality" evoke "an etymological link to visibility and vision, to that which is both *looked at* (as fascinating spectacle) and *looking* (in the sense of examining), suggesting their suitability for exploring and illuminating phenomena other than the putative return of the dead" (2; original emphasis).

The importance Derrida places on the gaze materializes in what he calls "the visor effect": "The specter is not simply someone we see coming back, it is someone by whom we feel ourselves watched, observed, surveyed, as if by the law: we are 'before the law,' without any possible symmetry, without reciprocity" (Derrida and Stiegler 2002, 120). Central to this definition is the inability to meet the specter's gaze when gazed upon, and the demand made by the "other," which, in Derrida's theory, is often the father/predecessor to whom one is indebted. This debt, this "owing to him and owing him everything," threatens to tie the specter to an authority that, in addition to being patriarchal, becomes incontestable (122). Derrida, however, takes it in a different direction; for him, freedom springs from this responsibility toward the unreachable other whose gaze "is spectrality itself" and demands respect for "the non-living" (123). And not just freedom, but justice, which for him is "a spectral business" and is the very thing that constitutes revolutionary movements.

It is thus unsurprising that Derrida's take on spectrality has been so productive in framing spectral operations that denounce injustices precisely by recognizing the lingering presence of a past that looks at us, that concerns us, and that always produces "something to be done." Yet, Derrida's specter also reflects the operations of a patriarchal form of authority—let us not forget that Gayatri Chakravorty Spivak in her critique of Derrida's *Specters of Marx* called it a "how-to-mourn-your-father book" (2013, 318). Because the specter's gaze cannot be returned, it becomes oppressive and uncontestable and the "freedom" resulting from finding oneself in his sight is limited, if not entirely illusory. As we read that the specter "is someone by whom we feel ourselves watched, observed, surveyed, as if by the law," would it be too far-fetched to imagine the eyes of George Orwell's Big Brother ([1949] 1950), rendered spectral by their continuing surveillance from telescreens?

Chávez's specter, I argue, exists in this overlap of Derridean/Orwellian eyes and the grin of Lewis Carroll's Cheshire cat as Jean Baudrillard describes it in *Why Hasn't Everything Already Disappeared?*—that is, as something that is continually disappearing, never gone for good, and leaving traces that seep back into our lives "in infinitesimal doses, often more dangerous than the visible authority that ruled over us" ([2007] 2009, 26). Like Derrida's specter, Chávez as specter materializes in a surveilling gaze that, as I will argue in chapter 2, is asymmetrical because it comes from the past—so returning the gaze is never truly possible—and because it comes with a demand that is sometimes clearly articulated and at other times left to the imagination of all those he gazes upon.

Chávez's specter behaves like the Cheshire cat's grin not only because it lingers but because it does so in a way that is not supposed to be frightening—even though many might think, along with Baudrillard, that the Cheshire cat's grin is in fact terrifying. If we think of Chávez's hologram, it is not meant to provoke fear but loyalty, admiration, and comfort in the knowledge that he is still here.[17] These feelings are of course scripted into the state's narrative of Chávez's presence/absence, but that does not mean that they are not the actual feelings of people who wish for Chávez to stay undead. Furthermore, these feelings coexist with the anger, rejection, and even disgust that the hologram triggered in those who do not identify as *chavistas*. Regardless of the spectator/citizen's affective take on the hologram, Chávez's specter is supposed to be entertaining; you can dance to the beat of the song that accompanies his journey as you let yourself be immersed in the fantasy of the revolutionary past that never passed and the promise of a new, radical future that materializes "right here." This authority, distilled in the ethereal luminosity of Chávez's spectral figure, despite looking out through a pair of Orwellian eyes, becomes pop, iconic, inviting, and—dare I say—*friendly*: you do not want to run away from Chávez's specter; if anything, you want to high-five it (if you care to pay attention to it at all).

While the hologram is unique in being the most literal rendition of Chávez's specter, it is only one of the many shapes Chávez's lingering takes in public and private spaces, where it molds the political, social, and affective landscape of the country by, as Baudrillard says, "seeping back into our lives in infinitesimal doses."[18] That process is sometimes assertive—as during official government events where Chávez is often blown up to gigantic proportions—but, most of the time, subtle, the lingering becoming an "unseen and barely audible hum" (Beasley-Murray 2010, 180) we can comfortably ignore and thus live with. Next to the hologram, and outlasting its eventful apparition, is the ever-present stencil of Chávez's eyes watching over people's comings and goings through cities and towns from walls, billboards, streetlights, T-shirts, hats, and phone screens, where it appears in memes shared by both government supporters and the opposition on digital platforms like WhatsApp, Facebook, and Instagram. Often accompanying the stencil of his eyes is his signature, which appears on the walls of the buildings and houses built by the Gran Misión Vivienda Venezuela (figure I.3). His image has been reproduced on clothing, jewelry, collectible phone cards, and toys—all objects that cross over the boundaries separating the public and the private, the stately and the intimate. His performance—his mannerisms, the informality of his speech, the epic tone of his proposals—continues to

I.3   Chávez's signature on a building.

be imitated by Maduro and by candidates from the opposition, becoming a force that dictates what political authority in contemporary Venezuela should look and sound like. These objects, images, and behaviors constitute Chávez's spectral remains.

The word "remains," in the most general sense, brings to mind that which is left behind after something else—the bigger whole—has disappeared. It evokes a materiality that seems to contrast with the specter's immaterial nature. Yet, the specter is not itself a void; it is symptomatic of a void—a void in power, for example—but it is not an ungraspable, empty form. It is, as Jonathan Gil Harris (2011) points out, matter that acts upon and shapes the present.[19] Understanding the specter alongside things and bodies brings us to the spatial/physical nature of haunting, which, in the context of Venezuela, occurs not abstractly but in a specific place, through the interaction with things, bodies, images, words, and behaviors that represent and re-present Chávez, that constitute that which remains of him and that in which he remains.

Birds, butterflies, coffee cups, holograms, memes, signatures, eyes, red T-shirts, key chains, necklaces, toys, posters, stickers, figurines, hats, collectible phone cards—Chávez's remains are varied and proliferate on a massive scale. They are spectral not only because they enable Chávez to linger—visibly and palpably—but because they themselves behave spectrally. This means that they are unstable, dynamic, and uncontained by either the structure or the logic of institutionalized and preserved archives; they differ from the statues, monuments, and documents typically created to commemorate a bygone figure of power. They appear and disappear suddenly and randomly, they circulate in private and intimate spaces as well as in public and official ones, they are open to alteration and interpretation, and they weave together individual and collective histories, the commonplace and the extraordinary, the people and the state. These remains comprise not only objects but also what Rebecca Schneider calls the "immaterial labor of bodies" engaged in and with an incomplete past. This labor includes "bodies striking poses, making gestures, voicing calls, reading words, singing songs, or standing witness," all acts that evince a "cross- or multi-temporal engagement with im/material understood to belong to the past in the present" (Schneider 2011, 33, 35). In the case of Chávez's remains, this bodily labor manifests in acts of doubling, mimesis, imitation, and impersonation by the government and its supporters and by the opposition, as we will see in chapter 4.

Many of these remains are also spectral because they are routinely made invisible and rarely taken too seriously; they move around without catching anyone's attention, "forgotten reminders"—to use Michael Billig's term from *Banal Nationalism* (1995, 38)—deemed too commonplace or too absurd to matter. Yet, I propose that it is precisely through those objects that haunting takes place, the invocation of the specter thus exiting the secret domain of the cult and the occult and going beyond official state rhetoric to become part of the everyday that unfolds in the streets, in plain sight. Thus, rather than simply dismissing the circulation of and engagement with these objects as inconsequential or the result of political propaganda, I view their ordinariness as key to how narratives and practices of memory are crafted, and how social, political, and historical relationships are established with Chávez's presence/absence and the authority he (spectrally) embodies.

To talk about specters is thus not only to talk about the sort of lingering that makes time layered, challenging a forward-driven linear temporality and complicating the view of death as irrecoverable loss. It is also to talk about haunted spaces as actual living spaces where people's daily routines are sometimes interrupted by, sometimes mediated by, and sometimes shaped around spectral remains. These remains invite us in and stimulate the imagination. They tempt our eyes to linger on torn posters and graffiti-covered walls, and our hands to hover over knickknacks sold on street vendors' tables—all objects that acquire meaning because we take them for granted, not in spite of the fact that we do. Lastly, these remains and the way they ground the specter and locate it within a specific context prevent it from being reduced to a superficial rhetorical figure. Exploring the dynamics around these remains—rather than limiting ourselves to a discussion of what the specter means—enables us to gain insight into what the specter can do, and what we can and cannot do in its presence and under its gaze.

The presence and circulation of these spectral remains contribute to the creation of an affectively charged and viscous atmosphere of temporal overlaps, political irresolution, social tensions, and magical spectacles that I call an "afterglow." Before turning to this concept in the following section, however, let us return to the distinction between ghosts and specters and to the question of why, in light of the conceptualization of the specter developed so far in relation to Chávez, I want to preserve that distinction. The state, I have argued, produces its own ghosts; these ghosts, *state ghosts*, are what I propose to call specters: figures of the past that linger in the present and lead a socially and politically dynamic afterlife that does not unsettle or challenge the way things are but that instead preserves the status quo with their affective purchase, surveilling gaze, and quotidian omnipresence. The specters of the state are not a metaphor for the violence of the state, which does not mean that they are not violent or, in Baudrillard's words, "more dangerous than the visible authority that rules over us" ([2007] 2009, 26). They are also not premodern figures allergic to new technologies; if anything, their spectrality is often powered by those technologies and the immediacy, virality, and tricks of animation that mediate their operations and our access to them.

Facing stately specters are *ghosts*. This term encompasses the disruptive energies, fragmented voices, and unsettling echoes that signal, as Avery Gordon ([1997] 2008) points out, that a past wrong needs to be righted, that the state needs to be held accountable, that history does not drive us in a straight line toward an innocent, always better future, and that it is possible to challenge militarized and patriarchal powers that thrive on social erasure.

Examples of these ghosts abound in Latin America. Argentina and Chile are haunted by the *desaparecidos* of the mid-twentieth-century dictatorships in the Southern Cone. Peru, Colombia, El Salvador, and Guatemala are haunted by the hundreds of thousands left dead by various armed conflicts. Mexico is brimming with the ghosts of the victims of drug-related violence and the war on drugs, the ghosts of the hundreds of women murdered in Ciudad Juárez, and the ghosts of the migrants who have died attempting to cross the border to the United States. Alongside all these ghosts are those that do not haunt a specific Latin American country but all of them: the ghosts left behind by a long, violent history of colonialism, the ghosts that speak of enduring racial injustice, the ghosts of an ongoing and continental femicide.

The extensive theoretical work developed around these ghosts repeatedly emphasizes their subversive nature when they appear in cultural works or as part of political and social acts of protest. Alberto Ribas-Casasayas and Amanda L. Petersen argue that, in postdictatorial contexts both in Latin America and in Spain, the ghost creates "new versions of the past that subvert official versions of history and recognize those who have been erased from it" (2017a, 3).[20] Juliana Martínez, in turn, proposes the term "spectral realism" to signal how the specter that appears in cultural works transforms narrative by changing how space, time, vision, and ethical concerns are portrayed and understood, ultimately setting the reader "into political, social, or artistic motion" (2020, 20).

Chávez's specter does not behave in this subversive way, as I will show in the following chapters. The substantial differences between the way he operates in the context of contemporary Venezuela and the unsettling way the ghosts mentioned above behave thus becomes an invitation for us to distinguish between ghosts and specters. Ghosts, I propose, show us our historical blind spots; specters encourage us to dismiss them as inconsequential. Ghosts disorient us; specters ensure we always know where we are—under their gaze. Ghosts discomfort us; specters reassure us that everything makes sense. The two figures are not mutually exclusive— ghosts can haunt specters, and specters can haunt ghosts—and they do not represent all the possible ways a past can linger. However, drawing this distinction, as antispectral as it might be—specters, Wolfreys insists, resist binaries—serves as a reminder that not all pasts that linger or are conjured up have subversive potential, even when they come with labels such as "new" or "revolutionary."

Afterglow

The word "afterglow" conjures up that which lingers, be it a gleam that remains after the light has disappeared or the effect or feeling—usually pleasant but not always—that remains after something is experienced or achieved. Thus, it differs from words meant to indicate a historical shift: it lacks the fixity of "the end of," the confidence of "post-," and the compass that often guides a "transition." These words appear out of place in the context of contemporary Venezuela where, as I argue in chapter 1, the alleged end—Chávez's death—was blurred by official and popular narratives that complicated processes of mourning and memorialization. Furthermore, Maduro's time in power has been characterized by an increase in political repression and censorship, the impossibility of holding democratic elections, the worsening of the economic crisis, and the "parallel state" that materialized with Juan Guaidó declaring himself Venezuela's interim president in January 2019, all factors that have made actual institutional change unimaginable.[21] The afterglow captures this state of political irresolution, which sets Venezuela's experience apart from other political changes and transitions that have taken place in contemporary Latin America and that execute more abrupt swings from socialism to military dictatorship to democracy and from far left to far right.

Key to those transitions is a concrete change in the face of power: somebody new arrives promising to govern with an agenda highlighting how things will be different from how they used to be. And while in the context of Venezuela, Maduro—Chávez's handpicked successor—is in fact somebody new, not only was his political agenda's main goal to continue Chávez's plans and dreams for the nation, but his own arrival in power was articulated in terms that made clear that it was not really him people were voting for, but Chávez. The official song of Maduro's 2013 presidential campaign—"Maduro desde mi corazón" (Maduro from my heart)—begins with Chávez's voice declaring that his choice for a successor was, without a doubt, Maduro.[22] The song then repeats slogans that tie Chávez and Maduro together: "Chávez por siempre, Maduro presidente" (Chávez forever, Maduro president); "Con Chávez y Maduro, el pueblo está seguro" (With Chávez and with Maduro, the people are safe); "Chávez, te juro, mi voto es pa' Maduro" (Chávez, I swear to you, my vote is for Maduro). This last slogan also featured prominently in murals and graffiti that popped up during the campaign. Like "Chávez corazón del pueblo" (Chávez, the heart of the people), the song that repeatedly played on every radio station and at every rally during Chávez's 2012 presidential campaign, Maduro's "Maduro desde mi corazón" was also a merengue-reggaeton mix. It was danceable, catchy, and "sticky" both because it invited people to dance in couples, and because it acted as a sort of glue that would adhere Maduro to Chávez to convince people to stick with Maduro, Chávez's vastly less charismatic successor/double/son.

I will return to these words—successor, double, son—and the different relational dynamics they establish between Chávez and Maduro in chapter 4. For now, suffice it to say, the fact that Maduro has performed all three of these roles as he grounds himself as the new leader of the country and the revolution reveals how limited that leadership truly is. There was never a move from Chávez to Maduro. Instead, Chávez remained by Maduro's side—in rhetoric and, as we will see, in practice—as Maduro appeared as the vice president/interpreter of the president's specter. For Lucia Michelutti, this relationship between the two marks a departure from "classical forms of charismatic transitions to power":

> The question is who is leading, Chávez or Maduro. The answer is both. What we are witnessing is the development of a charismatic leadership system that does not fit classical forms of charismatic transitions to power. The charismatic relational bond between the people and the leaders (Chávez and Maduro) needs to be constantly reenacted by public and private performances of revolutionary divine kinship. (Michelutti 2017, 246)

Michelutti defines divine kinship as "descent from common deified revolutionary ancestors" (236), a central trope of Chávez's discourse, which emphasized his connection with Bolívar and other revolutionary figures such as Guaicaipuro and Ezequiel Zamora. For Maduro, however, it is his ideological/familial relationship with Chávez that needed repeated performing, as Michelutti points out. But he is not the only one performing this relationship. Michelutti's study speaks of "mini-Chávezes," local leaders who have "replicated and routinized Chávez's charisma by performing his divine kinship repertoire (made up of words and government programs) at the local level" (241). To this cast of mini-Chávezes we could also add the people who choose to wear clothing and accessories with his face, eyes, or words printed on them, people who dress to look like him during political rallies, and people who imitate his gestures and speak like him.

In many instances these acts of doubling are articulated through a rhetoric that centers on affective excess: boundless love, infinite gratitude, deeply felt loyalty, all enabling the blending of leader and people that right after Chávez's death became visible in posters with slogans such as "Chávez, más que amor, frenesí" (Chávez, more than love, frenzy) and "Amor con amor se paga" (Love is paid with love). These slogans are representative of the collective nature of Chávez's illness, discussed in chapter 1, and cast new light on Eric Santner's theorization of the "flesh of the sovereign": "the spectral yet visceral surplus immanence" that detaches from the sovereign's "sublime physiology" once they are no longer living to then reattach to "the people," the new subject-bearer of sovereignty (2011, 103). For Santner, this surplus immanence triggers forms of biopolitical control over the body by appearing both to bind and to threaten to dissolve the body politic of modern nation-states.

Santner's argument and how it might speak to forms of biopolitical control in contemporary Venezuela merit further discussion; however, for the purposes of this introduction, I would like to linger on the image invoked in Santner's description of the detaching of the sovereign's sublime flesh, a detachment that is best captured in his analysis of Jacques-Louis David's oil painting *The Death of Marat* (1793). The painting depicts the dead body of Marat in the bottom half of the composition and a large, seemingly empty upper half painted in shades of black. For Santner, this upper half—not a vacancy but "the site of an excess of pressure" (2011, 93)—represents the flesh that can no longer be figured by the body of the king but that also does not manage to fully represent and adapt to the concept and the body of the people.

This nonvacancy that, as we see in the painting, thickens the atmosphere, making it dense with the weight of something that is and is not there—a sort of ectoplasmic substance—encapsulates the viscosity of the affectively charged afterglow that, I argue, followed Chávez's death. This afterglow becomes visible, in a way that echoes David's painting, in some of the most iconic images that were reproduced on posters after Chávez's death: the famous scene of the speech he gave during the closing of the 2012 presidential elections where, standing on the stage drenched in rain and covered in confetti, he lifts his right arm to people presumably cheering him on (figure I.4), and a photoshopped image that shows him in the form of clouds in

I.4   Poster featuring the closing of Chávez's 2012 presidential campaign.

the sky, watching over the people walking alongside his coffin (figure I.5). In both images, the air is thick: thick because of the combination of rain, sweat, and fog in the case of the former; thick because of the clouds that hover above and envelop the people in the latter. In the previous section, I argued that part of this thickness comes from how Chávez's spectral remains circulate and saturate everyday life, which enable the past to impress itself on the present, giving weight to spectrality. Here, I would propose that, in addition to the physical presence of these remains—and intrinsically connected to how they operate—there is a sort of affective excess that further anchors Chávez's specter in the present.

In figures I.4 and I.5,which have appeared in public spaces (as posters) and in private spaces (as calendar illustrations), this affective excess is shaped by a narrative of gratitude, love, admiration, and a complicated form of nostalgia that captures a longing for the past where Chávez was alive and rejects its pastness by claiming he is still here, not entirely dead.[23] This narrative is essential to the state but does not originate only with the state; people from all social classes and backgrounds, inside and outside Venezuela, continue to feel all sorts of warm feelings for Chávez, particularly since the multidimensional crisis that has affected Venezuela since Chávez's death can so easily be blamed entirely on Maduro, thus leaving Chávez's legacy somewhat intact. Circulating with these feelings are those that arise from an understanding of the Bolivarian Revolution as an aberration, a mistake, and the worst tragedy that could have befallen the country. These feelings

I.5   Poster featuring Chávez's coffin and Chávez's shape in the clouds.

often turn into what Svetlana Boym (2001) calls "restorative nostalgia," a craving for "before" Chávez, a time that, as the crisis worsens, becomes more and more desirable and utopian. The polarization that so frequently defines academic debates and general discussions about Venezuela is fueled by these feelings, which also affect scholars who have made Venezuela the subject of their research. Venezuela as a topic always touches a nerve; writing about it without thinking of family members (and the millions) who have suffered profoundly or perished because of the multidimensional effects of the crisis and without thinking also of the valid claims for justice and social participation that became rightfully audible and pressing in the years of the revolution is, if not impossible, at the very least extremely difficult. When I speak of affective excess, I speak of these feelings too, excessive because of their intensity and because of their stubborn lingering, because of the way they stick to us and threaten to overcome us.

Afterglow, as I define it here, captures this enhanced sensibility, the rawness of feeling something *a flor de piel*. In that sense, my use of the term points to one of the more erotic meanings of the word: the glow that lingers after a sexual encounter. Here, however, I am not interested in limiting the glow to one kind of, presumably pleasurable, experience but, instead, in viewing the afterglow as a glow/flush that appears on the skin because of the anger, love, sadness, joy, indignation, and many other feelings that the past as embodied by Chávez awakens. The glow is thus evidence of how this past is, in fact, still present, of how it still affects us. In referring to a secondary glow, one which is no longer brightly incandescent but has not disappeared, the term also captures less intense affects, what Jon Beasley-Murray, following Pierre Bourdieu's theorization of habitus, calls a "micropolitics of affect":

> There is, then, a politics of habit, which persists even as ideology wanes. We might consider it a micropolitics of affect, of a regularized low-intensity affect, closely associated with ethics. . . . Habit drives and is driven by the unseen and barely audible hum of micropolitics that pervades our daily routines; it is like background noise in that we are almost oblivious to its ongoing importance, the ways in which it structures our all too familiar, endlessly repeated quotidian activities. (Beasley-Murray 2010, 180–81)

We got a glimpse of this routinized, low-intensity affect in the reaction of the passersby who encountered Chávez's hologram but were not particularly disturbed by its presence. We will get many more glimpses in the following chapters as we linger on the virally reproduced stencil of Chávez's eyes and his magnified signature on the walls of apartment buildings. Both images are so commonplace that ignoring them—passively accepting that they are there—has become part of everyone's daily routine. That normalization, I argue, does not stop these images from shaping habits and the visual vocabularies mobilized in support of the Bolivarian Revolution and in acts of resistance to it.

Lastly, the glow in afterglow is also the glow of computer and cell-phone screens where tweets, WhatsApp messages, Facebook posts, and Instagram pictures capture the attention of millions of users, trigger strong emotions, enable various forms of political organization and social resistance, archive forgotten events, give hope that things will change, and almost immediately crush that hope. This role that new technologies and social media play in shaping the political landscape of contemporary Venezuela cannot be understood outside Chávez's own use of them, particularly his prolific presence on Twitter.

Using the handle @chavezcandanga, Chávez joined Twitter on April 24, 2010, and four days later, posted his first tweet: "How is everyone? I showed up like I said I would: at midnight. Heading to Brazil. And very happy to be working for Venezuela. We will be victorious!!" (Chávez 2010). Chávez's Twitter presence marked a significant change in the political and technological life of the country. By 2012, Venezuela ranked thirteenth in the world in its number of Twitter users. Moreover, it had the highest proportion of mobile internet usage in Latin America at over 30 percent of total connections because social media use on mobile phones was so widespread (Morales et al. 2015, 7). While alive, Chávez was considered the second most influential world leader on Twitter, preceded only by Barack Obama. The opposition also found on social media a channel to freely speak to their supporters and protest against the government, and, as both Chávez and Maduro censored or shut down the majority of television channels and newspapers that were critical of their policies, the internet progressively became the opposition's "lifeline" (Rendon and Kohan 2019).

Social media platforms—and the internet in general—also became Chávez's digital haunting ground while he was alive and after his death. Citizens-turned-users have seen their home pages and WhatsApp groups flooded with links to YouTube videos, memes, GIFs, and stickers featuring Chávez (as well as Maduro, members of the government, and representatives of the opposition), all of them shareable and modifiable, thus encouraging a level of creative participation that has yet to stop growing. In fact, Chávez's death seems to have led to an increase in the production of this sort of digital content; he "afterlives" in an endless stream of memes created by both *chavistas* and *opositores*, who combine in their digital creations political demands and cultural references that are both local and global. Chávez's "memeification" emerges alongside (and feeds off) the creation of digital archives such as Todo Chávez en la Web, which gathers and provides free access to almost everything Chávez ever said or wrote, from his 1,824 tweets to every episode of *Aló Presidente*, to a poem he wrote for his grandmother when she passed away. Yet, unlike this archive, the memes imbue Chávez with movement and animation, making him feel "current" in spite of his death. The afterglow I have discussed so far thus also encompasses this technological glow emanating from the screens where Chávez continues to be shared, his words and his images still dictating the terms in which the political life of Venezuela is virtually represented, criticized, mocked, and understood.

The glow in "afterglow" therefore has an affective dimension that mixes with, fuels, and is fueled by the luminescence of new technologies and that perpetuates a sort of shared temporal malaise intensified by the presence and circulation of Chávez's spectral remains. This temporal malaise is born out of the suspicion—confirmed over and over by those remains—that the past lingers in a way that is fragmentary and ongoing, which enables it to be dragged into "a negotiated future that is never simply *in front of us* (like the past is never simply behind us) but in a kind of viscous, affective surround" (Schneider 2011, 37; original emphasis). The afterglow I have proposed here to characterize the decade following Chávez's death aims to capture that viscous, affective, and cross-temporal surround. It underscores the affective exchanges that continue to take place between Chávez and the people while speaking to the country's state of political irresolution and the various forces that enable the government to stay in place, prolonging the life of a revolution that falls short in responding to the needs of the Venezuelan people as a whole. If we consider the afterglow in relation to the light that lingers in the sky after the sun has set, it suggests a combination of light and shadow, of visibility and invisibility, that invites us to reconsider not only how we experience time but also how we perceive and experience space and what remains in it.

Afterglow, as I have outlined it, is not a hermetic or fixed concept. The following chapters, which will take us through streets and buildings as we pursue different manifestations of Chávez's spectral remains, will offer us ways of understanding time, affect, and technology that will add to and change, however subtly, our understanding of afterglow. Accompanying it, rather than working against it, is what would appear to be its opposite: aftermath. The word, which refers to the consequences or aftereffects of a significant unpleasant event, captures the rhetoric, affective energy, and aesthetic of a corpus of contemporary Venezuelan fiction (and the scholarly works written about it) that fixate on ruins and what was ruined in the years of the Bolivarian Revolution. Gustavo Guerrero, in his analysis of a selection of contemporary Venezuelan poetry that he calls "catastrophic and/or postcatastrophic poetry," speaks of the recurring allusion to "a past that there may not be much to rescue from and a future that seems to relentlessly close in on itself" (2020,

40). This understanding of time, very much in line with aftermaths, becomes particularly pressing in Juan Cristóbal Castro's acclaimed novel *Arqueología sonámbula* (2020), in which fiction, autobiography, essay, and photography overlap, speaking of and showing ruins to the reader who sees spaces that are fractured, stained, abandoned, or simply no more. The possibility of choosing "aftermath" instead of "afterglow" has haunted this project since its very beginnings; this haunting has intensified with the worsening of the crisis and with the frustration at the invisibilization, misinterpretation, and manipulation Venezuela has endured in academic and nonacademic contexts, particularly since Chávez's death. Yet, I insist on afterglow because it contains something aftermaths do not: the possibility of something else taking shape, the memory, however faded, of a relationship, of *relationality* itself, of being with an "other" yet to be known. I will return to this possibility in chapter 5 and in this book's coda. For now, suffice it to say that, as I have worked on researching and developing this project, I have held onto the hope that, even in the suffocation of an all-encompassing afterglow such as this one, something always escapes.

Ghost H(a)unting: The Practice

The specter not as rhetorical device, as the product of a delusion, or as a symptom of trauma: *the specter as a social, political, and material figure.* This is the premise with which we embark on the task of exploring the various dimensions of Chávez's afterlife in contemporary Venezuela. Yet it is still unclear what this means in terms of methodology. Put differently, if the specter is not metaphorical, then shouldn't ghost hunting as a research modality not be metaphorical either? Consistency would demand that we answer yes. That answer, however, does not tell us exactly how we should go about conducting this research-as-ghost-hunting project.

We could follow the anthropological route and, like Taussig did in *The Magic of the State*, go on a pilgrimage that would lead us to the rituals of popular cults that bring Chávez back as a spirit, his apparition witnessed only by those involved, in the privacy of peripheral spaces. We could also track down the people who have claimed to see Chávez's specter and collect their testimonies, perhaps hoping to witness the specter's apparition ourselves. Yet pursuing these alternatives would mean subscribing to the idea that haunting is a private, peripheral, and/or individual phenomenon, an experience that can only be accessed behind closed doors and that does not leave any traces—or if it does, those traces can be dismissed as meaningless, irrational, or unbelievable by those who, in characterizing them as such, clearly draw a line that separates and protects them from the reality of being haunted. However, I have proposed that, in the afterglow of Chávez and the Bolivarian Revolution, we see haunting as a collective and remains-oriented experience, one mediated by and mediating the relationship between subjects and the social, political, economic, and historical structures that sustain the everyday life of the nation. We are thus not going to hunt for the specter in places hidden from the public eye or in the secret realm of individual imagination. Nor are we going to turn ghost hunting into a study of memory and politics among *chavistas* and *opositores*; this project is not about how one particular group remembers Chávez in one particular place, even if in many ways those group-constructed narratives and practices do shape the spectral afterlife Chávez leads. This is instead an exploration of haunting—in the words of Giorgio Agamben—in "some lane, in some piazza, in some street, on some sidewalk along a canal, in some back alley" (2013, 476).

Agamben is referring to places in Venice, a city he describes as existing in the state of "the specter, of the dead who appears without warning, preferably in the middle of the night, creaking and sending signals, sometimes even speaking, though in a way that is not always intelligible"—a city, he says, that "whispers" (2013, 473). Venezuela is not Venice, though its name, a variation of the Italian *Venezziola*, does coincidentally mean "little Venice." Nevertheless, Agamben's way of characterizing the encounter with the specter of Venice, in terms that bring to mind not so much a determined pursuit but a strolling, casual way of wandering around, is how I propose to approach hunting for Chávez's specter. Some street, some corner, some wall, some building, some back alley; the random "some" locates the spectral anywhere and thus everywhere, for if it is in some object in some street, then it can be in any object, in any street. Randomness thus distances haunting from the temporal and spatial specificity of a single event and turns it into an all-encompassing and shared reality that exists both as a given and as a possibility, and that invites us to embark on ghost hunting some place/ any place.

Over the course of three months in the summer of 2016, I traveled between Caracas and Mérida (my hometown) chasing after Chávez's specter by gathering photographic and physical evidence of his material and digital remains. While preparing for the trip, I developed a research agenda that included visits to places I was sure were "haunted" by Chávez: his resting place at the Cuartel de la Montaña, the Biblioteca Nacional, the Panteón Nacional, the Museo Bolivariano, and the headquarters of the Partido Socialista Unido de Venezuela (PSUV) in Mérida.[24] These places did not disappoint in terms of providing me with a wide selection of materials that spoke to the strength of Chávez's posthumous presence in the country's social and political landscape. However, it was the conversations, unexpected encounters, and accidental findings during the journey from one place to the other that yielded some of the most compelling discoveries. The number of times I accidentally "ran into Chávez" (at the airport, at a bakery, in a traffic jam) was only matched by the number of times I found evidence of his haunting in the form of graffiti, phone cards, and toys because someone—a relative, a friend, an acquaintance, a vendor, a library employee, a curious passerby—told me where to find them. Not only do these "tips" speak to the generosity of the people of Mérida and Caracas, without whom more than half of the spectral remains I analyze in this book would be missing, but they also evince a certain automatism when it came to recalling where Chávez was, one not contingent upon political allegiances. Both people who self-identified as *chavistas* and those who self-identified as *opositores* could think of "some wall, some street, some lamppost" when asked if they had seen graffiti, a poster, or any image of Chávez as they went about their daily routines. I interpret this automatic recall as part of Chávez's spectrality, which, I have proposed, is not confined to the spectacular and eventful but also manifests itself in the ordinary and quotidian.

Embracing the unexpected, random, and seemingly irrelevant as I hunted down Chávez's specter meant that the line separating ghost hunting and ghost haunting was, if not entirely gone, then at least heavily blurred. The result, a hybrid I refer to as "ghost h(a)unting," underscores the particularities of researching objects and practices *in the present*. After all, ghost h(a)unting, when carried out in a nonmetaphorical fashion, cannot be a retrospective practice; the specter does not exist in the past resting in peace but rather stands before and around us, restlessly copresent. Thus, writing about it requires writing *with it*, letting yourself be part of it, affected by it, and—it bears repeating—haunted by it. In practice, this means coming to terms with the fact that, just as specters signal that which is not over and done with, the "nonarchive" of spectral remains that render specters visible and interactive is equally incomplete.[25] New memes featuring Chávez are shared every day via WhatsApp and Facebook, his image reappears every time Maduro addresses the Venezuelan people, and red T-shirts and red hats with the stencil of his eyes continue to multiply in plazas and on streets. Simultaneously the symptom and the source of Chávez's spectrality, the "ongoingness" in the production and circulation of these remains, makes finding where to put the full stop in this ghost h(a)unting endeavor impossible, at least for the time being.

Also incomplete is the compilation of spectral remains in the following chapters. From the many objects, images, and performances that I encountered in those months of research and the many I have accessed virtually since, only a few have made it into this book. Those included were selected based on how frequently they made an appearance in public spaces (as is the case with the graffiti of Chávez's eyes and the reproduction of his signature), the high value placed on them by the people who collected or wore them (as with the phone cards), their virality (as with Chávez's memes), and, in some instances, the way they stood out as uniquely spectral (as with the hologram). Together, they form a constellation that, in its current configuration, transforms the specter into a point of departure to reflect on questions regarding not just the lingering of the past in the present, but how the copresent past weighs on the future. The spectral remains we will look at and the relationships constructed with and through them link ancestry and posterity in a narrative that defines a way of being in and of the nation; therefore, they engage practices and narratives of memory as much as they engage the act of imagining ourselves, politically and otherwise. Imagination, then, is not invoked to deny the specter its connection to a collectively shared reality— the specter as a "figment of someone's imagination"—but rather to emphasize that connection, ghost h(a)unting thus appearing as a practice that intervenes in the construction of political subjectivity and shared acts of imagination.

This appeal to the imagination is also connected to the stability and "graspability" of spectral remains: to our ability to capture them fully by creating frames that contain them in all aspects of their social and political existence. The reality of ghost h(a)unting calls into question the possibility of putting those frames in place and, more generally, the desirability of having them at all, when what they are meant to capture is, by nature, fleeting. One morning a street vendor would set up a small table with Chávez-themed memorabilia; the following morning the same vendor and his merchandise would be gone. A gigantic poster of Chávez would decorate a plaza in Caracas for an entire week, and the following week it would appear ripped to pieces. In each instance, the specter's appearance, produced by engagement with these kinds of remains, is preceded, followed, and permeated by the inevitability of its disappearance. The specter is, above all, liminal: existing between light and shadow, presence and absence, and visibility and invisibility. To approach it means to acknowledge the voids that define that liminality and that become pressing when we, for example, wonder what happened to the graffiti we once saw on some wall. These questions point to the "before," the "after," and the "around," of the encounter with Chávez's spectral remains, and while the possibility of pursuing a definite answer is always there, doing so would mean switching the focus from h(a)unting to tracking down and recording the social life of remains that would no longer be spectral, but would instead become objects existing in a stable and clearly outlined temporal trajectory. I thus choose the hybridity of h(a)unting over the paralyzing effect of only being haunted and over the goal-oriented task of hunting down, to preserve the overlap of familiarity and unexpectedness, of certainty and uncertainty, that comes with engaging with rather than capturing and archiving spectral remains—both actions that would flatten them to the point of rendering them inanimate. And, rather than seeing the questions and gaps that come with this engagement as shortcomings, I present them as essential in triggering the exercises of imagination that underlie Chávez's spectral afterlife.

Ghost H(a)unting: The Method

Three months of ghost h(a)unting left me with a flash drive storing over four hundred photographs, two notebooks filled with comments about my encounters with Chávez's specter, a suitcase containing my own personal collection of Chávez's spectral remains (a gifted coffee cup, pin, and flag from the chapel Santo Hugo Chávez del 23, a DIY cardboard Chávez, a key chain, and a few posters), and two pressing questions: What theoretical tools and methodological frameworks exist to read such a diverse constellation of objects? And, since the specter haunts me just as it haunts others (though perhaps not in the exact same ways), how can our critical language recognize and engage with the reality that the scholar is as vulnerable to the object (of study) as the object (of study) is vulnerable to the scholar's "reading" of it?

I developed the methodology of this book while attempting to respond to these two questions by drawing on an interdisciplinary corpus that brings together contributions from affect theory, cultural studies, performance studies, media studies, new materialism, and memory studies. Diana Taylor's theorization of performance, archive, and repertoire, and Rebecca Schneider's conceptualization of performing remains have been key referents to think about nonlinear ways of understanding temporality that ultimately allowed me to propose haunting and afterglow as productive categories to read the affective and material lingering of the past in contemporary Venezuela. Furthermore, Taylor's understanding of performance as a vital act of transfer that transmits "social knowledge, memory, and a sense of identity through reiterated actions" (2016, 25) shapes my reflections about a collective state of being haunted that, I propose, is powerful and enduring precisely because it relies on the routine repetition of certain behaviors that create a sense of (individual, collective, national, popular, official, revolutionary) identity grounded in the cohabitation with a familiar specter that those behaviors conjure up and animate. Beyond illuminating the operations of Venezuela's theatrical and necromantic state, performance as a concept and a practice has also allowed me to foreground my understanding of the research that I conducted for this book as performance, and thus as epistemology: a way of knowing, understanding, and theorizing the world—or a corner of it—that takes as a point of departure and as a valuable source my own participation in and performing of the ghost h(a)unting that is my object of study.

Also central to my analysis of the images and objects that make up Chávez's spectral remains is a theoretical approach that acknowledges their ability to "stare back" (as James Elkins [1996] and Marianne Hirsch [(1997) 2012] propose regarding images and photographs) and "do something" (as Bill Brown [2004] and Daniel Miller [2010] suggest regarding things and stuff). I treat Chávez's spectral remains as "actants" that make demands and do things—including routinely bringing Chávez back from the dead—that shape our behaviors, set our expectations, and intervene in how we might imagine ourselves and others.[26] In doing so, I follow the path established by Chiara Bottici, whose work on images, imagination, and the imaginary in *Imaginal Politics* (2014) served as a fundamental referent for one of the key arguments I put forth in this book: that being haunted leads, among other things, to a crisis of political imagination. I also draw inspiration from the work of scholars of new materialism such as Bruno Latour, Karen Barad, and Jane Bennett, as well as by those who pay close attention to the potential contained in the most ordinary of things, including Walter Benjamin, Roland Barthes, and Kathleen Stewart.[27] I take the works of Benjamin, Barthes, and Stewart as models of the kind of thinking I am interested in performing in this book, and also as models of the sort of writing I want to offer the reader who will accompany me in this ghost h(a)unting project: a writing that craves company and close contact, that loses itself in the vibrancy of things, and that, in Stewart's words, leaves both author and reader "with an embodied sense of the world as a dense network of mostly unknown links" (2007, 6).

Establishing dialogues between these theorists and their work allowed me to construct a methodology to read Chávez's spectral remains that reflects a view on interdisciplinarity I first encountered in Avery Gordon's groundbreaking *Ghostly Matters*. Gordon's proposal that we see the ghost as a social figure and haunting as part of our social world leads her to advocate for a new and transformative way of seeing what lies (visibly or invisibly) around us, and a new way of doing things grounded in a "method attentive to what is elusive, fantastic, contingent, and often barely there" ([1997] 2008, 26)—a method that is interdisciplinary not because it gathers three or four disciplines but because it produces a "new object that belongs to no one" but that leaves room to "claim rather than discipline its meaning into existence" (7). It is, without doubt, a method that invites trouble—and Gordon herself admits it has gotten her into some trouble—and the only one that, I believe, allows us to recognize the specter as a powerful social figure (as opposed to a metaphor, a delusion, or another word for trauma). Inspired and guided by Gordon's methodological approach to ghostly matters, my theorization of the specter is also unconcerned with disciplinary boundaries or disciplinary loyalties. I made this choice based on the belief that ghosts, even hypervisible, omnipresent, and state-made ones, rarely obey our methodological rules and our disciplinary organization of social life, and on the conviction that, in Gordon's words, "we need not . . . find the loss of this deluding innocence so terribly frightening" (27).

A Note on Vulnerability

Vulnerability is at the heart of this project and its embrace of ghost h(a)unting as a scholarly practice. The most explicit sign of it is my resistance to give up the "I" as I analyze the images, objects, and behaviors that make up Chávez's spectral afterlife, an analysis that includes and engages with my own personal narrative, my own reactions to the materials both while I was in Venezuela hunting them down and being haunted by them and after I left the country and returned to the United States. My use of the first person highlights my commitment to what Susanna Paasonen calls "self-reflexive scholarly agency": the acknowledgment that "analysis is always directed by one's reactions and values" (2011, 23) and that, because of it, as a theorist one is never really outside, above, beyond, or disconnected from that which one investigates. Situating oneself "above" the topics, phenomena, and materials studied is, Paasonen argues, a way of escaping vulnerability, of denying or ignoring resonances and the possibilities they open up. Aboveness "blocks from view both the power of those materials and the phenomena to move oneself, as well as the ways in which this motion affects acts of interpretation" (23).

I thus write about haunting not as a disembodied and detached scholar—one that can see specters from outside and remain unaffected by them—but as a *haunted* scholar who moves between proximity and distance, affectation and contemplation. I see the vulnerability that comes from this state of being haunted and writing in that state as evidence (and as a frequent reminder) of the agency embedded in the materials I analyze, the power that they exert over those who encounter them whether occasionally or regularly, the forces that they mobilize as they shape and reshape political, social, and urban landscapes. I also see it as an invitation, a hand that reaches out to you, the reader, to bring you in—so that you, too, feel haunted, so that you read about haunting while haunted—but also to remind you that the analysis that follows is one among many, that there is not only one way to be haunted, nor is there only one story that can be told about the spectral remains that we will encounter. Much like Chávez himself, the stencil of his eyes, his signature, the collectible phone cards, the toys and memes mean different things to different people, and the connections that can be drawn between these materials change depending on how they are grouped, each grouping shedding light on something new. What I offer you then is *one* ghost story, *one* set of constellations, *one* way of ghost h(a)unting. Not a point of arrival but a point of departure, the beginning of what I hope will be a long conversation.

Afterlife and Afterdeath

This book has two parts: the first part is a long journey into the afterlife, and the second, much shorter one is a peek into the afterdeath. The afterlife comprises the first four chapters. Chapter 1 analyzes the official and popular narratives that circulated in Venezuela after Chávez was diagnosed with cancer in 2011. I argue that these narratives created an atmosphere of uncertainty that complicated processes of mourning and memorialization and allowed Chávez's death to be "postponed," thus facilitating his spectral lingering in the nation's landscape. In chapters 2, 3, and 4, I develop an analysis of Chávez's spectral remains, which I have organized into three constellations, each illuminating a different dimension of his afterlife.

Chapter 2 focuses on the stencil of Chávez's eyes, which first appeared during Venezuela's 2012 presidential elections. I discuss the ubiquity of the image of the eyes and connect it to what I call Chávez's "pre-posthumous haunting," a term I use to refer to the excessive reproduction of Chávez's images and words in Venezuela in the years preceding his death as shown in the documentary *FANtasmo*, directed by Jonás Romero García (2009). I then analyze the memory narratives and practices shaping the creation and reproduction of the eyes by members of the government and the opposition, the characteristics of their spectral gaze, and the authority that materializes through them and that operates, I propose, through an act of temporal dislocation.

Chapter 3 engages with collectible phone cards that re-present Chávez's life and that were the result of a collaboration between graphic designer and cartoonist Omar Cruz and the state-owned telecommunications company CANTV. It also analyzes the afterlife of Chávez's handwriting, focusing on the reproduction of his signature as a tattoo and on the walls of apartment buildings constructed by the Gran Misión Vivienda Venezuela, and on the transformation of his handwriting into a font through the app TC Chavez Pro, developed by the state-sponsored art collective Trinchera Creativa. These objects, I argue, place Chávez's haunting in relation to affect, excess, and acts of collection and recollection, miniaturization and amplification, inhabitation and habituation. I conclude that they create a form of spectral intimacy that locates the future in the past and the past in the future, thus encouraging a form of imagination that operates like déjà vu.

In chapter 4, I analyze the connection between spectrality and acts of mimesis, playfulness, and imagination, in relation to a selection of Chávez's doubles. These doubles include: the hologram that walked around Caracas in December 2016, the bird that Maduro announced was the spirit of Chávez attempting to communicate with him, Maduro himself as he imitates Chávez's rhetoric and mannerisms, a man and a woman who "went viral" because of their uncanny resemblance to Chávez, and the Chávez dolls that appeared on posters placed around Caracas after the announcement of his death. I argue that the official and stately efforts to double, imitate, and reproduce Chávez repeatedly fail and lead to the widening of the gap left by his absence. Threatened with the imminence of its collapse, the state, I propose, appeals to people's playful imagination as a way to reanimate the specter in which it has grounded its legitimacy and authority.

Before reaching the afterdeath, we stop at an interlude that looks back at the specter that took shape in the previous chapters and discusses the central role imagination plays in the way it operates politically, socially, and historically. As an operation of the state, haunting, I argue, requires rendering the specter and the status quo attached to it comfortable, familial, and intimate. This takes a toll on political imagination and the possibility of testing out new visual and political languages that would go beyond the limits of the specter's gaze and enable forms of resistance that could lead to new political futures and figures. With that argument in mind, I ask: What, then, to do with the specter? To answer this question, I turn to contemporary performance art and, specifically, to the work of Venezuelan artist Deborah Castillo.

In chapter 5, I analyze four of Castillo's performance pieces: *The Emancipatory Kiss*, *Demagogue*, *Slapping Power*, and *The Unnamable* (2013, 2015b, 2015c, 2015d). Castillo, I propose, reckons with the specter by inserting it in an afterdeath where it turns into something material, malleable, and dead. As such, the specter becomes an opportunity to think of the future as an unshaped potentiality, which activates an agency that only exists in the hands of the present and that is born out of an unsettling, uncomfortable, and disloyal relationship with the past.

Lastly, the book's coda takes the unsettling provocations, uncomfortable affects, and calls for a raw kind of imagination found in Castillo's performance work as an opportunity to identify, in the fields of performance art and visual arts and among Venezuelans both inside and outside the country, other instances where, I believe, a certain futurity is articulated that escapes the boundaries established by the spectral gaze of the country's distant and recent revolutionary past. I introduce these examples as vignettes that pay homage to people who are working hard for something that has yet to take shape but that will not be disciplined into form or meaning by either the stale discourse of an epic past that we know has run its course, or the dystopian insistence that in Venezuela there is nothing left but ruins.

Chronicle of a Death Postponed   1

> To manipulate absence is to extend this interval, to delay as long
> as possible the moment when the other might topple sharply
> from absence into death.
>
> Roland Barthes, *A Lover's Discourse*

An Ailing Power

On the night of June 30, 2011, after days of speculation, rumors, and suspicious absences, Hugo Chávez announced that he had cancer. In a televised speech he gave while in Havana—the place where he would receive most of his treatment under the supervision of Fidel Castro's chosen medical team—the president stood behind a podium, next to Venezuela's flag and Simón Bolívar's portrait, and briefed Venezuelan and international audiences on the status of his health.[1] In the speech, he shared details of the surgeries he underwent interlaced with words of praise and love for Castro who, according to Chávez, had been among the first people to notice that something was wrong with him.

The short length of the speech—less than fifteen minutes—and Chávez's robotic, subdued delivery created a striking contrast with the charismatic demeanor that had won him admiration in Venezuela and abroad. His words, however, were those of a soldier readying himself for battle. He used military rhetoric that, as Susan Sontag (1989) points out in her study of illness and metaphors, often frames discussions of cancer and that in this case fit seamlessly within the epic narrative that grounded the Bolivarian Revolution and Chávez's own rise to power. In fact, a key element in Chávez's speech was the idea of the return from the abyss, which he underscored as he recalled his return to the public stage after being imprisoned for leading the 1992 military coup against former president Carlos Andrés Pérez, and then again after being ousted from office for forty-seven hours during the 2002 attempted coup d'état against him.[2] This time, he said, he would speak to his people as he returned from yet another abyss—his illness—with the help of God and Jesus Christ, and he then invited those listening to join him in a recovery that he appeared to take for granted, as reflected in the new slogan that he introduced at the end of the speech, which replaced the well-known and widely popular "Patria, socialismo o muerte" (Fatherland, socialism, or death): "Por ahora y para siempre viviremos y venceremos" (Now and forever, we will live and we will be victorious).

Chávez's announcement marked the beginning of months of uncertainty, confusion, and paranoia that continued even after Nicolás Maduro, his appointed successor, officially announced Chávez's death on March 5, 2013. In fact, the decade following Chávez's death saw the publication of books such as Ludmila Vinogradoff's *El ocaso del Comandante* (2015), David Placer's *Los brujos de Chávez* (2015), Francisco Olivares's *Los últimos días de Hugo Chávez* (2020), and Juan Carlos Zapata's *Chávez a la hora y en la hora de su muerte* (2021) that aimed to uncover the truth behind Chávez's illness and death through extensive research, primarily interviews, that only made the cancer seem more mysterious.[3] The conspiracy theories and semiconfirmed rumors recorded in these works circulated alongside the government's own theory that Chávez had been infected with cancer as part of an operation that involved the United States and the Venezuelan opposition, a theory that Chávez himself proposed and found compelling given that cancer had also affected other Latin American leaders of leftist governments such as Luiz Inácio Lula da Silva, Dilma Rousseff, and Fernando Lugo.[4]

While Chávez was ill, these theories were fueled by the lack of concrete medical information regarding his health and by the confusion caused by photos of Chávez in various newspapers and on social media platforms that were incorrectly dated or digitally altered, or showed a man who resembled but was not actually Chávez.[5] After his death, these images were revisited and spread with newfound vigor partly in response to the country's social, political, and economic crisis, which led to questions about the past and who was responsible for the catastrophic state Venezuela found itself in after 2014. While books like Placer's and Olivares's do not explicitly answer those questions, they hint at an explanation that would link the crisis to various forms of manipulation (political, economic, ideological, and supernatural) on the part of the government under Chávez and Maduro, an explanation that further radicalizes political discourse in the country and the dangerous conviction that the years of the Bolivarian Revolution in Venezuela can only be understood in terms of irrationality and as the result of foreign forces from a threatening and not fully knowable "outside."[6]

While it might be tempting to dismiss these theories as unfounded, biased, and unworthy of serious academic consideration, they constitute one of the key factors behind an atmosphere of uncertainty that, in Roland Barthes's words, prevented Chávez from "toppl[ing] sharply from absence into death" ([1977] 2010, 16). What follows is not a definitive, detailed chronology of Chávez's illness but an exploration of the fictions that materialized in the absence of such a chronology and that ultimately enabled Chávez to linger in the political and social landscape after March 5, 2013, neither dead nor alive but as something/someone in between. These fictions allowed bodies to overlap in symbolic and material ways, blurred the boundaries between public and private spaces, and complicated processes of mourning and memorialization. Together, they shed light on those uncanny moments in history when past, present, and future collide and conspire to suspend death and create a pulsating, never-empty void from which a specter can be born.

In the Flesh

In *Illness as Metaphor*, Susan Sontag argues that, throughout history, cancer has been overlaid with mystification, often described in a metaphorical language that appeals to the supernatural and to warfare, that hints at the possibility of contamination and contagion, and that triggers fear and paranoia. The mobilization of this language—reflected in descriptions of the tumor as "malignant," "alien," "invasive," or "colonizing"—is not surprising if we consider what the disease is at its core: the growth of mutating cells that immunologists often class as a "nonself" and that ultimately take over the host body, replacing "you" with a "non-you" (Sontag 2001, 67). This transformation of "you" into a "non-you" recasts the ill body as excessively material and thus robbed of all capacities for self-transcendence. In Sontag's words, "cancer, as a disease that can strike anywhere, is a disease of the body.

Far from revealing anything spiritual, it reveals that the body is, all too woefully, just the body" (18). Cancer is, as she also points out, often perceived to be obscene in the original sense of the word: "ill-omened, abominable, repugnant to the senses" (9).[7]

Taking Sontag's observations as a point of departure, this section turns to the metaphors that mediated the way Chávez's cancer was introduced, spoken about, and collectively experienced. In doing so, it also explores the political and bodily effects of these metaphors, and the ways in which they enabled the construction of a fleshy bond between Chávez's body and the body of the people, a bond that was central to his victory in the 2012 presidential elections and, as we will see, essential for the materialization of his spectral afterlife.

These metaphors appeared for the first time in the speech where Chávez announced his cancer:

> That was how a strange formation in my pelvic region was detected, which required an emergency surgical procedure due to the imminent risk of infection spreading. . . . After that operation, which in principle succeeded at draining the abscess, an intense antibiotic treatment was begun, which led to a positive evaluation, I mean, a positive evolution, and brought about a noticeable improvement. However, despite the overall positive report, throughout the process of draining and healing, there began to be some suspicions of the presence of other cellular formations that had not been detected before. Therefore another series of special studies was begun immediately—cytochemical, cytological, microbiological, and studies of pathological anatomy—which confirmed the existence of an abscessed tumor, with the presence of cancerous cells, which required a second surgical intervention that allowed the tumor to be entirely removed. (Reuters 2011)

Chávez's words reflect several of the elements Sontag mentions as she analyzes the metaphors that erupt when cancer is detected. Using medical jargon that creates a striking contrast to his well-known epic rhetoric—where death, when present, was always anachronistic or metaphorical—Chávez refers to the cancer as "alien" cell formations that had not been detected before and that require urgent interventions.[8] In this account, we hear an echo of the military language that is common when speaking of the "battle" against cancer, an echo that will become stronger when Chávez transitions from speaking about his medical procedures to discussing his victorious "returns" to the political stage after the military coups of 1992 and 2002. We also see—if we focus on Chávez's delivery and not just on his words—an unfamiliar Chávez: one that, subdued and reading from a script words that do not seem to be truly his, appears to reveal the lingering presence of a "nonself." And as we witness this "other" Chávez recounting his medical odyssey, we also feel our gaze become embodied, "tactile" in the sense Maurice Merleau-Ponty ([1968] 2004) proposes when he talks about our tendency to clothe what we see in its own flesh. This is because Chávez's words are dripping with fluids, abscesses, and cancerous cells; fleshy matter that does not allow us to distance ourselves from the body in question but that pulls us into it, as if we too were part of it, as if we too had been ill and could be again.

This movement from standing before to being with Chávez's ill body is something Chávez himself reiterates in the last part of the speech:

> And finally, my beloved compatriots; my adored sons and daughters; my dear young *compañeros*, girls and boys of my people; my forever valiant soldiers; my courageous workers; my dear women patriots; my beloved people, all are one in my heart, and wanting to speak to you today as I make a new ascent to return has nothing to do with me, but with you, *pueblo patrio, pueblo bueno*. (Reuters 2011)

As he appeals to his people, Chávez makes clear that his words, and therefore his illness, are not just about him: they also concern the "good, patriotic people." By the time the new slogan is introduced ("Now and forever, we will live and we will be victorious!"), the stakes are high: Chávez had to live because if he did not—his words seem to suggest—no one would. Thus, in less than fifteen minutes, Chávez's cancer contradicted its own noncontagious nature and spread, the body of the leader and the body of the people metaphorically becoming one, the illness developing into a collective experience.

The collective experience of Chávez's body and his cancer did not stay within the realm of the metaphorical; soon after the speech, a number of performances would take place among different groups of people for whom their own bodies (and the bodies of others) would become the ground where Chávez's fate would be decided. However, before turning to these performances, it is important to recognize that the discovery of Chávez's cancer was not the first time his body was exposed to the diagnostic gaze of the people—both those who supported him and those who opposed him—nor was it the first time that, in the years of the Bolivarian Revolution, the body of the nation was thought to be ill or monstrous.

Luis Duno-Gottberg and Javier Guerrero both trace the development and popularization of a "somatic narrative" that framed how the Bolivarian Revolution, its supporters, and its leader were described and perceived by the opposition, and how the opposition was portrayed as "the enemy" in *chavista* discourse. Taking as a point of departure the Hobbesian metaphor that ties the notion of sovereignty to the organic body of the monarch and the health of the nation to the health of his political/human body, Duno-Gottberg analyzes several newspaper articles and political cartoons by opposition writers who speak of Chávez's leftist ideology in terms of lethal viruses and contagion threatening to corrode the body of the nation. This somatic narrative also circulated among *chavista* groups, which created graffiti and political cartoons that denounced Globovisión—a television network known for being critical of Chávez—as an illness affecting the minds of the opposition (Duno-Gottberg 2015, 294), whom Chávez and his supporters often called *escuálidos*—a word that refers to a frail, ill body.

Guerrero in turn identifies three episodes in the country's recent history—the damage to the statue of the Venezuelan goddess María Lionza in 2004, the murder of the Faddoul brothers in 2006, and the appearance of a "gay Bolívar" in a 2005 carnival parade in Brazil that was sponsored by the Venezuelan government—as disruptions of what he calls the "Venezuelan holy family," disruptions that, he argues, had to be quickly brought under control so as to restore the healthy, familiar, nonhideous body of the nation. In Guerrero's analysis, these disruptions were the result of a fight for political power inscribed on the nation as a material body:

> The anxiety related to the powers of the body as representations of the Nation is skin deep. A polarized Venezuela builds a hideous family group composed by bodies that disfigure the—*mestiza*—national *Holy* Family to report the poor management, the disagreement between the different political sectors towards power, executive or symbolic, of the adversary. The political polarization and its violence, undeniable signs of these revolutionary times, act in a direct manner on these bodies and shape their representation. The body is a sensible area for the operations of the nation. (Guerrero 2012a, 28; original emphasis)

Fixing those "disfigured" bodies—repairing the broken goddess, making the bodies of the Faddoul brothers vanish, and "unqueering" Bolívar—was a necessity that all the groups involved in various political confrontations agreed on. For Guerrero, this evinces a shared insistence on not letting "other" bodies—particularly sexual bodies that challenge the heteronormative paradigm—be recognized as bodies of the nation.

Duno-Gottberg and Guerrero show how, from the early years of the Bolivarian Revolution, the nation as a body and the bodies of the nation became the raw material used to test out and inscribe political discourses, often with the purpose of transforming the "other"—*chavista* or *opositor*—into not just a political enemy but a diseased and contagious one. While this pathological reinscribing of the enemy relied heavily on metaphorical language encompassing entire groups of people where bodies blended together as they were compared with dengue-carrying mosquitos, kissing bugs, and parasites, when it came to Chávez, the language used to describe and diagnose his body went beyond the abstraction of metaphors.

Years before Chávez's cancer was detected, there were already newspaper articles that spoke of "Hugo Chávez's illness" (Duno-Gottberg 2015, 289), an illness that allegedly affected his spine, was connected to his consumption of coffee and tobacco, and manifested itself in his irritable mood. One article that discussed this illness—which included a graph with arrows pointing to areas on Chávez's body where the symptoms could be recognized (289)—was joined by several other articles and blog entries that claimed Chávez was mentally unstable and by the prophecies of well-known astrologer Walter Mercado, who insisted Chávez was going to die of a rare illness affecting his head. The government responded to these theories with a statement from the Ministry of Health warning against giving unfounded medical opinions about Chávez's health.

These debates over Chávez's mental and physical health, which started as early as 2002, reflect the common belief—one that Hobbes had already identified in his *Leviathan*, as Duno-Gottberg points out—that the health of the sovereign body is connected to the health of the nation and all its bodies. In the case of the obsession with diagnosing Chávez, this connection was strengthened by the omnipresence of Chávez's image and words, reproduced ad nauseam in public and private spaces through graffiti, posters, figurines, T-shirts, and hats, and on his famous show *Aló Presidente* during extraordinarily long episodes that monopolized television and radio channels.[9] Overexposed and readily available, Chávez's body thus did not seem to be just part of the landscape; it became the landscape (and the soundscape) itself and, as such, it easily pulled in the gaze of viewers who were compelled to constantly imagine and reimagine it.

By the time Chávez announced the discovery of his cancer then, there was a firmly established national practice of examining and diagnosing Chávez's body in order to understand and explain the body of a nation torn apart by the heavily polarized discourse Chávez himself promoted and the widespread populist rhetoric that divided Venezuelans into *chavistas* and *opositores*. As the polarization increased, so did the visible manifestations of people's political allegiances. Those who identified as *chavistas* would often wear red clothing and accessories that reproduced the military uniform associated with Chávez or that featured Chávez's image and words, and those who identified as *opositores* would appear at protests and public gatherings wearing blue and white or a baseball cap with the colors of the national flag.[10] Of the two groups, however, it was the former's choice to consistently wear red T-shirts—even outside the context of protests and presidential campaigns—that rendered the clothing item iconic and made it the visual link that joined the *chavista* people together and connected them to Chávez, who made red the color of the Bolivarian Revolution and who also often wore red clothing. Red represented not just an ideological bond but also a filial and organic one; after all, red evokes blood as much as it evokes more abstract concepts such as love, passion, and revolution. This organic bond, however compelling, remained for the most part metaphorical; that is, until Chávez announced that he had cancer.

Chávez's insistence on the collective nature of his illness in his 2011 speech did more than win him sympathetic nods and prayers. According to Beatriz Lecumberri, presumably healthy people rushed to the offices of oncologists, urologists, and proctologists to get checked, following the rationale that if Chávez was ill, they could be ill too, and members of his official entourage switched their diets and lifestyles to mirror Chávez's own determination to eat better and sleep more. Chávez's cancer thus behaved like a phantom limb: it became a "something" that people all over the country could feel even though it was not and had never been part of their own bodies in the first place. This phantom sensation was incorporated in the slogan of the 2012 presidential campaign: "Chávez, corazón de mi patria" (Chávez, the heart of my fatherland). This slogan—reproduced on walls, posters, T-shirts, and cups, and made into a song—turned the fatherland and everyone in it into a body with Chávez as the heart, the blood-pumping organ responsible for the body's survival.[11] The connection between Chávez and the people that emerged went beyond the abstraction of politics and ideology to become organic—tangible, bodily, vital—and, with the heart's symbolic tie to love, it drew strength from his supporters' affective responses to the illness.

In fact, there were those who felt Chávez's cancer so deeply that they shaved their own heads as an act of faith and solidarity with the president, who had lost his hair from chemotherapy. This took place in Miraflores as part of a massive healing ceremony attended by Chávez, Maduro, and religious leaders who stood in the audience giving blessings while people chanted "Cristo sana" (Christ heals), a woman sang prayers, and the men and one woman who had volunteered for the occasion sat smiling at the camera while the electric shavers left them bald.[12] The video of the ceremony then showed Chávez standing next to the newly bald individuals and hugging them, their bodies turned into echoes of his own ailing body. The group, it was announced, was following the example set by members of a Christian group, Paz Dominicana, from the Dominican Republic, who were also in the audience and who had shaved their heads "because that is what God showed us, because with the power of this vow that has spread to other nations moving the soul, moving the heart of so many human beings, this is because God has imbued with his grace this act of faith that we have carried out with love" (Todo Chávez 2011).[13]

This ceremony—broadcast live on national television and made available on YouTube—was the most public demonstration of people sacrificing parts of their own bodies to save the president. Other sacrifices were not as public, taking place behind closed doors or at night as part of the rituals of religions such as Santería, which had become more popular thanks to Chávez's support (Michelutti 2017). It was rumored that, during these rituals, both human and animal bodies became battlegrounds where supernatural forces were invoked to ensure Chávez's survival. These rumors, which proliferated after his death and found support in books such as David Placer's *Los brujos de Chávez* (2015), pointed to local news reports of animals disappearing from zoos, corpses being stolen from cemeteries, and homeless people floating in rivers all with the same fatal wound in their necks—all presumed to be raw materials used during sacrificial rituals performed to save Chávez's life. The desire to save Chávez no matter the cost intensified after he appeared live on national television praying to Christ and offering to carry his cross in exchange for more years to live.[14] Chávez's moving speech, which took place in a small church in Barinas during a Holy Thursday Mass that he celebrated with his family after he found out the cancer had reappeared in

April 2012, revealed a vulnerable side to him that appealed to the love of the people—a love, he emphasized, that was indispensable for his survival. Perhaps the most extreme manifestation of that love was the decision of a man named José Alberto Alviárez to kill, dismember, and set fire to his mother to save Chávez's life, a crime he committed, he said, following God's orders (El Comercio 2013; Semana 2013). This took place in January 2013, two months before Maduro announced Chávez had died, and was reported in several newspapers in Venezuela and abroad.

Chávez's cancer thus triggered bodily performances ranging from bodies fearing that they too might have cancer and therefore rushing to see oncologists, to bodies engaging in sacrificial acts in Chávez's honor, sometimes with fatal consequences. What they all have in common—other than Chávez—is a sort of material "excess," a "too-much-ness" that cannot be easily explained away as political propaganda or ideological "brainwashing," nor can it be contained within discourses of empathy, an emotion that, as Sara Ahmed points out, ultimately maintains the distance between the subject who wants to feel the other's pain and the one feeling it. In her words: "This is love as empathy: I love you, and imagine not only that I can feel how you feel, but that I could feel your pain *for you*. But I want that feeling insofar as I don't already have it; the desire maintains the difference between the one who would 'become' in pain, and another who already 'is' in pain or 'has' it" (Ahmed 2015, 30). Chávez did not focus on the pain of his cancer; in fact, signs of it were hidden. He would speak in detail about his diet and exercise regime, but he needed to conceal the painful deterioration of his body in large part because he was running for reelection, and the possibility of somebody else in his party running instead of him was out of the question. The invisibility of Chávez's pain and the lack of detailed records from his medical team thus bolstered the perception that anything—human sacrifice included—could work to help him. The task was not to empathetically feel Chávez's pain but to occupy/share his body with him: a bodily continuity, a "withness" performed on the flesh of the sovereign that was also the flesh of the people.

We cannot speak of this expansive, sticky, shared flesh without briefly referring to what Eric Santner calls the "sublime flesh, the sacral soma, of the monarch" (2011, xv). In Santner's theorization—a compelling revisiting of Ernst Kantorowicz's seminal 1957 work *The King's Two Bodies*—when the "sovereign thing, whether phallus, father, or king, can no longer discharge the duties of its office, it discharges the remains of the flesh it has heretofore pretended or appeared to embody . . . a kind of chronic, spectral secretion of the social body at large, one registered as a surplus of immanence that oscillates between the sublime and the abject" (81). The context for his analysis of this "discharge" is European post-monarchical societies where the people, in becoming the bearers of sovereignty, continue to struggle in various ways with the flesh of the monarch, a context that, needless to say, diverges significantly from the Venezuelan one. And yet, inasmuch as Chávez succeeded at portraying himself as the embodiment of the people, he became a sovereign-like figure whose impending death triggered a crisis of the body of authority and of authority as a body that strongly resonates with the concerns regarding transference, substitution, and discharge that both Santner and Kantorowicz address in their work. In the case of Chávez, however, these concerns manifested *before* his death, during an illness that, in becoming a collective experience, enabled a "common flesh" to materialize where the boundary separating the body of the sovereign and the body of the people repeatedly collapsed, which meant that, in the end—when the sovereign was declared "officially dead"—it was not entirely clear who lived and who died, or if anyone had died at all.

The bodily excess that marked the years of Chávez's illness and of the Bolivarian Revolution as a whole is represented in Duno-Gottberg's use of the term "embodied politics" (2015, 12) and in Paula Vásquez Lezama's allusion to "somatic culture" (Vásquez Lezama 2019, 104) to talk about Bolivarian Venezuela.[15] This bodily excess gave metaphors a materiality that, as we have seen, made them literal. "Chávez corazón del pueblo," (Chávez, the heart of the people), "Todos somos Chávez" (We are all Chávez), and Chávez's famous "Ya yo no soy yo, yo soy un pueblo" (I'm no longer myself, I am a people) became metaphors performed *in the flesh*, sometimes publicly in front of television cameras, sometimes behind closed doors. Mediating this performance were beliefs that made it not just a bodily performance but a magical one as well.

Magic, Unleashed

There is no doubt that every nation is magical in some way or the other; however, the scholarship on Venezuela seems to be particularly adamant in stating that Venezuela is a "magical state." Two widely cited works can be credited with coining the expression: Fernando Coronil's *The Magical State* and Michael Taussig's *The Magic of the State*, both originally published in 1997. In Coronil's work, the magic of the Venezuelan state comes from its main natural resource: oil. "Oil is fantastic and induces fantasies"—argues

Venezuelan playwright José Ignacio Cabrujas in Coronil's introduction to *The Magical State*—and the state that controls it acquires a "providential hue" thanks to its staging of awe-inspiring spectacles funded by Venezuela's seemingly infinite oil reserves (Coronil 1997, 1). In Coronil's analysis, the state acts as a "magnanimous sorcerer" that manufactures dazzling development projects that engender collective fantasies of progress, seizing "its subjects by inducing a condition or state of being receptive to its illusions—a magical state" (5). Contributing to the magical properties of the Venezuelan petrostate is a significant body of cultural production that feeds off (and occasionally challenges) a metaphorical language that infuses oil with magical allure. "Black gold," "devil's dung," and "black magic" are just some of the ways to (not) name oil in Venezuela, all deeply ingrained in the national imaginary and all effective in strengthening the illusion that oil—invisible yet omnipresent—comes from a supernatural, potentially life-threatening, "nonplace."[16]

Taussig presents a different take on where the magic of the Venezuelan state lies. In *The Magic of the State*, he explores the sacred underpinnings of modern sovereignty through an anthropological study that draws connections between two characters: the Spirit Queen and the Liberator. In the preface, Taussig explains that he uses these fictional names in part to evoke and better grasp the elusive nature of stately being. However, as one joins him on his journey, it becomes clear that the Liberator is Simón Bolívar, the Spirit Queen is María Lionza, and the magical state is, indeed, Venezuela. Venezuela, Taussig's study shows, is an ideal site to witness the workings of the magic of the state, which relies heavily on the effect that the image of Bolívar has on a populace that has been trained for over a hundred years to respect and obey his commands. This populace invokes his spirit and communicates with it through the practice of the cult of María Lionza. The cult combines African, Indigenous, and Catholic beliefs and allows followers to seek guidance from the souls of dead people summoned into a living body. This communication with the dead—organized in groups called *cortes* (courts)—has historically been seen by the practitioners of the cult as a solution to the problems that the state and its institutions are unable to solve. Therefore, the cult and the spirit of Bolívar it invokes appear separated from the operations of the state and its official uses and representations of Bolívar. Yet, Taussig's argument goes, the two feed off each other. The official and the unofficial enter in a circuit whereby the iconography of the state populates the cult's altars and reinforces the power attributed to the Liberator. In turn, the magic of the cult invoked in the periphery animates and empowers the state's kitschy self-representation, which places the image of Bolívar—reproduced endlessly in all public spaces—as the source of its legitimacy and authority.

The Venezuelan state is thus magical in two ways, and both have been central to the political agendas of every president that has governed since the early twentieth century, including Chávez. Chávez, like his predecessors, also acted as a sorcerer capable of staging dazzling, oil-funded spectacles; in his case, however, these spectacles were not connected to the twentieth-century promise of modernity but to his aspirations to make twenty-first-century socialism a Venezuelan (and continental) reality.[17] Also like his predecessors, Chávez appealed to the magic of the Liberator, making Bolívar's unfulfilled dreams the center of his political project—the aptly termed Bolivarian Revolution—often quoting his words in and out of context and ensuring a portrait of him was in the vicinity whenever he addressed his Venezuelan audience. However, unlike those who came before him, Chávez took his relationship with Bolívar to a new, magical level that broke the permeable yet historically persistent boundary Taussig identifies in his work between the peripheral space of the Spirit Queen, where magic is literal and embodied, and the public space of the state, where magic is metaphorical and translated into an ostentatious display. In Taussig's words:

> A crucial feature of this theater of spirit-possession is that the circulation of spirits of the dead through live human bodies is a movement parallel to the circulation of the ghostly magic of the Nation-State through the "body" of the society—as when the President of the Republic invokes as part of the daily round of statecraft the "spirit" of the Liberator, and Ofelia, the healer on the spirit queen's mountain, in her turn, invokes the spirit too, but as "literal fact." *Here everything hinges on the necessity and impossibility of collapsing spirit into literal fact.* (Taussig 1997, 139; emphasis added)

This collapse is precisely what Chávez staged in his political performance through the magical encounters he claimed he had with Bolívar. Venezuelan historians, anthropologists, and cultural analysts who have studied the cult of Bolívar and, more recently, the ways the national hero has been mobilized within the context of the Bolivarian Revolution, have repeatedly underscored the magical excess that is present in Chávez's political performance. Rafael Sánchez comments on the compulsive reproduction of the image, name, and thoughts of Bolívar under Chávez, noting that, "with his name literally on everyone's lips and his icon everywhere cloned and compulsively dissemi-nated, it may be said that Bolívar under Chávez finally arrived to lay claim to his nation" (2016, 3). Ana Teresa Torres reflects on how Chávez's attempts to revive the epic of the glorious past of the independence wars compare with similar efforts by his predecessors, concluding that "this project is not an invention of the present; it is instead a desire that has beat at the heart of Venezuelan-ness for two hundred years. Hugo Chávez has been its best interpreter and boldest enactor through his political proposal: the Bolivar-ian Revolution" (Torres 2009, 17). Lastly, Coronil introduces his analysis of Chávez's relationship to and production of history, stating that he believes that "Chávez's is a magical state, perhaps the most magical of all, and he is the most magical of our presidents" (2008, 5).

One anecdote, among many, that encapsulates this magical excess ap-pears in what Venezuelan historian Elías Pino Iturrieta in *El divino Bolívar* calls the "chapter of the empty chair":

> While discussions unfold, working plans are written up, and proj-ects are developed regarding immediate actions, the solitude of the chair is a testimony to the hero's presence. Sometimes, the coman-dante will stare at this space that no one occupies, as in reality there is just a solitary chair there, an empty hole, a useless trapping, a small empty surface, a useless object, but he observes it with solemnity and courtesy. (Pino Iturrieta [2003] 2006, 191)

Pino Iturrieta is referring to a meeting that took place among the mem-bers of the MBR-200 (Movimiento Bolivariano Revolucionario 200)—the political and social movement founded by Chávez in 1982—after the failed attempt to overthrow former Venezuelan president Carlos Andrés Pérez in 1992. According to the people the author interviewed, in these meetings Chávez insisted on leaving an empty chair for the ghost of Bolívar to sit on and oversee the proceedings. For Pino Iturrieta, Chávez's theatrical interac-tion with Bolívar's ghost and the many other ghostly encounters between the two figures that took place during his presidency were not just another political strategy meant to manipulate a society whose entire collective iden-tity was defined by the image, thoughts, and deeds of the Liberator. In his analysis, the "chapter of the empty chair" enabled the coming together of the world of politics and the world of the supernatural. It showed Chávez's willingness to publicly embrace necromantic practices that his predecessors would either keep hidden, conduct while maintaining a respectful temporal and physical distance between them and Bolívar, or ensure would be seen as nothing more than a calculated political performance.[18]

Pino Iturrieta's reaction to Chávez's seemingly spontaneous and genuine act of spiritism is one of uneasiness and rejection. He considers such behavior disquieting as it "is divorced from normalcy" (Pino Iturrieta [2003] 2006, 194) and fueled Chávez's aspirations of bringing the nineteenth century into the twenty-first, thus continuing the saga of the country's fight for independence through the Bolivarian Revolution.[19] While this reaction goes hand in hand with and supports Pino Iturrieta's overall rejection of Chávez and of the excessively creative license he took with the figure of Bolívar, it also speaks of a more general discomfort—particularly on the part of those who opposed Chávez's political project—with his seemingly shameless mobilization of magic.

This magic was not just connected to his literal and often theatrical invocation of Bolívar's spirit. During his time in power, Chávez engaged in what Lucia Michelutti calls a process of "de-folklorization of Venezuelan myth/history" through the revitalization of popular religious cults—such as Santería and spiritism—that, though present in the country since colonial times, had typically been practiced in secret, rarely spoken about in public because they were considered "un-Catholic" (2017, 240). These cults were revitalized in Chávez's celebration of his Indigenous and African roots and the spiritual and cultural practices that came with them and that allowed him to establish strong connections with several Indigenous and Afro-Venezuelan communities. As part of this celebration, the government launched the Misión Santería and began a dialogue with Asociación Yoruba de Cuba, which sponsored religious activities including the founding of local cultural houses and university-based centers for the study of Afro-Cuban religion (240).

In a highly polarized society with a strong Catholic tradition, the visibility and the celebration of these cults unleashed a stream of rumors and conspiracy theories that combined political opposition to Chávez with racist and classist discourses that redefined the cults and Chávez's public use of them as forms of "black magic." The term—which commonly refers to supernatural powers mobilized for evil, selfish purposes—appeared in an article published in *El Mundo* in 2011 titled "Magia negra contra la enfermedad de Chávez," about the rituals conducted by leaders of various Indigenous communities to heal Chávez's cancer (*El Mundo* 2011). However, it was the publication of David Placer's *Los brujos de Chávez* in 2015 that gave the connection between Chávez and black magic weight and validation.

Placer's book purports to shed light on Chávez's hidden role as "*santero, sorcerer and spiritist*" (Placer 2015, 9) and to reveal the magical undercurrents of the Bolivarian Revolution. While detailing each of the magical practices and encounters attributed to Chávez exceeds the scope of this chapter, a few of the images that Placer conjures up are worth mentioning:

Chávez in a trance, breathing heavily, body contorted, invoking the spirit of Maisanta in front of his cellmates while imprisoned after the 1992 military coup (60).[20]

Chávez addressing the country in 2003 and complaining about a dead animal with fangs that had been left by the door of the Palacio de Miraflores, the presidential residence, presumably by somebody in the opposition. "They've hired 200 sorcerers from all around the world to take me out," he stated (87).

Bones and bodies stolen from Venezuelan cemeteries as part of a corpse-trafficking operation linked to the ritual of Palo Mayombe, a branch of Cuban Santería (101).

Chávez bathing in Miraflores with lion's blood and dropping magical potions at night over Caracas to put the citizens to sleep before elections took place (139).

Alligator bones, a woven basket with fruits, a turtle shell, and flowers: all displayed in a *Santero* altar built in the middle of Miraflores (191).

Chávez digging up the bones of Bolívar—on national television, in the early hours of the morning (the "hour of the dead")—and, in doing so, unleashing a curse that would take the life of several renowned *chavistas*, including Chávez himself (112).

The attitude that Placer's reader is asked to adopt with respect to these images is summarized in the words of Venezuelan anthropologist Michaelle Ascencio, whom the author interviews: "Everything that people who were close to him and people in the streets say, all of it is true. At least, it is a truth from an anthropological point of view because it is what people say on the street and it is a generalized belief. Because if not, what is the truth? What the government tells you?" (Placer 2015, 140). Ascencio's statement frames truth as connected to generalized beliefs and "what people say on the street"; truth, thus, not as proven fact but as shared tale, a tale that, populated with unsettling images such as those cited above, is difficult to ignore or forget. Placer's book is itself built upon this way of conceiving truth. Chávez's magical practice is proven through conversations with those who were close to him (but are not anymore), the hard evidence included in the appendix being a letter from Chávez to his "first witch" Cristina

Marksman next to a prayer to Chávez that became popular after his death, and five chapters are narrated in the first person, the person being Chávez himself.[21] Rumors, confessions, revelations, and Chávez's own voice thus come together to surround (and perhaps scare) readers, to make them feel uncomfortable as they realize that they are (and have been for a while) "in the world of sorcerers. Of the occult" (11).

This brief account of Chávez's "magical side" and its representation in books like Placer's is not meant to center the question of whether Chávez was a sorcerer. The purpose is instead to point out that, just like there was a "somatic culture" that, as Guerrero (2012a), Duno-Gottberg (2015), and Vásquez Lezama (2019) note, mediated the political discourse that organized the bodies of the nation—including Chávez's—before he announced his cancer, there was also a magical atmosphere heavy with whispered rumors that passed as truths, transformed Chávez into someone/something "otherworldly," and repeatedly alerted the public to dark forces acting on public spaces and altering reality—political and otherwise.[22] While there was a time when this magic would have remained confined to a known yet largely concealed periphery—Sorte Mountain, cemeteries past midnight, séances performed behind closed doors—by 2011 that periphery had gone digital and thus ceased to be a secret.

Twitter became one of the privileged digital spaces for the operation of magic. In his book, Placer refers to @MuiMona, the Twitter account of an anonymous user claiming to be a witch, who started commenting on the relationship between witchcraft and the political future of the country with the announcement of Chávez's cancer. Her thousands of Twitter followers were informed of Chávez doing spells with the help of Cuban *babalawos* to placate his enemies and of the "actual" death of Chávez in December 2012, months before it was officially announced. These visions came to MuiMona from a candle: "through it, she sees images, signs, and scenes that she cannot corroborate or verify, but after she sees them, she has no doubt that they took place. And the visions are transformed into truths through her tweets" (Placer 2015, 139). MuiMona was not alone in her determination to shed light on the magical forces surrounding Chávez and share the information with her Twitter followers. Well-known astrologers—Ramses, Reinaldo dos Santos, Mhoni Vidente, Adriana Azzi, and Walter Mercado—also used social media platforms to make fateful predictions that inevitably concluded with Chávez's death and fueled other rumors such as the one linking Chávez's illness to "the curse of Bolívar's pantheon" (Alba 2011). According to the Tutankhamen-inspired legend, the desecration of Bolívar's tomb, which took place when Chávez decided to exhume his remains in 2010 and live tweet the event to his thousands of followers, unleashed a deadly curse that took the lives of important members of Chávez's party (Willian Lara, Alberto Müller Rojas, Guillermo García Ponce, and others), brought down two military helicopters and the Conviasa flight 2350, caused a series of natural disasters, and gave Chávez the cancer that would eventually kill him.

The circulation and popularization of these "magical truths" turned Chávez's body into a space of fiction that was simultaneously familiar and mysterious, hypervisible and occult (in both senses of the word), ill but also protected by otherworldly forces, near death and also already beyond it. Thus, death as a concrete, organic, recognizable event was expelled from the realm of possibilities, such that not only did a very ill Chávez win the presidential elections of October 2012, but it was his absence, interpreted by the Asamblea Nacional and the Tribunal Supremo de Justicia—Venezuela's Supreme Court—as an extraordinary form of presence, that was sworn into office in January 2013. In fact, the day before Chávez was due to take the presidential oath, the Tribunal Supremo de Justicia decided that his not being present did not count as what the Constitution calls a "temporal or absolute absence," arguing that the requirement to be present for the oath was a mere formality when it came to a reelected president.

This liminality constructed around Chávez's presence/absence material-ized in the circulation of Chávez dolls during and after the 2012 presidential campaign, a phenomenon that had already occurred in 2006 and that Javier Guerrero has interpreted as symptomatic of the "dollifying" of Chávez as head of government and figure of authority. In a 2012 article in the Ven-ezuelan newspaper *Tal Cual*, Guerrero highlights how essential Chávez's figure—and, more generally, the figure of the leader created in the likeness of Simón Bolívar—has become in the Venezuelan tradition and collective imaginary; so essential, in fact, that "Venezuelans do not seem to mind if Hugo Chávez continues governing or not. The debate among citizens takes place along different lines. The leader is so firmly built on Venezuelan tra-dition that, as we know, it is not even necessary that he be there. A doll is sufficient" (Guerrero 2012b).[23] This idea Guerrero proposes of being gov-erned by a doll (an idea I will return to in chapter 4) captures the fiction-alization of Chávez's body discussed so far, and points to the only question that seemed to matter in January 2013—Is Chávez dead?—and the only question that should have mattered, but did not—Is there someone (anyone) governing at all?

The answer to the first question was far from straightforward. Just as there were many theories regarding Chávez's cancer, there were also many theories regarding his death. In his interview with Ludmila Vinogradoff, Dr. José Rafael Marquina—forced into exile for his diagnosis of Chávez's cancer—stated that, as a result of the fourth operation performed on Chávez in Havana in December, the newly reelected president suffered a stroke that left him without any neurological functions. According to Vinogradoff's chronology—which appears at the end of her book and supports Marquina's theory—Chávez would have been declared brain-dead on January 16, disconnected from life support on January 22, and, after being put in a hermetically sealed coffin, returned to Caracas on February 21. This would mean that everything the government said Chávez was doing after December 29—exercising, signing decrees, and actually arriving in Caracas alive—was false.[24] The official timeline of Chávez's last days differs significantly: Chávez, who in this version had been actively governing the country from his hospital bed in Havana, finally returned to Caracas on February 18, 2013, as was announced on his Twitter account—"We have reached the Venezuelan fatherland once again. Thank you God!! Thank you beloved People!! We will continue the treatment here"—and died at 4:25 p.m. on March 5. Fueling the confusion created by these significantly different timelines is the photographic evidence that was produced in order to prove that Chávez was dead when it was believed he was still alive, and that he was alive when many thought he was dead.

On the morning of January 24, 2013, the Spanish newspaper *El País* published a photo of an intubated Chávez that suggested the president was in a critical state. It took only a few minutes for people to call the photo a fake on social media platforms, with some even including in their posts a link to the YouTube video they believed the photo had come from—a video that showed a man who looked somewhat like Chávez undergoing surgery. Soon it was proven that the photo was in fact not of Chávez, and the newspaper had to remove it from its website and publicly apologize for the mistake (*El Mundo* 2013). This was the first of many controversial photos that circulated in the two months preceding the official announcement of Chávez's death and that showed the extent to which his passing had stopped being a biological phenomenon to become instead a fiction produced by uncertainty, high political stakes, and the magic of Photoshop. Another photo of Chávez—this time seemingly dead and in a coffin—circulated on social media and was picked up by a number of news websites, which led to a state of collective panic that was short-lived since it was once again quickly established that the photo was a poorly executed Photoshop of a scene from the US television series *Lost* (Red Ética 2013b).

Just as there were photos "fabricating" Chávez's death, there were photos of him moving around and fully conscious, which were also considered fake. The first photo of him walking in Havana allegedly after his operation—which appeared in the Argentinian newspaper *El Diario 24* in January 2013—proved to be an old photo taken in 2011 (Red Ética 2013a), and some argue that the well-known photo of Chávez reading the Cuban newspaper *Granma* with his two daughters that appeared in February 2013 was just a digital manipulation meant to make people believe he was recovering when in fact he was in a coma.[25]

Which of the many photos that circulated in those two months were real and which were fake is, in the context of this analysis, not as important as the oscillation between fiction and reality, life and death, that characterized not just those two months but the entire time Chávez battled his illness. This oscillation, powered by new technologies and how easy they made altering time, transforming space, and disregarding the connection between an image and its referent, reworked the temporality of Chávez's ailing body, making the possibility of his death unreal—a figment of a magically inspired and highly active imagination—such that, when the end officially came, it surprised no one that it was quickly turned into another blurry fiction.

The (hi)story of Chávez's illness could have gone very differently. Medical reports could have been released early on with accurate information regarding the evolution of his cancer, Chávez could have withdrawn from the presidential race and let someone else from his party run against the opposition's candidate, Henrique Capriles, a plan to prepare the country for his eventual death could have been drafted and publicly shared, and, when the time finally came, he could have just died the death of any mortal man. The fact that none of these things happened reveals the degree to which Chávez had become essential for the Bolivarian Revolution to be perceived as a legitimate and successful project both inside the country and abroad. The revolution without Chávez—*chavismo* without Chávez—was at the time of his illness inconceivable. There was no one in his party or political entourage who could have taken his place and had the same connection with those who saw Chávez as both leader and advocate, their "creation" (Ciccariello-Maher 2013) but also the man/people whose words, like magical spells, could change reality and history quickly and spectacularly, and whose body was the body of the people, not just in a metaphorical way but also in an intimate, affective, and material way.

However, it was not just *chavistas* who worried about the future of the revolution without Chávez; the opposition, in addition to being internally divided, could not present a candidate that could match Chávez's pull among the poor and working class. More importantly, during his years in power Chávez had done more than just embody a revolution and the people who took part in it; he came to define how political authority looked, sounded, and behaved in Venezuela. The true challenge, then, that everyone regardless of their politics and ideology had to face when his illness was announced and his death started looming on the horizon, was to imagine political authority differently, separated not only from him but also from the long, familiar tradition of hypermasculine, authoritative *caudillos* (military leaders/ dictators) he so masterfully represented. It was a challenge no one had prepared for—or asked for—and one that was thus put off, along with Chávez's death, through the production and circulation, as we have seen, of a particular kind of magic, what Michael Taussig would call the "knowledge of knowledge that has to remain inaccessible . . . if we wish to go on thinking and talking" (Levi Strauss and Taussig 2005). This magic did not disappear when Chávez's death was officially announced; it became the foundation on which the memory of Chávez was collectively constructed, a memory that was charged with the contradictory task of simultaneously acknowledging his death and repeatedly bringing him back to life.

Dead, Sort Of

In his award-winning 2015 novel, *Patria o muerte*, Venezuelan writer Alberto Barrera Tyszka presents the following description of the journey of Chávez's body to the Academia Militar—the military center located in Caracas—after the announcement of his death: "The crowd seemed like a hot, humid, wounded wave. It was a red procession, filled with pain, wrapped in an irreparable sadness. The movement was so slow that the wave did not seem to move forward but simply rolled, coming and going, with no destination, around an empty box" (Barrera Tyszka 2015, 246). Read quickly, there appears to be nothing unfamiliar in the description; it has all the elements expected in a typical funerary rite: a death, grieving mourners, visible pain, a casket, and, presumably inside that casket, a body. That presumption, which fuels and gives meaning to the entire performance, collapses, however, in Barrera Tyszka's account. *The box is empty*, he informs us, but only at the end of the sentence—almost as an afterthought—and after we have already accepted the reality of the (presumed) ending. A tension grows out of these final words: the empty box forces us to reread the entire description, with some discomfort, for now the pain, the wound, and the mourning of the people appear absurd, yet also heartfelt and real. Is it true? Was Chávez really not there? And if so, where was he? Barrera Tyszka does not answer those questions; he is content with planting seeds of doubt that leave us with a story without a final page, haunted by thoughts about the body that might not have been there because, as the protagonist of the novel—an oncologist named Miguel Sanabria—points out, Chávez's corpse would not have been able to endure the heat and the duration of the slow procession without rotting.

While this image—Chávez's corpse being somewhere other than the casket, Chávez being something other than dead—belongs to a work of fiction, it captures the ontological anxiety that mediated the relationship with Chávez's body after his death, a body that, as the image of the empty box seems to suggest, was both there and not there, visible and invisible, static and animated, alive and dead. This anxiety is not rare when it comes to what Margaret Schwartz calls "iconic corpses": "corpses of people . . . whose deaths occasion public narratives about the nation, suffering, the other" (2015, 6). Two corpses that have acquired that iconic status are those of Eva Perón and Vladimir Lenin. Like Chávez, Perón and Lenin came to embody the promise of a revolution and the will and love of a people for whom they were always more than just remote political figures. Also like Chávez, their deaths were not *just* deaths easily overcome with a funeral, a grave, and a heartfelt but brief mourning period; they triggered national crises of political legitimacy and affective explosions that shrouded their bodies in an atmosphere of fantasy, conspiracy, obsession, and mystery. Unlike Chávez, however, Perón and Lenin were visible, material, and *visibly material* corpses.

Tomás Eloy Martínez's *Santa Evita* (1995)—a novel that blends fact and fiction—gives a detailed account of all that happened (or was rumored to have happened) to Perón's body, including its embalming, the odyssey of its kidnapping and disappearance, acts of necrophilia, the missing ends of its fingers, the squashed nose, its dents and marks, and its final resting place in Los Olivos—five meters underground, in a fortified crypt meant to prevent another kidnapping. Her embalmed corpse was photographed several times, thus enabling the creation of a visual corpus that lives on in films and documentaries and in the ever-expanding archive of the internet, where a quick Google search will turn up hundreds of results showing her corpse from different angles.[26] Her power as an icon in life thus continued in her afterlife, where her body—her actual material, broken body—took center stage, "gendered, doubled, lost, found, and hidden in plain sight" (Schwartz 2015, 40), its image forever imprinted on the Argentinian collective imaginary such that, though Perón remains underground, her embalmed body is never not on display.

Lenin is also always on display—at least the top part of him—in Lenin's Mausoleum in Red Square thanks to generations of scientists who have worked to preserve his body for almost a century. The procedures of re-embalming and reconstruction are complex and require not just scientific knowledge and artistic sensibility but an extraordinary amount of dedication, as Alexei Yurchak points out: "Some procedures are repeated daily, some weekly, and the most complex and lengthy (taking about two months) are repeated every one and a half years. They are part of an elaborate science of the body that is located between art and biology" (2015, 136).[27] Yurchak's account of these procedures is striking. He invites us to visualize every detail of Lenin's materiality: the wrinkles that must be smoothed out, the falling-out eyelashes that had to be replaced with fake ones, the spots that appeared on the outer side of his left forearm, the organic fats injected to keep him from getting thinner. This is a labor of memory executed in the realm of the physical, and one that merited the creation of a special commission in 1939—the Commission of the People's Commissariat of Health for the Examination of Lenin's Body—and of a bank of anonymous "experimental" bodies where the procedures performed on Lenin are first tested and perfected (142). This labor did not stop with the fall of the Soviet Union; it carries on, albeit with less funding, which means that the body continues to be endowed with "a future-oriented, emergent, perpetual momentum" that prevents it from decaying and that maintains the congruence of the sign and the object, of Lenin and Lenin's body (148).

Embalming the body—"freezing" it in time, turning it into a body-object—ties mourning and memorialization to a hyperawareness of the body's "thereness." This does not mean that the person the body belongs to does not get to experience a dynamic afterlife in the imagination of the living. However, preserving the body (and the knowledge that the body has been preserved) restricts the scope of that imagining because, wherever it might take us, it will inevitably return us to the incontrovertible fact that the body is dead, stable, immobile, nowhere else but *there*. We can pretend that this is not the case and speak of Lenin or Evita as being among us (as people often do given their strong symbolic grip on society), yet we will always know that this is a metaphorical presence because we know where their dead bodies are and what they look like. With Chávez's body, the story unfolded differently.

While the archive of images of Chávez alive is immense and has yet to stop growing, the archive of images of his corpse is nearly empty. There are a number of photographs that show his coffin: in them, we get merely a glimpse of Chávez's face. There are also the memories of those who said their goodbyes while the coffin was exhibited in Caracas's Academia Militar for ten days before the final state funeral on March 17, 2013, yet those memories too are glimpses, for each mourner had less than five seconds to pause in front of the body. Lastly, there is a black-and-white sketch—an identikit picture or *retrato hablado*—drawn in 2013 of what he might look like, available on Univision Noticias's YouTube channel, that shows him in full military uniform, his face serene, indistinguishable from the face of a sleeping man (Univision Noticias 2013a).

This absence of Chávez's body *as a body* is partly due to the impossibility of having him embalmed, an option that had to be dismissed in light of a scientific report asserting that the Russian and German teams of experts who had been consulted could not embalm his body given its state and how late the Venezuelan government had made the decision. The other alternative that Maduro's government considered was to place Chávez's body next to Bolívar's in the Panteón Nacional, which would have confirmed the special, intimate connection Chávez had always insisted they shared while also endowing Chávez with the immortality historically granted to Bolívar. This alternative was also discarded since it would have violated the constitutional article that dictates that twenty-five years must pass before the bodies of those considered national heroes can be moved to the Panteón. In the end, it was decided that Chávez would stay in the Cuartel de la Montaña in a setting that mirrors how Bolívar's remains are currently displayed in the Panteón: in a black granite coffin guarded by four soldiers in red uniforms (figure 1.1).[28] In Chávez's case, the coffin sits on top of a "flor de los cuatro elementos": a design by architect Fruto Vivas of an orchid that incorporates the four elements, meant to symbolize the new patria that was born thanks to Chávez and the Bolivarian Revolution. However, since Chávez's body cannot be displayed for visitors, this closed coffin cannot be entirely divorced from Barrera Tyszka's empty box. Looking at it (and seeing no body), we cannot help but wonder if Chávez is even there, or feel unimpressed by how

1.1 Chávez's black granite coffin in the Cuartel de la Montaña.

simple—how unepic, boxlike—the coffin is: a weak and anticlimactic ending to what had promised to be an extraordinary (hi)story.

As if to distract from this disappointment, the space around the coffin is bursting with all things Chávez. In the chamber adjacent to the room with Chávez's coffin, visitors find themselves surrounded by huge posters capturing some of the key moments of his presidency. One of these posters shows a picture of a smiling Chávez of gigantic proportions. His head—occupying almost the entire poster—towers over the visitor, and the plastic surface that protects it gives it specular properties that allow visitors to see their own blurred reflections projected on Chávez's face. The poster's specular quality is further emphasized by the inscription that accompanies it, which tells anyone standing in front of it: "You too are Chávez" (figure 1.2). There is also a display of Chávez's personal objects behind glass, familiar not only because Chávez was frequently seen holding them but also because they are part of daily life in Venezuela. These objects (figure 1.3)—Chávez's coffee cup, red

1.2   "¡Tú también eres Chávez!" poster.

pen, map—stage an atmosphere of intimacy with Chávez that overlaps with the narrative of historical significance articulated through the presence of other less intimate objects, such as the cannon that sits outside the main building, the replica of Bolívar's sword, and the miniature copy of the Constitution that Chávez was holding when he declared the end of the Cuarta República.

Together, these objects work to trigger an emotional response in visitors, who feel embraced by an omnipresent Chávez looking at them from every corner, his image repeatedly "frozen" as if to compensate for the unembalmed body and rescue it from its inevitable decomposition. And visitors do cry, moved by the words of the tour guides, the solemnity of the chapel built for those who want to pray for and with Chávez, and the opportunity

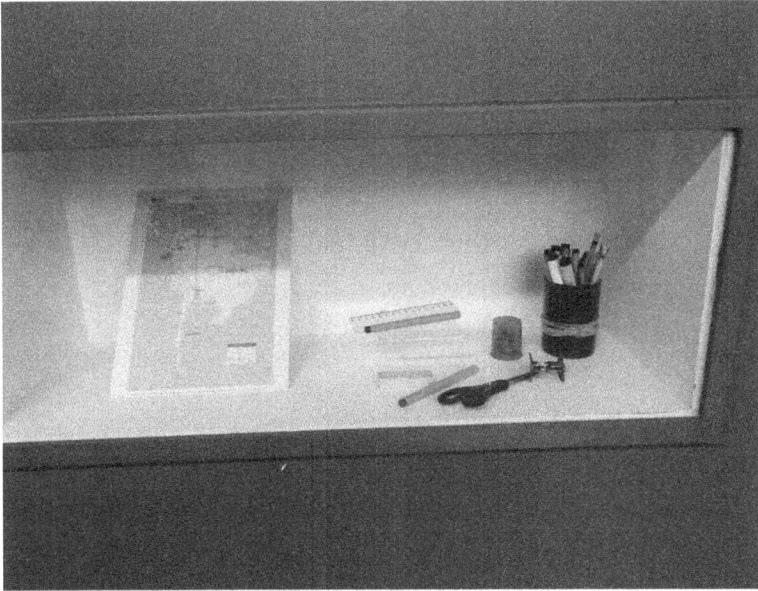

1.3   Display of objects that belonged to Chávez.

to briefly place their hands on his coffin.[29] However, while there is no doubt that the sentiment is real, the display of these Chávez-themed objects—all polished and looking like new—comes across as excessive, overly staged, and detached from the actual life of the man to whom they belonged. In other words, they leave what Taussig would call a "sort of state-inspired vomiting of His image" (1997, 111) and what Celeste Olalquiaga calls "the debris of the aura," an "irregular trail of glittery dust" (1998, 291) that fills the void left by Chávez's death until we cannot see it anymore. This is partly because the role of the Cuartel de la Montaña is never entirely clear: Is it a museum or is it a memorial? Is it a military barrack or a chapel? Does the coffin belong to the "aftermath of grief" or to the "futurity of hope" (Harrison 2003, 109)? Should we walk away with the certainty that Chávez is dead (as the coffin suggests) or with the conviction that he is alive (as the military guards shouting "Viva Chávez" around the coffin propose)? Are the tears tears of joy or of sadness? If the coffee cup in the glass case is the one Chávez always had by his side, why does it look like it has never been touched? Is it a replica, like Bolívar's sword (also on display)? Is the coffin—already a sort of replica of Bolívar's new tomb—also a replica, a prop, an empty box? Left unresolved, these questions ultimately underscore the lack of a "proper ending," one

1.4   Santo Hugo Chávez del 23 chapel.

anchored to a body that would be indisputably, visibly dead and *right there*, immobile, stable, obstinately self-referential.

But Chávez does not seem to be completely there; in fact, if anything, he seems to linger a few feet down the road from the Cuartel de la Montaña, in a small chapel called Santo Hugo Chávez del 23 (figure 1.4), which invites visitors to leave offerings for a miracle-performing Chávez. This according to Elizabeth Torres, the woman who cares for the chapel and arranges all the offerings left there and who kindly shared with me stories of these miracles when I visited the chapel and the Cuartel de la Montaña in 2016. She also mentioned that Chávez regularly drinks from the same coffee cup he drank from when he first visited her house in the 23 de Enero parish during the days of the 1992 military coup. When I looked inside the cup, I saw it was filled with cold dark coffee with the carcass of a beetle floating on top—its death by drowning a sort of fortuitous sacrifice in miniature to please, appease, and prolong Chávez in his miracle-performing afterlife. Evidence of gratitude for those miracles surrounded the coffee cup in the form of flowers, plaques, plants, and heart-shaped cards filled with loving words (figure 1.5). Together, these objects created a charged atmosphere where religion, politics, and affect circulated unconstrained and met in that cup,

1.5 Objects brought to the chapel to thank Chávez for miracles he performed.

whose vanishing liquid content was taken as a sign that the offerings and prayers—the unconditional love—were not in vain, for Chávez was (still) there and (still) drinking his coffee.

The proximity between the chapel and the Cuartel de la Montaña establishes a connection between the two commemorative sites. This connection is strengthened by the fact that, according to Torres, some of the offerings and gifts that visitors bring to the Cuartel de la Montaña are "stored" in the chapel in order to preserve the stately aesthetic of Chávez's official resting place. Furthermore, an ongoing act of doubling becomes evident in the display of the same objects in both places. The old, stained coffee cup in the chapel reappears in the Cuartel, seemingly new and pristine (figures 1.6 and 1.7). The statues of the Virgin Mary (gifts from official representatives visiting from other countries) decorating the entrance to the room where the coffin is are replicated in miniature in the chapel. Chávez's official portrait in the Cuartel appears again in the chapel, as a framed poster version, illuminated by the glow of the candles lit around it. This glow animates and gives access to the (dead) Chávez of the mausoleum, thus transforming visitors' experience from one of passive commemoration to active invocation. Within the chapel, the narrative that frames the visit to the military-guarded Cuartel

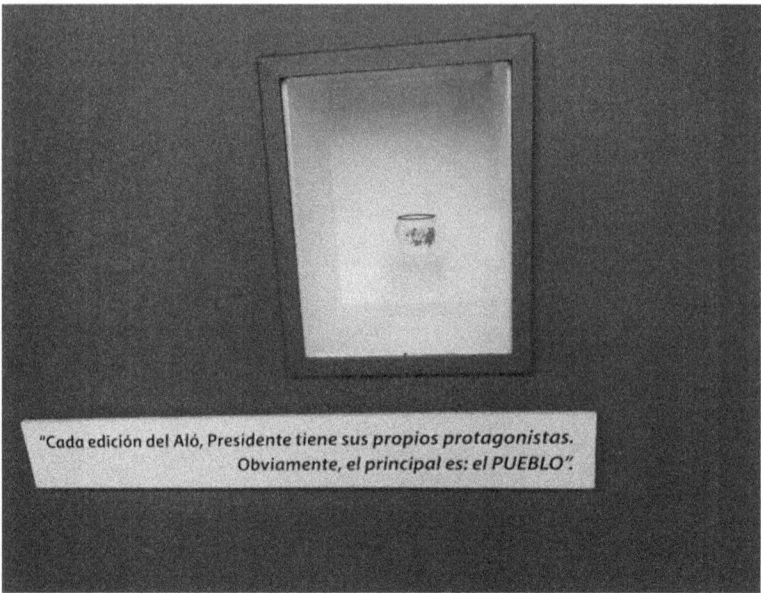

"Cada edición del Aló, Presidente tiene sus propios protagonistas. Obviamente, el principal es: el PUEBLO".

1.6 Chávez's coffee cup at the Cuartel de la Montaña.

and that claims Chávez is alive loses its museum-like artificiality and becomes not only authentic but also animated and magical. Chávez continues to listen to the people and help them through miracles that are attested to in a collection of objects that overflow the chapel. The chapel thus provides a space outside (though not disconnected from) the more formal, restrictive commemorative space created by the state, where Chávez can keep on doing, listening, and helping.

The empty space produced by the absence of Chávez's visible body in the Cuartel is then re-presented in the chapel, where he is no longer a dead body but a spirit that emerges, "infinite concentration in itself, the breath or wind that alone fills up holes" (Nancy 2008, 75). Jean-Luc Nancy's words hint at the possibility of the void itself becoming a subtle kind of body, one that cannot signify *as matter*, that cannot decompose and disappear, that is "here, in the where of nowhere, and nowhere else than this 'where' without elsewhere" (75), and that, therefore, complicates processes of mourning and memorialization that depend on there being no doubt regarding the ontological status of remains. As Jacques Derrida points out, "nothing could be worse, for the work of mourning, than confusion or doubt: *one has to know* who is buried where—and it is *necessary* (to know—to make certain)

1.7 Chávez's coffee cup at the chapel.

that, in what remains of him, *he remain there*. Let him stay there and move no more!" (1993, 9; original emphasis). But Chávez cannot stop moving, cannot just remain there, dead. The words spoken during his funeral reveal this restlessness. The speeches given in his honor and the spontaneous chanting of the people waiting in line to say their goodbyes all ended with the words: "Chávez vive" (sometimes replaced by "Viva Chávez"). Some of the speakers—such as Maduro, Chávez's daughter María Gabriela Chávez, and Major General Jacinto Pérez Arcay—further emphasized the meaning of those words by using the second person, addressing Chávez as if he were standing next to them, overseeing his own funeral.

After the funeral, local newspapers filled their pages with Chávez's name. Every other news item paled alongside the ubiquitous poems, artwork, and articles about Chávez's life, his legacy, the monuments and parks the government was planning to build for him, his close relationship with Maduro, and the personal anecdotes of regular people whose lives he had changed. These articles—stored in the archives of Venezuela's Biblioteca Nacional—reflect the desire of both the new government and the people to mourn Chávez's absence. Yet, they ended up foreclosing the fulfillment of that desire by turning Chávez into a current event so anchored in the present—and thus so present—that such mourning became almost absurd. The same contradiction permeated all the other acts of mourning that followed his death. The improvised altars that appeared in the streets of cities like Mérida had banners with messages where the sadness felt for his absence was accompanied by the comfort of his eternal presence such that, in the end, both found a way to coexist: "I swear I will never forget you, I will always hold you in my heart, and you will live on in me, you have not died for me; may you rest in peace."[30] Chávez's "undeadness" was further staged aurally, through songs that incorporated Chávez's voice (like Omar Acedo's "Chávez seguirá contigo"; see Acedo 2013), repeatedly played at official events and government-organized marches, on the radio, and during drills at military headquarters all over the country.

Chávez thus did not stay confined to his official resting place in the Cuartel de la Montaña, nor did he limit himself to performing miracles and drinking coffee in Santo Hugo Chávez del 23. Without a visible, material, and visibly material body anchoring him to either place, he "exploded" all over the country, dead but animated, dynamic, and corpse-less, unable to decompose or disappear, endlessly consumed rather than ritually mourned. This consumption acquired an unsettling literality in the tattooing of his signature at events that took place in March and April 2013 (ABC 2013).[31]

During these tattooing sessions, people lined up and offered their own skin as a place for Chávez to rest. With each stab of the ink-injecting needles, Chávez penetrated the body, causing physical pain. Pain, Jan Assmann argues, is what guarantees that something stays in the memory, which is why in ancient Egypt laws were burnt directly into the flesh until state institutions, literary and legal texts, and school instruction manuals became symbolic substitutes for the body (2006, 91). Assmann's argument regarding the connection between pain and memory draws from Friedrich Nietzsche's assertion that "a thing must be burnt in so that it stays in the memory: only something which continues to hurt stays in the memory" (quoted in Assmann 2006, 88). In the case of the tattoos, the pain of the needles and the scar left behind did exactly what Nietzsche claimed: they turned Chávez into a memory permanently imprinted on the bodies of those who got tattooed. In the process, however, they also allowed death and life to come together in a fleshy grave where the dead could share with us "the extension of its *here lies*. Not the one, as a being-*toward*-Death, but the writing of the horizontality of the dead as the birth of all our bodies' extension" (Nancy 2008, 55). As a form of remembrance, the tattoos of Chávez's signature complicated mourning by making it impossible for Chávez to be either gone, since he would remain irrevocably present in the skin, or dead, since he would become an inseparable, organic part of the living body carrying him. A "mutuality of being" (Michelutti 2017, 236) in its most literal sense, a burial for a death postponed: the tomb and the wound, one inside the other.

A Specter Is Born

How we treat, engage with, and speak of a fatally ill body; how we prepare the corpse, lay it to rest, and mourn its passing—these are highly symbolic and culturally relevant practices that dictate how death and memory are understood, how we deal with issues of legacy and continuity, how we organize social and political life around the void left by a deeply felt absence, and what kind of afterlife the dead can have among the living. It matters what kind of metaphors erupt from an illness and how they are understood and, most importantly, lived. It matters whether a body is or is not embalmed, whether the corpse decomposes privately or publicly (or at all), whether the coffin is above- or underground, and whether it can successfully contain the dead or not. The words spoken and the songs sung at a funeral matter, and so do the objects and voids, the presences and absences, that we encounter in a final resting place—if there is one. What we do with the bodies of the dead dictates whether they have a political life (as Katherine Verdery [1999] suggests) and what sort of futures those who are still alive can access (as Robert Pogue Harrison [2003] proposes). Thus, to understand Chávez's afterlife in contemporary Venezuela—an afterlife that, I propose, is spectral in nature—we have to go back in time to the moment his cancer became publicly known and to the moment his death was officially announced, and look at the bodies (Chávez's and everyone else's): what they were doing, what was being done to them, and how they were put to (un)rest.

　　In this chapter I have identified and discussed some of the key ways that Chávez's illness and death blurred the boundaries between the private and the public, reality and fiction, and the body of the people and the body of the state. The announcements of his cancer and of his death, I have argued, were marked by a collective feeling of confusion that resulted from circulating fragments of information that frequently contradicted each other and that ultimately removed Chávez's cancer from the realm of facticity and medical precision and located it in the world of imagination, affect, and mystification. Technologies old and new were key in fictionalizing Chávez's illness—the process by which that illness became a space of creation that freely combined medical facts with hopes, fears, superstition, and magic. Rather than clarifying and thus putting a stop to a seemingly endless stream of rumors, the news articles and videos that circulated online and on social media further complicated the possibility of distinguishing what was true and what was false, due in part to the media's own political allegiances, which in many cases dictated which "truth" each channel, newspaper, and radio station reported on.

The articles and videos referenced in this chapter are only a small sample of the many narratives that attempted to make Chávez's illness legible for a Venezuelan people that struggled to make sense of its social, political, and affective implications. Taken together, they created not a unifying narrative or objective chronology that ended with Chávez's death, but an atmosphere pregnant with doubts and thus possibilities, including the possibility of Chávez's afterlife. This afterlife could have taken many forms; had Chávez died suddenly and thus unexpectedly, perhaps his death and the mourning and memorialization that followed would have acquired a different, less spectral nature. Yet the fact that he died of a lengthy illness that did not have an immediately clear end, that was malleable and easily adaptable to different stories, and that never truly excluded the hope that he could survive it, made it so that death became one more fiction from which Chávez's specter could be born.

And a specter *had* to be born. The desire and the need for Chávez to afterlive as a specter respond, on one hand, to the specific political context of contemporary Venezuela. There, Chávez's spectral lingering is in part a result of Maduro's poor governing and lack of popular support, which have made him a mediocre successor unable to live up to the yet-to-be-fulfilled promises of the Bolivarian Revolution.[32] It is also symptomatic of a divided opposition that has been unable to commit to a single candidate or truly challenge the Maduro regime's monopoly over the political and judicial institutions. On the other hand, Chávez's spectrality is also connected to a much broader (and more global) concern with the future of the Latin American Left. With the election of far-right candidates like Jair Bolsonaro in Brazil's 2019 presidential elections, and with what appears to be a global return to a violent, exclusionary nationalism inspired by the political performance and populist rhetoric of leaders like Donald Trump—elected president of the United States in 2016—Chávez's Bolivarian Revolution and, therefore, Venezuela, represent for many one of the last bastions of socialism and anti-imperialism on the continent.

This hope placed in what Chávez promised—and, for some, in Maduro's regime—has certainly fueled grassroots movements that have continued to give agency and visibility to marginalized sectors of the Venezuelan population. Yet it has also led to a misunderstanding (and sometimes dismissal) of Venezuela's multidimensional crisis and the factors that have contributed to it, which are directly connected to the current government's operations and to foreign interventions, and which force us to reconsider the limitations and blind spots in the *chavista* project.[33] Furthermore, this hope has, to a degree, deviated the conversation from much-needed critical self-evaluation that would invite a rethinking and reshaping of the Left (and a questioning of whether categories such as "Left" and "Right" truly exhaust the field of critical thought and political imagination among communities and social movements). This is particularly true in Venezuela against the backdrop of current feminist, Indigenous, and ecocritical movements that are creating substantial structural change in several Latin American societies and that call into question forms of political authority that rely heavily on individualism, epic military narratives, and the spectacularized glorification of masculinity and patriarchal capitalism. As we move forward with the analysis of Chávez's spectrality in the following chapters, we cannot lose sight of those challenges, and thus of what we might be giving up when we routinely consent to live comfortably haunted by the authority, words, vision, and deeds of the eternal caudillo.

Under the Specter's Gaze

2

The specter enjoys the right of absolute inspection. He is the right of inspection itself.

Jacques Derrida and Bernard Stiegler, *Echographies of Television*

Do You Know the President?

"¿Conoce usted al presidente?" (Do you know the president?). The question is deceptively simple. In Spanish, the verb *conocer* has two meanings that, though similar, reflect two levels of proximity to the thing that is known. The first way of knowing something is to be familiar with it, to know of it, to be aware of its existence. The second one is to know something (or someone) directly: to meet them, to interact with them, perhaps even to touch them. The fact that these two meanings coexist in the same word is what makes "¿Conoce usted al presidente?" so fitting a question for the interview that triggers the interactions captured in Jonás Romero García's short film *FANtasmo* (2009). Produced by the group Kinoki and directed by Romero García, the film introduces itself as a "dokumental" (dokumentary). The *k* in place of the *c* alludes to the name of the production group (Kinoki), but it also unsettles the documentary genre to underscore the tension between reality and fiction that is present in the film and its protagonist: Hugo Rafael Chávez Frías, whom the film introduces as playing "the role of 'el Presidente.'"[1] In this "role," Chávez appears as both a political figure and a performer, a known image and an unknowable body, his governance an "act" that simultaneously persuades, controls, and entertains.

This choice to "cast" Chávez in a role resonates with José Ignacio Cabrujas's words: "We never had to build many theaters in this country. Why should we? The normative structure of power was always our best stage. . . . Where did we get our public institutions and our notion of 'state' from? From a hat, from a routine trick of prestidigitation" (quoted in Coronil 1997, 1). This theatrical characterization of power that Cabrujas puts forth is connected to the twentieth-century development of the oil industry and how it transformed the state into a "magnanimous sorcerer" that, Coronil writes, "astonishes through the marvels of power rather than convinces through the power of reason, as reason itself is made part of the awe-inspiring spectacle of its rule" (5). Following this introduction, Coronil moves on to craft what remains a groundbreaking analysis of the life of the Venezuelan petrostate, highlighting the "magic" of the dazzling projects developed under the dictatorships of Juan Vicente Gómez and Marcos Pérez Jiménez, as well as during the two terms of Carlos Andrés Pérez's presidency, and the economic, social, and political issues concealed by that magic.

Lisa Blackmore further analyzes the spectacular nature of the "magical state." She proposes the concept of "spectacular modernity" as a lens to analyze the relationship between space, spectacle, and modernity under the Pérez Jiménez dictatorship.[2] Her analysis draws from Guy Debord's understanding of spectacle as going beyond a mere "decoration added to the real world," constituting instead an ideologizing conduit "for the ruling order's non-stop discourse about itself, its never-ending monologue of self-praise" (Debord, quoted in Blackmore 2017, 103). In the case of Pérez Jiménez, this "never-ending monologue" was translated into spatial and visual terms in the monumental scale of novel infrastructure and state-funded construction that staged "impressive displays of rapid change" (Blackmore 2017, 103). The spectacular visual regime served as confirmation of the leader's magical power and indispensable presence, and inserted the citizen-turned-spectator in a dynamic of "scopic reciprocity" (171). This term, which Blackmore borrows from Tony Bennett's work on the history of museums, describes how "public spaces gave rise to the proliferation of gazes that exposed people to the scrutiny of others and, in so doing, led to the self-regulation of behavior in line with prevailing social mores" and, in the case of the Pérez Jiménez dictatorship, in line with "the politics of control exerted through military statecraft" (171).

Coronil's and Blackmore's focus on the development of Venezuela as a modern nation and the historical periods they center mean that the objects they present as constituting this stately spectacle are mostly monumental constructions and, in the case of Blackmore, public exhibitions and advertisements for commodities associated with wealth and progress.[3] There is, however, another kind of spectacle that does not rely on the monumental or the exceptional but that instead materializes in the everyday and the taken for granted. Romero García makes this "quieter" spectacle visible in the many shots of Chávez that appear in *FANtasmo*: his likeness, his gestures, and his words reproduced ad infinitum in graffiti, posters, advertisements, figurines, radio segments, and television shows. There is no major event triggering or framing the virality of the president's image, though every event is necessarily absorbed by it. It is simply the status quo, so ingrained in the landscape and soundscape of the capital—and of other cities, to varying degrees—that no one is astonished by what feels like Chávez's never-ending monologue.[4] This does not mean that, in Chávez's Bolivarian Revolution, there was no room for monumentality. As Blackmore points out, the massive social-housing project initiated during his governance and, I would add, the construction of Simón Bolívar's new mausoleum certainly reflect the magical state's adherence to its long-standing tradition of grounding its authority in architectural spectacles built with oil revenue. Yet, in between spectacles, there is not a void but an ongoing and, as Romero García shows, multisensory interpellation that locates Chávez in a central position from which he shapes space and, in doing so, molds the itineraries, interactions, and identities of those who navigate it.

In proposing the centrality of Chávez's figure in Venezuela's urban landscape as a point of departure, I may appear to be following a trend that George Ciccariello-Maher sharply criticizes in his book *We Created Chávez*. Ciccariello-Maher attributes the focus on Chávez in discussions of contemporary Venezuela to a "myopia" that applies to "opponents on the conservative right or the anarchist left or supporters in between" (2013, 6), which, he argues, has led many people to overlook the fact that "*the Bolivarian Revolution is not about Hugo Chávez. He is not the center, not the driving force, not the individual revolutionary genius on whom the process as a whole relies or in whom it finds a quasi-divine inspiration*" (7; original emphasis). Instead, he proposes an approach to the revolution "from below," whereby it is the people who created Chávez and not the other way around.

Ciccariello-Maher's point and his analysis of various popular movements— and the tensions between their autonomy and their loyalty to and affiliation with the state—is a valuable contribution to our understanding of the complex social and political dimensions of the Bolivarian Revolution. However, while the revolution is doubtlessly not *only* about Chávez, I argue that we cannot deny the centrality of his figure and the various—sometimes subtle, sometimes overt—ways it has been fundamental in shaping the imaginary of the contemporary Venezuelan nation, the individual and collective identity of its citizens, and the performance that currently defines how political authority is conceived of in the country.[5] The exchanges between the people (from both sides of the country's political spectrum) and the state are nuanced, and it would be a mistake to assume that the people are just passive, naive spectators of a performance that an all-powerful leader created for, and not with, them. Yet what García Romero underscores and what, I would argue, has become even more evident in the years following Chávez's death, is the fact that Chávez's ordinary omnipresence matters. His posters, his graffiti, the radio stations that play his *cadenas*, the television sets that replay fragments of *Aló Presidente*, are not just "decoration added to the real world" (to cite Debord); they *do something*, even if no one is actively paying attention to them and even when those routinely exposed to Chávez's audiovisual presence do not agree with or support him.[6] What is that "something"? In his documentary, García Romero answers this question by rendering visible the coming into being of a pre-posthumous specter and showing how his haunting enables a relationship between the people and the state—a state embodied by Chávez—that develops in the realm of affect and imagination.

This pre-posthumous specter is not disconnected from the posthumous spectrality that defines Chávez's afterlife and the politics that permeated the narratives surrounding his memory in the years following his death. In fact, I would propose that one of the reasons Chávez was able to continue afterliving as a specter was because the feeling of being haunted by him was already deeply ingrained in the collective consciousness of the Venezuelan people, even before the announcement of his illness and death, because of the excessive reproduction of his image and words in urban spaces.[7] I thus begin this chapter by discussing Romero García's film and the dynamics that defined Chávez's pre-posthumous haunting and that, as we will see, center on the realm of imagination, affect, and the sensorial. In the second section, I focus on one particular image that has acquired a symbolic status in the years following Chávez's death and that frequently reappears in visual productions coming from both the government and the opposition: Chávez's eyes. I trace the memory narratives and practices shaping the creation and reproduction of the eyes, the characteristics of the spectral gaze that they stage, and the authority that materializes through them and that operates through an act of temporal dislocation. Lastly, I engage with some of the most recent iterations of Chávez's eyes and analyze what their endurance, adaptability, and virality in the visual language of the nation say about the coming into being of the political subject, the functioning of political authority, and the relationship between spectrality and the exercise of political imagination.

FANtasmo

Though not much has been written about Romero García's thirty-minute documentary, the film—his senior thesis for the Escuela de Artes of Venezuela's Universidad Central—garnered substantial recognition, with awards such as an honorable mention from the Universidad Central, best picture at the 2009 Altos Mirandinos Film Festival, and best documentary at the 2009 Documenta Caracas Film Festival.[8] The film's release in the country was not without controversy: it was banned from both the Cinemateca Nacional and the Centro Cultural Chacao because of its "ambiguity."[9] The ambiguity that these institutions—the former favorable to the government, the latter critical of it—cited speaks of the film's refusal to take a clear political stance: it gives equal weight to a cast of "characters" with a range of opinions about Chávez, from love and devotion to rejection and indifference. In the context of a highly polarized country where you are routinely asked whether you are *chavista* or *opositor*, this noncommittal stance was, unsurprisingly, unsettling.

However, I would suggest that there is something else unsettling about the film that has to do with how it renders visible and uncanny the way power operates outside the momentous: outside marches in favor of or against the government, outside spectacular displays that accompanied Chávez's public appearances, and outside the violence of repression and censorship. This "outside"—a temporal and spatial ordinariness—reveals power's sensorial dimension, which goes beyond the formal patterns of discourse employed by the presidents and dictators that preceded Chávez (who, unlike him, appeared to talk *to* the people rather than *with* them), and beyond the stable, hermetic nature of monuments and buildings that have historically served as visible and seemingly permanent reminders of power's presence and role in shaping the daily lives of the Venezuelan people. In *FANtasmo*, García Romero gives us an explosion of images and sounds that virally reproduce

Chávez, easily enter private spaces (like dreams) and public spaces (like the streets), and are imbued with a dynamism that makes it impossible for them to "stay put" in one specific place or time. The interviewees in the documentary repeatedly underscore this omnipresence, as does Chávez himself. In fact, in a scene in the film that begins in a barbershop, Chávez appears on television in one of his lengthy *Aló Presidente* episodes sharing the anecdote of a reporter who interviewed a six-year-old boy during carnival celebrations and asked him about his costume. Surprised, the boy answered, "You're silly, don't you see that I'm Chávez?" Chávez, laughing with his audience at the boy's response and at what he calls the "naivete" of the reporter, finishes the anecdote by saying that the reporter then asked the boy, "And who is Chávez?" and the boy answered: "Chávez? You don't know who Chávez is? He's hidden in the trees."[10]

The boy's response is illuminating. Saying that Chávez is "hidden in the trees" suggests his presence is felt and presumed rather than simply seen or heard. That presence has the ability to shape the body, as reflected not only by the boy's costume—dressing up like Chávez had become a widespread phenomenon that the reporter was investigating—but also by the way Romero García frames the shot of Chávez sharing this anecdote. Chávez appears on a television screen as several men are getting haircuts (figure 2.1). The simultaneity of these two actions—Chávez talking about people dressing up like him and men altering their appearance with new haircuts—suggests a link between them. Chávez's words, like the barber's scissors, shape the body, a change that is powerful not because it is overtly spectacular but because it is subtle and, therefore, easy to accept. The camera then moves to the inside of a grocery store, where there is also a television showing Chávez sharing the same anecdote. We see people coming and going, shopping without pausing to pay attention to the screen or showing signs of acknowledging the president's words. The television is on, it seems, by default. Nothing terribly important is happening: Chávez is not announcing a major change or passing an important law, his voice is simply a mindlessly consumed background noise.

Chávez's audiovisual omnipresence and the casualness of his discourse contrast with the delivery of previous political leaders who addressed the people in a more formal, distant manner. García Romero underscores this contrast at the beginning of *FANtasmo*, which opens with Alejandro Izaguirre, Carlos Andrés Pérez's interior minister, on national television, unable to read the bulletin in his hands that stated that "the situation was under control" during the 1989 riots that came to be known as "El Caracazo."[11] Against a backdrop of blue curtains, standing in front of a

2.1   Chávez on TV in a barbershop. Taken from *FANtasmo*.

podium, Izaguirre, visibly shaken and struggling to catch his breath, ends up stopping midsentence, apologizing, and leaving the stage. In the following shot, loud lighthearted music—"Comely Row," by Dutch musician Solex—accompanies the camera as it travels around Caracas in a car, filming walls covered with posters for Chávez's presidential campaigns, murals featuring him, and graffiti reproducing his name. During this sequence, the music mixes with Chávez's voice speaking about magical realism, then about Bolívar, then claiming repeatedly "no one here understood anything." The movements of the handheld camera then become more abrupt, shaking the image and zooming in and out until everything—Chávez's voice, the song, the streets, the posters, the people walking and driving—blends together and fades to a white screen.

The theatricality of the magical state—a theatricality that spoke the language of the monumental and the spectacular, as Coronil points out—is replaced by an entertaining, irreverent performance that could seep into the everyday life of Venezuelans regardless of their political position, and that did not seek to astound but rather to become taken for granted. Hence the question that drives *FANtasmo*: "¿Conoce usted al presidente?" The people the crew interviews are puzzled by the question, not because they do not understand it but because it strikes them as odd—if not entirely inappropriate—when, surrounding them, there is an explosion of Chávez-themed imagery.[12] After the question is asked, the camera stays focused on the face of the interviewees, who point to a poster or graffiti of Chávez "over there"—"There he is," "Don't you see the photo?" "He's there, in red," "So you haven't seen him?"—where the camera refuses to go. This refusal, rather than acting as a challenge to the interviewees' statements about Chávez's omnipresence, confirms it: the camera does not need to show the place they are pointing to because there is no doubt that Chávez is obviously, indisputably there.

After the requisite affirmative answer to the question, the crew asks the interviewees if they *know* the president—that is, if they have touched him or know what he is really like. This second question triggers acts of storytelling that mirror Chávez's anecdotes about his life tied to the life of the people, Bolívar, the revolution, and the Venezuelan nation. The president's overproduction of words is the focus of Coronil's article "Magical History: What's Left of Chavez?" In it, he revisits his arguments about the magical state and suggests that, with Chávez, "it is different. It is a matter of qualitatively changing Venezuela—it is not just more 'development,' or more modernity, but a different kind of development and modernity. If other presidents, to use Cabrujas's imagery, would bring progress to Venezuela out of a hat, Chávez claims to bring out a different Venezuela out of a hat" (2008, 9). He does this primarily with words: the revolution, according to Coronil, "is verbal before it is social, it is anticipatory—the narrative of revolution prefigures or perhaps even replaces revolutionary transformations" (15). Chávez needs to verbally frame events so that they meaningfully fit within the narrative of a revolutionary history that solidifies antagonisms that prove the urgency of a never-ending "cosmic battle" (18).

A change thus happens in history and of history: the race to catch an always elusive modernity has been replaced with the urgency of the revolution, the overproduction of monumental buildings with the overproduction of monumental words, the magician with the storyteller. And while the effects of this change are most evident in the nation's division into two apparently irreconcilable groups—each finding reaffirmation of its ideological position in the marches that, while Chávez was alive, became increasingly frequent, and in the inflammatory discourses articulated by both sides—there are other effects that have to do with individuals and the stories that shape their everyday lives. These stories are as central to *FANtasmo* as Chávez is; they articulate a narrative centered not on what the president does or how he governs, but on who he is to the people, a people that, as the title of the documentary suggests, are his "fans."

The word, emphasized by its capitalization in the title, appears as an alternative to a political terminology that conceives of people as citizens, political subjects, followers, and, in the specific context of Venezuela, *chavistas* and *opositores*. Here, *everyone is a fan*; that is, everyone—regardless of political affiliation or lack thereof—has strong interest in and admiration for not really (or not only) Chávez but the ghost he embodies, a *fantasmo* that, as the documentary's repeated allusions to Gabriel García Márquez's work seem to imply, is none other than the ever-present Latin American caudillo, who has gone from being a bloodthirsty, ruthless dictator, to a sort of spectacular celebrity: popular, *pop*, iconic—someone everyone is compelled to routinely imagine, whether driven by love, hate, rejection, or desire.

The first person the film crew interviews is a young woman who calls herself a member of the "leftist fashion party": a group of women who, she says, make themselves pretty and wander around La Casona—where the president resides—looking for Chávez. When asked why, she answers: "Because the president is hot, he's sexy, we all want to have him." Her express desire for the president *as a body*—as opposed to as a distant authority figure—evokes similar statements made by several of the other interviewees, both men and women. An older woman claims that, though she has not touched the president, she is sure she will soon, because she is "his grandmother." A young man claims that Chávez is "his father." Another woman notes that Chávez, unlike the interviewer, is strong and virile, a "real man." Another says that he is her "platonic love" and that she had a dream where she was fixing his tie. Proudly standing in front of one of Chávez's many campaign posters, a street vendor refers to him as "mi comandante" and tells the interviewer Chávez comes third in a hierarchy where God is at the top and Bolívar comes second. Another vendor claims Chávez is a happy, cheerful, sincere man, who speaks from the heart and whose love for the people can be felt in the skin, like goose bumps. Some interviewees, however, do not hold Chávez in high regard. An elderly woman, sitting by her display of candles, rosaries, and statues of saints for sale, describes Chávez as "insane" and says that she would not like to touch him because she does not like Black people. Later on, a man describes him as intransigent and authoritarian, another claims that he has tricked the people and given away the country's oil, and yet another says he has good intentions but is inconsistent and cannot do the things he wants to do properly.

The last man interviewed imagines Chávez on top of a sports car "blowing kisses to the ladies" and notes that everyone has their own "cuento" (story) as he does about Chávez. This observation calls attention not just to the fictional nature of these accounts that give Chávez a human and tangible presence—one people can develop an intimate connection with—but also to the fact that everyone has to have a story about Chávez: that amid the ubiquitous images and sounds, not imagining him is not an option. As if to confirm this, the film shows a collage of pictures of Chávez from newspapers from all over the world where he appears dressed in uniforms and costumes, photoshopped in Michelangelo's famous *The Creation of Adam*— Chávez as Adam and Fidel Castro portrayed as God—and in posters where he is shown receiving a kiss from George W. Bush, dressed as Indiana Jones, as the pope, as Batman, and in his signature pose and uniform next to Bolívar's blurry portrait. A multiplicity of voices in multiple languages accompanies this visual collage, all talking about Chávez and creating stories about him that complement and expand the reimagining of his image.

In capturing all these stories about Chávez, *FANtasmo* resists reducing the social dynamics that routinely develop around his figure to the fanaticism the title alludes to and that tends to characterize people as passive, homogeneous masses standing, as Coronil would say, with their mouths hanging open, as the leader performs his enthralling magic tricks. To have a story about Chávez is, in fact, to create and recreate him, and to evaluate where one stands vis-à-vis his promises and actions. This act of creation is, as the film shows, affective; it triggers and fuels—in some cases, not all—a form of love that has played a role in the production of the revolution and in the complex dynamics that developed between the people and the state while Chávez was alive and, as we will see, after his death.

The revolution is not just about that love, but it is also not independent from it. Reminders of that love are central to the imagery the revolution has produced from the start and the language it created to narrate itself. It is true that, as Coronil points out, the history that Chávez created was filled with inflammatory language of wars, battles, and enemies, but it is also true that it underscored love for the people, the nation, and Bolívar. The posters and television segments advertising the achievements of the *misiones*—the social programs implemented under Chávez's administration that were hailed as one of the most significant accomplishments of the revolution— emphasized that love: children hugging Chávez, Chávez hugging the elderly, Chávez among the mothers of the barrio. Chávez saying, "Más que amor . . . frenesí" (More than love . . . frenzy) and repeating José Martí's "Amor con amor se paga" (Love is paid with love) as he recognized the "infinite love" he received from the people during the closing of the 2006 presidential campaign (see "Comandante Chávez" 2017). While previous presidents and dictators certainly enjoyed the people's support to varying degrees, it would not be far-fetched to claim that none of them capitalized on affect the way Chávez did. Overlooking or denying this creates a significant void in accounts that applaud what Chávez did and those that condemn it, and, more broadly, in the understanding of twenty-first-century populist movements that emerge amid the popularization of technologies (old and new) and the unprecedented visibility, virality, and accessibility that they grant to political leaders.[13]

This love and the other affective responses to Chávez are, as *FANtasmo* shows, encouraged by daily exposure to the excess of Chávez's imagery, which ultimately renders his audiovisual presence something everyone must routinely engage with, not physically—for, as the film shows, few really get to *touch* Chávez—but through an act of imagination. However, if, as the film shows, there is no space where Chávez is not present, if his voice becomes the unit of time and his face the measure of space that determine the pace and the dimensions of the city, then imagination, that individual faculty that promises to free us from our social context, merges with the demands of that context, and something that is not only individual or social, but both, takes shape. Chiara Bottici calls this "the imaginal." In *Imaginal Politics*, she defines the imaginal as "that which is made of images and can therefore be the product both of an individual faculty and of the social context as well as of a complex interaction between the two" (2014, 5). As such, it does not concern itself with the distinction between the real and the fictional, and it becomes a tool for exploring the connection between imagination and authority that takes shape when the former blends in with and is subtly regulated and circumscribed by the latter.

In Bottici's analysis, the imaginal emerges in the context of the unprecedented technologically enabled visibility of contemporary political leaders. She argues that our political world is inundated with images of those who govern us. Whereas before, ordinary people rarely had the opportunity to see their rulers, today's rulers "are constantly in front of us: their images dominate our screens, nourishing, soliciting, and perhaps even saturating our imagination" (Bottici 2014, 1). Furthermore, she notes that there is a gap between the mass production of images—aided and transformed by new digital technology—and the reality that those images purport to represent. This gap has allowed virtual images to create their own reality, cutting ties with the "here" and the "now" and thus occasionally replacing "the real thing" that gave rise to them in the first place (2).

Bottici's point regarding virtual images and their ability to create their own reality is reflected in the last scenes in *FANtasmo*, where multiple realities involving Chávez are rehearsed using collages and Photoshop. These scenes underscore the blurring of the boundaries separating reality and fiction, and subject (who imagines) and object (which is imagined). In fact, the images shown are a combination of real photographs of Chávez in traditional national dress from other countries—a practice he adopted as a way of showing empathy and familiarity with other political leaders and their people—and pictures that have been manipulated so he appears to be wearing costumes and as part of photoshopped artistic and historic scenes. These collages emphasize the difficulty in distinguishing which images are "real" and which are not. The one showing him and Fidel Castro in *The Creation of Adam* is evidently a montage, but the one of him receiving a kiss from George W. Bush, or even the one of him dressed as Batman, is not as blatantly fake. The message that thus lingers at the end of this sequence is: "he is not but he could be," as underscored by the last image, where a close-up of Chávez's eyes and then his whole face appears, unadorned, as if ready to be something (anything) else, somewhere (anywhere) else. The words of the boy dressed as Chávez during carnival acquire a newfound resonance: Chávez is not truly hiding in the trees, *but he could be*.

This liminality brings us to the title of the film: *FANtasmo*. It could have been "FANtasma," the Spanish word for "ghost." Yet the choice to change the ending from the gender-neutral "a" to the masculine "o" suggests that the protagonist is not just any specter but a specific, *male* specter. This relationship between gender and spectrality is central to how Jacques Derrida theorizes the specter and to critiques of his theory. I will return to this in the following sections and in the following chapters; for now, suffice it to say that, in the context of Romero García's film, there are many instances in which the interviewees point to Chávez's virility, expressing a desire to know him as a man, not (or not only) as the president. The film emphasizes this desire in a shot where we hear Chávez's voice coming out of an old radio that sits on a store counter. Behind the counter is a wall covered with pornographic pictures of women, their provocative poses openly performing a desire for another body that never arrives because no one actually walks into the store. Thus, what is left is Chávez's disembodied voice, incapable of fulfilling the desire the pornographic display conveys, and thus making it more acute. This shot—which takes us back to the woman in the first interview and her craving for the president's body—not only shows the gap between the president's voice and his body but, by making the desire for the body explicit, also introduces the question of how to fulfill that desire: how to bridge the gap between the image and the body. The answer, we have seen, is through an act of imagination and storytelling that only partially succeeds, thus ensuring that the desire for the body is ongoing.

However, the title of the film is also an invitation to think about Chávez as a specter and about his presence in the landscape and soundscape of the city as a form of haunting. This specter is pre-posthumous: in 2009 (the year of the film's release), Chávez had not yet been diagnosed with cancer. The term "pre-posthumous" appears in Cuban writer Severo Sarduy's essay "El estampido de la vacuidad," which he wrote in 1993, a few months before he died of HIV-related complications. In it, he calls the exercise of looking back at the life he lived a "pre-posthumous assessment," a choice of words that underscores his awareness of his imminent death (Sarduy 1994). In her doctoral dissertation, "'Balance prepóstumo,'" Cristel Jusino Díaz takes Sarduy's phrase as a point of departure to explore a temporal state that "is produced through an awareness of the imminence of one's own death" (Jusino Díaz 2015, 1–2). She uses this temporal state to read a selection of texts by Latin American writers who died of HIV-related complications and frames her analysis in the period of the HIV crisis—a time when contagion, survival, and the awareness of the imminence of one's own death marked the day-to-day life of the gay community. She argues that, in these texts, the pre-posthumous becomes an invitation to explore other ways of life and of understanding communities that deviate from a normative temporality that emphasizes reproduction and child-oriented futurity.

Sarduy's understanding of the pre-posthumous and Jusino Díaz's theorization of it resonate with the temporality of Chávez's cancer, discussed in chapter 1, an illness that, like HIV at the time Sarduy was alive, makes those who have it hyperconscious of the inevitability and in many cases proximity of their deaths. Yet in the context of *FANtasmo*, the pre-posthumous is connected to a specter that appears through the viral reproduction of images and the liminality they produce, in between reality and fiction, here and there, now and later, which ultimately dislocates Chávez spatially and temporally. This dislocation becomes visible in the introductory scenes of *FANtasmo*, in the postponement of its ending, and in the choice of colors, which remain the same throughout the film.

The entire film is shot in black and white. Chávez and the people interviewed appear drained of color, which not only visually reaffirms the connection between them that emerges through the stories told during the interviews, but also makes the film atemporal: it is suspended, much like the specter, in a time that is not bound to the past, present, or future. Just when the first shots of Caracas appear in varying hues of gray, a voice—Chávez's voice—begins to speak. Unlike the other shots where we see the radio or television where the voice is coming from, in this shot the voice has no concrete origin: it "floats" above the city, simultaneously present and absent, as it discusses the concept of magical realism and cites a fragment of García Márquez's seminal novel *Cien años de soledad / One Hundred Years of Solitude*. The voice thus appears to reflect on its own—and on Chávez's—status in the urban landscape of Caracas, where it emerges as this magical, supernatural, fantastic thing that blends in with everyday reality, ultimately becoming part of it.

The film returns to this scene toward the end when Chávez's voice, García Márquez, and Solex's "Comely Row" reappear as Chávez talks about Arturo Uslar Pietri and the advice the renowned Venezuelan politician and author gave him: how one exits the stage—understood in both the theatrical and political senses—is as important as how one enters it. This reflection seems to conclude the film. However, we soon realize that the film keeps on going, postponing the end by introducing several "end-like" shots until ending becomes impossible and Chávez leaving the screen/stage unlikely. In fact, he reappears reading a fragment of García Marquez's historical novel about Simón Bolívar's last days before his death, *El general en su laberinto / The General in His Labyrinth*, where the main character, believed dead by his servant, José Palacios, turns out to be just meditating, in a state of ecstasy that made it seem he was not of this world. In the same way, Chávez appears to be not of this world in the following shots, where the music turns suspenseful and uncanny, its intensity increasing as a sequence of posters with Chávez's face is shown at high speed, merging into a supernatural-looking blur that leads to a white screen. From the screen, a shadowy Chávez emerges talking about the difference between *ser* and *estar* (figure 2.2). "I am Hugo. . . . That I am serving as [*estoy de*] president is a different matter, but I am not [*no soy*] president." His words slowly fade, but the message remains: *¿Está de o es presidente?* It does not matter; as a specter, Chávez is already beyond this linguistic (and ontological) technicality.

In *Ghostly Matters*, Avery Gordon conceptualizes haunting as those singular yet repeated instances when "what's been in your blind spot comes into view" and proposes that the essence of the ghost is that "it has a real presence and demands its due, your attention" ([1997] 2008, xvi). Gordon's point is illuminating when it comes to *FANtasmo*: a documentary that oscillates between reality and fiction and that is not just about a specter— Chávez's pre-posthumous specter—but in its title suggests the film itself is a

2.2   Blurry Chávez. Taken from *FANtasmo*.

sort of *fantasma*. In what way could we say *FANtasmo* is a ghost? Following Gordon, we could argue that the film acts as a ghost because it calls our attention to a blind spot in debates about Chávez and, more broadly, about contemporary Venezuela. In many cases, these debates reproduce in their rhetoric the same inflammatory antagonism that defines the country's polarization and either attempt to exclude Chávez to focus on the people—who nevertheless often invoke Chávez as they speak of their grassroots movements and organizations—or propose an almost pathological approach to Chávez that underscores his authoritarian and populist characteristics, occasionally projecting traces of it onto what then appears as an excessively passive and/or fanatic people. *FANtasmo* resists going in either direction and instead underscores what Sara Ahmed calls the "affective economies" (2015, 8) that in quotidian ways structure the relationship between the people (from both political sides) and the state Chávez came to embody, a relationship that cannot always be reduced to fanaticism or to blind hate. This relationship of course changes; emotions are malleable in that way. In the context that *FANtasmo* captures, these affective economies do not stay locked inside a body or object but move between bodies, between bodies and objects, between images and sounds. They also attach themselves to objects; as Ahmed points out, emotions are "about attachments or about what connects us to this or that" (11). It is in that circulation and not outside of or independent from it that power relations are formed and that we become invested in social norms. In Ahmed's words, "emotions 'matter' for politics; emotions show us how power shapes the very surface of bodies as well as worlds" (12).

Ahmed's point brings us to a scene in *FANtasmo* where one of the interviewees—a man wearing a bandana that says "Chávez ¡es un vencedor!" (Chávez is a winner!)—tells the director that Chávez's love for the people can be felt in the skin: "when he speaks, you can feel in your skin that he is speaking with love, that he's speaking with sincerity." As he says these words, the man points to his own arm, to the goose bumps triggered by Chávez's voice that is projected loudly, making it impossible to hear the interviewer's question. Goose bumps—which do not have a predetermined positive or negative connotation—are exactly the kind of effect that Chávez's pre-posthumous haunting achieves. They are the materialization of a sensibility connecting the body of the people—not "Chávez's people" but all people—and the body of power, which attunes them such that they accept that Chávez, real or imagined, for better or for worse, *is there*. And he stayed there, after his death, through images and sounds that proliferated with newfound strength in an effort to trick if not the mind then the senses into believing that Chávez, though absent, was not truly gone. In fact, as the image discussed in the next section shows, not only was Chávez not gone but, in his temporally dislocated lingering, he continued to watch (over) us.

All Eyes on You

Chávez's death on March 5, 2013, triggered a substantial increase in the efforts to reproduce his image. That image ceased to be just political propaganda or a sign of political loyalty and became a form of spectral remains—something that circulated in honor of his memory but that also "revived" him, challenging the reality of his death. The weight of Chávez's posthumous omnipresence could be felt everywhere around the country, as I discovered when I arrived in Caracas in the summer of 2016. Chávez greeted me as I transferred from the international terminal to the domestic one and accompanied me as a sticker on my luggage cart. As I left the airport and drove to the city, on the walls and in improvised altars on the streets: Chávez. In downtown Caracas, on cars and roofs, on the ground, and glued to lampposts: Chávez. On necks, torsos, hands, and heads: Chávez. "Chávez vive" (Chávez is alive), "Los amores de Chávez" (Chávez's loves), "Chávez por siempre" (Chávez forever), "Chávez corazón de mi patria" (Chávez the heart of my fatherland).

2.3   Chávez's eyes in Caracas.

Chávez as graffiti, inflatable Chávez, Chávez the toy, Chávez's eyes, Chávez and Bolívar. Always and everywhere: Chávez. While after a couple of hours these images, slogans, and objects all started blending together—forming a sort of loud, blurry collage that seemed to take over the city's landscape—one particular image repeatedly stood out: Chávez's eyes (figure 2.3).

Not only did they appear more frequently than any of the other images but, unlike those images where Chávez's entire face was visible, the eyes were not easily legible; there was no exact meaning to them and no indication of the message they were supposed to convey, only the suspicion that they were, in fact, watching. This feeling—which I had attributed to how unfamiliar the eyes seemed to me after spending over a year outside the country—was later echoed in a conversation I had about them, when the anecdote came up of a woman who was convinced that there were cameras behind them that allowed the government to know who you were voting for.[14] While this was not the case, the fact that the eyes could trigger that suspicion brings us to a point visual studies scholars like James Elkins and W. J. T. Mitchell have repeatedly made: images are not just the passive objects of a gaze, surfaces that stay still, indifferent as the eye glides over them. Images, to quote Mitchell, "want something" (2005, 7); more importantly, as Elkins argues, they stare back, they "see us back," even when they do not have actual (human, animal) eyes to do so. In Elkins's words, "in the end, seeing and vision do not depend on eyes at all. A bright stripe, a shining color, a fragment of a face, a 'coat upon a coat-hanger'—they are all things that see" (1996, 84–85). In this case, the fact that eyes make up the totality of the image makes its ability to see even more explicit. The stencil of Chávez's eyes sees because every image and object does, as Elkins argues, but also because it is the only thing it can do: it is the only meaning that can be objectively attributed to it, and it is, as we will see, a powerful one.

The eyes appeared for the first time as part of Chávez's campaign during the 2012 presidential race.[15] According to Rodrigo Navarrete (2015), it was José Miguel España, a member of the Comando Carabobo, who first came up with the design.[16] Against a red background—the signature color of Chávez's political party—a rectangle appears with a stenciled sliver of the president's face featuring his eyes and eyebrows drawn in black at the center. The black coloring of the eyes contrasts with the ghostly whiteness of the skin, and this contrast, along with the positioning of the face (which is turned slightly to his right), makes them seem as if they were, in fact, watching whoever finds themselves in their field of vision. It was a simple, easily reproducible design, sometimes accompanied by Chávez's well-known signature or by one of his party's many slogans, and it became particularly popular among Chávez's supporters. As soon as the eyes appeared on the first hundred red T-shirts, people started reproducing them on walls all over the country, baseball caps, backpacks, necklaces, billboards, and their own skin. Chávez's eyes thus quickly multiplied and positioned themselves at different angles, sometimes looking down from the highest points in the city—from billboards placed on apartment buildings built thanks to government-sponsored housing projects like the Gran Misión Vivienda Venezuela—sometimes looking up from flyers covering the ground, and sometimes looking straight at you from the chests, backs, and heads of people who wore them on their clothing, and in doing so not only made visible their political affiliation but also enabled Chávez to "see" more people, from more places, at all times.[17]

Though in many cases the design was reproduced without the president's signature, there was no doubt that the eyes were Chávez's. The obviousness of the design's referentiality was yet another reason for its popularity, and it took only a couple of black lines on an empty surface for Chávez to materialize and look at/watch over people. This was no small feat if we consider that the months before the election were marked by Chávez's frequent absences for cancer treatments in Cuba. Thus, not only did the eyes provide Chávez's supporters with yet another tool to visually reaffirm their allegiance in the upcoming elections, but they were also one of the many ways in which Chávez's political party ensured that his absence was never fully felt as such. Furthermore, they synthesized and acted as reminders of the main goal of the Bolivarian Revolution: to see the poor who had historically remained invisible as the upper classes achieved political dominance and economic progress. The eyes became the visual confirmation of the accomplishment of this goal, joining and widening the reach of other institutionalized forms of "seeing" such as the president's television program, *Aló Presidente*, and, later on, his Twitter account @chavezcandanga, both platforms developed with the goal of not only providing Chávez with a movable and thus omnipresent place from which to see (and reprimand, and praise) the people of the revolution, but also to provide them with a screen on which they could see themselves *being seen*. As Elkins argues, "to see is to be seen," and what I see sends "my look back to me" (1996, 51). Chávez saw the people and the people saw Chávez seeing them. The authoritarian, unidirectional gaze thus turned into a multilayered exchange of gazes where both parties shaped each other. Worn as accessories, drawn and shared by the people (and thus not only owned and distributed by the state), the eyes were a quick, effective reminder of that interaction and helped conceal the fact that Chávez, ill, was rarely there, on the other side of the gaze.

The ubiquity of Chávez's eyes puts them in dialogue with another set of eyes that have watched over the Venezuelan people since the mid-nineteenth century: those of Bolívar. Bolívar's omnipresence in Venezuela has been studied by several scholars who have explored in depth the political, historical, social, and cultural dimensions of what they refer to as the cult of Bolívar.

The fact that Bolívar is everywhere is evidence of that cult: it is difficult to go anywhere in Venezuela without encountering him in the form of a statue, a painting, a mural, a figurine, and so on. However, his omnipresence is not perceived as an uncanny intrusion but rather as the welcome—and, as Rafael Sánchez points out, indispensable—companionship of the country's greatest hero.[18] This was the case at least until Chávez came to power and, through his political rhetoric and practice, changed Bolívar's image and made him foreign to the segment of the population that opposed Chávez's government. Even then, the question was never about whether Bolívar should be everywhere but rather about *which one*: Chávez's Bolívar or the "original." Because they have been reproduced with a frequency that seeks, but fails, to make Chávez's eyes as ubiquitous as Bolívar's (in many cases they appear side by side), Chávez's eyes seem to tap into the symbolic and nearly magical power Bolívar's image has historically been imbued with. Michael Taussig captures this magical power in the following description of Bolívar's eyes:

> But this is no panopticon of visual pursuit, no visible or invisible eye perusing you wherever you are wherever you go. If anything it's the reverse. This is an eye more like the Sacred Heart of Jesus festooned with thorns and set beating maladroitly in the middle of His chest setting up some hypnotic image which demands being looked at and, in that exchange of looks, obeisance. Of course one does not really look, just as one does not really look at the sacred heart of Jesus. It's just there in its thereness because remembrance demands the image, loses itself in the image, and the image then proliferates as the populace through some strange compulsion seeks out his empty gaze in a pursuit doomed to eternity. (Taussig 1997, 111)

In Taussig's description, Bolívar's eyes appear infused with a magical quality that, on one hand, explains their seemingly spontaneous proliferation, and, on the other, lends them a hypnotic power that compels people to look for them even if they never "really look" at them. A key element that enables the eyes to have this kind of power is the fact that Bolívar's gaze is, as Taussig puts it, "empty," a "blank nothingness" (112) that seems to trigger the "pursuit doomed to eternity," for it acts like a vacuum of meaning that pulls you in, asking you to answer a question that is never articulated.

This vacuum also materializes in the stencil of Chávez's eyes, which appear as just that: two black voids deprived of any immediate context that would give the gaze any specific meaning outside the act of looking itself and the identity of the man to whom the eyes belong. In that way they are also reminiscent of Big Brother's eyes in George Orwell's *1984*: "The black-mustachio'd face gazed down from every commanding corner. There was one on the house front immediately opposite. BIG BROTHER IS WATCHING YOU, the caption said, while the dark eyes looked deep into Winston's own" ([1949] 1950, 2). This description underscores the darkness in the only two features of Big Brother's face that are mentioned: the black mustache and the eyes. This darkness is what stands out for Winston Smith, becoming what Roland Barthes in *Camera Lucida* calls the "punctum" of a photograph, the element that rises from the picture and unintentionally fills the whole image ([1980] 1981, 43). As it spills out of the eyes and the mustache, the darkness pierces and envelops Winston, allowing Big Brother's eyes to escape the inanimate two-dimensionality of the poster and actually "look deep into Winston's own eyes." There is thus a compelling excess in the darkness of Big Brother's eyes that also materializes in Chávez's, animating them and making visible the emptiness within them that seems to want, demand, ask for something.

We are reminded once again of W. J. T. Mitchell's provocative question: "What do pictures want?" In his book of the same title, Mitchell frames this question within what he calls our "incorrigible tendency to lapse into vitalistic and animistic ways of speaking when we talk about images. It is not just a question of their producing 'imitations of life' (as the saying goes), but that the imitations seem to take on 'lives of their own'" (2005, 2). The vitality and animism that Mitchell sees in the images themselves resonate with Chávez's afterlife and with the proliferation of his image. The fact that there was not just one official, static image of Chávez created by the government to commemorate him, but rather a sort of visual explosion of his face, body, and words all over urban spaces—sometimes accompanied by recordings of his voice—increased the image's "animistic quality," with seemingly endless repetition both creating the illusion of movement and making the question "What does [Chávez's image] want?" even more pressing. To reckon with this question—and with the question of images' desires more generally—we need to account for not just the power of images but also their powerlessness, or, in Mitchell's terms, the "paradox of the image": "that it is alive—but also dead; powerful—but also weak; meaningful—but also meaningless. . . . To ask 'what do pictures want?' is not just to attribute to them life and power and desire, but also to raise the question of what it is they *lack*, what they do not possess, what cannot be attributed to them" (10; original emphasis).

While this paradox might be embedded in every image, it seems particularly relevant when it comes to Chávez's eyes and their gravitational pull on those who look back at them. Drawn in black and white, separated from the face, the eyes are both meaningful and meaningless. They are meaningful because they are Chávez's eyes, they "bring him back," and they synthetize the central promise of the Bolivarian Revolution. They are meaningless because they are, at the same time, entirely open to meaning: they can mean anything, which means—as we will see below—they can mean *everything*. The answer to the question "What do pictures want?"—and, specifically, "What do Chávez's eyes want?"—turns out to be quite straightforward: what they want is to be given a meaning, any meaning.

In fact, giving Chávez's eyes a meaning became one of the ways the narrative of his memory was crafted among the government and members of his political party after his death was officially announced. The eyes that before had just been a synecdoche—the part representing the (still living) whole while also distracting from its absence—became a way for Chávez to linger among the people not only as their deceased yet still present leader, but as their father and protector. This grandiose interpretation is synthesized in Navarrete's essay "Los ojos de Chávez," included in *Rostros y rastros de un líder* (2015). The book, published by the Fundación Centro Nacional de Historia, uses several images of Chávez and accompanying essays to show how Chávez became one with the people, while simultaneously paying homage to his memory. The eyes not only feature prominently in these pictures, but they also appear on its very first page, ensuring readers know "they are being watched."

In his analysis of the eyes, Navarrete identifies as their immediate predecessor the famous eyes of Ernesto "Che" Guevara, a figure that occupies an important ideological position on the altar of the Bolivarian Revolution: "Even though his imposing presence makes us forget about those who came before him, this image is derived from an earlier, similar presentation of the eyes of Che" (Navarrete 2015, 55–56).[19] Navarrete then proposes that Chávez's eyes are, first, the eyes of the father of the nation. Through the many reproductions of his eyes, Chávez watches (over) his children, combining familial love and paternal authority: "Just as Chávez, because he loves you, must maintain control and a responsible watchful gaze over the internal and external dynamics of the family, in our case, the nation" (57). They are also the eyes of a god, their ubiquity a sign that Chávez has become omnipresent and worthy of prayers, as demonstrated by the version of the Lord's Prayer that was made for him and distributed after his death on pocket-size prayer cards with his picture.[20] This religious side of the eyes is captured by Leonardo Ramírez in his award-winning photo-essay "Los ojos que te ven," a project that Ramírez says was born when he suddenly discovered that the eyes were everywhere (Ramírez 2014). In one of Ramírez's photographs, they appear on top of a residential building against a blue background that seems to blend in with the sky so that the eyes seem to be floating there, signaling the godlike presence of a Chávez who watches over the people and who welcomes and monopolizes the gaze of those millions of eyes that, in a religious country such as Venezuela, look up every day to say a prayer.

Navarrete's interpretation of the eyes strategically ties them to two figures that are central to the private and public lives of the Venezuelan people. On a private level, Chávez overlaps with the father that sits at the head of the family table and with the figure of Jesus Christ on the cross that tradition-ally hangs at the entrance of many Venezuelan homes.[21] On a public level, he is linked to the family unit, the foundation of Venezuelan society, which expands to include the entire nation.[22] In Navarrete's analysis, Chávez's supporters respond to this affective interpellation by wearing clothing such as red T-shirts with the eyes on the chest. As they "put the eyes on," they let Chávez take over their bodies, filling them with a sense of revolutionary obligation toward him. In Navarrete's words: "Moreover, their location on a clearly visible part of our body that is also a symbolically significant site, the chest, which houses our heart and lungs—air and lifeblood—proclaims that it is necessary to put our heart into the struggle and that the heart of the patria is in me, is in Chávez" (2015, 66).

The photographic collage that Navarrete includes in his essay displaying the eyes' many locations—T-shirts, murals, posters, earrings, buildings—further emphasizes their ability to blur the boundaries between public and private and, most importantly, between the state and the people. Rather than just forming part of official state-organized rituals, the eyes also show up on people's bodies and on objects people have made informally and spontaneously. Without dismissing people's agency and their desire to remember Chávez by reproducing his eyes on their persons, I would argue that, within the narrative Navarrete builds around the eyes, this spontaneity and informality become part of the state's repertoire; the state reproduces itself and legitimizes its contested authority precisely through the spontane-ous and unpredictable ways in which the eyes are reproduced, not in spite of them. Therefore, in the context of the ongoing imperative to remember and honor Chávez that shapes political and social discourse in Venezuela, ordinary acts such as getting dressed and putting on jewelry have the potential to become, at least to an extent, "rituals of thralldom for the state" (Navaro-Yashin 2002, 119).[23]

In his conclusion, Navarrete expands his interpretation to include "a thousand other meanings": "Visionary. Authority. Paternalism. Protection. God. Identity. Love. State. Transcendence. Thousands of meanings seem to progressively pile up on a simple but dense design" (2015, 73). Each of these meanings points to different ways of remembering Chávez through his eyes, and together they compose a straightforward, politically charged narrative that turns Chávez into everything that is good, admirable, desirable, and necessary for the nation. Since Chávez's death, this prepackaged and easily digestible—not for everybody, but definitely for many—narrative of memory has also become one of the current government's survival strategies. With record-breaking inflation rates, widespread scarcity, and a significant drop in popular support, Maduro's regime brings Chávez back from the dead both as a threat—"Remember, Chávez is watching"—and as a reminder of his love and the promises he made regarding the future of the Bolivarian Revolution.[24]

Though Navarrete's summary of this narrative certainly provides insight into the ways in which *chavismo* defines itself post-Chávez and into the intimacy that characterizes the sort of relationship the dead president established—and continues to establish—with his most fervent followers, it does not fully address the dynamics of memory and surveillance that the eyes take part in and that engage citizens in their daily life. After all, the many meanings that Navarrete gives to the eyes—all working together to transform Chávez from a public figure of the past into a familiar lingering presence—only become compelling in the context of public events and marches in support of the government. On those occasions, the eyes are magnified and take over the screens as Maduro talks about and sometimes to Chávez, thus performing the central message of his government: that Chávez is still among us, watching (over) us, and that therefore everyone who is part of the revolution must continue showing their loyalty and support. Outside these events, the eyes lose the array of meanings that Navarrete and Maduro attribute to them, and become empty, *silent*. Silence, however, does not imply powerlessness, nor does it mean that the temporally dislocated surveillance the eyes perform comes to a complete stop. If anything, it is precisely when they are silent, not joining in the loud spectacle Maduro's regime relentlessly stages to legitimize itself, that the eyes' surveillance is most strongly felt.

This is partly because when we think of the eyes appearing not on the government's signature red T-shirts or on the walls of the stage from which Maduro addresses his audience, but on any and every wall on any and every street, we encounter the "obtuse presence" of an image that is there without reason.[25] It will, therefore, be there (a movable "there") again. Put differently, the eyes' "random" appearances are not only a matter of the now—a face-to-face encounter unfolding in the present—but are also a matter of the future: the promise of an unexpected yet entirely predictable "againness" that imbues the eyes with an agency that threatens to overpower us because we cannot control it and, more importantly, because we cannot control our always imminent encounter with it. Surveillance in this context then has less to do with the act of surveilling itself—the actual "looking at"—and more with the form of omnipresence attributed to a gaze that looks into both present and future.

This monopoly over time, the "againness" that the viral reproduction of Chávez's eyes promises, is felt alongside the atmospheric "thickness" that materializes when *everything* suddenly has eyes: the walls, the streets, the lampposts have eyes, people have (extra) eyes. The reproduction of the eyes varies in intensity: in times of elections or protests, they multiply virally; other times, they are here and there, not necessarily everywhere. What does not change, however, is the randomness of the "there" where they appear, or, perhaps more accurately, their ability to make anything have a gaze— Chávez's gaze. In that sense, the effect they create is reminiscent of the one produced by the nineteenth-century painting that represents a sentient universe crowded with seeing stars that James Elkins discusses in *The Object Stares Back*.[26] For Elkins, this painting captures the "terrifying, smothering claustrophobia" (1996, 49) we feel when we realize that everything seems to be watching us: "Every object sees us; there are eyes growing on everything. In daily commerce we don't think about objects, but a half dream or a childish fear or an old man's lonely mind can bring back their power. To see is to be seen, and everything I see is like an eye, collecting my gaze, blinking, staring, focusing and reflecting, sending my look back to me" (51). Reproduced on all sorts of surfaces and objects, Chávez's eyes do not require the dreamlike, childish, or lonely way of seeing that Elkins mentions; they are effortlessly visible, which means they are not terrifying when encountered daily. However, like the eyes in the painting, they are suffocating: they thicken the atmosphere with the weightless, never-ending gaze of the specter. And the specter, Derrida reminds us, is "the right of inspection itself" (Derrida and Stiegler 2002, 121), which means that not only are we suffocated by endless repetition but also by an act of surveillance that, though unfolding in the present, originates in the past and has no concrete ending in the future. Before turning to Derrida and the imbalance that characterizes the encounter with the specter's gaze, let us explore how surveillance has been built into the design of the eyes itself.

Though at first glance there seems to be nothing extraordinary about the design, its simplicity—the fact that the eyes appear without the white space that surrounds the iris—and the implied angle of the absent face allows them to have what is known as the Mona Lisa effect. This artistic effect—made famous by Leonardo da Vinci's painting—is connected to how we perceive three-dimensional objects painted on a flat surface. While real three-dimensional objects look different depending on the angle because of the change in the way the light falls on them, on a flat canvas, shade and light are fixed and the image looks the same from every angle. Thus, if an image is painted to look straight at you, it will do so regardless of your position. In the case of the design of Chávez's eyes, this effect is achieved through the black color filling the eyes, which, by doing away with the pupil that would point in a certain direction, makes them seem like they are watching anyone who looks at them. Thus, to look at Chávez's eyes is to be subjected to a field of visibility that, though fictional, creates an effect of surveillance that structures the relationship between the state (represented by Chávez) and the subjects whose daily routines—walking down the street, going to the bank, buying groceries—are framed by the eyes' uninterrupted gaze.

In his discussion of "panopticism," Michel Foucault explores the relationship between power and visibility through his analysis of Jeremy Bentham's panopticon penitentiary. The panoptic mechanism arranges spatial units so that the inmates of an institution can be observed by a single watchman without being able to tell whether they are being watched or not at any given moment. In Bentham's original design, the watchtower is at the center of a circular structure and the cells occupy the perimeter. For the inmates not to know when and if they were being watched, Bentham imagined blinds and mazelike connections around the central tower that would block any light and noise that could betray the presence of the watchman. According to Foucault, the structure of the panopticon subjects inmates to a state of conscious, permanent visibility that ensures the automatic functioning of power. Because power appears as simultaneously visible and unverifiable, the inmate has to assume responsibility for the operations and constraints power places on him:

He makes them play spontaneously upon himself; he inscribes in himself the power relation in which he simultaneously plays both roles; he becomes the principle of his own subjection. By this very fact, the external power may throw off its physical weight; it tends to the non-corporeal; and, the more it approaches this limit, the more constant, profound and permanent are its effects: it is a perpetual victory that avoids any physical confrontation and which is always decided in advance. (Foucault 1995, 202)

The ubiquity of Chávez's eyes presents us with a scenario that inverts the structure of Bentham's panopticon; rather than having one potentially present yet invisible set of eyes watching many bodies within the confines of a prison, we have many hypervisible eyes standing in for an absent body and surrounding people as they engage freely in their daily routines. Nevertheless, the scenarios have two things in common: a power that, in its watching, "tends to the non-corporeal," and subjects who inscribe in themselves the power relation that engenders the principle of their own subjection. The noncorporeality of power in the case of Chávez's eyes is twofold: on one hand, there is the physical absence of the body the eyes purport to represent and replace; and on the other, there is the absence of a living body of power, since Chávez is dead. Chávez's eyes thus acquire a spectral quality—evinced in the white coloring of the background behind the eyes—that is absent in the power dynamics at play in the panopticon. However, I propose that this spectral quality has an effect similar to the uncertainty of whether or not the watchman in the panopticon is at their post: it establishes an imbalance in the act of looking that becomes the basis of power's surveillance.

Rather than staying buried in his grave or frozen in immobile statues and monuments, Chávez returns again and again from the dead in the form of eyes whose presence is both unpredictable—every day new ones appear while old ones are erased or painted over—and ubiquitous, and that make it seem like he is always watching without ever allowing anyone to return his gaze. This impossibility of returning the gaze relies, first of all, on the obvious fact that the eyes are not real eyes. Second, they signify a way of looking that is located at a temporal disjunction; they are the visual configuration of an afterlife that suspends the limits between past, present, and future as it frees itself from the biological temporality of the body. Put differently, they are the eyes of a specter, which means they cannot be reached by the bodies whose lives—and eyes—are anchored in the present, and who are therefore reduced to being looked at. This imbalance in the spectral gaze is what Derrida calls the "visor effect":[27]

> The wholly other—and the dead person is the wholly other— watches me, concerns me, and concerns or watches me while addressing to me, without however answering me, a prayer or an injunction, an infinite demand, which becomes the law for me: it concerns me, it regards me, it addresses itself only to me at the same time that it exceeds me infinitely and universally, without me being able to exchange a glance with him or with her. (Derrida and Stiegler 2002, 120)

Though unreachable, the spectral gaze—as Derrida notes—cannot be dismissed, for it constitutes an address that places the subject always in relation to the eyes, regardless of whether they engage with them or not. The eyes often appear in places that demand attention: on the pages of a personal planner (figure 2.4), on the corner of newspapers, on the ballot of the 2015 parliamentary elections, on military headquarters, to name but a few sites. In those cases, the subject is interpellated and forced to acknowledge that both personal and national events are mediated by Chávez's presence. Additionally, the simplicity of the eyes makes them at once easily recognizable and inviting, as the design is waiting to be filled in. And it can only be filled in by first recognizing that the eyes are watching us.[28] What comes after, meaningful as it might be, is secondary. Depending on political allegiances, we might say Chávez is watching us lovingly and revolutionarily, or we might say his eyes are those of a despot or an insignificant corpse. These meanings assigned to the eyes—that proliferate in the cartoons and memes I will analyze in the following section—are not where power relations are constructed. That occurs much earlier, in the moment when we look back and see not only the eyes (and Chávez), but *ourselves* being seen, ourselves as watched subjects, trapped within the field of vision of a gaze that cannot be challenged because it precedes, exceeds, and succeeds us. Elkins's words come to mind: "seeing is self-definition. Objects look back, and their incoming gaze tells me what I am. Our sense of ourselves is like a television station always going out of focus, and we tune and clarify ourselves by seeing. . . . All this happens unnoticed, even though it is the common thread of vision" (1996, 86). And what are we, we who *look back*? Objects of a gaze, watched subjects, the "principle of our own subjection"—to return briefly

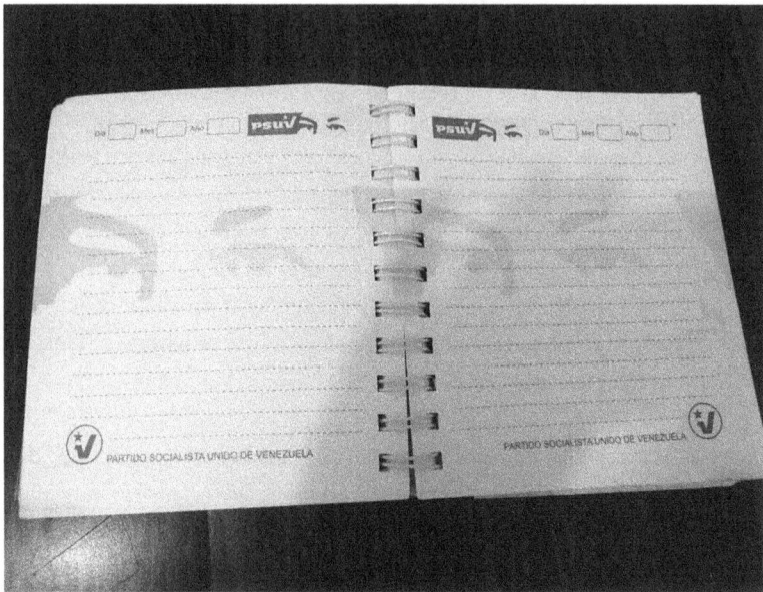

2.4   Chávez's eyes in a psuv planner distributed in Mérida.

to Foucault—being the acceptance of a form of relationality that visually chains us to an ongoing past embodied in the revolutionary male leader: Chávez (now) and Bolívar (always). Thus, looking at Chávez's eyes is never "just looking" but is always looking back, even in acts of defiance.

If looking at Chávez's eyes is never just looking, not looking at them is also a mnemonic act pregnant with political implications. Not looking at them is in fact what people do daily (figure 2.5), the ubiquity of the eyes having rendered them too ordinary to repeatedly catch the attention of passersby who look past them, knowing they are there (somewhere, anywhere) and resigned to their presence. While this indifference is not surprising—there are too many eyes for people to be bothered by them anymore—it is not inconsequential. As Michael Billig points out in *Banal Nationalism*, it is in the forgotten re- minders that make up the habits of social life that politically relevant and rarely harmless concepts such as nationalism take shape and are mindlessly reproduced by the citizenry. In his words: "The metonymic image of banal nationalism is not a flag which is being consciously waved with fervent passion; it is the flag hanging unnoticed on the public building" (1995, 8).

I would argue that the image of Chávez's eyes that does not attract any- one's attention is similar to the unnoticed flag Billig talks about in that it too

2.5   Fading image of Chávez's eyes on a wall in Mérida.

configures a whole system of power relations that relies on its banality and
its activation of forgotten reminders. Drawing on Pierre Bourdieu's notion
of habitus—which refers to the "second nature which people must acquire
in order to pass mindlessly (and also mindfully) through the banal routines of daily life" (Billig 1995, 44)—Billig argues that banal nationalism
operates with common words and symbols that, while reminding us over
and over again of our national identity, are through their endless repetition forgotten and thus become "enhabited," the result being that "the past
is enhabited in the present in a dialectic of forgotten remembrance" (42).
Through their ubiquity and banality, Chávez's eyes also become enhabited;
they quietly reconfigure the landscape and permeate people's daily routines, and, in the process, they render living with them a habit that makes
Chávez part of a shared and unremembered form of memory. Thus, Chávez
is everywhere by default, seen but unnoticed, recalled as he is forgotten.
His presence is taken equally for granted by those who continue to support
him and by those who do not, which means that the past—represented by

him and by everything he once stood for—can keep on living beyond its expiration date.

In the following section, we will turn to a selection of Chávez's eyes that appeared in some of the artistic and political work produced by the opposition to criticize Maduro's regime. These works seek to point out the failures of the regime's political project and denounce its acts of political oppression and its human rights violations. These examples not only reveal the "enhabited" nature of Chávez's spectral gaze but, in doing so, invite us to ask: What does it mean for the same image to be mobilized by two opposing groups as they each look to reclaim their place on the country's political stage and in public space?

Whose Gaze Is It Anyway?

In *Dancing Jacobins*, Rafael Sánchez briefly discusses the ghostliness of Chávez's eyes and the signature which often accompanies them and which, he argues, "is there to make redundantly clear that what is at stake in these representations is not a flesh-and-blood Chávez, but the ruler reduced to what is most essential to him as a putatively unique, transcendental entity abstracted from the here-and-now and charged with ruling over Venezuela, so to speak, from the grave" (2016, 330). He also argues that, while the regime's aim with the eyes is "to communicate that, contrary to appearances, the ruler is still alive . . . what it has achieved may be just the opposite" (330). In fact, in their "obsessive reiteration and sheer otherworldliness, Chávez's uncanny eyes may very well provoke in everyone's mind the nagging suspicion that in Venezuela today, sovereignty is just so much make-believe" (330).

Sánchez's reading of the eyes is linked to his broader argument regarding what he identifies as the withdrawal of the theologico-political in Venezuela.[29] This withdrawal, which he traces back to the start of Venezuelan republicanism, is marked by "the insistent retraction of the figure (of 'Bolívar' and, as happens to be the case, of 'Chávez') as the communal locus of identification, or the projecting screen on which Venezuelans may see themselves reflected as a single 'people'" (Sánchez 2016, 328). Fueled by the current globalizing predicament, this "catastrophic withdrawal" (328) has led to a "boundless coexistence among singularities, in which selves and identities are constantly being remade in ever-renewed settings. . . . Such a 'being-with,' by definition, not only does not express a putatively preexistent, presumably sovereign instance, whether this be 'Bolívar' or 'Chávez,' but it is highly resistant to being vertically absorbed as a collection of discrete 'particulars' by any such instance" (328).

Sánchez's argument provides a critical lens to read the sort of ongoing shapelessness of the social fabric of the Venezuelan nation that, according to him, manifests, first, in the complex and at times antagonistic relationship between the state and popular organizations, and second, in the "becoming crowds" of the Venezuelan middle classes.[30] We could add to this list the over seven million Venezuelan migrants who, since 2014, have been forced to reconfigure their understanding of their national identity and their relationship to the Venezuelan state as they integrate into new contexts with new languages, cultures, and social and political norms. It is precisely in relation to this uncontained/uncontainable shapelessness that Sánchez proposes the state's insistent reproduction of Chávez's eyes fails at its primary goal: to prove to everyone that Chávez is still alive and sovereign and that he is still the communal locus of identification. Sovereignty—which, following Michael Naas, Sánchez notes is already a phantasm—becomes a fiction threatening to reach its limits when it is distilled to its most minimal expression: the gaze and the signature. With both reproduced everywhere in Venezuela, sovereignty loses the disguise that hid its always fictive nature: Chávez, the images confirm, is dead and sovereignty today in Venezuela "is so much make-believe."

While Sánchez's argument is compelling, I would propose that there is an element that it does not take into account: the fact that the eyes (Chávez's and Bolívar's), though certainly part of the state's official and perhaps stale symbolic repertoire, have been and continue to be mobilized, shaped, and reinvented by the people, and not only by those who self-identify as *chavistas*, but also by the opposition. The ghostliness that he reads in the eyes, rather than anchoring them in the past and leaving them (and Chávez) there, as a thing of the past, becomes, as I have argued, an invitation: a trigger of imagination that "animates" Chávez outside official state narratives, enabling him to continue to shape social and political relationships and also the visual language that is used to challenge and protest against the Bolivarian Revolution, Maduro's regime, and Chávez himself.

Evidence of the eyes' many lives can be found, for example, in the tents of street vendors selling merchandise featuring Chávez's eyes in a way that departs from the polished, grandiose aesthetic with which they are reproduced by the government and government-affiliated groups. In one of those tents—one I visited while walking around Plaza Lina Ron in Caracas in

2.6   Patch of Chávez's eyes on a hat.

2016—they appeared as small pendants that could be attached to necklaces and bracelets, the emphasis thus placed on intimacy and proximity, on a sort of bodily contact where the question of whether Chávez was alive or dead did not seem as important as the personal acknowledgment and appreciation of him being simply there, copresent. A different store inside a small shopping center also in downtown Caracas sold a variety of Chávez-themed memorabilia. The vendor offered keychains, T-shirts, hats, figurines, jackets, and many other objects featuring Chávez's eyes that accompanied more typical souvenirs (cuatros and maracas, the Venezuelan flag, mini-Bolívars, etc.). While the design of the eyes was the "official" one, they were on sale as something to be adapted and personalized, mixed and matched with other objects associated not only with the country but also with the routines, commodities, and behaviors of daily life (figure 2.6).

The eyes are also frequently reproduced and reinvented in murals, graffiti, and posters whose creators—often members of groups such as the Ejército Comunicacional de Liberación, Trinchera Creativa, and Comando Creativo—take Chávez's eyes (and Chávez himself) and make them "their own," with variations that reference but also exceed the official narrative of the state.[31] Commenting on Chávez's presence in these forms of artistic expression, José Leonardo Guaglianone points out that, while before his death Chávez appeared in political murals and graffiti only occasionally—the most common historical figure being Che Guevara—that changed, "to the degree that today—particularly after his death and after being sown in that urban monument in today's Caracas that is the Cuartel de la Montaña . . . he is undeniably the most widely portrayed historical and political figure on the walls of our urban social memory, following only Simón Bolívar" (Guaglianone 2015, 85). These murals and graffiti of course do not remain untouchable. Existing on the streets (and not inside a museum or other institutionalized archive), they are subject to being painted over and modified in acts of spontaneous engagement that confirm, rather than obliterate, the eyes' power of interpellation.[32]

Navarrete, in his essay on Chávez's eyes, anticipated this lingering and the changes that the eyes would undergo: "Your reconfigurations have surpassed even the limits of time and have adapted to new contexts. In fact, you seem to have now transcended the limits of immediate and personal memories of events to leave a mark on collective memory and to become an identitarian element that will be a part of a more permanent and transcendent cultural legacy" (2015, 73). These changes are the subject of Jessica Velásquez Urribarrí's article "Resemiotisations across Time, Space, Materials and Modes," where she identifies four trajectories of Chávez's eyes. The first one is connected to the proliferation of the eyes during the 2012 presidential elections, the second one to their usage after his death, and the third and fourth ones to the ways they have been adapted and mobilized during the protests of 2014 and 2017. The latter two draw from examples that Velásquez Urribarrí takes from public Instagram accounts of Venezuelan photojournalists, where we see Chávez's eyes being reappropriated by opposition groups as they denounce the country's economic crisis and the repressive violence of Maduro's regime. In those examples, the eyes appear surrounded by two lines of text: the one on top of the eyes typically reads "Ay Nicolás!" and the bottom one tends to change, though two recurring phrases are "Veo escasez" (I see scarcity) and "Veo desastre" (I see disaster) (Velásquez Urribarrí 2023, 36). The opposition's reappropriation thus consists of changing who the eyes watch and who is behind them: rather than seeing through Chávez's eyes, Maduro and his leadership are put "under the scrutiny of the eyes of Chávez" (36), which breaks the continuity between the two leaders and aligns Chávez with the sentiments of a people that are no longer just *chavistas* but everyone who feels affected by the crisis. In another example, we see a stencil of Bolívar's eyes redrawn to resemble the design of Chávez's eyes and printed on a shield held by a protestor with the phrase "Maduro dictador" above them. For Velásquez Urribarrí, replacing Chávez's eyes with Bolívar's seems to have the intent of "stripping away the symbolic power of the image of Chávez and finding a figure to better represent the voices and sentiments of anti-government groups" (38).

The impulse to search for this other figure of resistance—the search for "other eyes"—also shaped the visual language denouncing the politically motivated arrest of opposition leader Leopoldo López in 2014 and then again in 2017.[33] People who attended the protests to demand his release carried posters with a stencil of López that mirrored the simplicity of the design of Chávez's eyes, though the López posters showed his entire face and a beard that served as a reminder of the time he had spent in prison while also giving him the look of a revolutionary hero. Other posters included cutouts of López's eyes so that people could wear them as masks.

The artistic work on violence by Sergio Barrios, known as "El Hase" and considered one of the pioneers of graffiti culture and urban art in Caracas, also centers on the image of the eyes. In his solo exhibition *We Are Violence*, he displayed pieces of wood with erratically drawn black lines or pieces of black cloth and black metal.[34] In the middle of the pieces of wood there were pairs of eyes that seemed to look right at the spectator. The pieces of black fabric evoked the sort of "uniform" worn by protesters who have resorted to the use of tear gas and rocks as a way to fight against the government's increasingly violent efforts to suppress any sort of political dissidence. They also bring to mind the increase in violence in daily life in Venezuela, where the lack of food and medicine has resulted in a significant rise in robberies and murders. Thus, the eyes in Barrios's pieces seem to look back at Chávez's eyes and threaten their authority (and Maduro's) with the unpredictable, unrestrained violence represented by the sharp black lines surrounding them.

A similar sentiment permeates Ricardo Arispe's *#Somos #Resilientes* (2017), which pays homage to the resilience and survival efforts of the Venezuelan people who take to the streets to protest scarcity and the government's repression. The book includes the photographic series "Somos muchos" (We are many), which Johanna Pérez Daza describes as challenging "the symbolic 'eyes of Chávez' imposed as homogenizing official propaganda, a reworking of the panopticon, an omnipresent gaze that stalks us. Instead, this series reveals and makes visible the eyes of the many, anonymous Venezuelans who, without taking center stage or having special distinctions or privileges, exist and observe in their particular ways" (Pérez Daza 2018).

However, this wave of eyes has not meant Chávez's eyes have disappeared. Not only because the new ones emerge *to look back at them* and challenge the authority of the figure they represent and bring back—reaffirming his presence by opposing or responding to it using the same image—but also because Chávez's eyes, modified in mockery and/or anger, continue to be reproduced in the memes and cartoons that criticize Maduro's regime. The killing of Venezuelan rebel leader and pilot Óscar Alberto Pérez in 2017 was denounced in a meme that showed a side-by-side comparison with Chávez's eyes—captioned "hate"—and Pérez's eyes—captioned "love." When the Guardia Nacional shot Venezuelan student Rufo Chacón in 2019 and left him permanently blind, images of Chávez's eyes crying circulated online and on the streets, as noted by Max Römer-Pieretti: "Chávez's eyes bled; they cried as the people cried. They cried of indignation, anger, and discontent. In that moment, the iconicity of the Revolution's leader disappeared and became a symbol of fight, protest, and a boomerang against Maduro's regime" (2021, 160). Lastly, the eyes have been portrayed as "rose-colored glasses" that *chavistas* and *maduristas* use to avoid recognizing the scarcity of food and the precarious state of the country's natural resources (figure 2.7).

The eyes—and Chávez's spectral gaze, more broadly—also make a recurring appearance in contemporary Venezuelan literature and film that take a critical stance toward Chávez, Maduro, and the Bolivarian Revolution. Juan Carlos Méndez Guédez's novel *Y recuerda que te espero* (2015) describes the disciplinary power of Chávez's spectral gaze and introduces a character whose own nostalgic gaze might condemn and resist Chávez and the Bolivarian Revolution.[35] His earlier novel, *Los maletines* (2014), also incorporates Chávez's gaze in a subtler way by following a trend that is also present in the work of renowned Venezuelan writer Alberto Barrera Tyszka: the choice to talk about Chávez without actually mentioning his name. In an interview, Méndez Guédez explains that he refuses to incorporate his name because "I'm superstitious. I haven't wanted my blood to turn by citing in my novel the name of this character who poisoned our existence and brought me and the country such bad luck" (Khan 2014). The result of this choice is that, rather than disappearing or becoming inconsequential, Chávez, unnamed, becomes an almost magical force that operates through a form of surveillance and control that is not contained by one person but is instead omnipresent, felt rather than seen, and thus particularly successful at permeating and shaping everyday life. Juan Cristóbal Castro's hybrid novel, *Arqueología sonámbula* (2020), includes Chávez's eyes as part of the photographic material that complements, illustrates, and/or challenges

11:04

Instagram

en el mundo etc, que se ha hecho de todo.. pero no ha funcionado. Eso es algo distinto. B [...]

Hace 5 horas · Ver traducción

elpotasio_

El mundo segun un chavista..

1.840 Me gusta

2.7   "The world according to a chavista." Instagram image shared via WhatsApp.

the written text, which moves between genres (fiction, essay, poetry, journal entry, newspaper reports). The eyes appear as part of the author's critical reflection on ruins, which recasts them as fading and forgotten—as ruins and as ruined—amid a landscape filled with trash, animal corpses, and unfulfilled architectural promises. Nevertheless, this ruinous state seems at odds with the rescuing and preservation of the eyes that occurs as they become part of the visual archive of the novel itself. Lastly, Flavio Pedota's zombie film *Infección* (2019) opens with a shot of an anonymous worker standing on the rooftop of a building and looking at the city of Caracas. On his left, on the walls of three of the buildings surrounding him, we see Chávez's eyes; in front of him, in red ink, there is graffiti with the words "Maduro dictador."

It is a lot of eyes. Too many. If we brought them together, as I have done in this section, it would be impossible not to see the resemblances between this set of eyes (Chávez's, Bolívar's, López's, Pérez's, the people's) and the eyes that make up the sentient universe in the painting Elkins discusses in *The Object Stares Back*. In both cases there is a sense of saturation, of overload: trapped in the ever-growing web built by a multidirectional and temporally dislocated gaze, what else could we feel if not suffocation? If everything is looking at us, and if Maurice Merleau-Ponty is right when he says that the gaze envelops the things (and the people) it sees, that it palpates them, that it clothes them "with its own flesh" ([1968] 2004, 2), then wouldn't this suffocation be painfully literal as our bodies feel the touch coming from all directions from a gaze that might belong to many but that ultimately has one origin—Chávez? And, with him, the hypermasculine, epic, undefeated, unreachable military man that refuses to stay dead? And, faced with the threat of this suffocation, shouldn't we be terrified, or, at the very least, disturbed? Perhaps we should be, but we are not. Sánchez, Castro, and Méndez Guédez all refer to Chávez's eyes as uncanny and sinister, but, as this section has shown, these qualities have not prevented people from getting used to, engaging with, reproducing, and remaking them. In some cases, people may succeed at occupying the space of the authority embedded in the eyes (by making the eyes be somebody else's, not Chávez's), but this leaves the principle by which that authority operates—the ever-proliferating spectral gaze itself—uncontested.

This brings us back to Sánchez's point regarding the reproduction of the eyes and the effect that he says they provoke: the nagging suspicion they leave in everyone's mind that, in Venezuela today, sovereignty is just so much make believe. I would argue that, in fact, this is not a suspicion anymore; it is a widely accepted fact. We have only to look at the growing corpus of works that insist on exposing the conspiracies, foreign interventions, power games, and corruption that have led the country to its current state. This includes works of fiction like Moisés Naím's well-received *Dos espías en Caracas* (2019)—advertised as a thriller, a romance, and an "almost-fictional story"—as well as works of investigative journalism such as Juan Carlos Zapata's *Chávez a la hora y en la hora de su muerte* (2021), both leading the reader to the same conclusion: not only is sovereignty in Venezuela make believe, as Sánchez argues, it does not even belong to Venezuela anymore but to foreign powers that have been governing the country from abroad since Chávez was first elected president.[36] Like the eyes, these works have been proliferating since Chávez's death, and there does not seem to be an end in sight. Their circulation fuels people's anger about the crisis and the government, and also leads to cynical distance and ironic laughter, some of which, as we saw, is represented in graffiti, political cartoons, and memes that manipulate the image of Chávez's eyes. So, we say again, with Sánchez, louder this time: it is all make believe.

And yet we cling to the eyes. Maduro's regime insists on reproducing them, blowing them out of proportion, because without them—without Chávez's specter—it would risk losing any claim to authority and legitimacy. People who still believe in Chávez and his social and political project make them, print them, draw them, and wear them: a form of temporally dislocated allegiance that can both support and challenge the current government, widening the crack within *chavismo* that separates *chavistas* and *maduristas*. People who criticize the current government, the Bolivarian Revolution, and Chávez himself, mobilize and adapt them to denounce political repression, censorship, and the economic and humanitarian crisis. It would be hard to say that anybody truly believes Chávez is alive and watching even as they use the eyes in this way, which does not mean that the feeling of being watched, at all times, is not real. We are aware it is all make believe: a game of pretenses where the country is ruled by a dead man. And still, we play it; we play it so well that it is hard to say we do not believe in it, at least to a degree. We laugh while playing it because we know it is all a game, and yet, the ironic laughter, the cynical distance, breeds more eyes, whose presence in our daily lives we accept because, well, who cares? *It is just eyes*; we have better, or rather, worse things to worry about. And through this dismissal, or, alternatively, through the insistence on playing with the eyes—and the eyes, being so simply designed, so meaningless, crave that playing—we fantasize about ideals of freedom: freedom from Chávez, from the government, from the opposition, from the crisis. And yet in doing so we end up recycling and restating rather than transforming the language and principles of domination that allowed the current state of oppressive violence and social and political crisis to exist in the first place. In other words, in making and remaking the eyes, and in our choice to ignore their ordinary omnipresence, we leave the spectral gaze untouched, and the dead, epic, hypermasculine military man lives to die another day.

Sánchez thus is right; Chávez, and Bolívar for that matter, do not contain us, do not operate as a common locus of identification. But that does not mean they do not *watch us*, that they do not remain copresent such that we always exist in relation to them, to their gaze, a relationship that does not have to be one of identification. It simply has to exist to become part of our everyday life, to act as a force that might not monopolize our national and political identity but that certainly shapes the language we use to describe and even contest it. The eyes thus leave us with a nagging suspicion: that our problem might not just be that sovereignty in contemporary Venezuela is so much make believe but rather that we might not have any alternatives. Thus, we keep making and believing: making more eyes and believing that, in doing so, we are creating something different, even if, in the end, it all looks the same.

A Crisis of Imagination

A stencil of Chávez's eyes decorates the headquarters of the Ejército Bolivariano, Venezuela's army, in Mérida, my hometown. Back in 2016, I drove past it several times before finally deciding to stop and take a picture of it (figure 2.8). Why the hesitation? Well, I was afraid. I felt like taking that picture was wrong, like I was doing something I was not supposed to. I had taken numerous pictures in the Cuartel de la Montaña, in the Panteón Nacional, in the chapel Santo Hugo Chávez del 23, even in the headquarters of the Partido Socialista Unido de Venezuela in Mérida (with the permission of the staff); in none of these highly politicized places did I feel the apprehension I felt when it came to stopping in the middle of the sidewalk or the street to photograph graffiti, murals, and posters featuring Chávez's eyes. And, it turned out, I was partially right to feel that way, for no sooner had I finished taking the picture than a security guard appeared and demanded that I showed it and the other pictures in my camera to him. He said taking pictures of the headquarters was not allowed due to security concerns, but he also asked me to explain why I had so many pictures of the Comandante's eyes. I told him it was for a research project on Chávez's presence in the

2.8   Chávez's eyes on the headquarters of the Ejército Bolivariano (the Venezuelan army) in Mérida.

urban landscape, but that did not erase his suspicious look, one I would see, again and again, during my research stay.

"Why are you photographing Chávez's eyes?" would later become "Why are you writing about Chávez's eyes?"—a question I would encounter more often than not when presenting these reflections to a mostly Venezuelan audience. Non-Venezuelans, meanwhile, would focus on how uncanny and terrifying having those eyes all around would be for them, which would free me from spending too much time explaining the "why" of my interest in them. It seemed then—and it still seems now, sometimes—that I should be writing about something else: the crisis, human rights violations, governmental corruption, or, on the other end of the spectrum, popular movements, the barrios, the history of the revolution from below. But I go back to the eyes because I take this implicit consensus to dismiss them right away—because they are *just* political propaganda, because nobody pays too much attention to them anyway, because they are too commonplace to matter—as evidence of how engrained they are in our collective imaginary, how much we have gotten used to them. In this scenario, looking at them, *really* looking and wondering about what they are, where they are, and how they function, seems unnecessary. And yet, when we do, when we believe, along with Billig, that the banal is rarely inconsequential, and thus proceed to call attention to the eyes and "frame" them, what we realize is, first, that we are haunted, always surveilled by a spectral gaze, and second, that, being haunted, we might be suffering from what Chiara Bottici calls a "hypertrophy of the imaginal" (2014, 106).

We encountered the imaginal at the beginning of this chapter, in the discussion of *FANtasmo*. Bottici defines it as "that which is made of images and can therefore be the product both of an individual faculty and of the social context as well as of a complex interaction between the two" (2014, 5). Looking at the nexus between politics and the imaginal in our contemporary world, she argues that we cannot help but perceive "a puzzling tension: the imaginal has been both exponentially inflated as well as paralyzed in the present" (106). This is because in a world overflowing with images that have become an end in themselves, "the very stuff that politics is made of" (106), a hypertrophy of the imaginal occurs that leaves us without the space or capacity to imagine things differently, to produce radically new images. In the context of contemporary Venezuela, the proliferation of Chávez's eyes makes evident and fuels this reality. Chávez's eyes, we have seen, "have legs"—an expression that, as W. J. T. Mitchell points out, advertising executives use to appraise whether an image has the potential to "go somewhere, to go on . . . leading into unforeseen associations" (2005, 87). The simplicity and reproducibility of the design and the eyes' openness to all sorts of meaning enable them (and Chávez) to keep on going, saturating the space and turning it into a visual field that, ultimately, has been rearranged to be legible only to a dead man.

There is thus a subtle kind of violence in being exposed to Chávez's spectral gaze, which highlights a dimension of political authority that is typically obscured by other more explicit forms of violence, such as repression and censorship. This violence is tied to the process of infinitization that the leader undergoes through the multiplication of his eyes. This process is fueled by their virality and unpredictability, their free transit between public and private spaces, and their spectral nature—which locates them in past, present, and future simultaneously. Chávez's eyes turn him into the only referent, monopolizing not only the national visual vocabulary but the political one as well, such that politics cannot be conceived of outside him, nor can the burden of his gaze be challenged precisely because it is not located in the "here and now" but rather in the "everywhere always." I have argued that one consequence of this effect is the coming into being of the political subject as a "watched subject," whose identity—political and otherwise—is shaped by everyday interactions with the surveilling gaze of a past that by afterliving strengthens the protagonism of the male revolutionary hero and our indebtedness to his unfulfilled quest. Bottici's arguments draw our attention to the other consequence of this spectral gaze, which is the loss of an outside, the impossibility of "stepping out" of the eyes' field of vision, to face what may lie in its blind spots. A crisis, thus, of the imagination, which is ultimately what I am proposing being haunted means when the specter that haunts us is one that has comfortably become part of our reality, so much so that we hate it, love it, forget about it, but never see beyond it, and struggle speaking about ourselves and to one another without it.

This does not mean that there is no outside, something else, something different, brewing in the barrios, at the borders overflowing with Venezuelan migrants, in the classrooms of universities struggling to keep afloat amid the many crises, in the new communities that Venezuelans, regardless of political affiliation, form every day out of necessity. But how can we access it, how can we see it play out, when everywhere we look we find ourselves under the specter's gaze?

(Re)Collecting Chávez 3

Just as the living room reappears on the street . . . so the street migrates into the living room.

Susan Buck-Morss, *The Dialectics of Seeing*

Haunting implies places, a habitation, and always a haunted house.

Jacques Derrida, "Archive Fever"

A Familiar Sight, Part I

Take 1: Family Portrait

It is a typical family portrait.[1] A young father smiles as he holds a sleeping baby; the mother, also smiling, stands next to them, her cheek gently caressing the baby's fuzzy head. If viewed from a distance, the arrangement of the three bodies evokes the outline of a house or the shape of a heart.

Who are they? Their names have been left off the poster, but that does not mean that they do not have an identity. They are—the poster explains to passersby and to those who, like me, are stuck in traffic and looking at the poster to distract ourselves—"los amores de Chávez": Chávez's loves, Chávez's darlings. It certainly looks that way. Chávez's eyes decorate the front of the father's gray T-shirt and the baseball cap the mother wears. The mother holds a photograph of Chávez wearing his presidential sash, right hand in a military salute. All three family members are, moreover, accompanied by Chávez's gaze, thanks to the happy coincidence of another poster just beneath theirs, captioned "Viven en nosotros" (They live in us), from which he gazes upward. The third-person plural in this second poster refers to Chávez and Bolívar, both alive inside the all-encompassing *nosotros* that brings together the Venezuelan people, Chávez's darlings, and whoever happens to lock eyes with the posters. It would be difficult to find a more accurate image of "porosity."[2] The private, intimate, and familial now rendered public, exposed, and stately; the state, condensed in the figure of Chávez—who, let us not forget, "lives inside us"—miniaturized, wearable, holdable, lovable. The living room reappears in the middle of the street, hanging from a lamppost; the state slides seamlessly into the family album.

Take 2: The Stubborn Collector

The traffic finally moved, and I was able to arrive at my destination: Plaza Lina Ron, also known as Plaza Andrés Eloy Blanco, in downtown Caracas.[3] I was there on a mission: to find, among the several street vendors, somebody selling the collectible phone cards featuring different moments of Chávez's life.

I had discovered these cards by accident. While waiting in line to pay for a book at the Centro Nacional de la Fotografía, located next to Caracas's Biblioteca Nacional, I caught myself staring at the ID holder hanging from the cashier's neck. While the holder itself was ordinary, what was inside took me by surprise. In lieu of the man's ID, there was a picture of Chávez as a teenager (figure 3.1), which I recognized because earlier that morning I had seen it in *Cuentos del arañero*, a book where Chávez narrates his life in a format that combines autobiography and children's literature (Chávez 2012). The man noticed me staring and asked if I wanted to see it up close. He took it off and put it on the table, and he told me that it was his amulet and that he had given others like it to his children and nieces and nephews so that they would never be without Chávez's protection. I asked him where I could find those cards, and he told me that everyone always asked him that but unfortunately he did not know and did not think it was possible to purchase them, as they were considered rare and priceless. He did, however, tell me to go to Plaza Lina Ron, where street vendors would be selling all sorts of Chávez-themed objects.

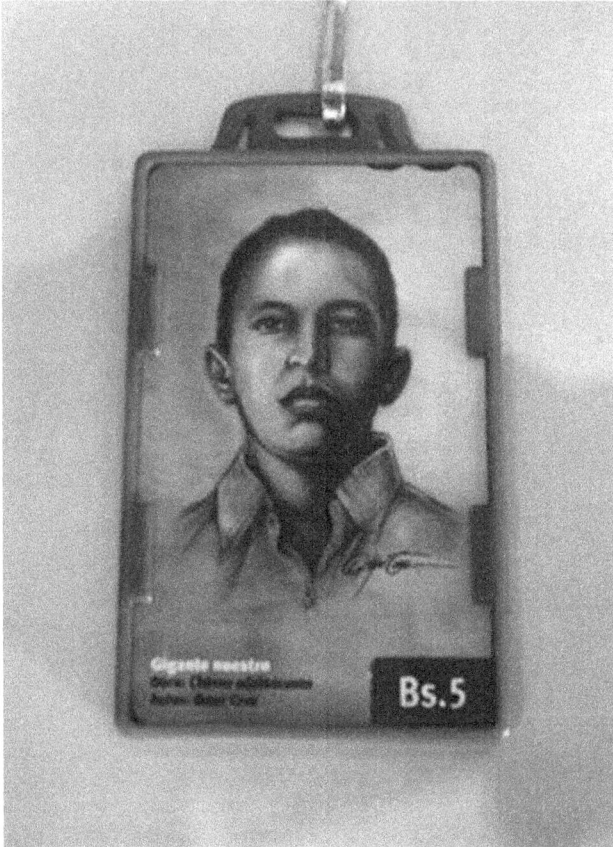

3.1 ID holder.

He was right. I found what I was looking for on the last vendor's table. Amid piles of knickknacks, there was a row of cards that stood out because of how carefully they were arranged, with the first one showing toddler Chávez, followed by teenage Chávez, and so on, until on the last card Chávez appeared at the closing of his 2012 presidential campaign (figure 3.2). I asked the woman if I could buy them, and she said they were not for sale. Her husband, irritated, told her to just go ahead and make the sale, but she refused, arguing that Chávez was her "gran amor" (great love). She then told me that it had taken her a long time to collect all the cards, which were prepaid phone cards that had appeared in July 2014. I thanked her for her time and asked if I could take a picture of her collection, to which she gladly

3.2 The ten phone cards in the collection "Gigante nuestro."

consented, arranging them so I could capture all of them in one shot. As I walked away, two questions lingered in my mind: What would I have done with the cards if she had let me buy them? Why did I even want to own them in the first place?

Take 3: Impressions

I look up and there it is: the *rabo 'e cochino*, also known as Chávez's signature. Stuck again in traffic, I spend my time trying to find the pig's tail in the squiggly lines. The conditions could not be better for this exercise: the signature is not on a piece of paper, small and difficult to read, but on the wall of one of the apartment buildings constructed by the Gran Misión Vivienda Venezuela (GMVV) (figure 3.3). It is huge, extending across the outer walls of seven floors. How, I wonder, is such a gigantic signature drawn? What sort of tools and expertise are involved in the process? Who draws

3.3 Chávez's signature and eyes on the walls of an apartment building.

it? What does it feel like to be welcomed home by it? And, perhaps more important, why draw it at all?

It is the excess that troubles me—how unnecessary it is, how random it appears when other, more commonplace options are so readily available. "Name the building after Chávez," I think. "Just print his name, or paint the walls in his party's signature red," I tell nobody.

It bothers me. The overlap of familiarity and strangeness, uniqueness and repetition, the miniature and the gigantic, the legal and the domestic. If there is a signature—not yours—on the wall of your house, who owns it? Is it the signature that appears at the bottom of a legal document, or is it the signature that appears on the card that comes with a gift? Are they the same thing? And what happens when someone asks for the signature to be tattooed on their arm, forehead, chest, or neck, not because they are forced, but voluntarily, even lovingly? What do we do when we encounter commemoration

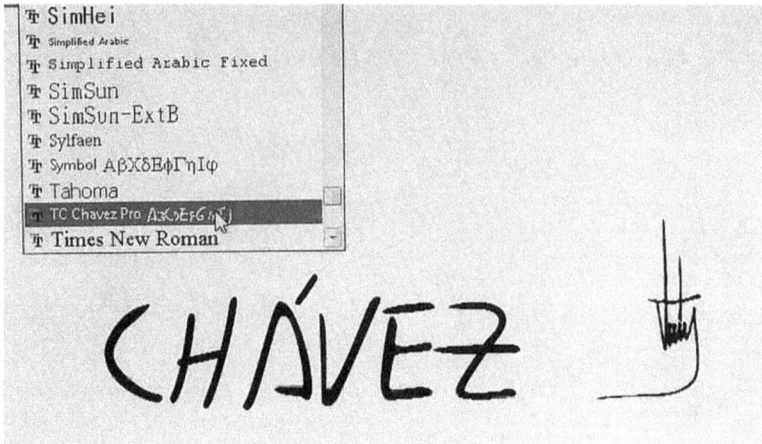

3.4   Font TC Chavez Pro, taken from ABC Internacional's web page. See ABC 2014.

and ownership, pain and love, the living and the dead, "you/yours" and "I/mine," all intertwined, all tangled up in flesh?

Take 4: Whose Hand Is It Anyway?

Can there be citation without quotation marks? Yes, we could answer, but we would call that plagiarism or common knowledge. And, in those cases, while the quotation marks might not be visible, that does not mean that they are absent: there is a void, a quiet interpellation, the intuition of the marks that should or could be there, the silent, always imperfect yet relentless return to the original. Chávez, while alive, fervently cited Simón Bolívar: in and out of context, accurately and inaccurately, with his words and with his body.[4] Maduro, in turn, fervently cites Chávez: the Comandante still has the final word in regard to the country's road to socialism, the future of the revolution, and the anti-imperialist struggle.[5] Copies citing copies, doubles doubling doubles, the original—if there ever was one—waiting on the other side of an endless performance of necromantic mimesis. Given all this, the existence of the app TC Chavez Pro—created by the collective Trinchera Creativa—should not be surprising.[6]

Yet it is—surprising and uncanny (figure 3.4).

The app allows its users to download a font that reproduces Chávez's handwriting, which was "copied" from various documents, most notably the letters he wrote while imprisoned in Yare during the two years following the

1992 coup against Carlos Andrés Pérez and the note he sent while detained after the 2002 coup against him. It is easy to use: after clicking on a link to download it, it appears on Word's list of fonts above Times New Roman. Tempted by the possibility of writing this entire book in that font, I downloaded it and began typing. I typed Chávez's name: it felt like impersonation, plagiarism, and spiritual possession. I typed "hello," "I am here," "I am alive," and wondered: *Who* is here? *Who* is alive? *Who* is the addressee? My words, my thoughts, but his handwriting. Every sentence I typed was like a spell, the hand that first drew the letters hovering above me, engaging me, against my will, in a conversation with the dead. The vast scholarship on citing and citation—with Jacques Derrida and J. L. Austin at the forefront—seems to have missed or, at least, not paid too much attention to handwriting outside the signature. The equally vast scholarship on handwriting, in turn, seems to reduce the topic of citation to the ethical, practical, and philosophical issues accompanying plagiarism. In between them is TC Chavez Pro, messing things up and destabilizing taken-for-granted ontological claims, creating an overlap between technology and incantation, print and trace, hand and screen.

A Familiar Sight, Part II

In the prologue to her analysis of longing, souvenirs, and collections, Susan Stewart describes walking around the city as experiencing

> the disjuncture of partial vision/partial consciousness. The narrativity of this walking is belied by a simultaneity we know and yet cannot experience. As we turn a corner, our object disappears around the next corner. The sides of the street conspire against us: each attention suppresses a field of possibilities. The discourse of the city is a syncretic discourse, political in its untranslatability. Hence the language of the state elides it. Unable to speak all the city's languages, unable to speak all at once, the state's language becomes monumental, the silence of headquarters, the silence of the bank. (Stewart 1993, 2)

This chapter is born out of a similar walk in the summer of 2016 around Caracas that started early in the morning and lasted until late in the afternoon. Like the walk Stewart describes, it was far from an anthropological or ethnographic enterprise. I did not have a list of questions or a preselected group of subjects from whom to gather answers. Objects and people indeed appeared and disappeared, our encounters for the most part fleeting. It was, as she calls it, "partial vision." As my eyes focused on something, I could feel the weight of everything else that would go unnoticed, that I would miss, but not regrettably so, because the goal was never to see it all and to frame it such that there would be no blind spots, fractures, or missing pieces. It was a walk that was driven by a craving for unexpected encounters and that embraced chance—in other words, what, in the introduction to this book, I called "ghost h(a)unting."

It was with that mindset—or, better yet, in that mood—that I happened to see the poster titled "Los amores de Chávez" and began noticing similar ones hanging from lampposts all over the city. The image of the father, the mother, and the baby, all three embracing and being embraced by Chávez, acted as the lens through which I saw the other objects and images I encountered that day: Chávez's magnified signature on the apartment buildings constructed by the GMVV and the collectible phone cards that captured different moments of his life. If we bring them together, as I have done above, what we get—what we hear—is something very different from the silent and monumental language Stewart attributes to the state. The state in this case, in this walk, is not silent; if anything, it screams as it enunciates words oozing with affect, as it slides into the intimate narratives built by and for family albums, as it takes part in private cell-phone conversations, and as it signs, in red (the red of love, of blood, of Chávez's party), the walls of homes. It is a language of "exaggeration, fantasy, and fictiveness," all operations that Stewart insists are not located in the domain of the authority invested in the state: "If authority is invested in domains such as the marketplace, the university, or the state, it is necessary that exaggeration, fantasy, and fictiveness in general be socially placed within the domains of anti and nonauthority: the feminine, the childish, the mad, and the senile, for example" (1993, xiii). Here, however, these operations are very much the domain of the state, and they are also the domain of the family: inside and outside, the private and the public, the stately and the intimate, all blend together as the state, condensed in the figure of Chávez, stops being familiar to become *familial*.

The interviewees in the documentary *FANtasmo* (Romero García 2009), discussed in chapter 2, had already alerted us to this. Jonás Romero García's decision to introduce Chávez as playing "the role of 'the president'" left a space open for us to consider what he would be, what he would do, outside that role—a space that several of the interviewees filled with fantasies where Chávez was their lover, their grandson, or their father. This familial rhetoric that frames the specter is not just limited to this one documentary in this one specific place. Derrida, "the father of spectrality," would not let the figure of the father go when developing his theory of hauntology, the "visor effect," and inheritance: "This father comes before me, I who am 'owing' or indebted. . . . The predecessor has come before me, . . . I who am before him, I who am because of him, owing to him" (Derrida and Stiegler 2002, 122). Fathers, however, are not the only ones who can become spectral figures; sons, daughters, and grandchildren have been invoked as subversive ghostly figures in Argentina and Mexico, and the figure of the mother haunts the continent through, among other examples, the various popular iterations of the legend of La Llorona (the weeping woman)—a ghost who mourns the death of the children she drowned to punish her cheating husband. Whatever shape the ghost or specter takes, what remains consistent is that ghostly matters seem to always be family matters, as made explicit by the word "familiar"—the ghostly spirit that typically adopts the shape of an animal and that serves a family across generations—and by Derrida himself, who, as the second epigraph of this chapter shows, argued that for haunting to occur, there needed to be "places, a habitation, and always a haunted house" (1995, 55). A haunted house that is/was/will be someone's home.

In this chapter, I examine the haunting that occurs in the overlap of the state, the public, and the official with the familial, the private, and the intimate. I explore this overlap by analyzing two objects/traces that, just like the eyes in chapter 2, act as Chávez's spectral remains. In the first section, I discuss the collectible phone cards that narrate and re-present his life in the worn-looking, nostalgia-evoking, family-friendly aesthetics of sepia. In the following sections, I look at his handwriting, which has experienced different afterlives as a tattoo and as an addition to the walls of apartment buildings constructed by the GMVV—in the case of his signature—and as a computer font—in the case of the application TC Chavez Pro. These objects exemplify the porosity that occurs when, as Walter Benjamin and Asja Lācis observed, the living room appears on the street and the street migrates into the living room. The cards render Chávez pocket-size, wallet friendly, and family-album worthy, while also suturing his image and his afterlife to the money that allows people to make phone calls and send text messages. The afterlives of Chávez's handwriting, in turn, allow the dead president to "sign" skins and walls of homes and to shape people's thoughts. Making, selling, and purchasing Chávez's collectible phone cards thus means making a piece of the living room—a piece of a family album—appear on the streets; typing on a personal computer with Chávez's handwriting means bringing the street—understood as part of the state's material language—into the living room.

While each of these objects could be given its own chapter or be put in dialogue with other remains from other chapters—Chávez's eyes could, for instance, be productive interlocutors for both the cards and the signature—analyzing them side by side brings to the fore certain operations that shed new light on the conceptualization of spectrality I have developed so far. In chapter 2, I explored the links between haunting, vision, and the power of a temporally dislocated form of surveillance; in this chapter, I look at haunting in relation to affect and excess, and to acts of collection and recollection, miniaturization and amplification, inhabitation and habituation. In the course of this analysis I will revisit the relationship between memory and the market and between the state and the archive, both relationships complicated by the liminal nature of the cards and of Chávez's handwriting. I will conclude by turning to Derrida and to the invitation he extends, in *Specters of Marx*, to future scholars: the invitation to learn to live with ghosts, talk to them, and give them back their speech. I will ask: What happens when we take this invitation at face value? What if living with specters becomes the *only* way of living available to us? What happens when being haunted becomes habitual and the relationship with the specter becomes intimate? When considered alongside the spectral remains analyzed here, the answers to these questions lead us to the realization that accepting Derrida's invitation might, in fact, come at a very high cost.

Family Matters

Though discussions regarding Chávez's legacy—and, specifically, who should be considered his true and lawful heirs—became heated and prominent after his death, the rhetoric that transformed Chávez from a political figure into a familial one had existed long before and was central to his political performance. The people Romero García interviews in his documentary *FANtasmo* make that clear: Chávez was the president, but, in their view, he was also their lover, grandchild, father, and brother (Romero García 2009). While all these roles were products of the interviewees' imaginations, spoken about jokingly or wistfully, they found resonances and, to a degree, confirmation, in Chávez's own words and in his public performances, which in several cases portrayed him participating in various family dynamics. Two episodes are particularly noteworthy, both featuring children.

The first one is an anecdote Chávez shared in a 2005 episode of his television show *Aló Presidente*, where he recounted a conversation with his youngest daughter, Rosinés Chávez Rodríguez. Rosinés, sick with a fever, asked her father why the white horse in the national coat of arms—which symbolizes the country's fight for independence—seemed to be looking back and standing still. Her question, he said, encouraged him to ask the Asamblea Nacional to revise the country's national symbols and "fix" the horse, which since 2006 appears running to the left—a left that is both literal and ideological. The decision to change the coat of arms—and to add another star to the national flag—caused outrage and inspired well-known humorist Laureano Márquez to publish a short article titled "Querida Rosinés" in the digital journal *Tal Cual*, where he proposes a series of questions for Rosinés to ask her father on behalf of the opposition (Márquez 2018). The journal, as a result, was fined for having violated Rosinés's intimacy, privacy, and integrity, according to the verdict by the district attorney of the state of Lara and the Consejo de Protección de Niños, Niñas y Adolescentes—the government entity in charge of protecting the rights of children and teenagers.[7] The story of Rosinés and the horse has primarily been discussed in relation to the restrictions Chávez's government placed on the media's freedom of expression and in relation to the president's insistence on performing, repeatedly, the founding of the nation through the manipulation of its symbols.[8] For the purposes of this chapter, however, I would like to focus on the family scene that Chávez's anecdote evokes: Chávez, the caring father, watching over his sick child, changing the nation's symbols—demanding a new horse be drawn—just for Rosinés.

The second, less controversial, family scene was also part of an episode of *Aló Presidente*, this time in 2008.[9] In it, Chávez asked a child who had been sent away by his security team to return, quoting Jesus from the Gospel of Matthew: "Let the little children come to me." The three-year-old approaches and stands near Chávez's lap, and when Chávez asks him what he is doing there, he says he is there to bring him cookies, to which Chávez responds: "Okay, so give me a cookie." What happens next sets off effusive applause and laughter from the audience: the child takes part of the cookie he was chewing from his mouth and feeds it directly to Chávez, who chews it and then wipes the gooey crumbs from his lips and the child's lips as he comments on the innocence of children and how it is later perverted by the selfishness of capitalism. What stands out in this scene is not Chávez's ideological rhetoric and denunciation of capitalism, but the child's saliva: the primal mouth-to-mouth feeding, the intimacy of an act meant to bond parents and children, which has now entered the public and political sphere, transforming Chávez from a distant authority figure into a father unafraid of a child—someone else's child, now his child—and his spit.

These are far from the only two instances in which Chávez's fatherly nature was publicly displayed for everyone in Venezuela to see; in fact, several *Aló Presidente* episodes feature children, and Chávez's daughters often accompanied him during his public appearances. I highlight them, however, because they render visible the crumbling of the boundaries separating the family, the nation, and the state. The symbol of Venezuela's fight for independence is transformed into a toy for the president's child; Chávez becomes not just the father of his children but of any child who lands on his lap; his political agenda and the fight against capitalism are condensed in a toddler and his willingness to share his cookie with the president. The Bolivarian Revolution is thus retold and reinterpreted as a family matter, and Chávez is reimagined as a father watching over his children.

The relevance of the family to the Bolivarian Revolution transcended Chávez's publicly performing his fatherhood. For instance, in 2001, the Ley Orgánica para la Protección del Niño, Niña y Adolescente was passed to protect and defend the rights of children. Through presidential decree, Chávez ordered the creation of the Misión Madres del Barrio—a social program designed to help homemakers from the barrios by providing them with social assistance, political activities, and microcredit—and the inclusion of article 88 in the Constitution, the first constitutional article in the world to recognize the value of housework for society.[10] The protagonism that the Venezuelan family acquired in the social and political agenda of the revolution accompanied the protagonism that Chávez's own family had on the political stage. Chávez's brother, Adán Chávez Frías, was governor of the state of Barinas from 2008 to 2017; before him it was Chávez's father, Hugo de los Reyes Chávez, who occupied the role from 1998 to 2008. Chávez often spoke of his grandmother, Rosa Inés (Mamá Rosa), with whom he had lived until he left to join the military, and he underscored his familial links to the country's revolutionary history by paying homage to Pedro Pérez Delgado, popularly known as Maisanta, a nineteenth-century Venezuelan revolutionary and politician who was also Chávez's great-great-grandfather.

The question of the family acquired new relevance and urgency after Chávez's death, when the decision regarding who should succeed him and be responsible for keeping his legacy alive became a family matter that resulted in several of his most fervent supporters claiming to be his rightful and only heir. Maduro, whom Chávez had named his successor months before his death, often referred to himself as "Chávez's son" (Michelutti 2017, 244). Opposing him was a subgroup within *chavista* officialdom that called itself "Los verdaderos hijos de Chávez" (The true children of Chávez) (Barráez

2017) and who proposed María Gabriela Chávez, Chávez's daughter, as his rightful successor.[11] As the months went by, more "children of Chávez" appeared. During carnival celebrations, children would dress like him and wear a sash with the words "Yo soy Chávez" (I am Chávez); there were also rumors regarding Chávez's extramarital affairs and the potential illegitimate children the president might have around the country.[12] Then, as Maduro proved to be a less-than-adequate substitute/heir, more members of Chávez's family began occupying positions of power, their presence a reassurance that Chávez was still alive and relevant in spite of Maduro's failure to convey the power and charisma of his predecessor. Jorge Arreaza, Chávez's son-in-law, became the country's vice president in 2013; his daughter (Arreaza's wife), Rosa Virginia Chávez, became the head of the Misión Milagro that same year; and his brother, Argenis, became governor of the state of Barinas in 2017.[13]

It was amid these debates regarding family, legacy, and the claim to power that the collectible phone cards featuring moments from Chávez's life began circulating in July 2014. While initially presented as a homage to Chávez (who would have been sixty years old that year) from CANTV—the state-run telephone and internet service provider in Venezuela—and the graphic designer and cartoonist Omar Cruz, who created the drawings featured on them, the cards, I propose, do more than just honor the dead president's memory.[14] They make Chávez "part of the family" by giving him a place in the family album. The album is a familial object that, as we will see in the following sections, demands physical, emotional, and mnemonic labor; imposes cohesion and relationality; collapses individual and collective time; and triggers acts of revival and animation that enable both the dead and their ideology to have a politically active, socially relevant afterlife.

A Market for Chávez

Omar Cruz first proposed the creation of the cards to CANTV on Twitter. He had started making drawings of Chávez the day his death was announced as a way to mourn him. However, drawing the president was something he had been doing for years, to the point where, he said, "I basically know it by heart" (VTV 2021a). Cruz's proposition was accepted by CANTV, and, on July 31, 2014, it put over two million cards in circulation. The cards were also displayed in an exhibit open to the public in CANTV's headquarters in Caracas, where visitors could see the drawings signed by Cruz next to an enlarged version of the cards. There are ten cards in total. In addition to the drawings, each of them shows how much they are worth (five or ten bolívares), Cruz's name, a caption ("Chávez comandante en jefe," "Chávez niño," "Chávez pensador," etc.), and the name of the series, "Gigante nuestro"—one of the many titles given to Chávez by his supporters after his death.

The first time I saw one of these cards—the one captioned "Chávez adolescente"—it was in the ID holder of the man who saw it as an amulet offering protection he felt compelled to share with his children, which is why he did not keep the cards he had collected but instead distributed them among the youngest members of his family. The second time I saw them, they had been arranged in chronological order and displayed among an explosion of knickknacks (figure 3.5). A collection of marbles, pendants featuring Chávez's eyes, a wooden dolphin and anchor, seashells, resin rings, Ernesto "Che" Guevara, the Venezuelan flag, the Virgin Mary, all side by side, piling on top of each other, forming what Jacques Rancière calls a "co-belonging": a "shared world where heterogeneous elements are caught up in the same essential fabric, and are therefore always open to being assembled in accordance with the fraternity of a new metaphor" ([2007] 2009, 57). There was no organizing logic, at least not an immediately visible one; there were also no prices displayed, which meant only the vendor knew what each item was worth, a number that—as tends to be the case in markets and among street vendors—was open to negotiation. The only objects that appeared "in order" were the phone cards, the order being the chronology of Chávez's life. Thus, they seemed to offer the "fraternity of a new metaphor," in Rancière's words. As if imbued with gravitational force, the cards appeared to attract all the other objects, to hold them together, and to provide the link between them—the link being, of course, Chávez. Chávez + Che Guevara, Chávez + the Virgin Mary, Chávez + marbles, Chávez + flag: all connections that never settled, that were never articulated but only insinuated or suspected, and that, therefore, granted Chávez an animation that emerged from the incompleteness, from the forward momentum of a yet-to-be-discovered link, and from the force of the random and the arbitrary.

What stood out in the case of the man's ID card holder and in the collection displayed among the knickknacks was that, in both cases, the cards seemed to be living all sorts of afterlives that took them beyond their basic function as disposable phone cards. For the man who worked at the Centro Nacional de la Fotografía, they were an amulet and a document that rendered his identity visible and legible. For the woman who displayed them in her tent, they were priceless, not for sale yet shown alongside things being sold; most important, they were hers and only hers, a collection built as an act of

3.5 Phone cards on a vendor's table.

commemoration and as an act of love. For Cruz, the cards were a homage to his beloved Comandante; for CANTV, a product that would bring in money. For everyone else, they were a means to an end; merchandise that could be turned into souvenirs; disposable things that could be kept, collected, and cherished. For me, they were reproductions of drawings of photographs taken of Chávez, the result of the act of turning a giant into a miniature, new things that looked like old things, ten family photographs in search of a family album. They were, thus, not (just) phone cards, but something else, something beyond, something better (or worse, depending on whom you asked).

If we take a step back, we will notice that they are also part of a growing market of Chávez-themed objects whose production, circulation, and consumption invite us to revisit the relationship between memory and the market, one that, in the case of Venezuela the year the cards started circulating, had to face the 2014 drop in oil prices that marked the beginning of an economic crisis that has only worsened with the years (Key and Villarroel

2018; McCarthy 2017; Weisbrot and Sachs 2019). In the context of the Latin American countries that emerged from authoritarian state repression in the 1980s and 1990s (Argentina, Brazil, Chile, Mexico, Peru, and Uruguay), the relationship between memory and the market has been studied and theorized extensively, with the concept of the "memory market"—a term coined by Ksenija Bilbija and Leigh A. Payne in "Time Is Money" (2011)—driving scholars to develop multiple understandings of memory narratives, practices, and goods. In this context, memory sometimes resists the logic of the market but at other times allows people to benefit from it, as the logic of memory and the market seamlessly blend. Central to these reflections is the link between memory and terror: the commodification, transaction, exchange, advertisement, and consumption of atrocity, sometimes in order to advance the fight for justice, reparations, and human rights, sometimes in order to move on and erase the traces left by state violence.

In the case of the "Chávez market"—the term I am using to refer to the Chávez-themed objects that circulated and were consumed in Venezuela and abroad after Chávez's death—terror and atrocity are not part of the equation, though this does not mean that the Venezuelan state has not repeatedly engaged in acts of violence that qualify as such.[15] The memory of Chávez does not oppose or disrupt the logic of the market; instead, it relies on it to acquire strength and relevance, and to circulate and become ubiquitous. The relationship between memory and the market thus operates more in the way Andreas Huyssen describes it—that is, memory providing comfort and the market rendering that comfort accessible. For Huyssen, however, this understanding of memory is tied to the "slow but palpable transformation of temporality in our lives, brought on by complex intersections of technological change, mass media, and new patterns of consumption, work, and global mobility" (2003, 21), which, in his view, make us desire the past in the first place and respond favorably to memory markets. While a case can be made for the relevance of these changes in Venezuela and in Latin America as a whole, in the years following Chávez's death, the transformation of temporality—which I have called an "afterglow"—also had to do with the uncertainty regarding the country's future in light of Chávez's absence and, as stated above, with the economic crisis that loomed on the horizon after the 2014 drop in oil prices. The desire for memory in this context thus was not, as Huyssen proposes, a "displaced fear of the future" (23), or anxiety regarding the speed of change and shrinking horizons of time and space, but rather the displaced fear of not having a future *at all* as a state, a movement, and a people. This widespread fear represented a threat to the legitimacy and authority of Maduro's government, and, more broadly, of the Bolivarian Revolution, which had to face economic restrictions that did not exist while Chávez was in power and the oil economy was healthy and booming. To assuage that fear, I argue, the market was saturated with Chávez, whose image appeared both in knickknacks like keychains and necklaces and on basic goods like milk and disposable phone cards.

This reference to milk is not an exaggeration. In 2015, the Asociación Cooperativa Empacadora Bolívar Vuelve R. L. produced the government-sponsored milk brand Bolívar Vuelve. The packaging declares that the milk is "hecha en socialismo" (made in socialism) and rich in vitamins A and D. It features Bolívar himself, drawn in red, who, the plastic bag states, "vuelve" (returns). *Vuelve* is also the imperative form of the verb, demanding that Bolívar come back. Already while Chávez was alive, there had been an increase in the "Bolivarization" of food, following the change to the name that took place months after he became president, from República de Venezuela to República *Bolivariana* de Venezuela. As Elías Pino Iturrieta points out, Bolívar went on to baptize everything from social programs ("misiones bolivarianas") to food products ("cultivos bolivarianos," "caraotas bolivarianas," "plátanos bolivarianos"), thus rendering the metaphor "el héroe está hasta en la sopa" (the hero is even in the soup) literal, for Bolívar was in fact in the ingredients used to make soup, "and we consume him every day with the help of our ordinary spoons" (Pino Iturrieta [2003] 2006, 249).

What exactly does one drink when one drinks this milk? Saying "just milk" feels like an oversimplification; saying "Bolívar/Chávez" feels too close to transubstantiation. Dismissing it as political propaganda—one more eccentricity of the government—does not undo the fact that it remains there, inside the home, the combination of Bolívar, Chávez (present in the red of the logo), ideology, and calcium rendered banal, desirable even, amid widespread hunger.

I rehearse in my mind hypothetical answers to the question: What did you drink today?

The government's milk.

Bolívar's milk.

Chávez's milk.

Bolívar comes back.

Bolívar, come back!

These imagined answers underscore how acts of consumption that occur on a daily basis, almost mechanically, might become forms of sociopolitical participation, even among those who strongly oppose the government yet must drink Bolívar's milk because it is the only affordable option. This lack of choice, the imperative to live with the specter shut in a cupboard, waiting to be poured into the morning's coffee, has become more pressing with the worsening of the economic crisis, which has led the government to be even more adamant in branding the things people consume—and the oil that makes their production and distribution possible—with Maduro's name or a reference to Chávez.[16]

Consuming the specter also takes place in the space of television, a space that has been progressively monopolized by government-sponsored channels such as Televisora Venezolana Social (TVES).[17] Chávez appears throughout TVES's regular programming both in shows and in advertisements and public service announcements. His face adorns the sets of the shows (figure 3.6), which during the summer of 2016 included several talk shows discussing his legacy along with daily contributions by Maduro talking to people while surrounded by pictures of Chávez and Bolívar. His voice also erupts during commercials, sometimes disembodied, other times in excerpts from old episodes of *Aló Presidente* that the channel keeps replaying, and other times in the messages delivered by artists and public figures who dialogue with the audience and remind them that they must remain loyal to Chávez and the Bolivarian Revolution. He is thus at once the topic of conversation and the product advertised in between conversations; his excessive televised presence is not only an insistent denial of his death but also a good to be consumed amid the scarcity of all other goods. Maduro associates this scarcity with what he calls the "unconventional economic war," a term that refers to intervention by a foreign country by means other than weapons of war, including instead political, economic, and social measures.[18] The shows dedicated to discussing this unconventional war spend little time detailing what those measures are and more time talking about how to respond to them. The most efficient solution, other than videos of Maduro in factories encouraging more production, is Chávez: it is the love shown for Chávez that will pull the country out of the crisis.

This message echoes in the stores that sell Chávez-themed objects, which often have a television or radio set tuned in to one of the government-sponsored channels. Inside these stores, both kinds of Chávez commodities—the material and the visual—coincide, reinforcing each other's value. Some of these stores are owned by the same people who make the objects that are for sale. This is another side of the process of commodifying Chávez: his direct intervention in the livelihood of the people who depend on making and selling him to survive (figure 3.7).

3.6   Chávez displayed on the set of the show *La hojilla*.

The need for the past to circulate in the market thus reveals itself to be twofold: not only are Chávez-themed objects necessary for Chávez to keep on living and, through his afterlife, ensure people's loyalty to the revolution and Maduro's administration, but they are also necessary for some people to make money to support their families. The woman *not* selling Chávez's collectible phone cards is a noteworthy exception to this more utilitarian approach to making and selling the Comandante. The man storing the phone card in his ID holder is also resisting the cards' (and the market's) disposable logic. Before turning to the cards in the next section though, it is important to recognize that the Chávez market has expanded beyond Venezuela. In September 2014, Labiofam, a Cuban laboratory, announced the creation of two perfumes: Ernesto (inspired by Che Guevara) and Hugo (inspired by Chávez). When applied to the skin, "'Ernesto' is woodier and sweet with fresh notes, while 'Hugo' is softer, with notes of tropical fruits, and less penetrating" (Voz de America 2014). As of March 2022, a number of stores on Amazon sold T-shirts featuring Chávez, and vendors on Etsy offered small busts and hand-painted dolls of him.

The creation and circulation of these objects—just a few examples in a market that grows as contemporary politics and governance lean more

3.7   Chávez figurines sold in a store in Caracas.

and more toward spectacle—point to a form of commodification of the political figure that seems to have become more intimate, moving from political posters and pins to T-shirts to scents that are absorbed into the skin. They offer a productive point of comparison with other forms of memory commodification—such as the objects made and sold by or on behalf of Argentina's Asociación Madres de Plaza de Mayo—and other ways of understanding the afterlives of commodities in different kinds of memory markets.[19] For the purposes of this chapter, however, I would like to stay with an understanding of the memory market as an afterlife space where the past can be animated rather than obliterated, infused with the energy spent making, selling, and buying, empowered by the intensity of nostalgic cravings and by the need for comfortable familiarity amid a lack of futurity that acquires a very concrete shape in the Venezuelan context.[20] There, after Chávez's death, the memory market finds itself in a paradoxical state of perpetual mourning that responds to Chávez's absence by turning him into a commodified presence subject to circulation, production, and consumption. The past is thus brought to life by the market, where it acquires a spectral quality that arises from the transformation of remains—Chávez's remains and Chávez as remains—into raw material used to fabricate goods, and from the hypervisibility and excessive accumulation of those goods. This excess, rather than being sterile and unsignifying, physically grounds Chávez in the present and gives rise to memory narratives that reflect the different ways that subjects/consumers establish a relationship with the spectral power they consume through the possession of Chávez-themed merchandise. These narratives are as varied as the people who choose to make, sell, and buy Chávez, and as those who choose not to do any of these things and nevertheless find themselves with Chávez in their home. The following analysis is not meant to flatten or condense all those potential narratives into one; further scholarship could productively pursue each narrative and give an ethnographic account of Chávez's lingering in individual and collective memories. What I offer instead is a reading of the commemorative phone cards that underscores the familial narrative invoked by their aesthetic and by the acts of collection and recollection that they seem to demand from those who purchase them, a narrative that, I argue, anchors the cards at the intersection of the gazes, encounters, and temporal gestures performed by the family album.

Family Album

In *On Longing*, Susan Stewart offers the following definition of a collection:

> In contrast to the souvenir, the collection offers example rather than sample, metaphor rather than metonymy. The collection does not displace attention to the past; rather, the past is at the service of the collection, for whereas the souvenir lends authenticity to the past, the past lends authenticity to the collection. The collection seeks a form of self-enclosure which is possible because of its ahistoricism. The collection replaces history with *classification*, with order beyond the realm of temporality. In the collection, time is not something to be restored to an origin; rather, all time is made simultaneous or synchronous within the collection's world. . . . The collection presents a hermetic world: to have a representative collection is to have both the minimum and the complete number necessary for an autonomous world—a world which is both full and singular, which has banished repetition and achieved authority. (Stewart 1993, 151–52; original emphasis)

This understanding of collections illuminates how time functions within the individual cards and in relation to their configuration as a collection.

Though this particular collection does privilege the past—Chávez's biographical past being the central topic of the collection—it also severs that past from its own linear temporality and folds it into itself, making it into its very own hermetic and autonomous world where death has been permanently banished. In fact, looking at the different stages of life depicted on the cards, we see there are no photographs of a sickly Chávez; the collection ends with a healthy-looking Chávez smiling at the closing event of his 2012 presidential campaign (figures 3.8 and 3.9). Thus, the world that the collection constructs is one where Chávez is meant to continue living, achieving eternal life not only through the promise of permanence in the immutability of each individual photograph, but also through a controlled passage of time that follows Chávez's growth across the cards and "freezes him" right before his death. This temporality imbues the collection with organic movement and vitality while also arresting time so that Chávez avoids encountering his own death.

Chávez's afterlife is further fueled by the logic of the collection itself. To collect is to agree to be driven by the obligation to keep hunting for the next piece—in this case, for the next Chávez. Thus, for those who collect these cards, Chávez exists in an anticipated future, not a long-lost past. Moreover, the cards challenge the "out with the old, in with the new" logic of the market because the value of collectibles encourages a different approach to consumption that protects them from being easily discarded. The cards thus stick around even after the money on them has run out, which means Chávez stays too as a valued and valuable remainder/reminder, exiting the disposable and public world of the market and entering the intimate and private spaces where personal collections and treasures are held. We saw this move from the public into the private in the ID holder, where the card with Chávez's teenage portrait served both as a sign of an assumed identity and as a talisman, and on the red tablecloth in the vendor's tent, where the card collection stood out as being above—both literally and figuratively—all the other small objects that were for sale.

The move from public to private is also represented by the miniaturization of the gigantic, which occurs in the phone cards in two ways. First, in the phrase printed on all of them, which gives the collection its title: "Gigante nuestro." In it, we see a relationship of ownership being established over Chávez, who goes from being an unreachable public figure to someone "possessed" by—someone who is part of—those who own the cards. Second, we see the process of miniaturization in the actual size of the card, which makes Chávez's image—typically displayed on huge posters and wall-sized

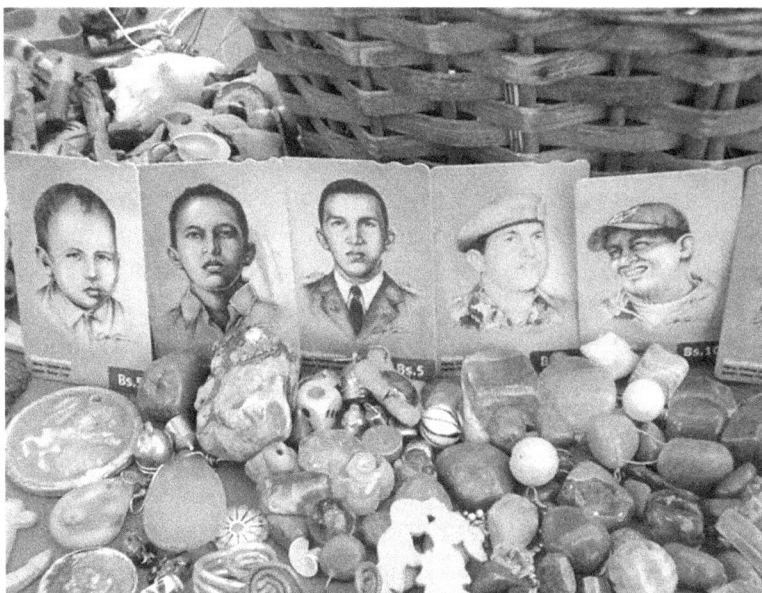

3.8   Display of the first five phone cards in the collection "Gigante nuestro."

3.9   Display of the last five phone cards in the collection "Gigante nuestro."

graffiti—pocket-size, thus encouraging its owners to place it in private spaces such as the ID holder, a wallet, an altar, and so on.[21] The combination of these two processes brings to mind Stewart's conceptualization of the miniature as "that which can be enveloped by the body" (1993, 137). Compressed by the dimensions of the phone card, Chávez is "enveloped" by the hands of those holding it, and as a result he acquires a tactility that the design of the card itself evokes through the use of sepia tones suggesting something worn and cherished—a feeling that is strengthened by the borders, designed to look like they have lost little bits over time. Stewart associates this "worn" quality with a type of souvenir—the personal memento—that speaks of individual experiences that, taken together, construct an autobiographical narrative:

> Such souvenirs are rarely kept singly; instead they form a compendium which is an autobiography. Scrapbooks, memory quilts, photo albums, and baby books all serve as examples. It is significant that such souvenirs often appropriate certain aspects of the book in general. . . . Yet at the same time, these souvenirs absolutely deny the book's move of mechanical reproduction. You cannot make a copy of a scrapbook without being painfully aware that you possess a mere representation of the original. The original will always supplant the copy in a way that is not open to the products of mechanical reproduction. . . . The acute sensation of the object—its perception by hand taking precedence over its perception by eye—promises, and yet does not keep the promise of, *reunion*. Perhaps our preference for instant brown-toning of photographs, distressed antiques, and prefaded blue jeans relates to this suffusion of the *worn*. (Stewart 1993, 139; original emphases)

The cards are designed to not only resemble but actually function like a memento; their "worn" quality and the intimate nature of the photographs erase their reproducibility, creating a feeling of uniqueness and familiarity that transcends mere acquaintance with and recognition of the cards and the person whose biography they represent. The copy thus reverses its own process of reproduction and becomes an "original" whose history is simultaneously biographical *and* autobiographical: it narrates Chávez's biography while also establishing a link between Chávez's life and the lives of the card collectors.

The biographical element of the cards is self-evident: they capture Chávez's growth from a baby into the fifty-nine-year-old man who won the presidential elections in 2012. Understanding their autobiographical nature, however, requires a more careful look. On one hand, there is the "worn" design, which conjures up a temporality constructed by the cards passing from hand to hand and from generation to generation, and by the feelings that materialize in that passage: the love and devotion that bring family members together, even those who might have never met and who nevertheless reconnect when one of them holds what was once in the pocket/wallet/nightstand/album of the other. We already saw how this hypothetical passage becomes real when the owner of the ID holder mentioned he gave similar cards to his children and nieces and nephews. This "family history" that the cards both evoke and construct also draws on the personal investment required not only by the act of collecting but also by the act of organizing the collection, which involves (re)constructing the narrative of Chávez's life by placing the cards in the proper chronological order, just as one would the photos of one's own children. Furthermore, the primary role of the cards—to provide people with money to make calls and send text messages from their phones—establishes a direct connection between them and the people who connect through them. Mothers talking to their children, aunts talking to their nieces, spouses talking to each other—all these intimate forms of communication among family members are made possible by the cards and the equally intimate and familial engagement with Chávez's life that they perform.

The cards thus blur all kinds of boundaries—between past and present, private and public, old and new, original and copy—and in the process articulate the promise of a reunion that reproduces all the elements of family reunions: a palpable and shared history, the physical and affective intimacy between bodies, the rituals that bring everyone together, and the exchange of looks that locates the individual within a family unit. This familial aspect of the collection is also accentuated by the cards' hybrid nature. As I mentioned, the images on the cards are reproductions of real photographs of Chávez, some well known, like the one where he appears wearing his red beret or the one at the closing of his 2012 campaign, and others less so, like the photograph of him as a toddler. Cruz used all these photographs to create his drawings, where the impersonal camera is replaced by the much more personal touch of the hand that draws the body, producing it while reproducing it. This overlapping of the photograph and hand-drawn portrait in the cards heightens the feeling of intimacy and interconnection that allows the Chávez of the cards to "stay in the family," not just as a recognizable image but also as the trace left behind by a body that was once there, sharing spaces and gazes as it actively participated in the handmade reproduction of its image.

A familial body thus materializes in the cards, its familiarity evoked not only by the familiar-turned-familial images of Chávez they capture but also through the recollections and behaviors that they trigger. This familial body calls to mind a quote by Roland Barthes that Marianne Hirsch returns to repeatedly in *Family Frames*:

> The photograph is literally an emanation of the referent. From a real body, which was there, proceed radiations which ultimately touch me, who am here; the duration of the transmission is insignificant; the photograph of the missing being, as Sontag says, will touch me like the delayed rays of a star. A sort of umbilical cord links the body of the photographed thing to my gaze: light, though impalpable, is here a carnal medium, a skin I share with anyone who has been photographed. (Barthes, quoted in Hirsch [1997] 2012, 5)

Hirsch argues that through the image of the umbilical cord, Barthes makes photography "inherently familial and material, akin to the very processes of life and death" (5). Furthermore, she points out that photographs, "as the only material traces of an irrecoverable past, derive their power and their important cultural role from their embeddedness in the fundamental rites of family life" (5). Before discussing those rites in more detail, let us stay a bit longer with the image of the umbilical cord and examine how it dialogues with the images displayed in the phone card collection. The umbilical cord is an instrument for Barthes to emphasize photography's role as a material emanation of the past; rather than being just a representation of the past, photography is a real, tangible link to it that burdens the present with the truth of what "has been" (Barthes's well-known "ça a été"). In the case of the cards, we saw how that link was visually incorporated in their design, through the yellowed surface and worn edges that make the truth of the past represented in each card as tangible as the card itself. But in Barthes's metaphorical description, that materiality is intrinsically tied to a sense of biological familiarity contained in the umbilical cord itself, a connection that in his case was inspired (and authenticated) by the Winter Garden picture of his mother that he is referring to, and the "mother/son/daughter" relationship that he reads in it (5).

In the cards, the umbilical cord as a biological thing is not as easily detectable, since there is no preestablished familial connection between the collector and Chávez. However, the cards seem to perform that familial connection both individually and as a group. Individually, their size, the close-ups, and the poses Chávez adopts make them *just like* the family photographs one carries around in a wallet, specifically those that parents have of their children, taken to mark their most important life events. Collectively, they are the (hi)story of a life told in the "family album" format, as exemplified by the captions that read: "Chávez bebé," "Chávez adolescente," "Chávez cadete," "Chávez deportista," and so forth. These inscriptions remind us of the narratives we construct when we choose, organize, and label photographs as we are putting together our own family albums. This performance of family results not in a spectacle to be watched but in a ritual to participate in through the act of collecting, which the cards turn into an act of *recollecting* that enables Chávez to descend from the gigantic posters, graffiti, and banners and move into the private spaces of the family circle and into the private stories of family life.

Photos like the ones we see on the cards thus not only capture snapshots of family life, they make that life and that family possible. As Hirsch points out:

> Now, more than one hundred years later, photography's social functions are integrally tied to the ideology of the modern family. The family photo both displays the cohesion of the family and is an instrument of its togetherness; it both chronicles family rituals and constitutes a prime objective of those rituals. Because the photograph gives the illusion of being a simple transcription of the real, a trace touched directly by the event it records, it has the effect of naturalizing cultural practices and of disguising their stereotyped and coded characteristics. As photography immobilizes the flow of family life into a series of snapshots, it perpetuates familial myths while seeming merely to record actual moments in family history. At the end of the twentieth century, the family photograph, widely available as a medium of familial self-presentation in many cultures and subcultures, can reduce the strains of family life by sustaining an imaginary cohesion, even as it exacerbates them by creating images that real families cannot uphold. (Hirsch [1997] 2012, 7)

This "imaginary cohesion" derives not only from the photographs holding people together inside their frame and in the contexts where photos are shared—at family gatherings where albums are passed around and commented on—but also from the look of recognition that allows those who view the photographs to see themselves connected to the people and the events captured there. In Hirsch's words,

> when I visually engage with others familially, when I look through my family albums, I enter a network of looks that dictate affiliative feelings, positive or negative feelings of recognition that can span miles and generations: I "recognize" my great-grandmother because I am told that she is an ancestor, not because she is otherwise in any way similar or identifiable to me. It is the context of the album that creates the relationship, not necessarily any preexistent sign. (Hirsch [1997] 2012, 53)

In the case of the cards, this familial look is constructed through the combination of two different narratives. On one hand, there is the narrative that makes Chávez recognizable as the figure repeatedly glorified in public and private spaces and that falls in line with the sort of memory practices promoted by Maduro's regime and Chávez's party—practices that include making Chávez a hypervisible and constant part of the landscape through posters, banners, statues, and so on. On the other, there is the more personalized narrative that the collection evokes and that is recognizable because it reproduces the kind of rituals families practice—such as looking at photographs together, making an album—along with the affiliative/parental feelings that are awakened by witnessing a little boy growing into a man. Together, they allow for the collectors and keepers of the cards to go from seeing Chávez's images as familiar to seeing them as familial: he becomes a member of the family and part of the family's history.

This familial look cast upon Chávez leads to his insertion in the family narrative and thus makes him part of the recollections that bind family members together and position them in relation to one another. This does not mean that Chávez necessarily acquires a predetermined role within those relations, but rather that he is an active part of the history that shapes them, occasionally filling in familial gaps. This transition from a state-endorsed, public, official memory narrative to the private, personalized memory narrative of the family is mediated by acts of creativity and imagination inspired by the cards themselves. In this way, the narrative that the cards construct and that keeps Chávez "in the family" is tangentially related to Hirsch's conceptualization of "postmemory" as "a powerful and very particular form of memory precisely because its connection to its object or source is mediated not through recollection but through an imaginative investment and creation"

([1997] 2012, 22). It is important to note that Hirsch defines this term in relation to the experience of those who grow up dominated by narratives belonging to previous generations shaped by traumatic events that cannot be understood or recreated, which is clearly not the context surrounding the collectible phone cards. Nevertheless, the concept illuminates both the distance between the biographical narrative in the cards and the autobiographical narrative of the collector, and the processes that bridge that distance. Those processes entail a creative and affective engagement with the cards that makes them familial and, as a result, burdensome.

This familial burden is one of the points Hirsch repeatedly emphasizes in her analysis, which sheds light on that burden and on different ways that photography allows for it to be alleviated. The burden that family pictures impose is tied to the "familial look," which is at once affiliative and surveilling:

> The familial look, then, is not the look of a subject looking at an object, but a mutual look of a subject looking at an object who is a subject looking (back) at an object. Within the family, as I look I am always also looked at, seen, scrutinized, surveyed, monitored. Familial subjectivity is constructed relationally, and in these relations I am always both self and other(ed), both speaking and looking subject and spoken and looked at object: I am subjected and objectified. (Hirsch [1997] 2012, 9)

The familial look becomes a "gaze" once the camera intervenes. In distinguishing between these two, Hirsch draws on Jacques Lacan and differentiates "a noninstrumental, embodied, situated, and mutual maternal look from the gaze-effect created by the conjunction of the mother and the camera, coextensive with the workings of ideology and with the ways in which society imagines authoritative vision" (156).

In chapter 2, I discussed the surveilling gaze in the context of Chávez's disembodied eyes. Now, with the cards, we encounter that gaze once again. If we look at the objects right next to the card collection on the vendor's red tablecloth, we will see a small pile of Chávez's eyes in bead form, waiting to be turned into charms for bracelets or pendants for necklaces. The proximity between the collection and the eyes, incidental but unsurprising given the ubiquity of the eyes, sheds light on the ideological narrative concealed underneath the family story told in the cards. With the familial recognition and affective identification with the little boy who grows into a man comes a familiarity with the state that imposes, on one hand, a set of demands and expectations—loyalty, behavior that would make Chávez proud, a sense of conformity tied to the confines of the family structure—and, on the other, a commitment to keeping Chávez alive within the personalized and private space reserved for family members.

Unlike the surveilling gaze associated with Chávez's disembodied eyes, however, the gaze in the context of the phone cards emphasizes tactility and reciprocity. In fact, through the textures mimicked in the cards' design, the specter becomes something to be *handled*; he (after)lives through the buying, selling, exchanging, touching, folding, rubbing, dirtying, and passing on of the cards, which then become more than images meant for mere observation. They become personal treasures that insert Chávez into the dynamics of familial inheritance. Furthermore, within those dynamics, the spectral gaze becomes reciprocal: not only is meeting the specter's gaze a possibility, but it is a familial duty that is fulfilled by creating the narratives that frame the collection and that make Chávez part of the family. Chávez's spectral authority then stops being associated with the impersonal command of the state and the law and becomes tangled with the affective burden of family obligations, which, as Hirsch suggests, are both hard to pinpoint and even harder to resist.

It is precisely this irresistible—though not unchallengeable—nature of family obligations that drives the state to create narratives and perform rituals that appeal to familial duty and love as it looks for ways to ground its legitimacy and authority. After all, blood, the saying goes, is thicker than water, which is why it was so central to Chávez's rhetoric. Chávez was all about blood. Not the blood spilled in battle—he, unlike Che Guevara, did not fight imperialism on the ground, with his body, holding a gun—but family blood, the blood that allowed him to insert himself, ex post facto, in revolutionary history and the nation's long tradition of insurgency. Hence his appeal to his great-great-grandfather, Maisanta, the outlaw who was converted into an epic hero thanks to the publication of José León Tapia's *Maisanta: El último hombre a caballo* in 1974. This lineage allowed Chávez to claim a place in a family history of revolutionary men, a link he repeatedly performed by wearing and exhibiting Maisanta's scapulary of Our Lady of Perpetual Help around his neck.[22] His own blood, in turn, externalized and re-presented in his party's signature red T-shirt, served as a unifying locus of identification for the people, *his* people, people dressed in red who, gathered around the president—also dressed in red—would vow to help him fight his illness, sometimes going as far as sacrificing their "real" family members to cure him, as we saw in chapter 1.

In Chávez's absence, the phone cards perform this connection through their invocation and evocation of family and, particularly, of the family album. The family album, we have seen, does not look back, at least not with the same intensity and stubbornness with which it looks around and looks forward. Creating, preserving, and sharing it are all forms of copresence, a "being with" that gathers people, alive and dead, old and young, and puts them always in relation to each other, always for and in each other, temporal and physical barriers collapsing as the family is brought into being over and over again. The photographs that belong in a family album—photographs like those adapted for the phone cards—thus function as a form of what Stewart in her exploration of longing calls "appurtenance": "an addition to the body which forms an attachment, transforming the very boundary, or outline, of the self" (1993, xi). The shape and size of the cards make them such an addition: the "missing bits" along the edges crave something (another card, another body) to complete them, and their pocket-size form seems to demand proximity to the body, which, as we discovered with the ID holder and the seller's collection, alters identities and generates new affective bonds. Furthermore, the cards capture a kind of Chávez that does not come with preconstructed and thus exclusionary narratives. The words in the captions are "raw" in that they can be used as building blocks in the personal narratives of the collector/family member: "bebé" (baby), "deportista" (sportsman), "café bendito" (blessed coffee), and "llovió en verano" (it rained in summer) are just the beginning of the story, not the whole of it.

Chávez afterlives in that narrative impulse, in that jump to the future where the family will carry on—and Chávez will carry on with it. He afterlives in the animating labor that goes into a family album: the energy that awakens the limbs and activates memory as photographs are gathered and held, as pages are written on and turned, as gazes—loving, authoritative, judging—are cross-temporally exchanged. The evidence of that labor, the proof that it is ongoing, is sweat: the kind that yellows images and that materially sutures past to present. *Sweat and not dust*—dust being the sign of a past preserved but forgotten, sweat being a symptom of animation, the secretion that alerts us to a past that haunts.

Chávez, the giant, thus afterlives as a miniature.

The reverse, too, allows for spectral lingering. In the next section, we will see how making the miniature gigantic can also conjure up a specter. First, however, one last thing about the family album, or rather, one last warning: it hides things. In a way, this is inevitable. In the name of harmony and the survival of the family, the album glosses over conflicts and absences, losses and fractures. In the context of Venezuela, however, what these cards hide, what they distract from, is the country's deteriorating telecommunications system. The CANTV that made the cards is the same CANTV that regularly fails to provide fast internet service, that carries on with malfunctioning infrastructure, and that has created a significant geographical divide in internet access.[23] The cards both conceal and reveal this reality. They conceal it by appealing first to the collector, then, maybe, to phone and internet users, and they reveal it by doing the same thing: the "Gigante nuestro" collection is just that, a series of collectibles, a gift from/for the Comandante. Why would we expect anything else from it? What better task for CANTV to undertake than honoring Chávez's memory? What more can a telecommunications company achieve than putting us "in touch" with the dead?

Parenthesis: Chávez and Me

I, too, collect Chávez (figure 3.10). In my office, a tattered box holds:

1   A small Venezuelan flag missing its plastic pole that someone once waved during a march in support of Chávez.

2   An old rusty pin with the words "¡Viva Chávez por siempre!" and "(1954–2013 QEPD)" (May Chávez live forever, 1954–2013 rest in peace) accompanying the portrait of a young Chávez doing a military salute.

3   A pamphlet featuring the same Chávez that appears on the pin, surrounded by the words "Maduro, desde mi corazón" (Maduro, from my heart), the slogan of Maduro's 2013 presidential campaign.

4   A plastic keychain displaying a smiling Chávez.

5   A large poster of Chávez with the words "Con Chávez siempre lealtad absoluta. ¡Socialismo o Nada! Mérida Gobierno Socialista. Lealtad con Chávez" (Always with Chávez, absolute loyalty. Socialism or nothing! Socialist government of Mérida. Loyalty with Chávez).

6   A chipped tin coffee cup: the twin of the one Elizabeth Torres sets out every day for her Comandante to spectrally drink his coffee in the Santo Hugo Chávez del 23 chapel.

I did not purchase or ask for any of these objects, and, up until the moment I received them, I did not want them. "Collecting" then might not be the right word for what I did: they are perhaps not a collection and I am not

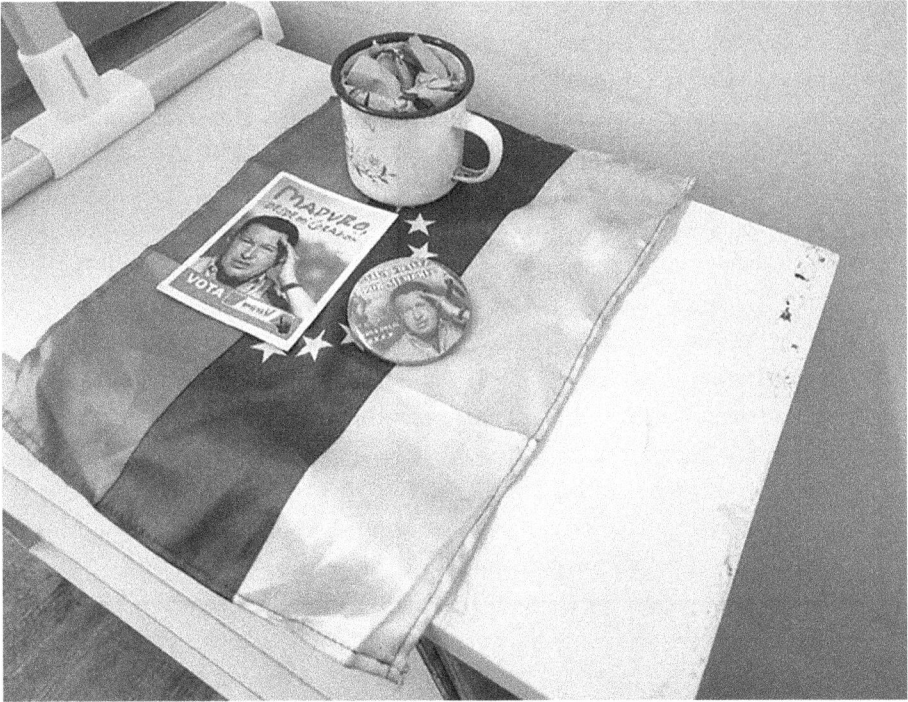

3.10   Flag, pin, voting card, and coffee cup.

a collector. True collectors, faithful ones, hold their breath as they imagine the delight and pride that comes with finding "the next one." They carefully build their collection a home: they polish wood and shine metal for the collected objects to be housed the way they deserve, properly displayed as the treasures they are. They invest time and money, their limits on both vanishing when they encounter the marvelous and the priceless. True collectors, faithful ones, gladly coexist with their collection and, in certain moments, give in to it, become part of it, and inhabit it.

Me? I did (and do) none of that.

I did, however, hold my breath when the aforementioned objects were placed in my hands by their previous owners. People—generous, kind people—who gave them to me because they could afford to do so, because they had many more objects that were similar and thus could spare these redundant pieces, because they were instructed to give them away, or because they wanted to end our conversation with a gift. I first politely refused to take them, but they refused my refusal. I then offered to pay for some of them, but that too was met with a strong no. So, I kept them. The box that holds them—previously, they were contained in a paper bag—has traveled with me from Mérida to Caracas to New York City to Ithaca. I often think of throwing it away. It would be so easy, I tell myself, as I look at the trash can and consider its tempting proximity. Easy, and yet impossible, completely out of the question. I feel indebted, infinitely so, to the people who owned them before me, people I will never see again, people who probably forgot we ever met and would likely not care what happened to these few objects, people whose loyalty to Chávez radiates from the objects themselves, making me perpetually uncomfortable. The discomfort never translates into surrender, though: I cannot give them up, a realization that hits me tangled up in Marcel Mauss's warnings about gifts and the strings attached to them ([1925] 2011). Warnings I ignored, consciously or not. Therefore, here we are, and here they stay.

Colleagues, family, friends, and acquaintances who happen to enter my office when the collection is on full display look at it, look at me, and look back at it. I can hear the question before they formulate it, sometimes angrily, sometimes not: Are you for or against Chávez? Or, more commonly, are you *chavista* or *opositora*? It is the question every Venezuelan and every Venezuelanist has to answer. Option A: *Chavista* (What does it mean to be *chavista* if Chávez is dead? I often wonder). Option B: *Opositora* (What exactly are we opposing anymore? And in the name of what?) Option C: *Nini* ("neither one nor the other"—and by far the answer that triggers the strongest rejection, the most deeply felt indignation, *plain old disgust*).

It sounds inconsequential, but it is not. For a scholar, A, B, or C might determine the publication of an article, an invitation to give a talk, the inclusion in a special issue. For everyone else, it is a personal matter: the beginning, the continuation, or the end of a relationship, of a family gathering, or of a friendship. Also, a work issue: being hired, being fired, being fired *and* sent to jail. And, a survival issue: receiving a box of food or necessary medicine.

A, B, or C.

When asked in the context of my Chávez collection, I always marvel at how strongly the question speaks of the bond between collector and collection. Whatever mastery the collector might believe they have over their collection is fictional: in the collection's proximity, the collector is one more object, the last object and the first, the only part of the collection that cannot truly leave it.

While Chávez was alive, I dutifully answered the question. Easily, heatedly, decisively, repeatedly, the way I, as a Venezuelan, was supposed to: pulse racing, no blinking. Now, Chávez is dead, and the question needs reformulation. While waiting for it, for a different question that I know will take its time to come—if it ever comes at all—I look at the Chávez on the keychain, frozen in a smile that does not reach me but that passes by me, a subtle gesture that speaks of the not so subtle persistence of his stubborn anachronism. Life and death neatly wrapped up in plastic, the shadow of a life that abruptly disrupts the present and burdens it with the weight of a past that, being spectral, weighs nothing and yet encompasses everything.

How long, then, until a new question is articulated? How long until Chávez, *deceased*, ceases to be part of the equation? The waiting, I realize, marks the lifespan of the specter—Chávez's specter—and of my collection as it stands now: something other than a pile of unwanted souvenirs, something in between a coffin and a Ouija board.

Yours, Chávez

What does a giant's signature look like? The answer is on the wall, more specifically, on the walls of housing complexes and apartment buildings built by the Gran Misión Vivienda Venezuela (GMVV).

Chávez proposed the GMVV program in 2011 with the goal of providing dignified housing for the homeless, the poor, and those living in geomorphological high-risk areas that often endure floods and mudslides. Like other *misiones* in Venezuela, the GMVV was funded in large part through Petróleos de Venezuela, the state-owned oil company, and like every plan Chávez proposed as he announced the epic transformation of Venezuela into a socialist society, the GMVV's task was extraordinarily ambitious: the construction of three million houses in ten years.[24] These houses could be individual units that, together, would form "villas socialistas" (socialist villas), or they could be apartment buildings of ten or more floors.[25]

Chávez's construction dream came true in 2020. The three-million milestone was televised on *Jueves de vivienda*, a show that films the "handing over" of the housing units, broadcast by the government-sponsored channel Venezolana de Televisión. In December 2020, the channel's web page posted the video, featuring the historic landmark of constructing over three million homes and showing the handing over of ninety housing units in La Gran Villa housing development.[26] Though the event was supposed to also highlight the commemorative plaque and plaza built in homage to Darío Vivas—governor of Capital District who died due to COVID-19 complications—Chávez remained, in rhetoric and in the space itself, the central figure. As the reporter, the mayor, and the family that received the first house thanked Maduro and Chávez for it—repeating the slogan "con Chávez y Maduro el pueblo está seguro" (with Chávez and Maduro the people are safe)—the camera showed the stencil of Chávez's eyes on the yellow walls of the buildings and on top of the gigantic billboard announcing the 3.3 million houses, a small poster of his face overlooking every house's living room, and a metal cutout of him near the entrance to the villa. The spectacular nature of the event was further intensified by repeated allusions to the United States' sanctions on the country, the pandemic, and the "fascist oligarchy": all factors that made reaching 3.3 million homes appear nothing short of heroic.

The spectacularity of this particular moment—and the spectacularity and monumentality of the task undertaken by the GMVV of building so many houses so quickly—can be read alongside similar projects carried out throughout Venezuela's history, particularly during the dictatorships of Juan Vicente Gómez (1908–35) and Marcos Pérez Jiménez (1952–58) and during the first term of Carlos Andrés Pérez's presidency (1974–79). Taken together, these projects constitute the visual and material manifestation of what Fernando Coronil called Venezuela's "magical state": a state that, fueled by the country's seemingly infinite oil reserves, "astonishes through the marvels of power rather than convinces through the power of reason," and manufactures "dazzling development projects that engender collective fantasies of progress" (1997, 3). In the years following Chávez's death, however, the state's magic underwent a transformation: it acquired a necromantic hue. The number and size of the buildings were only half of the magical act; the other half was the conjuring up of Chávez, whose spectral presence became visible, part of both the inside and the outside of the buildings. Inside, we see him in the living room, in between a poster of Simón Bolívar and one of Maduro, a layout that reproduces the way the three figures must appear in official buildings and public offices. Outside, he lingers on the walls, in the magnified reproduction of his signature.

We have seen Chávez's signature before. In chapter 1, we saw how, as part of the commemorative events following the announcement of Chávez's death, a number of people chose to have it tattooed on their bodies, which then became fleshy graves where the Comandante could carry on living. Now the signature reappears, drawn in red on the walls of apartment buildings where it spans seven floors. Its dimensions "decompress" the giant miniaturized in the phone cards: Chávez, "gigante nuestro," exits the family album and grows in our imagination until his hands can grasp a pen big enough to draw such a signature.

Whereas the miniature awakens in us the impulse to create an environment for it, the gigantic, as Stewart argues, "becomes our environment, swallowing us as nature or history swallows us" (1993, 89). And the signature does contain us, as part of the environment and as the environment itself, both because its gigantic dimensions and its location deny us the opportunity to truly confront it, and because behind it people have made homes: homes that the signature on the wall simultaneously certifies (legally speaking), hides, points to, protects, and, we could argue with Stewart, swallows. Though just a metaphor, the idea of Chávez's signature "swallowing" the homes underscores the subtle violence that permeates the choice to draw it where it cannot be reached and thus erased. In fact, while strikingly visible to passersby, the signature is not what the inhabitants of the buildings see when they stand on their balconies or look outside their windows. It is only when coming home, when standing in front of the building or passing by it on the street, that the signature occupies their field of vision—a "welcome back" they can soon leave behind. The signature thus is and is not there, and it is that liminality—the conjuring up of a presence that lingers without becoming too disruptive—that guarantees it is forgotten and, once forgotten, routinely accepted.

Accepting its presence also comes easily because it is not a foreign, unrecognizable image but one that is familiar and effortlessly recollected. In fact, before it landed on walls and skins, the signature had already become a recurring feature of the Bolivarian Revolution's visual rhetoric. As Lisa Blackmore points out, the ceremonial signing of documents during televised meetings and events "became a common part of the repetitive syntax of *cadenas nacionales* . . . that were a commonly used media platform during Chávez's government" (2014, 242). Moreover, when it came time for Chávez to activate his encrypted electronic signature, he did so on live television, sharing with the audience the password he had chosen to activate the card he received as part of the process: unsurprisingly, "maisanta2021."[27] A few minutes before the activation occurred, Chávez had signed a document by hand and the camera had zoomed in for a close-up of the signature, which appeared drawn in red ink next to the words "máxima eficiencia" (maximum efficiency) that he had also scribbled on the page. With enough practice, anyone could reproduce Chávez's signature, and that seems to have been the point. Instead of keeping it hidden, afraid of identity theft, Chávez chose to repeatedly show himself drawing it, the power contained in it seemingly put at the service of anyone and its referential nature blown up to encompass no longer just Chávez but everyone else too. Chávez's signature was the people's signature: both the people and Chávez could, technically, sign "Chávez."

It is thus not surprising that the signature outlived the signer, that it kept being drawn long after Chávez's death was announced. That is, after all, what signatures are for. Drawing them, Derrida reminds us, implies the "actual or empirical nonpresence of the signer" (1988, 20). But why draw it on the walls of the GMVV apartment buildings? Buildings that all share the same design and leave little room for confusion regarding who was responsible for their construction—Chávez, Maduro, the government, the Bolivarian Revolution—thanks to spectacular inauguration events, commemorative posters, the names given to them (like Villa Socialista Hugo Chávez), the *Jueves de vivienda* episodes, and Maduro's frequent reminders on live television. Moreover, why Chávez's signature and not something else, like his name printed in big red letters or a blown-up reproduction of his face? The answer, I propose, has to do with the signature's inherently spectral nature: the temporal juggling that allows it to conjure up a presence, to invoke rather than evoke, and to conflate past, present, and future.

Signatures, like all forms of handwriting, are distinctively intimate. As Sonja Neef points out, in spite of digital writing equipment,

> handwriting holds its own within the bastions of private and personal correspondence—as formal condolences or (even still) as intimate love-talk—as also in the manifold practices of signing, from signing one's name in an autograph, via the engraving or tattooing of one's skin as a mark of authenticity, through to spraying on walls: everywhere it is a matter of establishing or maintaining one's unique identity. Now as much as in the past, handwriting . . . remains the means of writing for the *aide mémoire*: one's diary, shopping list and a quick note on the phone. (Neef 2011, 25)

In her work, Neef, following Derrida, problematizes the signature's claim to uniqueness by highlighting its iterability: the fact that, for a signature to be a signature, it has to be reproducible. Before addressing that argument and its implications for Chávez's spectrality though, let us stay a bit longer with the intimacy that the signature exudes regardless of how many times it is drawn. This intimacy is not tied to the signer's unique identity—which the signature (re)presents and reaffirms—but rather to our understanding of the signature (and of handwriting generally) as a *bodily* gesture, as the mark that materializes when a body (hand) presses an object (pen) onto a surface. While the eye moves easily across typed letters as it reads the words they form, it gets "stuck" in the twists and turns of a signature both because the signature is not to be read but to be decoded and because the eye cannot help but notice the (now invisible) signing hand that hovers above it. Put differently, the signature never appears by itself: it always drags with it the hand that created it. Hence why love letters and condolences, as Neef points out, tend to be handwritten, at least in part: while the message conveyed is important, it is not as important as the *presence* of the sender, the need/demand to be *with* the message's addressee. Not only does the handwriting and, specifically, the signature, convey the message "I am with you, here, accompanying you, from a distance," it performs the message by being the proof of presence, the imprint left by a hand that is too, to a degree, trapped in the imprint.

In the case of Chávez's signature, this intimacy is further emphasized in two ways. First, in the process of recollection that the signature, being well known and widely reproduced, triggers. Encountering it on the wall is not a surprise but a form of déjà vu: we recognize it, we have seen it before. This familiarity intensifies precisely because the signature has been enlarged, rendered excessively legible to leave no room for confusion. Thus, like Chávez's eyes discussed in chapter 2, the signature does not appear as exceptional or eventful but as ongoing: one more link in an infinite chain that makes clear that it was already there and will be there again. The ordinary is blown out of proportion so that its ordinariness is noticeable but not shocking, so that it pulsates with a familiar hum that has the potential to transport us to that moment when Chávez activated his electronic signature and the camera recording the event was angled so that we—the viewers—would be *right there*, close to Chávez, as close as a child sitting on his lap, his signing hand almost our hand too. We thus know the signature as if our very own hand had drawn it; that is, we know it intimately.

The intimate nature of Chávez's signature is intensified by the color it is frequently drawn in and the associations that come with it. While the signature has been drawn in black and in white—a palette that reproduces that of Chávez's eyes—it is often also drawn in red, the color of Chávez's party, evoking blood. What Neef calls the "somatic dimension of writing" (2011, 119)—a dimension underscored by the comparison between the flow of ink and the flow of bodily fluids—becomes even more evident as the red gives the impression that the signature could have been drawn in ink or in blood. The blood, of course, could only be metaphorical—no one would believe that Chávez's signature on the walls would ever be drawn using actual human blood—but that does not make the association any less powerful. As Thomas Fechner-Smarsly argues, compared with ink, "blood seems much more auratic, even frightening, because blood is directly related to the body, either to the body of someone who voluntarily gives blood or has a blood test, or someone who has been wounded" (2006, 200). In the case of Chávez's signature, it is the presence of the body (rather than the state it is in) and its authenticity that the ink/blood highlights. It is not only a form of handwriting—and an appeal to the intimacy that it evokes—but also a *hand, writing*: a hand containing blood vessels, one of which could have accidentally broken and thus allowed for ink and blood to mix and leave a biological trace, a trace containing a bit of body in it.

This "bit of body" comes back to us with each iteration of Chávez's signature and the differences that make them unique. The differences are subtle: they stand out only if you look for them. They are an assault on the original and, simultaneously, a confirmation of its power and proof of its authenticity. When placed side by side, Signature A (figure 3.11) and Signature *A* (figure 3.12) do not engage in a battle between the genuine/original and the false/copy. The differences in the spacing, in the sharpness of the *V*, and in the ninety-degree angles on the top and bottom, are not evidence of forgery, of a different hand, a non-Chávez hand, tracing a fake signature. It is always his hand, and always his signature, as confirmed by the fact that many of the signatures also have the word "Chávez" in printed letters separate from the cursive flourish. Whatever irregularity catches the eye is precisely the proof that the signing hand is, in fact, human: vulnerable to the impossibility of drawing each letter identically each time. The relationship between the two then, as Neef argues, cannot be "covered by the dual concepts genuine/false, original/copy, individual piece/series, but integrates these oppositions into a dialectic third term, 'which connects the same kind with the different and the different with the same kind'" (2011, 151).

This "dialectic third term" also does something else: in going beyond the binaries Neef identifies, it allows us to focus on the physicality of the signatures, the heat that radiates from the brushing of hand, pen, and paper/wall against each other, tied to the suspicion that something of the signer remains, trapped in the twists and turns of his signature, vibrating, agitated, bearing witness to and also completely disregarding the irrevocability of his absence. Each signature—a copy and an original in its own right—can thus

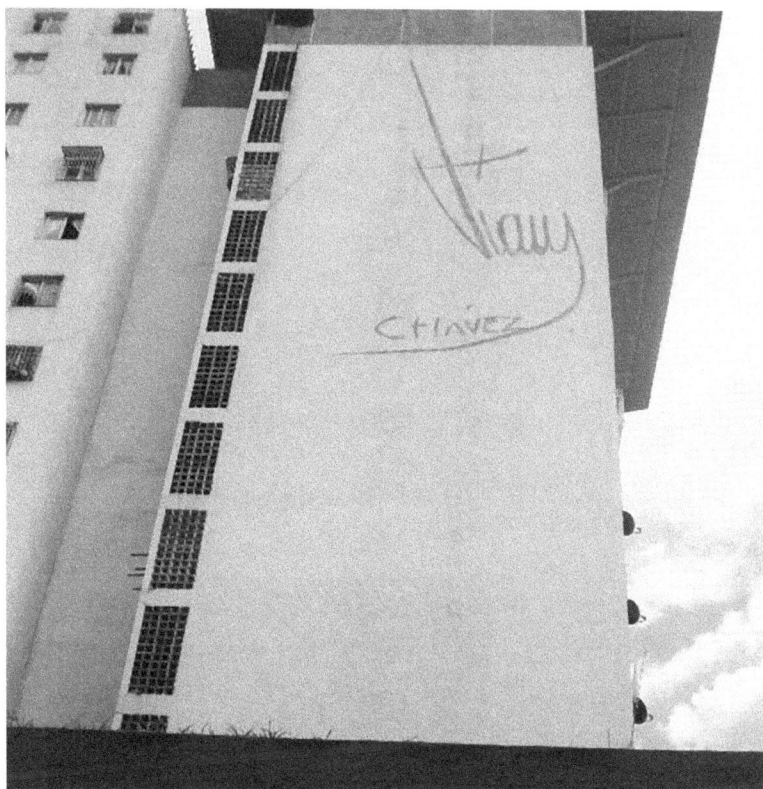

3.11 Chávez's signature in red ink on the wall of an apartment building.

be thought of as a preserving jar conserving the "auratic here-and-now of the physical touch emanating from the 'original'" (Neef 2011, 208), a touch that reaches out, stretching across past, present, and future, anticipating an always imminent and intimate encounter with the eyes of a reader who comes to it from the future present. In the case of Chávez's signature and its recurring appearance on the walls of GMVV constructions, however, the preserving jar is more than that: it is a genie's lamp, and the genie inside it, the *specter* it holds, is the kind powerful enough to make houses appear seemingly out of thin air.

Though Chávez visibly haunts the reproduction of his signature—in the handwritten "Chávez" lingering above the long line trailing below the vertical scribble—all signatures are spectral, performing the sort of temporal juggling that wraps presence and absence around each other and drags both past and future into the here and now. Derrida argues as much in "Signature

3.12 Chávez's signature in white on the brick wall of an apartment building.

Event Context." He defines the signature as implying "the actual or empirical nonpresence of the signer. But, it will be claimed, the signature also marks and retains his having-been present in a past *now* or present [*maintenant*] which will remain a future *now* or present [*maintenant*], thus in a general *maintenant*, in the transcendental form of presentness" (1988, 20; original emphasis). This temporality of the signature, the continuity it establishes between past and future, both coexisting in "a general *maintenant*," is tied to the signature's paradox: the fact that while it must retain its absolute singularity, which evinces the uniqueness of the signer, it must also be reproducible. As Derrida argues, in order to function, "a signature must have a repeatable, iterable, imitable form; it must be able to be detached from the present and singular intention of its production. It is its sameness which, by corrupting its identity and singularity, divides its seal" (20).

Derrida's conceptualization of the signature underscores a form of temporality contained in the *maintenant*, which can be translated into English as "now," "already," and "henceforth." This suggests a multidirectional temporality that is also spectral because it projects the past into both present and future, and because it animates the past, making it seem alive thanks to the ongoingness—the *maintenant*, the "transcendental form of present-ness," the promise of iterability—that the signature performs. At the same time, the signature repeatedly points to the singularity of the signer who simultaneously asserts their presence and ensures that their presence will be unnecessary at a later time, the signature both signaling that they were there and guaranteeing that their words will carry on without them in the near and distant future.

Taken together, these characteristics illuminate a compelling argument for the reproduction of Chávez's signature on the walls of the GMVV buildings. While a historically relevant date or simply Chávez's name on the buildings would be forms of commemoration looking back to a past that has already passed and therefore is no more, using Chávez's signature gives him an afterlife, the possibility of an "ongoingness" that is spectacular—the spectacle of the gigantic, of the impossible made possible—and relational. Relational because, while the signature is a seemingly inconsequential (yet gigantic) "final touch" added to the buildings, it is embedded in the process of creation of a site that will become a home. This process is represented by the signed document that commands the apartment building or housing complex be constructed; once the document is signed, construction begins and, after a certain amount of time, a house will be built and delivered. However, this sequence of events is collapsed by the act of placing the signature on the outer wall of the house or apartment. The authorization, the construction, and the final product are made to overlap and become simultaneous; power, represented by Chávez, appears twice as powerful because its promises are fulfilled immediately.[28]

This temporal collapse is accompanied by a spatial collapse that, Blackmore argues, turns the residential buildings into archives and, consequently, into sites for commemoration and memory:

The buildings, decorated with the giant signature, proffer a testimony (document) of Chávez's authority to have them built, while this *commandment* and, by extension, the commencement of more dignified life that these buildings were tasked with are returned to the domestic scene. What this gesture thus seeks to imply is a direct link between power—via the personalist iconography of *chavismo*—and *el pueblo* (the people) who inhabit the building/document/monument that is proposed as a stimulus for commemoration. (Blackmore 2014, 245)

For Blackmore, the coming together of the archive, the document, and the monument through the reproduction of the signature on the buildings allows for an act of "capturing life" that enables Chávez to keep on living as that "original auratic object" that the building/document/monument promises to bring us closer to. For that capture to occur, however, the archive, the document, and the monument have to be tampered with so as not to succumb to the monumental stillness that would deactivate Chávez's power, understood as an ongoing, compelling, and effective act that demands more than commemoration precisely because *it is not done and over with*. Hence why the signature in particular is essential: its multidirectional temporality animates the monument just as it "completes" the residential building and promises the construction of a new one, making Chávez—the signer, *always*—a political and social actor who continues performing his official duties after his death.[29]

Furthermore, there is something "nonofficial," "unstately," pulsating in the signature as it is reproduced on the buildings' walls, an aesthetic element that takes it away from the document and the archive and aligns it more with graffiti, with the irreverence of a form of writing that is less about communication and meaning production and more about marking territory and producing an act of address directed at a second person, a "you" that the graffiti, like an unruly—and gigantic—hand, shamelessly touches. This marriage of the irreverent and the stately, authority and disobedience, archive and home, and document and graffiti staged by the signature injects it with a vibrancy, a liveliness that transforms Chávez from an object of commemoration to the subject of an address. The link that Blackmore argues is implied in the signature thus does not just tie together power/Chávez and the pueblo but puts them in touch in a form of relationality that, cherished or not, desired or not, comes with a burden that disguises itself as gratitude.

This gratitude is an act of ongoing remembrance that does not look back— at a dead Chávez, anchored in the past—but instead stays in a temporally dislocated present, directed at a Chávez who is right there, always on the wall, a potential family member and co-owner of the house for, as Yaneira Wilson Wetter in her study of the GMVV points out, many inhabitants of these buildings refer to them as "Chávez's houses" (Wilson Wetter 2020, 14). And because he is right there, that gratitude demands loyalty, gets lost in loyalty, and reaches beyond Chávez to the current government whose survival partially depends on the strength and endurance of that loyalty.

This gratitude grows loud at events such as the celebration of the construction of three million homes, discussed above. Outside those televised, spectacular, and highly advertised events, it carries on as what Jon Beasley-Murray calls the "unseen and barely audible hum of micropolitics that pervades our daily routines; it is like background noise in that we are almost oblivious to its ongoing importance, the ways in which it structures our all too familiar, endlessly repeated quotidian activities" (2010, 180–81). Habits, according to Beasley-Murray, drive and are driven by this "barely audible hum," which, in the context of Chávez's signature and the gratitude that it aims to trigger, is in fact boomingly loud, reproduced in space with a frequency that makes it too banal to be noticed, its presence accepted not (or not only) because of political allegiance to Chávez and the revolution, but because it does not cause any violent disruption. Yet, as Beasley-Murray reminds us, what is habitual is rarely inconsequential. Habits form our sense of time and place, our being in the world; they reproduce "our corporeal assent to power's legitimacy" (192), which, in the post-Chávez era, depends, among other factors, on Chávez's ongoingness, on him *still* being there, *still* engaging with people, guaranteeing the fulfillment of the promise of the Bolivarian Revolution. Living with his signature, accepting (actively or passively) its thereness, is thus consenting to live with the subtle yet incessant imperative to be grateful to the (not-so-dead) man who allowed the house to be built and to share with him the right to own it.

Chávez's signature, then, acts as the signature at the bottom of an official document, as graffiti, and as the signature on the card accompanying a gift, reminding the recipients, kindly but firmly, whom they need to thank for it.[30] We cannot think of gifting in this context and not think of Marcel Mauss and his widely cited argument regarding the obligations that come with receiving gifts: "The obligation attached to a gift itself is not inert. Even when abandoned by the giver, it still forms a part of him. Through it he has a hold over the recipient, just as he had, while its owner, a hold over anyone who stole it" ([1925] 2011, 9).[31] This "hold" becomes visible in the Chávez haunting the signature, and, less explicitly but perhaps more strongly felt, in the "invisible hand"—his hand—that hovers above it. A giant's hand, a *giant hand*, one that, large as it is, does not just have a hold over those living under it: it enfolds them, wrapping around them, holding them up, and, most important, not letting go.

I feel the impossible weight of this invisible hand as I drive past the apartment building where it lingers. Who owns these apartments? Legally, the inhabitants, once they finish paying the mortgage. But that straightforward answer does not seem sufficient, at least not while Chávez's signature remains on the wall. Perhaps the uncertainty, the inability to identify a single owner, is the point of the signature, one aligned with the socialist goals of the GMVV and the Bolivarian Revolution: to encourage us to consider private property and collective ownership outside the individualistic, capitalist framework we have grown used to. Or, it might be a subtle form of subjugation and control: the transformation of a right—to dignified housing—into a gift, which produces a sense of obligation, demanding the sort of blind loyalty that would keep an increasingly unpopular government afloat. It might easily be both. The question though remains unresolved, the "who" split into two: an I and a you, a people and a spectral giant, living under the same roof. This form of co-ownership and copresence, the doubling of the I, reappears in two more afterlives granted to Chávez's handwriting: the app TC Chavez Pro and the signature-turned-tattoo. We will look at them together in the final section of this chapter, where we move away from the miniature and the gigantic to focus instead on the average-sized body trapped in between, enveloping one and enveloped by the other.

The Flesh, the Screen, and All the Hands In Between

THE FONT TC Chavez Pro was born from a tattoo. Marcelo Volpe, its creator and designer and part of the collective Trinchera Creativa, developed the idea when he had the slogan "Hasta la victoria siempre" (Always to victory) tattooed on his body in a font that reproduced Chávez's handwriting, which he described as transmitting "urgency and haste with a rather unusual asymmetry, which makes it a good choice for efficiently spreading a message" (Aporrea 2014).[32] The font became available for download in July 2014 as a gift for Chávez and the people on his birthday, a gift that expanded the commemorative pile of presents that included the collectible phone cards and that were shared with Venezuelan audiences during the televised transmission of the birthday party Maduro organized for Chávez. To create the font, Volpe used the letters Chávez wrote while imprisoned in

Yare after the failed coup against Carlos Andrés Pérez in 1992 and the note he sent clarifying that he had not renounced the presidency during the 2002 coup against him. In addition to imitating Chávez's handwriting, TC Chavez Pro offers keystroke shortcuts that produce a number of Chávez's signature phrases—like "Por ahora y para siempre" or "Hasta la victoria siempre"—and, if one clicks on the @ key, Chávez's signature appears on the screen (*Diario Extra* 2014). While the app would be most appealing to people who self-identify as *chavistas*, it is, Volpe clarifies, for everyone, *chavistas* and *opositores* alike, to be used by graphic designers and anyone interested in making art about—and, we could add, with—the Comandante.

Before words were typed instead of handwritten, and barring acts of forgery and cowriting, the traces forming the letters written by a hand as it pressed against a surface were interpreted as being unique to the writing individual. So unique, in fact, that an entire field of handwriting analysis emerged with the promise of catching criminals by reading the traces they left behind in their writing, and books were written with the exclusive task of preserving the (sacred) handwriting of kings and queens.[33] Then digital technologies arrived and called this uniqueness into question by allowing us to write electronically, the choice between fonts a matter of preference rather than proof of an identity. Now comes TC Chavez Pro to put the question of uniqueness and identity back on the table/screen. My thoughts, but Chávez's handwriting, as interpreted and designed by Volpe. Our writing (Chávez's and mine), which is also everyone's writing (or at least everyone who uses the app). Not a sui generis font but one that migrated from a document without fully leaving it and that therefore is here and there (and there, and there, and there). A punctured archive bleeding out not content but form.

It only takes one element of this sequence to set heads spinning.

The implications of the tattoo of Chávez's signature (figure 3.13) are equally noteworthy. Though people had already had Chávez's signature tattooed on their bodies before his death (Blackmore 2014, 243), the practice became an official act of commemoration when, from April 1 to April 5, 2013, the *chavista* youth organization Fundación Fuerza Integradora de la Juventud (FIJU) organized sessions where people could get a tattoo of Chávez's signature for free, with the option of getting it in the president's signature red ink (243). Commenting on the reasons the interviewees in FIJU's promotional video gave for getting the tattoo, Blackmore argues that there are three key factors that explain the perceived resonance of the signature: "First, the tattoo is presented as an internalisation of Chávez and his

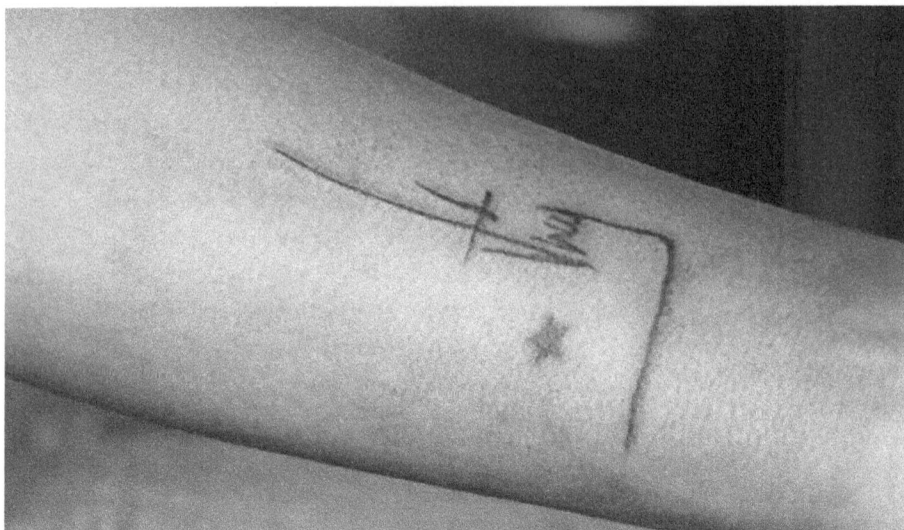

3.13 Tattoo of Hugo Chávez's signature on a woman's arm. Taken from ABC News web page. See Rueda 2013.

enduring presence through its inscription on the social body. . . . Secondly, the authority connoted by the signature is presented in a positive light. . . . Finally, the tattooed body is presented as an extension of the writing of history" (243). She concludes that the practice of tattooing the signature on one's body "posits the body as a living archive by virtue of the enduring temporality of the tattoo/document, tasked with stimulating collective, 'living history' by incorporating citizens' bodies into the act of inscription" (244).

Blackmore's analysis of the tattoo presents it as a document as understood by Jacques Le Goff—that is, as a vehicle that captures life and can be transmitted via sounds, images, or other means (Blackmore 2014, 236). I would like to push this argument further by taking a closer look at the act of tattooing itself—the injection of ink, the escaping of blood, the replacement of blood by subcutaneously injected ink—and by reflecting on the identity issues that arise when what is being tattooed is someone else's signature. The latter point brings us back to Derrida and complicates his understanding of the signature by dismantling the assumption that a signature lives on outside the body and that it is this split between the signature and the signer that guarantees the power of the former and the spectral return of the latter. In the case of the tattoo, the signature not only reattaches itself to the body—though not Chávez's body—but actually *penetrates it*, blood and ink corporeally merging in a way that was only metaphorical in the repro-duction of Chávez's signature on the walls of buildings. Viewed in this way, the process brings to mind the final scene of Franz Kafka's 1919 short story "In the Penal Colony," the law actually carving the body as it becomes part of it and punishes it, as well as other instances of power tattooing bodies—slaves tattooed by Roman and European colonists, or the tattooed prisoners of Nazi Germany's concentration camps. These resonances recede, however, in light of the testimonies of the tattooed, who see the process as a way of inserting themselves into the living history embodied and inaugurated by Chávez and who voluntarily chose to have his signature become part of their bodies, *as a scar.*

The tattooed signature, like regular tattoos but unlike regular signatures, is, in fact, nothing more than a scar. Getting tattooed is to have one's skin "simultaneously divided and united, pierced and repaired, wounded and healed," operations that involve two bodies: one's own body and the hand of whoever holds the tattoo gun (Neef 2011, 244). In the case of the tattooing of Chávez's signature though, we see more than two bodies. Two hands (not a pair), one skin: Chávez's spectral left hand (he was left-handed), the tattoo artist's tattooing hand, and someone's skin, all three choreographed into a *danse* that is no longer *macabre* but *vivante*, with Chávez folding into a body split into three. All of this times four hundred, perhaps more. In her analysis of the tattoo, Blackmore mentions that an article published by the Agencia Venezolana de Noticias announced that an estimated four hundred tattoos of Chávez's signature existed worldwide, though it did not provide the source for that information (2014, 243). Four hundred tattoos: eight hundred hands (half of them spectral), four hundred scars, four hundred flashes. "Flash" is the term for predrawn tattoo designs: it is also a word that allows us to briefly revisit Walter Benjamin's thesis that "the past can be seized only as an image which flashes up at the instant when it can be recognized and is never seen again" (2006, 391). The tattoo is in fact the successful seizing of the flashing image, but it does not stop there: it seizes the flash and turns it into injectable ink, the ink then becomes blood, the flash turns into a scar, the dead is safely folded into the living. The past is thus not only recognized by the present as being one of its own concerns—to go back to Benjamin's point—but as being present, copresent, a growth on the skin that interlaces old and new tissue and that vibrates with the movement of the blood/ink pumping through it.

Tattooing Chávez's signature on one's body thus shatters the unity and self-containment associated with the autographic signature and complicates the understanding of the tattoo as a technology of the self. What comes out of it is a specter that haunts from within, one that, wrapped up in flesh, ink, and blood, makes oblivion irrelevant and recollection redundant. And what about the subject? The one with the skin where the enfolding of the inside and outside is performed? As time goes by, the itching, the redness, and the pain that follows a freshly inked tattoo subside and the bumpiness progressively disappears, leaving the skin as smooth as it was before. Smooth yet changed by the permanence of a blended-in other that remains present though undetectable by a caress. This subject is thus mostly themselves, but not completely, growing a scar tissue that alerts them to a foreign trace, which connects them to the living history Blackmore talks about, one whereby "Chávez's presence (real or reproduced) is a prerequisite for the continuation of history, or at least for the narrative that accounts for the Bolivarian Revolution" (2014, 243–44). Continuation: a flow that started before, elsewhere, with someone else, and that the tattoo—and the Chávez in it—provides access to. Another entry into this flow is TC Chavez Pro and the way it toys with archives and citation.

A citation is a bracket, a frame, a cut. A bloodless yet rarely clean surgical removal that takes away as much as it repeats and that can invoke—and thus confirm—the power of the cited original, transform it into something slightly or vastly different or entirely new, or subdue it so that it becomes, in our minds, an inconsequential or repulsive carcass.[34] It thus intentionally looks back, at least in contexts outside plagiarism or accidental repetition, and, in doing so, it makes us look back too, to something we see as if through a glass that always distorts it a bit. On the other side of the glass we find words, images, and behaviors, all available to be claimed and put to use in the present. However, TC Chavez Pro does not show us any of these. It shows us lines, letters drawn in a certain way; it shows us the urgency behind those letters, and the moment that demanded that urgency: not Chávez's writings, but the writing of Chávez's hand, at a point in history when what mattered most was the promise of his return. That is what we cite when we download and type anything with TC Chavez Pro: a potentiality, a bodily readiness, a moment of holding our breaths because something different—and arguably better—is about to happen. This is Chávez's famous "por ahora" (for now) and the hope that materialized with it.[35]

While Chávez's "por ahora" was first articulated in the televised speech he gave on February 4, 1992, after the failed coup against Carlos Andrés Pérez, the two words reappeared in the letters he sent while imprisoned in Yare and became relevant once again during the 2002 coup against him that ousted him from office for forty-seven hours before he was restored to power.[36] That Volpe chose letters written during these moments to create TC Chavez Pro means that the app gives us access not only to a creative way of commemorating Chávez but also to an atmosphere of anticipation that translated into the urgency that Volpe says he reads in Chávez's handwriting at those times. The app thus does not capture the relief and the certainty of a victory—the first time Chávez was elected president in 1998, for instance, or the moment he returned to power after the 2002 coup—but what comes before, a moment of doubt, uncertainty, and hope that, because of its partly unactualized state, becomes an invitation, a living history people can take part in, are eager to take part in, in spite of now knowing the outcome, or precisely because they do.

The intimacy that has been at the core of Chávez's spectrality as we have seen it operate throughout this chapter reappears there, in the reliving of the hypothetical, in the reanimated corpses of butterflies from the past that find themselves fluttering around in a stomach in the present, in the recollection of half-formed trajectories that, Kathleen Stewart argues, are ultimately the most compelling because in them the body is still unanchored, and, therefore, feels "most intimate, familiar, and alive" (2007, 212). In her words, "when the body is beside itself, it pulses in the mutual impact of dream and matter, hesitation and forward thrust. It wants to be part of the flow. It wants to be in touch. It wants to be touched. It flexes its muscles in a state of readiness, hums like a secret battery kept charged, registers stress in a back spasm or a weak limb" (212).

"A body pulsing in the mutual impact of dream and matter." Isn't that the body that lives in the GMVV buildings where Chávez, the man who collapsed dream into matter, also lives? "A body that wants to be part of the flow." Isn't that the body of the collector chasing after the next Chávez phone card, and also the body of Chávez, chasing after a family album? "A body that wants to be touched, and that wants to be in touch." Isn't that the body of the possibly more than four hundred people that had Chávez's signature tattooed on them? "A body that flexes its muscles in a state of readiness." Isn't that the body typing with TC Chavez Pro?

It all comes down to intimacy, to the familiarity born out of the encounter of two bodies that do not occupy the same temporal dimension. Two bodies, both anchored in the present, touching each other, is an intimate act, no doubt; it is also the very picture of fleetingness. Two bodies (or more), one anchored in the present, one in the past and also the future, in touch with each other, is also an intimate act, one that, cross-temporally, always delayed, and always postponed, promises to last forever. In the encounter, one body (or more) holds its breath in excitement/anticipation/doubt, and the other enters death backward, so that what lies before him (Chávez) is the past, so that what the future promises us all is what (he, Chávez) has been, seen, and done. Venezuelan poet Eugenio Montejo, though thinking about Bolívar, said it better: "no one remembers if all of us were him or if we will be. . . . His life becomes a horizon" ([1976] 1988, 90).

Spectral Intimacies

In "Space and the State," Henri Lefebvre asks: "Is not the secret of the state, hidden because it is so obvious, to be found in space?" (2003, 87). The state and the territory, he then argues, interact in such a way that they can be said to be mutually constitutive. For Lefebvre, the state binds itself to space through a series of complex relations that pass through critical points, one of which is the creation of what he calls "social space":

> During the course of its development, the state binds itself to space through a complex and changing relation that has passed through certain critical points. Born in and with a space, the state may also perish with it. The moments of this relation can be described as follows: . . . (2) The production of a *social space* as such, an (artificial) edifice of hierarchically ordered institutions, of laws and conventions upheld by "values" that are communicated through the national language. This social architecture, this political monumentality, is the state itself, a pyramid that carries at its apex the political leader—a concrete abstraction, full of symbols, the source of an intense circulation of information and messages, "spiritual" exchanges, representations, ideology, knowledge bound up with power. (Lefebvre 2003, 84; original emphasis)

As it produces this social space, the state imposes a rationality of its own that regulates social relations among individuals, groups, and classes, and that privileges the identical and the repetitive, generating a homogeneous geography that is "the same throughout" (86), which ensures that natural differences and particularities are abolished. Though Lefebvre's analysis focuses on capitalist states and the capitalist spaces they produce, his arguments also shed light on the spatial transformations that took place after Chávez's death, transformations that, as we have seen throughout this chapter, focused on rendering the state, condensed in Chávez's spectral figure, intimate. This intimacy demanded the creation and repetition of a familiar language and the mobilization of familiar spaces and family rituals as the social space was reimagined as a living room and as the walls of living rooms all over the country were made porous enough to let the state seep in, find a place in the family album, take over computer screens, and penetrate deep into the skin. Are these operations not concrete proof of what it means, as Derrida put it, to learn to live *with* ghosts "in the upkeep, the conversation, the company, or the companionship, in the commerce without commerce of ghosts" (1993, xviii)?

We could answer, "No, they are not," and point out that Derrida, in spite of his constant revisiting of ghostly fathers and attention to Marx, did not mean for the specter to become *this concrete*, for the conceptual metaphor at the center of hauntology to become *this literal*, for ghostly matters to go beyond temporal disruptions and demands for justice and actually materialize in specific spaces inserted in specific political, social, cultural, and historic contexts—spaces like Venezuela where, as we have seen, metaphors have the bad habit of becoming shamelessly literal. We could also answer, "Yes, they are," and point out that while Derrida was certainly not envisioning a Chávez tattoo, the lingering presence of the Comandante on skin, walls, and everywhere else is a reminder of the need for justice and responsibility and the sort of ethical demand that, in Derrida's reading of spectrality, must keep pressing onto us in order to stay relevant and to continue fueling the revolutionary struggle that, in the case of Venezuela, created Chávez and that Chávez, too, created. Both answers end the conversation too soon and somewhat disappointingly. Instead, we might consider that, whether or not this is what Derrida imagined when he invited future scholars to learn to live with ghosts, this is still one way that living with ghosts—with a specter in particular—might happen, and it is one where the relationship with the specter moves beyond Derrida's "visor effect" and the simple act of talking with the specter and letting it talk back, and into the realm of intimacy.

In this chapter, we have seen how living with the specter—when habitual, almost mindless—can become an intimate affair. This intimacy became visible and palpable in the narratives that inserted the specter into the family album through collectible phone cards, in the possibility of being enveloped by the gigantic, invisible hand that signed the walls of houses and thus made homes possible, in the tattoo that turned the specter into ink and then into a scar, and in the temporally dislocated act of cowriting that TC Chavez Pro enabled. Less explicitly, but central to these examples, intimacy appeared in the incompleteness, in the blurred boundaries and unresolved issues, in the unanchored and split subjects, in the anxiety and the expectation that materialized as part of the encounter with these spectral remains and the promise they carried: the possibility of becoming part of living history.

Which history? Chávez's and the Bolivarian Revolution's, both wrapped around each other in these spectral remains that made the past—his past, what he did, how he did it—a future we can return to, again and again, relishing it with excitement, imagining it as something simultaneously familiar and new. The collectible phone cards, the signature on the skin and on the wall, and TC Chavez Pro thus fold time onto itself, with two consequences. On one hand, Chávez lingers in the present as a presence that is socially active, politically relevant, familial, and intimate. On the other, future and past overlap so that the future appears as déjà vu and the past can be remembered not with nostalgia but with anticipation, as something yet to come. We hold the phone card featuring baby Chávez and think of the man he was/could be. We look at his signature on the wall and think of the home that was/will be built. We do not obsessively look at the tattoo because we know it is there, always, waiting. We type with TC Chavez Pro and imagine the changes made possible by Chávez, who will/did return. Was, is, and could be. A multidirectional form of time travel embedded in the banality of the everyday, imagination and memory collapsing into each other in the routine repetition of an anticipatory response that the cards, the signature, and the app want to trigger, and that has the potential to make us forget that, if the future is the past, *if everything is déjà vu*, then perhaps there is no future at all.

Toying with the Comandante   4

> Even feared and hated objects excite pleasure when mimicked
> on a small scale.
>
> Susan Stewart, *On Longing*

The Talking Bird

It took less than a month for dead Hugo Chávez to rejoin the world of the living. The lucky witness to the Comandante's return was none other than Nicolás Maduro, who announced it during a conversation with Chávez's family that was broadcast nationally by Telesur on April 2, 2013—the day that marked the beginning of the presidential campaign against opposition candidate Henrique Capriles.[1] Inspired by the intimacy of the encounter— which took place in Chávez's family home—Maduro shared with his audience what had happened to him in a small wooden chapel he had visited by himself that morning to pray for and remember Chávez. As he was standing there, accompanied by a photograph of Chávez that had been placed next to images of José Gregorio Hernández and Jesus Christ, a little bird entered the chapel and circled Maduro's head three times.[2] "He landed on a wooden rafter and started to whistle," said Maduro, reproducing the bird's whistle for his audience, "and then I was watching him and I also whistled at him, I said, if you whistle, I'll whistle," and he whistled as he had done that morning. He then said the bird had looked at him strangely, whistled for a bit again, circled him, and then left, and at that moment he had felt in his soul the spirit of Chávez "blessing us, saying to us: today the battle commences, go forth to victory."

Watching the clip from this event, it is difficult to gauge the reaction of the members of Chávez's family, all sitting in a semicircle around Maduro as he tells his anecdote. Unlike Maduro's wife, Cilia Flores, who smiles encouragingly as her husband whistles, Chávez's family members appear straight-faced, and their reaction—or lack thereof—leaves viewers uncertain as to how they should respond to the news that the new presidential candidate communicated, by whistling, with a bird he claimed embodied Chávez's spirit. It did not take long, however, for this moment of confusion to give way to an endless stream of mockery, to which Maduro's supporters responded by defending the candidate's spirituality and rejoicing at the fact that Chávez was still present among them—a defense that was nevertheless accompanied by concern from members of the government regarding possible claims of insanity that could damage the party's image in the upcoming presidential election.[3] Though the mockery came primarily from sectors of the opposition, the tale of the bird crossed national borders, reaching newspapers globally and even appearing in a Chilean commercial for a cell-phone company where, while the face of the "bird whisperer" is not shown, the actor's haircut and build resemble Maduro's, and the bird's feathers display the colors of the Venezuelan flag.[4]

Chávez qua bird once again made an appearance that Maduro witnessed and shared with a national audience during celebrations honoring Chávez's sixtieth birthday (July 28, 2014). This time, the little bird told Maduro that Chávez "was happy and full of love for the loyalty of his people" (*La Nación* 2014). As he was telling this story, the television screen showed an image of Chávez superimposed over the image of Maduro talking—seeming to bolster the credibility of Maduro's tale and of Chávez's politically active afterlife. The day's celebrations also included fireworks, a birthday cake decorated with a design of Chávez's birthplace (which Maduro cut as he sang "Happy Birthday"), the unveiling of a new Chávez statue, and the launch of the application TC Chavez Pro, discussed in chapter 3.

Maduro's account of Chávez's feathery reincarnations is, or at least should be, familiar, for Chávez (the man, not the bird) while alive also engaged in several necromantic performances that gave the impression he was communicating with the person he saw as his predecessor: Venezuela's liberator, Simón Bolívar. This communication occurred in connection with the gaze (Chávez looking at Bolívar sitting on what to everyone else appeared to be an empty chair), through conversations (Chávez talking to Bolívar's bones after he ordered the exhumation of his remains), and in bodily re-enactments (Chávez reenacting Bolívar's Monte Sacro oath).[5] Though the excessively theatrical nature of this necromantic exchange made Chávez stand out among the parade of presidents and dictators who governed the country before him, it also confirmed that he belonged among those lead-ers, for he, like them, though perhaps much more creatively, tied his claim to authority to the spirit of Bolívar. Chávez, thus, was not the exception but the embodiment of a rule as old as the Venezuelan nation itself: that in order to be recognized as having authority and legitimacy, political leaders tasked with governing Venezuela must cite Bolívar, honor him, and hold on to him lest we forget how much we owe to his battles and accomplish-ments, how much our identity is tied to his name and exceptionality, and how much our future as individuals and as a nation mirrors, still, his heroic hopes and dreams.[6]

Then came Maduro, who did almost the same thing Chávez had done—but it was not Bolívar who appeared on the other side of his necroman-tic performance, but Chávez qua bird. That switch made all the difference. Where once there was admiration, fear, cynicism, suspicion, recognition, and disgust—all blended together so that no individual component completely challenged Chávez's relationship to Bolívar—now there is laughter and the nagging anxiety that takes over an audience who, sneaking behind the cur-tain, encounters the messy backstage of the state's specter-making factory. The laughter that follows Maduro's tales thus is not just cynical; it is a nervous laughter that reveals, as Rafael Sánchez reminds us laughter often does, "the unknown that dwells within the known, ruining from within any reasonable construct, in this case the state" (2006, 403). In the specter-turned-bird, the state's aura was reduced to feathers, the solemn command of the nation's epic and revolutionary past distilled into a whistle. A glitch thus appeared in the functioning of Venezuela's necromantic state, one that threatened to turn its magical power—a dense mix of oil and epic spectrality, as Fernando Coronil and Michael Taussig have pointed out—and the Bolivarian Revolu-tion it was fueling into dust. To fix it, I argue, the government turned to the people, more specifically, to the sort of animating, life-infusing labor that materializes in people's playful and quotidian acts of imagination.

This chapter explores this animating labor and the ways the state sought to capture and redirect it back toward itself in an effort to ensure its survival amid the economic, political, and social crisis that followed Chávez's death. I argue that the need for this labor led to the production and circulation of a number of Chávez's "doubles," which were meant to trigger acts of imagination, playfulness, and creativity that would fuel his afterlife and, through it, the life of the revolutionary project he championed and that of the state responsible for making that project come true. These doubles include Maduro in his acts of imitating and reviving Chávez; the hologram of Chávez that walked around Caracas in December 2016; Chávez's "accidental" doubles (a meme, an impersonator, and the opposition); and a selection of Chávez-themed toys. Each of these doubles operates in its own way; however, taken together, they reveal the workings of a kind of popular agency that is, to a degree, spontaneously generated to reproduce the state and contribute to its survival.[7] This agency relies on a certain kind of playfulness in the relationship established with state power and the way of imagining it that blurs the lines between resistance and subjugation, spontaneity and enforcement. I propose that, although state violence and the government's authoritarian measures are, without doubt, effective at perpetuating the status quo and neutralizing popular discontent, the ultimate foundation of state power is its ability to capture the popular imagination, for, far from simply producing reverie, imagination, as David Morgan points out, manufactures "what people take to be real, want to be real, and make real by concerted belief and practice" (2018, 29). And what more can a necromantic state want than for the specter it conjures and talks to—the epic one that promises to make it magical, legitimate, and popular again—to be real?

The Awkward Double

In April 2017—four years after Chávez's first feathery apparition—Maduro found himself once again under the Comandante's wing. However, this time around two aspects of the story changed. First, rather than disguising himself as a bird, Chávez chose to reappear as a butterfly. Second, rather than revealing his true nature to Maduro behind closed doors in whistles that only the president could understand, he chose to land on Maduro's bright-red shirt on camera, his apparition thus witnessed by those attending the event, by those watching it on television, and later on by everyone who watched the video on YouTube or saw it featured in online articles.[8] Just days before, Maduro had posted on his Facebook page a video where a soft piano soundtrack served as the background for his reflections on butterflies and his skills as a butterfly charmer. We see him pointing at them admiringly and calling them God's miracle, and, in the last few seconds, we see him instructing one of them, "Come here. Stay." The audience claps and cheers as the butterfly obediently follows Maduro's commands. Staying still so that the butterfly on his shirt does not leave, Maduro refers to that Facebook video by saying, "Butterflies [*mariposas*] often visit me: it must be that they recognize me as a *mariposón*."[9] He repeatedly orders the camera operator to zoom in on it—we get a close-up of the small yellow butterfly—and then asks the audience, "Who is it?" to which they reply in cheerful unison, "Chávez!" After which he adds: "The immortal spirit of our Comandante Chávez."

This assortment of winged creatures Maduro claimed were the spirit of Chávez are just one of several shapes the president has publicly given to his predecessor, who came to be known in the country and around the world not only because of the radical nature of his social and political reforms but also because of his unparalleled charisma. Though almost everything about Chávez—his political agenda, his ideology, his mannerisms, his rhetoric, his physical and mental health, his relationship to magic and religion—became a point of contention ever since he was elected president in 1999, his charismatic qualities have rarely been up for debate. He had what theater historian and scholar Joseph Roach has succinctly called "it": a protean combination of magnetism, charm, and the sort of charisma that Max Weber (1968) defined as one of the necessary qualities for powerful, inspirational leadership and authority. In his theorization and historization of "it," Roach ties it to the power of "apparently effortless embodiment of contradictory qualities simultaneously: strength *and* vulnerability, innocence *and* experience, and singularity *and* typicality among them" (2007, 8; original emphasis), and the equally contradictory responses "it" provokes, such as "drawing toward the charismatic figure as *attraction*; radiating away from him or her as broadcast *aura*" (7; original emphasis). The coexistence of these contradictions (and several others) was, as Alejandro Velasco (2022) has argued, central to both *chavismo* and Chávez, who in life sought to embody both the people *and* the state, to the detriment of the latter's institutional strength and integrity, and of the former's ability to radically contest official narratives and practices.[10] The tensions in the relationship between the people and the state, and, more broadly, the tensions that materialize when oppositional forces remain in play, are what for Roach generates "an intense, charismatic radiance that emanates from their fissionable source" (2007, 9).

This radiance, in Chávez, was sometimes literal, as in the glow of television and cell phone screens where he would appear for several hours discussing a wide variety of topics, singing, and dancing on his talk show *Aló Presidente*.

Maduro also dances often, particularly salsa.[11] In fact, in November 2016, he announced the launch of *La hora de la salsa*, a radio show that mixed music and politics that he would occasionally host. The episodes were uploaded in part or in whole to Facebook, Twitter, Periscope, and/or YouTube and, together, comprised more than twenty hours of audiovisual material, spanning a period from November 2016 to December 2017, at which point Maduro no longer appeared on the show. This show, as Sean Bellaviti argues, helped Maduro solidify his political power by drawing on notions about salsa widely shared by Venezuelans: "the idea that salsa (i) is the music of poor and working-class Latin Americans, (ii) has a special connection to Venezuela and (iii) is capable of offering people a form of escape from the rigours and hardships of their everyday life" (2021, 395). It was also a short-lived attempt to reproduce Chávez's media presence or, at least, to establish echoes that would make viewers think of Chávez as Maduro spun his wife, Cilia, around and addressed them in the intimate, playful tone Chávez had once utilized. Yet the people (at least the people whose commentary and reactions Bellaviti analyzes) had mixed feelings about Maduro's salsa, in part because in dancing he also seemed to be dancing *around* the worsening of the economic crisis and ignoring the hardships that everyone, regardless of political positioning, had to face daily because of the record-breaking hyperinflation and scarcity of basic products. This criticism carried with it a haunting question: If Chávez had been alive, would he have done the same? Would things be as bad as they are? The answer is irrelevant—as Chávez is dead—but the question is not. It underscores the game of comparisons Maduro has had to play since Chávez named him his successor, one he keeps losing at, no matter how hard he tries to be (like) Chávez.

And he tries hard. During his 2013 presidential campaign, Maduro mentioned Chávez's name around seven thousand times (Norman 2017, 183). He has referred to Chávez as "the redeemer Christ of the Americas" and to himself as his apostle and son (Michelutti 2017, 244; Norman 2017, 182). He often surrounds himself with portraits of Chávez and of Bolívar, and reproduces Chávez's incendiary rhetoric and dramatic gestures. At the inauguration of the transportation system Transmaracaibo in the state of Zulia in 2015, he put on Chávez's eyes painted on a pair of plastic sunglasses he took from a woman in the crowd that surrounded the bus he was traveling in (figure 4.1). All this in addition to conjuring birds and butterflies. Each of these acts

4.1 Maduro wearing Chávez's eyes. Taken from Lapatilla Patillavideo 2015.

gives Maduro a different role: he is Chávez's son, but also Chávez's apostle; he is Chávez's successor and also his conjurer; he is not like Chávez, but he imitates him; he has vowed to continue the Comandante's legacy while also ensuring that the Comandante himself keeps on living, which has condemned him—de facto if not de jure—to forever being the vice president to the president's specter.

If we linger on the image of Maduro wearing Chávez's eyes, we do not see the successful union of the two men—an effortless blending of Chávez's eyes on Maduro's face. Instead, we see the gap: the space marking the distance between two skins of the state—one fleshy, one plastic and spectral—that fail to merge, producing a grotesque image that shatters any possibility of charismatic radiance. This distance widens the more the awkward double succeeds at reproducing certain elements of the original, in large part because Maduro's many different acts of doubling and imitation prevent a single recognizable performance from cohering. Put differently, Maduro does not settle for one role. The changing nature of his relationship to Chávez, the many masks he tries on in an effort to find the one that will resonate most with a people still longing for the Comandante make it so that, in the end, the only thing that is clear is the fact that he is very much *not* Chávez. And not only is he not Chávez, but it is questionable how persuasive his necromantic exchange with the Comandante can be said to be. Not much aura radiates from a bird no one but Maduro saw, or from two fragile butterflies. At least not if we compare these acts of invocation with the performance Chávez staged in 2010 around Bolívar's exhumed remains, a performance that was certainly controversial but that also capitalized on the affective and mnemonic power Bolívar has historically held and that, for that reason, was not met with the same laughter or indifference Maduro has so often encountered.

Maduro's failure to properly channel Chávez represents a significant problem for a political and social movement that relied heavily on the Comandante's charismatic presence and guidance. However, *chavismo*—the name itself confirming Chávez's centrality and of Maduro's lack of place— is not the only movement that struggles with Chávez's less-than-adequate successor. As he turns the state into a laughingstock through a performance that is less the awe-inspiring spectacle of a magical state or an epic revolution and more the sort of cheap trick a birthday party magician performs while wearing an ill-fitting hat, Maduro inadvertently calls attention to the backstage maneuvering of the state's complex specter-producing factory. The laughter thus fades as we realize that it is not just about Chávez coming back as some winged creature but that it is also about the historical reliance on the specter as the modus operandi of the country's national memory and as the source of the state's legitimacy and authority. In Maduro's clumsy hands, the whole process of spirit invocation historically conducted by the state becomes farcical and sparks a crisis: where once there was a specter—the obedience-inducing, power-granting, and familiar specter of Bolívar—now there is just a cheap pair of sunglasses, a bird, a butterfly, and the nagging suspicion that the Liberator's magical bones might not be all that different from these ordinary objects.

Faced with the "gaping hole in the auratic balloon of the Venezuelan state," two responses take shape (Sánchez 2006, 408). On one hand, there is the reaction of the opposition, which, in addition to wholeheartedly joining in the laughter at Maduro's performance, also presents it as further evidence of his incompetence and, metonymically, of the failure of the Bolivarian Revolution. Additionally, it has responded with a spiritual performance of its own, publicly turning to well-known figures of Catholicism, whom they invoke on social media—on Twitter, Facebook, and WhatsApp—asking followers and contacts to join in a collective prayer for Venezuela. This move seems to challenge the chaotic world of magic and superstition unleashed first by Chávez—through acts like the exhumation of Bolívar's remains and the performance conducted in Miraflores with various religious leaders to help him fight his cancer—and later, less successfully, by Maduro. On the other hand, there is the reaction of the government itself, which turns to the people, to Chávez's beloved "pueblo," tasking them with the responsibility of reanimating not only the Comandante but also the lost aura of the state. We thus return to the scenario that Taussig describes in *The Magic of the State* (1997)—a scenario I discussed in this book's introduction—in which the people produce the magical surplus the state needs to cement its authority. Yet, this time, the rituals will not take place in the secrecy of the hidden corners of Venezuela's spiritual landscape, but out in the open, in public space.

Luminous Chávez

On December 8, 2012, at 9:34 p.m., Chávez addressed the Venezuelan people *live* for the last time. Having won the presidential elections two months earlier, he had had to depart for Cuba soon after to continue his cancer treatment and would have to do so again on December 9. Thus, he only had this moment—thirty minutes, to be exact—to put his affairs in order, which included making sure people knew that, if his illness were to prevent him from fulfilling his role as president, they were to vote for Maduro in the next elections. In his words, "my firm opinion, as clear as the full moon, irrevocable, absolute, total, is that—in a situation that would require, as the Constitution commands, that presidential elections be held again—you elect Nicolás Maduro as president of the Bolivarian Republic of Venezuela. I ask you this from the depths of my heart." (VTV 2021b). Four years later, the Venezuelan people would once again hear these words—this time from Chávez's holographic specter.

On the night of December 8, 2016, residents in the central and western areas of Caracas discovered Chávez walking beside them. Taller than everyone around him and displaying an ethereal luminosity, he walked with determination and did not stop to greet or scare anyone (see *Clarín* 2016). His apparition was thus startling but not threatening. While he walked around Caracas, he was also walking the digital streets of Twitter; videos of the spectral parade were uploaded by then minister of popular power for communication and information Ernesto Villegas to his Twitter account and the account of VTV—the government-sponsored television channel. With hashtags such as #AmorYLealtadAChavez, #PlenoComoLaLunaLlena, and

#ChavezLuminoso, Villegas and vtv followed the specter's journey, which ended at the Panteón Nacional, specifically at the sail-shaped wing of the new building holding Bolívar's remains. There the specter delivered his message—or rather his request—in the form of a projected video presentation of Chávez's last speech accompanied by photographs of him and Maduro. It was a simple request: to remember him, to love him, and to be loyal to him by being loyal to Maduro—all tasks that seemed fitting for a day that Maduro had declared Día de la Lealtad y el Amor a Chávez (Day of Loyalty and Love for Chávez) through a presidential decree signed on November 4, 2013 (vtv 2021b) (figure 4.2).

Chávez's specter was the product of video mapping. Also known as projection mapping and spatial augmented reality, video mapping turns two-dimensional and three-dimensional objects into display surfaces for video projection, and it is used for adding extra dimensions, optional illusions, and movement to previously static objects. Though this technique is evident in the videos that circulated online, the articles that featured them and the title of the videos themselves referred to this luminous Chávez as a hologram—that is, as a three-dimensional image formed with lasers or other light sources. This technical error is telling of the aspirations that surrounded the production of Chávez's technological specter: the possibility of freezing the past—of freezing Chávez, who could not be embalmed—and then releasing it/him when necessary, the need to render absence inconsequential, and the hope that, as Jean Baudrillard feared, everything that disappears can in fact "seep back into our lives in infinitesimal doses" (2009, 26). Theories of the hologram often center on these issues and on the fascination that holograms, regardless of how rudimentary they might be, trigger among those who have the opportunity to see them in action.

In fact, Sean F. Johnston argues that, regardless of how a hologram is used, it is always a source of childlike fascination. There is something about how it appears to weave together the rationality of science with the mystery of magic that makes looking at a hologram unlike anything else. This was particularly true early in its development, when viewings of holograms were rare and mostly confined to conference rooms where the science behind them was explained, though the audience was often more interested in looking at the hologram than in understanding it. Two quotes exemplify this fascination, both from the 1970s, when regular audiences started gaining access to holograms. The first one is from a 1979 article titled "Off the Wall," in which the author, Randy James, argues that the idea of holography was "imbued with a breathless sense of being on the threshold of some new

4.2 Chávez's hologram. Taken from *800 Noticias* 2016.

form of consciousness" (quoted in Johnston 2016, 121). The second one is from a 1973 *Rolling Stone* article titled "Do-It-Yourself Holography": "The hologram is as likely as anything technological to push your subliminal awe and wonder button and leave an ancient message flashing somewhere below the surface of consciousness: Here we have some Powerful Magic" (quoted in Johnson 2016, 127). What stands out in both is the feeling of getting a glimpse into something that is at once recognizable and extraordinary, primitive and modern.

The hologram thus embodies what David Nye calls "the technological sublime" (1994), a concept that presents the sublime—traditionally associated with a supreme or extraordinary being that provokes fear and wonder (as established in theories of the sublime by Edmund Burke, Immanuel Kant, and Arthur Schopenhauer)—as manifested by modern technology and, as Johnston adds, by the imagery that it produces.[12] Thus, the hologram is imbued with a power that arises from how it plays with our disbelief. Looking at it—or rather into it—we notice the autonomy it seems to have suspended in space, disconnected from its source, and we are forced to struggle with two competing feelings: the feeling of security that derives from knowing that this is the product of man-made technology and the disconcerting suspicion that there is a chance this might in fact be old-fashioned magic.

The hologram's visible yet impalpable three-dimensionality along with the exactitude with which some holograms reproduce an object or body bring to mind recent discussions regarding the state of contemporary bodies that, finding themselves traversed by the sorcery of digital technology, appear to have lost their analog sturdiness and become permeable, projectable, and programmable. Such discussions are at the center of Paula Sibilia's *El hombre postorgánico*, which incisively analyzes how technological advancements have called into question the three elements that previously shaped our understanding of the human body and its place in the world: "the organic nature of the body, the material nature of space, and the linear nature of time" ([2005] 2010, 52). As the possibilities of humans living without these elements become more and more realistic, information threatens to replace the mass of the body, which means that sooner rather than later death will become obsolete: "As the Australian artist Stelarc—one of the main representatives of technology-inspired body-art—suggests, death would be an 'out-moded evolutionary strategy' because now the human body 'must become immortal to adapt' to the new context" (44).

In this context, then, holograms emerge as a sort of preview—a very rough draft—of what this alternative way of being would be like, and of the uncanny, intriguing temporality that would come with it. Although seeing a hologram locates it in the present, the fact that it is a copy of something gives it a past, and its sci-fi look along with its untouchability imbue it with futurity. Hence why Baudrillard spoke of it in terms of dreams and the afterlife: "We dream of passing through ourselves and of finding ourselves in the beyond: the day when your holographic double will be there in space, eventually moving and talking, you will have realized this miracle. Of course, it will no longer be a dream, so its charm will be lost" (quoted in Johnston 2016, 161). Baudrillard's comment, as Johnston points out, endows the hologram with supernatural powers that differentiate it from the copies of ourselves we normally encounter, such as photographs and our reflection in a mirror. It implies that we have been outlived by ourselves and thus can finally experience what it could be like to be "on the other side."

Holograms thus appear to be magical; they cast an ethereal light that plays with our imagination, our beliefs, our willingness to evaluate critically, and our sense of time. This last point is perhaps the most crucial: the hologram's purpose is not—or at least not only—to trigger remembrance but to show time as layered, to add to its infinite length equally infinite depth. It thus requires us to develop a new form of temporal literacy to read *into* time. This change in temporal logic requires in turn a change in how we understand the dynamic of remembering; its spatial trajectory—the motion of metaphorically going backward in time—is replaced by the feeling of witnessing a temporal collusion whereby past, present, and future are right there in front of us, hanging in space in the form of an ephemeral image that has depth and a technologically bred magic that immerses us in a state of childlike wonder.

The fact that the Venezuelan government took part in the creation, circulation, and advertising of Chávez's hologram is both a reminder of Taussig's observation that magic plays a fundamental role in the consolidation of the modern state, and a testament to the ways in which power operates temporally, manipulating assumptions about time and in doing so engineering the conditions for political subjection. In this context, power's temporal operations ground political authority in disappearance rather than presence because disappearance, unlike presence, is not fixed in a particular time and leaves behind traces that can seamlessly penetrate daily life, shaping it in ways that go unnoticed. As Baudrillard has noted: "Everything that disappears seeps back into our lives in infinitesimal doses, often more dangerous than the visible authority that ruled over us" (2009, 26). Dangerous because of the impossibility of fighting back or even fully grasping the reach of an authority that, like the Cheshire cat says in Disney's *Alice in Wonderland* (1951), is "not all there."

Chávez is also "not all there" when it comes to his holographic reincarnation, which, I would argue, is the source of the strength and persuasive power of the state's performance. Had he been all there—embalmed, for instance—he would have been anchored to a specific place, his waxlike flesh and immobility a reminder that yes, Chávez remained, but as little more than a well-dressed, revolutionary carcass. As a hologram, however, he could not only haunt both physical and digital spaces, but he could also offer onlookers the feeling of fantasy, radical change, and "newness" that, Ryan Brading (2013) argues, keeps a populist project going and that was condensed in a luminous body that sought not to frighten but to entertain.[13] In fact, if we return to the videos that recorded the journey Chávez's hologram took, we can hear the beats of a techno song presumably coming from the vehicle that carried the projection machinery, and, if we wanted, we could see in Chávez's steps something reminiscent of a dance move. On top of the Panteón Nacional, his magnified face was poster-ready, inviting, and iconic, seemingly removed from the fear-inducing eyes of Big Brother and the obvious indoctrination of military parades. He was, simply put, pop: popular and populist. The words of his last speech—played as a soundtrack to the sequence of pictures projected on the building—confirmed this: "Chávez is not only this human being. Chávez is a great collective. Chávez is the heart of the people, and the people are in the heart of Chávez."

Yet, the people seemed to barely notice the Comandante's holographic return. Nobody stopped, paralyzed with emotion or the childlike fascination the hologram is supposed to trigger. The lucky witnesses to Chávez's specter simply carried on with what they were doing, their pace undisturbed by any sort of desire to chase after him. Online, Villegas's tweet accumulated over six hundred retweets and over three hundred replies, which included messages of anger at what users called an unnecessary expense given Venezuela's shortage of medicine and basic products, insults directed at the government and at Chávez himself, and, occasionally, echoes of Villegas's enthusiasm. Someone—user @JunduJuan—tweeted that he wished Chávez were indeed walking the streets so he could yell at those responsible for the failure of the Misión Ribas.[14] The hologram, then, did not fare any better than Maduro's birds and butterflies. Like them—and as the tweets that complain about the cost of this production show—it drew attention to its own fabrication, to the fact that its radiance was made of money that could have been spent elsewhere. Furthermore, the spectral light on the buildings Chávez passed by also happened to hit cracks, stains, and holes, the material evidence of the country's multidimensional crisis, which Chávez's specter—upbeat, determined, state-made—refused to see. It is perhaps for all these reasons that the hologram never appeared again. But Chávez certainly did.

The Memeification of Chávez

"Here is Chávez! Chávez lives!" said Maduro, excitedly, to the audience that had gathered for the closing of his 2013 presidential campaign in the city of Valencia (Carabobo), as he pointed to the Chávez that was standing among the people, startling some of them, making a few others cry with emotion, and taking selfies with anyone who asked. From a distance he truly looked like Chávez; up close, he did as well. Not 2012 Chávez, but a younger, skinnier version of him. In that moment, no one cared about who this man really was, though later, articles about the presidential campaign would inform readers that his name was Alí Bazán (figure 4.3), that he worked as a taxi driver, and that he lived in the city of Güigüe (*La Tercera* 2013). In those articles, he would be referred to as "Chávez's double," a hypothesis that Maduro seemed to confirm as he invited Bazán to the stage, where he

4.3   Maduro and Alí Bazán. Taken from *Libertad Digital* 2013.

stood raising his fist just like Chávez used to do, while the audience cheered. The ensuing image was nothing short of spectacular: Maduro, the presidential candidate whose campaign slogan was not even about himself but about Chávez—"Chávez, lo juro, mi voto es por Maduro" (Chávez, I swear, my vote is for Maduro)—dressed like Chávez and talking about Chávez's multiplying presence as he excitedly pointed to Bazán, who was not only dressed like Chávez but looked like Chávez, both in front of an audience covered in Chávez-themed memorabilia. No theory of doubles could possibly contain this climax of mimetic excess where bodies, times, and spaces all came together, traversing, touching, and mimicking each other until all that was left was an endless echo and the suspicion that, perhaps, Maduro was right: that Chávez was (still) alive and multiplying.

Though most newspaper articles on Bazán focus on this specific performance as Chávez's double, this was not his first public appearance at an important event on the government's political agenda. Bazán was first seen during the closing of Chávez's 2012 presidential campaign, and he appeared again at the inauguration ceremony on January 10, 2013 with Chávez in absentia. He was there with Chávez, instead of him, and as him: he performed Chávez's remains, understood both as an act—Chávez remaining in power in 2012 and then remaining as a presence after his death in March 2013—and as a form of bodily lingering, a continuity in the flesh that had nothing to do with kinship and everything to do with luck, and such luck was nothing short of magical.

More magical still was Chávez's second double, who appeared wearing a swimsuit in a photograph that went viral in 2014, generating several memes and the hashtag #ChávezNoMurió, and causing such a stir in online communities in Venezuela that certain news channels actually commented on it.[15] The reason behind the commotion was not only the extraordinary resemblance this double's face bore to Chávez's, but also the fact that the double was a woman, whose name, background, and political allegiance, along with all other biographical information, were unknown. Unlike Bazán, who intentionally performed Chávez, this woman—engaged in conversation with two other women while standing in the water on a beach—does not even seem to be aware that her picture is being taken, let alone that, captured in that exact moment, her features are so similar to Chávez's that they risk making Bazán look like a poorly manufactured copy of the Comandante. This striking similarity, discovered accidentally and in a woman, led to consultations with Photoshop professionals, who confirmed the authenticity of the picture amid an endless stream of mockery occasionally interrupted by moving comments from those who actually believed her to be Chávez reincarnated.

Bazán and the unknown woman implode our understanding of original and copy, of reenactment and remains. Bazán's public appearance during Maduro's presidential campaign complicates these categories not only because of the emotional and political scene it triggered, but also because of what his existence and performance of Chávez suggest about how we understand the material and bodily lingering of a past believed to be over and done with. To think through this question, I turn to Rebecca Schneider and her conceptualization of performing remains. Drawing from the temporal and interpersonal possibilities that have arisen from the "affective turn" and from works that shed light on the archive outside the archive and inside the body—such as Diana Taylor's *The Archive and the Repertoire* (2005)—and inspired by US Civil War reenactments, Schneider provocatively calls into question what we understand by "remains":

> If the past is never over, or never completed, "remains" might be understood not solely as object or document material, but also as the immaterial labor of bodies engaged in and with that incomplete past: bodies striking poses, making gestures, voicing calls, reading words, singing songs, or standing witness. Such acts of labor over

and with the past might include a body sitting at a table in an archive, bent over an "original" manuscript or peering at a screen, interacting with history as material traces positioned as evidence. Or such bodily labor might be—though this is a far more contested problematic—a twenty-first-century body interacting with traces of *acts* as history; carrying a replica nineteenth-century musket on a historic battle-field, uttering the "phonic materiality" of a cry to arms, or engaging in surgical amputation practices of the 1860s. (Schneider 2011, 33–35)

Schneider's suggestion that we might understand the immaterial labor of bodies as a kind of "remains" certainly resonates with Bazán's performance, which transcended the boundaries of representation and managed to estab-lish contact with what existed "on the other side" thanks not only to the gene-tic cocktail that made him physically similar to Chávez but also to Maduro's official discourse, which publicly confirmed this resemblance. Performance thus yields remains, and those remains perform their own remaining. How-ever, in the case of Bazán, this performance becomes all the more complicated because of the bodily side of it, which introduces a new element that puts Schneider's theory of remains in dialogue with Taussig's conceptualization of mimesis in *Mimesis and Alterity*.

Taussig argues that "the wonder of mimesis lies in the copy drawing on the character and power of the original, to the point whereby the representa-tion may even assume that character and that power" (1993, xiii). For this to occur, we must recognize what is sticky, bodily, and sensuous in the act of copying; that is, we must see the mimetic faculty as a moment of contact where the copy and the original interpenetrate, unleashing a sort of bodily innervation that cuts through both. Bazán thus stands at the crossroads of Schneider's performing remains and Taussig's mimetic faculty; he is made to be part of Chávez's remains both through a theatrical performance with heavy political undertones that disrupts any attempt to establish a linear temporality where the past is past and done with, and through a bodily re-lationship with the original that arises from but also exceeds resemblance.

We have thus moved from Maduro as the double wannabe and from Chávez's hologram as the luminous yet inconsequential double to Bazán and his success at not only performing Chávez but also being a bodily remain-der of him. The bodily nature of Bazán's act of doubling confronts us with the possibility of encountering a spectral version of Chávez that animates not his image but his flesh. Put differently, Bazán and the unknown woman make it possible for Chávez's body to linger without Chávez. In the case of the woman, this lingering seems to carry on indefinitely in the digital world where she and Chávez have been turned into a meme and thus recreated, updated, and shared. This is Chávez's body—not Chávez's corpse. As we saw in chapter 1, his corpse disappeared from the public view after his death, creating a void that productively bred an ever-expanding archive of images of his life, which draw our eyes away from his death as they capture our imagination from corners, streets, and walls all over the country. These images do not remain in the realm of the visual; as Bazán's act shows, they can materialize and produce a body that, lacking the decomposing and distance-producing flesh of the corpse, invites manipulation and playfulness. That is, after all, what we see in Bazán's decision to walk around political rallies, hug people, take selfies, and reproduce Chávez's gestures: the will to play with Chávez, to dress up and act like him, and, in the process, to become a vessel for people's nostalgia and love for the Comandante and a prop mobilized by the government to back up its official rhetoric—that Chávez is alive—with material evidence.

The memes of the unknown woman—baptized on social media as "el doble de Chávez" (Chávez's double)—and the resulting viral hashtags (#ChávezVive, #ChávezNoMurió) are another form of playful engagement with the Comandante. First coined by evolutionary biologist Richard Dawkins in *The Selfish Gene* (1976) to explain the spread of ideas and cultural phenomena using evolutionary principles, the term "meme" has more recently been applied to internet phenomena that are "widely appropriated and creatively adapted by internet users" and that "appear to spread and mutate via distributed networks in ways that the original producers cannot determine and control" (Gratch 2017, 5). What characterizes the meme, then, in addition to the popularity it acquires as it is shared, is its mutating nature; as it jumps from one corner of the internet to the other, the meme changes according to the whims of users who take advantage of the participatory nature of online platforms to deframe and reframe it. In *Adaptation Online*, Lyndsay Michalik Gratch argues for memes—which she renames "online adaptations"—to be considered within the framework of performance. Drawing on the work of performance studies scholar Michael LeVan, she notes that digital methods and contexts provide an opportunity to rethink notions of audience, stage, movement, space, and time, and the way such notions shape our understanding of what performance is and does. To the extent that memes belong to the category of adaptation—a practice that, she argues, is at the center of performance work—they speak to how people perform themselves, perform others, and "perform themselves through the performance of Other" (15). Thus, memes enter into dialogue with reenactments—as defined by Schneider—and the knotty and porous temporality associated with them.

The connection that Gratch allows us to draw between memes and reenactments invites us to think about memes against the backdrop of Schneider's conceptualization of remains. Memes are remains both because they are what is left of an original and because they *remain*, they stick around, circulating freely in online spaces where they often show up unexpectedly and where their survival depends on their ability to adapt to different discourses and creative interventions. Their way of remaining depends simultaneously on their capacity to change and to stay the same, on preserving an "original" whose power is enhanced by the changes and manipulations it undergoes. The picture of the unknown female Chávez lookalike evinces this act of preservation through creative and active cocreation; deframed so as to underscore the uncanny similarity to the deceased president, the picture was then reframed over and over, more often than not in humorous ways that widened the act of doubling to draw in parody and its subversive potential.[16] The online world thus becomes a space of afterlife that enables the haunting of Chávez's specter—as evidenced by the meme's virality and unpredictable apparitions—but that also transforms the nature and tone of its authority, which ceases to be hierarchical, auratic, and fear-inducing and relies instead on the ongoingness of a disappearance that never comes to an end and that, thanks to the participatory nature of online platforms and social media, becomes "user-friendly."

The result of the sharing, updating, and remaking of this meme—and of any viral meme—is an invisible bond with a community, "a sense of membership in a privileged group" (Shifman 2014, 26) that creates what Simon J. Evnine calls "a vast susurration" (2018, 303) for which not one single member can claim full credit and which has a certain power of animation that operates through affect and "memoricity." Memoricity "facilitates evocation of affective responses by re-activating feelings associated with past experiences" (Makhortykh and González Aguilar 2020, 344). Enhanced by digital media's unparalleled capacities for storage, manipulation, and circulation, and operating through memes' intertextuality and remixing of mnemonic symbols, memoricity allows for a contextualization of current events in light of the affective responses evoked by drawing parallels with past sorrows and triumphs (347). In the context of Chávez's female double, the sorrow of Chávez's death appears intertwined with the triumph of his afterlife, both traversed by the irreverence and playfulness of mockery and amusement.

What the meme generates then is not so much a specific emotion, strictly codified and oriented toward a concrete goal, but a mood: a feeling of and around an absence that, somehow, refuses to be absent, insisting on remaining in ways that not even Maduro's government—so eager to see Chávez alive—could have predicted.

And yet, the mood, the "vast susurration," like a chant or a spell, gives the government's rhetoric new life, repairing, if only for the duration of the meme's virality, the frayed stitches and tears in the specter of Chávez it sloppily manufactured. The birds, the butterflies, the hologram, and Maduro, all found lacking, lose importance alongside Bazán and the unknown woman, who, for better or worse and as if by magic, prove that in fact Chávez, his body at least, is there—not as a carcass but as a living, moving, viral person-thing.[17] The meme, with all the emotions it triggers, helps us deal with, rather than make sense of, this lingering, one that could have gotten lost in the vast ocean of images that populate the internet, dismissed as pure coincidence, but did not. While the resemblance of both Bazán and the woman are indeed coincidence, in the afterglow and the social and political uncertainty following Chávez's death, that coincidence acquired meaningful proportions, amplified by the fact that neither Bazán nor the woman was a product of the government's spectral machine—they were not "made" by the state but by people and through popular engagement with digital media—though in the end they fueled the state nonetheless.

A tension thus permeates the performance of Chávez's posthumous doubles, one that brings us to the question of popular agency and to the phrase/slogan that distills this question both in political rallies and in academic works on the topic: "We created Chávez" (see Ciccariello-Maher 2013). A version of this statement appeared at an event during the closing of Maduro's 2013 presidential campaign in Caracas. In the live televised transmission of the event, thousands of people wearing all sorts of Chávez-themed memorabilia—including T-shirts featuring Chávez's eyes—appear as the force moving Maduro forward, wearing fake mustaches in his honor and carrying posters that depict him next to Chávez and, in some cases, next to Bolívar. One of the commentaries featured in the transmission came from María Pilar Hernández, minister of popular power for the youth, who started her intervention by speaking fondly about Chávez and his legacy, stating that everyone who was there who loved Chávez was willing to do whatever it took to avoid losing that legacy. Then she said, "those who believe that this revolution was one man's revolution are mistaken. This revolution was led by one of the most marvelous men this nation ever produced, Hugo

Chávez, but the revolution does not belong to Chávez, it belongs to the people" (Aporrea 2013).

"The revolution does not belong to Chávez, it belongs to the people." The force of that popular power can be seen in the emotions and endurance of the people rallying for Maduro at the more than five-hour event. And yet this power cannot be understood as separate from the repetitive script that framed the live transmission and Maduro's speech, which made Chávez the center of the movement, called everyone "los hijos de Chávez" (Chávez's children), spoke of Chávez as having rescued the country's political conscience and Bolívar himself, and ultimately located him in the place Maduro was supposed to occupy. In the words of Maduro, who during his speech held Chávez's photograph in his hand: "Chávez is going to be around for a while in the future history of this free and independent nation. . . . This is the people of Chávez, this is Chávez's role, Chávez is still leading us with his example, with his love" (Aporrea 2013).

What emerges from these words and from the bodies gathered at the closing of Maduro's campaign, and what becomes visible in Bazán and the unknown woman, is the other side of "We created Chávez," which is the other side of every act of creation. "We created Chávez" is undeniable; in fact, not only did the people create Chávez, they brought him back to life. The people responsible for this reanimation include those at the rally with their T-shirts and energy, Bazán and his performance, and, involuntarily, the female double and her digital virality. But "Chávez created us" is equally true, as summed up by the words repeated at the rally: that all the people there, including Maduro, were "Chávez's children." After all, creations create back, a point Daniel Miller underscores when he argues that, every time we create something, "by the very same process we also create a contradiction, a possibility of oppressing ourselves if the thing we made then develops its own autonomous interests" (2010, 59). It is not so much Chávez's "autonomous interests" that might become oppressive—though his legacy certainly weighs heavily on people—but the impossibility of his absence, the fact that he is *both* creator and creation, and the fear of what might happen if his name were simply not spoken.

It could be that fear that drove Diosdado Cabello in January 2017 to launch a campaign that asked people who worked in public offices, who were part of the military, who lived in government-built houses, or who drove the taxis delivered by the Misión Transporte, to hang a sign saying "Aquí no se habla mal de Chávez" (No badmouthing Chávez here).[18] "So long as we keep Chávez up there above us, this revolution is going to go forward," said Cabello, in a statement that seemed to indirectly address the worsening of the economic crisis and the lack of popular support for Maduro, which, apparently, only Chávez, in name, could solve (*El Universo* 2017). I would argue that the purpose of this initiative was not so much to punish everyone who spoke badly of Chávez as to ensure Chávez's name continued to echo—both praise and insults evidence that he still mattered.

Chávez's name is not the only aspect of him echoing across Venezuela. His mannerisms, fiery rhetoric, and insistence on merging with Bolívar in various creative ways have also permeated the performance of the leading figures of the opposition. Leopoldo López, who in 2008 was mayor of Chacao, Caracas's wealthiest district, and who became the first real threat to Chávez after his rise to power, boasted that he was Bolívar's great-great-grandnephew, which further increased his popular appeal. Moreover, at that time and for several years after, the opposition responded to the figure of a messianic Chávez, and his bodily and linguistic reenactment of a war that is over a hundred years old, with the lengthy saga of López's imprisonment, ordered by the government. After the December 2013 local elections delivered disappointment to the opposition, María Corina Machado, Venezuelan politician and then member of the Asamblea Nacional, stated that "183 years after the death of the Liberator, our generation will defend his legacy: independence, liberty, and republic" (Norman 2017, 215). Henry Ramos Allup, leader of the opposition party Acción Democrática, became known during his tenure as president of the Asamblea Nacional for his order to discard the portraits of Chávez and of "Chávez's Bolívar" that decorated the building and replace them with the "real Bolívar," and for his bombastic speeches that evoked, in their passionate tone and unfiltered honesty, Chávez's own.

More recently, as Juan Guaidó was sworn in as interim president of the country in January 2019, he held in his left hand a small copy of the Venezuelan Constitution with a portrait of Bolívar drawn in black and white, the lack of color underscoring his spectral quality while also subtly but efficiently banning Chávez's Bolívar—and therefore Chávez—from the political stage. The connection between Guaidó and Bolívar did not stop there. In an article published on the news site *EsCaracas* and titled "Las enigmáticas similitudes de Juan Guaidó con Bolívar" (The enigmatic similarities between Juan Guaidó and Bolívar), the unnamed author argues that Guaidó appears to be "on the right path" because of his similarities with Bolívar, which include being born exactly two hundred years apart, sharing the same zodiac sign (Leo), their fathers having the same name (Juan), and being the same age when becoming president (thirty-six) (*EsCaracas* 2019). While these connections were irrelevant to Guaidó's preparedness as a politician, pointing them out seemed necessary to his success and popular appeal. Though Guaidó is in many ways an outsider whose political origins tie him to the student movement and not to the opposition's all-too-familiar representatives, and although that outsider status was a welcome change on the Venezuelan political stage, the fact remains that for him to enter that stage, he had to do so, it appeared, like Chávez did: hand in hand with Bolívar.

Thus, like any movement that defines itself against something else, the opposition has managed to create a world of parallels that, in turn, has prompted the government to respond with even more parallels, ultimately turning the country's political, social, and economic landscape into a deafening and disorienting echo chamber. In addition to the doubling acts of its political leaders, the opposition responded to Chávez's signature red with their signature white (and occasionally blue), historically charged language has been answered with more historically charged language, and even the Chávez that Maduro resuscitates has found a contender in the Chávez that the opposition brings back as it quotes Chávez's words in WhatsApp messages to show the extent to which the current government's repression deviates from the initial revolutionary project.[19] I mention these examples not to gloss over the complexities of each political project or to minimize the efforts that opposition groups have made to alleviate a crisis that has affected the majority of the population. My purpose is simply to call attention to the fact that, in the afterglow of Chávez's death, doubling became an imperative both among those who remained loyal to Chávez and those who opposed him, and whose doubling, like that of a shadow, became tangled up with the determination to be something entirely different.

In the context of Chávez's afterlife, then, remembering is not an act of consciously retrieving something or someone from the dusty corners of the mind, nor is it the violent attack that body and mind experience as a result of the return of an elusive trauma. It is something in between. It is a bodily echo, a performance at the crossroads of recurrence and reenactment, whereby remains are not there to be exhibited, buried, preserved, or mourned, but rather created and recreated, and where the body of the sovereign (past and present) and the body of the people (always present) find themselves in a shared state of sensuous mimesis. In this context, then, to remember is to perform over and over—sometimes consciously, other times unconsciously—the body of power that is not there; it is an endless supply of physical and creative labor that makes the void overflow with a spectral energy and that suggests, as Schneider points out, that "the bygone is not entirely gone by and the dead not completely disappeared nor lost, but also, and perhaps more complexly, the living are not entirely (or not only) live" (2011, 15).

The fact that news and memes of the doubles I introduced in this section circulate and become accessible online adds a virtual layer to the performance of remains that puts practices of remembering and doubling in dialogue with the participatory and playful nature of digital media. Often relying on humor, irony, and sarcasm, the memeification of Chávez strips the double of its uncanniness and the specter of its mystery as it invites the pueblo-turned-users and the opposition to play around with Chávez's image, to deframe and reframe him, to find him in the most unlikely places, to mock him, praise him, curse him, and love him. In other words, to cocreate him and recreate him through tools that give him a dynamic and visible afterlife where the body of power operates and is remembered through the playfulness and creativity of a digital manipulation that masks the tyranny of authority's ongoing, never-to-be-completed disappearance.

This process of memeification is, I propose, an alternative to and the consequence of Chávez's failed mummification. As I pointed out in chapter 1, one of the first ideas that circulated after Chávez's death was officially announced was to have him embalmed so his body could be forever exhibited to the public. Had this proposal been implemented, the creative proliferation of Chávez's doubles would have been limited by the constant presence of the "original" and the respect commanded by his frozen-in-time corpse. This does not mean that there would not be all sorts of creative rituals performed around it, but the presence of Chávez's embalmed body would have provided a stable referent to which all the questions would be addressed, and to which all the doubles—condemned to always fall short—would be compared. With Chávez's body out of sight, the possibilities of doubling become infinite as they transcend temporal, spatial, and bodily boundaries. Chávez can be simultaneously here and there, everywhere and nowhere; he can be a woman or a man, a bird or a butterfly; he can roam the streets and haunt the internet. As an embalmed body, he would have just been one man, here, for now.

That is what I thought, at least until I visited Caracas's Panteón Nacional in the summer of 2016. The building holds the sacred remains of national heroes, and, for a while, it was considered for storing Chávez's remains, an option ultimately dismissed because the Constitution establishes that a body can only be buried there twenty-five years after the person's death. Like any tourist attraction, the Panteón has its own gift shop, filled with books and souvenirs featuring the heroic men and women buried in the building as well as artisanal objects made all around the country. In a corner near the register, a stack of cardboard caught my eye due to how cheap it looked in comparison with the artisanal crafts on display that sought to capture the solemnity of the Panteón itself. Each piece of cardboard showed a historical figure, their paper body parts drawn separately so that children could put them all back together. There was a small picture near the corner of what the end result was supposed to look like—a three-dimensional figurine capable of standing on its own, the head disproportionately big and grotesquely square—and, on the side, there was a brief biographical note accompanied by the instructions, which included asking for the help of an adult to complete the project.

The cardboard cutout was certainly reminiscent of paper dolls that had been popular when I was growing up, except that those—at least the ones I had—had pictures of cartoon women and an entire cardboard wardrobe. It also reminded me of the toys that would come inside treats like the Kinder Surprise, which you had to put together before you could play with them. It was while thinking about those toys from my childhood that I began wondering: What sort of games are children supposed to play with these historical cardboard figures? Do they playfully recreate the wars of independence? There was unfortunately no child in the gift shop to ask. In any case, as I kept going through the pile, I found him: a little cardboard Chávez in his military uniform and red beret. Holding him in my hands, my first thought was that he had not escaped the fate of embalming after all, nor had he lost his spot in the Panteón. He just went through a different kind of embalming, the sort that produces not frozen-in-time corpses, but toys.

Parenthesis: Putting Chávez Together

It is not true that I found Chávez in the souvenir shop of the Panteón Nacional. He found me.

I was not looking for his dismembered body on a piece of cardboard, anxiously visiting every place that might sell it the way I did with the phone cards discussed in chapter 3. In fact, I did not even know a DIY Chávez existed, nor did it ever occur to me to include him, or something like him, in the possibilities that I imagined in preparation for my trip to Venezuela and that featured seemingly endless iterations of Chávez's eyes and signature, many of which I did end up finding and photographing. I knew when I arrived in Caracas and then in Mérida in 2016 that I wanted to find as many eyes and signatures as possible, and so I developed what for lack of a better term I will call a "Chávez radar." This radar heightened my attention and emboldened me to ask people to guide me, to take me to "that corner, that plaza, that building, that park" where they knew—and I knew with them, preemptively—that I would find Chávez. There were of course surprises—I was not expecting to find Chávez's eyes looking down at me from the army headquarters in Mérida, for instance—but nothing to topple the certainty I had about the objects themselves, the *sought-out* objects, the ones I cared about in advance and could easily and solemnly call "the objects of my research."

The DIY Chávez was a *found* object. Was this an oversight on my part? Perhaps. Perhaps I could have done more research, gotten more creative about what I could imagine I would find back home. Or perhaps the DIY Chávez existed to be found because in that state—not beautiful, not sublime, not loud, not remarkable in any obvious way, not sought—Chávez could conduct his haunting unnoticed, peacefully, more like a whisper than like a scream. A scream, after all, scares children, but a whisper plays with the imagination.

And the DIY Chávez is for children, is he not? The instructions say as much: "With scissors and the help of an adult, cut along the white lines labeled with letters." There were no children in the store that day, no one to fight with me over who should be the one to take Chávez home (as there was only one of him in the pile of cardboard figures). So I have to imagine them: the children who would have been dragged to the Panteón by their parents, bored and possibly indifferent to all the glorious dead people, and brought to the store—the only place they could actually touch anything—where they would pick everything up. It is for those moments that the DIY Chávez lives, at least in this imagined scenario. He waits for the excessively curious and possibly sticky little hand that does not care about accuracy or perfection but is instead drawn to the odd, the grotesque, and the weirdly square, the hand that will place him as if by accident on the checkout counter and convince the paying adult to bring him home because he is just a piece of cardboard, and so cheap.

As I imagine this, I realize that I am not only talking about imaginary children but about myself, by all accounts an adult. I could have just taken a picture of the DIY Chávez and been done with him. Instead, I went ahead and bought him, already imagining the gluing and cutting, how big he would be, and where I would place him once I finished making him. W. J. T. Mitchell anticipated this outcome when he spoke of the moment of finding the found object as the moment when one feels oneself to be "about to adopt something" (2005, 122). This, I would argue, is even truer when the object is meant to be a toy, when the toy is meant to be a doll, and when the doll is meant to be the miniaturized version of someone familiar. Leaving it behind would mean leaving him behind: tiny, vulnerable, cardboard Chávez, odd Chávez with his square head, affordable Chávez. Really, who could resist taking him home?

However, for all the excitement I felt when I purchased him, it took us six years (more or less) and an hour (exactly) to finally cut out his feet, his right hand, his left hand, his body, and his face, and glue them all together. "Us," because, as the instructions predicted, I did end up needing the help of an(other) adult. We cleared off a table and placed the cardboard next to two pairs of scissors, a bottle of glue, a ruler, and tape. Then, we started to carefully cut out each of Chávez's body parts, asking each other: Is this his right or his left hand? Where are his feet? His uniform is facing the wrong direction, no? Is his wart under his hat or did they forget to draw it? We laughed and made jokes, but at some point, we grew silent, completely focused on making sure Chávez was properly built and on following every step in the instructions, which we read several times, almost as if we were performing some sort of ritual. Almost.

One hour later, Chávez was done and we were thrilled (figure 4.4). My mother—the other adult in question—made a little red platform for him to stand on, amused in spite of the fact that her feelings about Chávez were as far from fondness as they could be. And yet it was she who saved Chávez from my cat, as she got ready to push his freshly glued body off the table.

Why did she—my mother, not my cat—do that? Because we had spent an hour making him and she did not want to see all that labor go to waste, and neither did I. Simply put, Chávez was *ours*, we had made him, and somehow that meant that we had, from then on, to care for him. So, when it rained the next morning as I walked to my office, I hid him inside my trench coat to keep him dry. Once in the office, I found him a spot among all the other Chávez-themed objects that make up my collection, but, before I left for the day, I hid him in a drawer, afraid he would somehow fall and lose a limb. In each of these decisions, obligation and imagination hold on to each other: I imagine an obligation that does not exist, just as I feel obligated to imagine a life for my cardboard Chávez who will not stop staring at me as I write these words, with a look of suspicion I know I am imagining.

And it is all so much fun.

4.4   DIY Chávez.

Toying with the Comandante

The cardboard image of Chávez was unsettling and grotesque.[20] The combination of an oversized head featuring dead-looking eyes with surprisingly thin and well-defined eyebrows and purple lips was far from the charismatic image of Chávez often featured in posters and murals. At the bottom of the cardboard rectangle, it says that it was produced by the Ministerio del Poder Popular para la Cultura, a branch of the executive government tasked with preserving memory, culture, and national identity.

The DIY Chávez was not the only Chávez-themed toy I saw the day I visited the Panteón Nacional. A smaller plastic Chávez was waiting for me in the Biblioteca Nacional, which is right across from the Panteón and next

4.5   Figurines of Ezequiel Zamora, Hugo Chávez, and Simón Bolívar.

to a field used for military drills—more than once while working there, I heard the squads chanting "Chávez vive, la lucha sigue" (Chávez lives, the struggle continues). The space was being filmed as part of a television show—I could not find out which one—and in addition to the cameras and the people operating them and shouting instructions, there were a couple of people bent over a display table, moving around three little figurines that I later learned were representations of Ezequiel Zamora, Bolívar, and, naturally, Chávez (figure 4.5). While they were definitely not playing with them, there was something in the way they were arranging them that seemed playful, particularly since they could not agree on who was going to stand where and thus kept walking them around, trying to find the arrangement that would best represent the ideological dynamic they wanted to capture. In the end, they settled for Chávez in the middle, with Zamora to his right and Bolívar to his left. As soon as they were done shooting, I took a picture of the little plastic faces, all asking—it seemed—for someone to choose their next move.

The third toy appeared on a poster I saw while driving through Caracas later the same day. In it, a young woman stood dressed in a bright-yellow T-shirt with a drawing of Chávez on it, her right hand holding what looked like a copy of the Constitution and, in her left, a Chávez doll: slender, tall, dressed in his green military uniform. I was startled by how the doll wove together childhood nostalgia and sexual playfulness, personal narrative and political power, indoctrination and games, the living and the dead, all glued together with that affective goo oozing out of the name at the bottom of the poster: "Los amores de Chávez" (Chávez's loves).

The toy had a name: Chavecito. It had been released a month before Christmas in 2005 and had been sold online and in a number of stores in Caracas for 60,000 bolívares (around twenty-nine dollars at the time). Made in China and measuring sixty centimeters, Chavecito came in two versions—one with the military uniform and one with the president's signature red T-shirt—and talked (figure 4.6). By pressing a button, Chavecito's owner could make him sing the national anthem and repeat, three times, phrases spoken by Chávez, such as: "I came here to do everything humanly possible to serve the Venezuelan people in their dreams, hopes, and determination to be free and equal" (see *El Universo* 2005; Morsbach 2005; Toothaker 2005). The doll's commercial success was recorded in several newspaper articles, where vendors stated that the toy would sell out as soon as it hit the shelves, purchased by both *chavistas* and *opositores*, sometimes as Christmas presents for children.[21] Chavecito's appeal was summed up by a woman interviewed for a 2006 article published in *El Mundo*, who said: "There is an energy of mutual attraction between Chávez and the children. . . . What child isn't going to like having a 'Chavito' that will talk to them in their house?" (*El Mundo* 2006).

These objects—the cardboard cutout, the plastic figurine, and the doll—occupied different spaces and played different roles, yet all three demanded an act of memory from their owner that, I propose, combines childish playfulness and a DIY dynamic through which the past appears not as something to be remembered but as something to be toyed with. By proposing that we approach these objects as toys, I am suggesting that we resist seeing them as religious figurines (which could be used to channel Chávez's spirit or to pray to/for him) or mere decorative knickknacks (to put on a shelf and quickly forget about). This is not to say that they could not perform either role; in fact, the little plastic figurine of Chávez that was on display in the Biblioteca Nacional was also sold in a spiritual store in Mérida, along with prayer cards, rosaries, and other items used in religious rituals. Yet these roles do not fully address the child who, whether we see them or not, materializes when we come into contact with any object that miniaturizes the human figure. Put differently, when we encounter something that looks like us, that fits in our hands, and that we can manipulate, we find ourselves feeling pleasure and becoming—some for just a second, others for much longer—children. As

4.6 Chavecito doll. Taken from Aporrea 2007.

Susan Stewart points out, citing pioneering psychologist Stanley Hall's *Study of Dolls*, "even feared and hated objects excite pleasure when mimicked on a small scale" (Stewart 1993, 112), which would explain why Chavecito, for instance, was also popular among members of the opposition, whose attraction to the doll was most certainly driven by the desire to mock the president by taking all sorts of creative liberties with his miniature version.

With Chávez literally in our hands, several questions emerge. What is at stake when we toy with the past? What sort of temporality frames our interaction with toys? What sort of subjectivity is configured in our games with the miniature of a dead man who continues to hold political power? What links toys and death?

That Chávez would eventually find himself turned into a toy is not as ludicrous as it might sound; in fact, this particular form of afterlife seems more than fitting for someone who took every chance he got to interact with children, be they his own or someone else's. Not only did he frequently take babies from mothers' arms to play with them in front of the cameras during political campaigns—a practice that has become a staple in any politician's repertoire and that people enthusiastically embrace, involuntarily perpetuating the centuries-old belief that the touch of the sovereign is somehow magical—but his own children, particularly his daughters, were often near him, playing around as he inaugurated new buildings or gave press conferences. Many of his campaign posters show him squeezed among dozens of children, and in the photographic compilation published in his honor by *Últimas Noticias* after his death, *Las 50 fotografías inolvidables de Hugo Chávez* (Riera and Gonzalo Jiménez 2014), at least five of the pictures are of him smiling or making funny faces with children. Playing with Chávez— innocently challenging the aura of power that surrounded him—was thus a practice that preceded his death and exemplified the kind of paternal relationship he aimed to establish with the people, one that was as affective as it was pedagogical and gave his political performance an intimate tone.

The toys I have mentioned are, first and foremost, the material echoes of a relationship that preceded their fabrication and thus a reminder of the sort of loyalty that is due to someone who was "like a father" to many in the country. Their role, however, and the actions they demand of those who own them make them more than simply a mnemonic device, as theories of the toy show. Taken on its own, the toy appears unattached to any historical time; unlike a photograph, which immediately takes us back into the past, the toy has no temporal drag, leaving us stranded in a dormant present waiting for us to activate it with touch, awakening a world of reverie. However, this does not mean that the toy does not have a bearing on our understanding of time, particularly the time that is connected to our own bodies. In fact, Stewart argues that the toy's transcendence, which allows it to endure beyond history, links it to the world of the dead, to "the end of organic growth and the beginning of inaccessibility to the living" (1993, 57). If we think of dying as the body's transformation into an object, then we can see toys, particularly those that resemble people, as a kind of "dead among us"—a possibility that the horror movie industry has ceaselessly and creatively exploited. Furthermore, we could see the stories concocted as part of the games that are played with toys as fantasies of the afterlife, children's involuntary answer to adults' most puzzling question.

The toy's intimate relationship with death—one that is rarely acknowledged on the playground and mostly comes into view in the context of voodoo practices where object and body merge—invites us to briefly consider its connection to the memento mori. Aesthetically speaking, memento mori are objects inserted in European Christian paintings—skulls being the most popular—as reminders of the transient nature of life and all earthly things, the Latin phrase meaning, "remember you must die." In a way, the toy too is a reminder of our mortality; having it around means being constantly in the presence of an object that anticipates our own inevitable objectification. Yet it is also the opposite: an invitation to ignore that outcome, to imagine and fantasize, to go in and out of various contexts and realities, all the while calling into question the limits that we place between organic and inorganic bodies. Thus, while it is true that toys are usually thought of as belonging to the realm of childhood, in reality the imaginative possibilities that they put on display are equally appealing to adults, for whom they become a means for defining their subjectivity.[22]

The kind of relationships that we establish with toys are as varied as the toys themselves. We do not engage with a teddy bear—whose big eyes and cuddly body are designed to trigger a parental response—in the same way we engage with a toy car or a doll. With dolls, specifically the Chávez dolls, our interaction is mediated by the fact that they are the result of a process of human miniaturization: Chávez, the giant whose presence enveloped the country, shrinks to fit in the hands of a child, his seemingly limitless political power converted into fuel for the imagination. This process collapses the public into the private, transforming the former into an experience that can be easily manipulated and triggering a second act of doubling: the creation of a fantasy world that runs parallel to the real one, sometimes mirroring it and other times remaking it into something entirely different. The sustainability of that world concocted by a playful act of the imagination is contingent upon belief in the toy's everlastingness: the little toy soldier can be shot and killed again and again, the doll can be dropped, the teddy bear can be grotesquely twisted to fit into a small backpack. All of that is possible because the injuries are as imagined as the game itself, and if they were real—if the toy were actually broken—then the game would immediately end. The toy thus inserts itself in a world outside lived reality that, as Stewart points out, "erases the productive possibilities of understanding through time" as it invites us to get lost in its presentness; we might envelop the toy with our bodies, but the toy's transcendence envelops us, tempting us with the pleasures of a state of infinite reverie (1993, 60).

In that state, imagining becomes an imperative. Unlike other objects that seamlessly blend into the background where they quietly accumulate dust and spiderwebs, the toy emphatically demands animation. Having been removed from the "please do not touch" world of the store, the toy now *must* be played with, for otherwise it would be not a toy but an ornament. Hence, beneath the illusion of mastery that the toy provides its owner, there is a demand for an attachment that resembles subjection. Once again, we are reminded of a distinctive element in the plot of horror films that involve objects, whereby the protagonists, having tried without success to destroy the evil doll, succumb to its demands and watch helplessly as it goes on its homicidal rampage.[23] Two conclusions can be drawn from these films: toys seem to own us as much as we own them (if not more); and playing with toys that resemble humans engages us—whether willingly or not—in an affective relationship.

Though each theory of affect introduces something new and debates have arisen regarding what affects are and what they can and cannot do, there seems to be consensus that affects are muddy, indeterminate, sticky, ongoing, and contagious in nature. Affects never seem to circulate in an orderly manner between bodies: they jump (Stewart 2007), they stick (Ahmed 2010), they resonate (Gregg and Seigworth 2010), they contaminate (Brennan 2004); they are the intensities and forces that corrode borders in subtle yet deeply felt ways that allow bodies of all sorts not so much to meet as two separate entities but rather to fold into and out of each other. This understanding of affect, which has been widely deployed in relation to queer theory, performance, political science, environmental studies, and the digital world, also strongly resonates with the world of childhood.

Childhood is essentially driven by affects; in fact, the neuroscientist Susan Greenfield has pointed out that, when we are infants, "feeling is not greatly tempered with individual memories, with cultural or private meaning, or, most important of all, with the self. Feelings just are" (quoted in Smith 2016, 118). The relationships that children establish with the world around them are unmediated and unfiltered; times, things, and bodies stick to each other; bodies of all sorts and all levels of reality find themselves mingling in fleeting relationships that are not linguistically or socially predetermined; mimesis is imperative yet unconscious; imagination renders boundaries not only unnecessary but also unrecognizable; and the protagonist of it all—the child—is the example par excellence of what it means to be unfinished in every way. Also at the center of this messy world—this mess usually glossed over by the trope of childhood innocence—is the toy, which sits across from the child and becomes both the target and the trigger of the child's affective way of being.

It is the toy that, from the child's very first moments of conscious existence in the world, is in charge of collapsing all temporal, physical, and spatial borders, all while aiding in the development of the child who uses it to play out and play with different scenarios and social roles. The toy's pedagogical role is then tied to its ability to bond with the child in a way that makes it part of their developing body. As Sara Ahmed points out in "Happy Objects," "objects that we like or that give us pleasure"—such as toys, although Ahmed does not mention them specifically—"take up residence within our bodily horizon. We come to have our likes, which might even establish *what we are like*. The bodily horizon could be redescribed as a horizon of likes. To have our likes means certain things are gathered around us" (2010, 32; original emphasis). The toy's incorporation into our bodily horizon is perhaps best exemplified by children's physical and emotional attachment to a specific toy that sometimes even survives childhood to exist as a nostalgic treasure throughout adult life. Baby blankets, worn teddies, toy cars: they are all dragged around by children who cannot imagine their lives without them—crying inconsolably when they cannot find them—and who fall asleep holding them close, thus achieving in this unconscious state the bodily communion of child and toy.

There is thus much more to the toy than meets the adult eye trained to see it as just one more object in the innocent world of children. In fact, works such as Marita Sturken's *Tourists of History* pinpoint the importance of toys for the development not only of the child but also of the narrative that brings together the nation. One of the objects that Sturken focuses on in her discussion of memory, consumerism, and kitsch are the teddy bears that were given to children and adults after the Oklahoma City bombing and the 9/11 terrorist attacks in the United States. Sturken highlights the teddy bear as a commodity of grief that contributes to the assimilation of a narrative of national innocence grounded in the comfort that the toy provides, which, as she argues, "doesn't promise to make things better; it promises to make us feel better about the way things are" (2007, 7). Purchasing or being gifted a teddy bear in the aftermath of the two attacks links loss to a sort of prepackaged sentimentality that, she proposes, allows us to gloss over the complexities of the tragic events and therefore walk away with feelings that might prevent us from asking ourselves what these events mean. While the context Sturken discusses seems far removed from the one that concerns us here, her observations regarding the political role toys are made to play are relevant to the dynamics surrounding Chávez-themed toys.[24] The characteristics that I have identified in the toy—a relationship with time that makes death both present and unprocessed, a form of ownership that is uncannily mutual, and the bodily as well as affective immersion the toy requires from the body that engages with it—make the Chávez toys active participants in the configuration of a national memory narrative that centers on the empty stage of political power, a void that the toys both conceal and reveal.

In the case of DIY Chávez, this narrative is tied to the agency that comes with crafting. Though the word "craft" has typically been associated with an occupation or trade requiring artistic skill or remarkable manual dexterity, recently crafting has become much more accessible and popular, with people watching tutorials online or heading to arts-and-crafts stores to purchase supplies to create objects that are not only individualized but in some cases end up being cheaper than their premade counterparts. In Venezuela, the widespread scarcity resulting from the economic crisis triggered by the drop in oil prices in 2014 has turned crafting into a necessity; people have been driven to make their own flour, their own soap, their own deodorant, and their own toothpaste, and to grow whenever and wherever possible the basic produce that is either impossible to find or too expensive to buy—fruits and vegetables mostly, but also medicinal herbs with which people try to compensate for the severe lack of medicine. The toy inserts itself in this informal economy of crafts and scraps, with the DIY dynamic responding not only to the appeal of creativity and family time, but also to the fact that people are more likely to choose it over the more expensive, sturdier figurines sold by artisans in specialty stores.

Accessibility is thus a key element of the DIY toy: not only is the price affordable but the figure the object represents becomes accessible. Chávez, the authority figure whose image was everywhere and whose body was nowhere—as we saw in chapter 2 in *FANtasmo*—suddenly appears at one's fingertips, his phantasmagoric body split into small, fragile yet tangible parts that subjects-turned-owners must now put together using the energy of their labor that, like godly breath, will infuse it with a life governed by the owner's imagination. Doing it yourself thus alters the political and economic order of things; the instant gratification promised by the commodity is exchanged for the lengthy process of crafting, and the political subject goes into labor, using their own body to put each piece of the sovereign's body together until it can finally stand on its own.

This act of laboring power into being—labor as a mix of crafting and birthing—has to be read alongside one of the central issues in theories of crafting: the fact that it is never just about hands making things; it is a way of being and becoming in the world. In *Crafting in the World*, Clare Burke and Suzanne M. Spencer-Wood present crafting as inherently informed by socially and culturally constituted knowledge, beliefs, and expectations. As an embodied experience, crafting involves "a diverse set of habitual practices, ways of being and processes of doing and becoming that shape both materials and people, through a reciprocal relationship in co-creating a meaningful material social world" (2018, 6). This emphasis on reciprocity is key; crafting not only brings into being a material object but also a subject whose body (and worldview) is shaped through the sensual experiences of handcrafting. In this process of cocreation, "not only individuals but their social relations, accompanying power dynamics, and worldview are mutually constituted through crafting" (2). Crafting something thus means being crafted in turn. Playing also involves this sort of reciprocal shaping; as Nathan TeBokkel points out, free play involves "determining things and being determined by things" (2017, 105). In that sense, an uncanny connection emerges between what goes on on the playground with DIY toys—and toys in general—and Michel Foucault's observation regarding power relations in the context of the panopticon.

Foucault (1995) argues that by rendering power at once visible and unverifiable, the panopticon requires subjects to inscribe the power relation in themselves, becoming the principle of their own subjection. Though the DIY toy seems far removed from the panopticon—indeed, nothing seems further from a prison than a toy—I would argue that it engages in a similar dynamic: power becomes the "it" in the do-it-yourself, with subjects not only willingly participating in its coming into being and thus in the crafting of the relationship that makes them subjects, but also—unlike in the panopticon—actually enjoying the whole process, giving in to the harmless, childish world the toy promises and the affects that the little paper figure awakens. In that sense then, the toy appears to be even more efficient than the panopticon at structuring long-lasting power relations; with fear and the impalpable magnitude of authority out of the equation, and with the prison displaced by the playground, the illusion of agency, which breeds subjection, is prolonged by the possibility of endless games—a power dynamic that nicely fits with the performance of a populist leader who relied on enjoyment and happiness to connect with the people, as shown by the many pictures of him dancing, singing, and playing baseball, and, after his death, by the creation in October 2013 of the Viceministerio para la Suprema Felicidad Social del Pueblo (Vice-Ministry for the Supreme Social Happiness of the People) in his honor (see Univision Noticias 2013b).

This power relation that the DIY toy constructs is interwoven with the act of memory that also takes place as the little pieces of Chávez are put together. In fact, memory is in the title of the collection that the toy is part of ("arte y memoria," art and memory); the child—and the adult that helps them—is supposed to engage with the cardboard Chávez in a way that combines entertainment, pedagogy, and ideology with a return of the past that endeavors to be Proustian, appealing not just to the mind but primarily to the sensuous knowing of the body, which is stimulated through the cutting, gluing, and folding of the pieces of paper. Remembering, then, is not so much expressed by a metaphorical hand that reaches backward in the hope of grabbing something fleeting but is a real hand in the present building a body that is gone. Paper and flesh—past and present—thus adhere to each other and leave marks on each other until the boundaries separating them become, if not invisible, then at least irrelevant.

This crafting of the past is then followed by the toy's (after)life in the worlds that the imagination builds for it; putting Chávez together is also to put together a future made up of stories where beginnings are real but endings are not. These stories that follow no rules—temporal, spatial, or otherwise—propel memory forward by turning facts into daydreams and speculations. As Abby Smith Rumsey points out, "memory records the world *as so*, imagination transposes it into the key of *as if*, transforming experience into speculation. That is why to lose one's memory means losing the future. Because imagination is memory in the future tense" (2001, 127; original emphasis). Life and afterlife are thus conflated in an act of childish imagination whereby Chávez's existence in the future is rehearsed over and over again, becoming as vivid as his existence in the past.

An example of this rehearsed futurity was the playful handling of the little figurine of Chávez in the Biblioteca Nacional, where it found itself engaged in a playdate with Zamora and Bolívar. The figurine was in no way special; it was part of the merchandise sold in both souvenir shops and spiritual shops, and it imitated the all-too-familiar design of the bust, with a little silver platform holding the reproduction of Chávez's upper body, which could be compared with the framed photograph of Chávez in his presidential sash in the background. And yet looking at the figurine and where it was positioned—in front of cameras and other television equipment—it became clear how different it was from a regular bust, a religious object, or the photograph it was mirroring. These objects, though different, share a certain auratic quality. Although all of them can be serially reproduced, in the specific space they inhabit, they acquire an air of uniqueness and solemnity that emphasizes their status as bridges between past and present. Walking in front of the severe gaze of a marble or bronze bust, praying to a religious figure to communicate with the world beyond this one, looking at a photograph that captures the irrefutable existence of a person or an event—all are acts that frame the past as something that demands reverence, which can be accessed only because it is somewhere else, temporal distance thus a prerequisite for the illusion of proximity that memory brings.

The figurine qua toy that concerns us, on the other hand, presents the past as something to be *toyed with*; that is, the past appears as something to be handled lightly, something to amuse oneself without having to be loyal to historical accuracy or anything but one's own whims. The very features of the figurines seem to capture this historical lightheartedness: both Chávez and Bolívar appear to be frozen in a smirk and Zamora seems startled—neither expression befitting the sacred associations of marble and bronze busts and statues, but both appropriate for the much more humble and malleable nature of plastic. The presence of the cameras further encourages this toying with the past by introducing a "live" element, which brings together the "live" of the spectacle of television and the "live" of being "alive," such that liveliness becomes performance and performance a proof of life. The past then is displaced to the here and now, and as the figurines walk around in the impossible space where historical figures who lived a hundred years apart meet, the future too becomes less temporal and more physical—a child's game that not only puts memory in the future tense, as Smith Rumsey points out, but also serves to define political subjects as children whose duty toward their government is to imagine it and thus to imagine the authority it holds over them.

In the cases of both the figurine and the DIY paper Chávez, this imperative to imagine is also an imperative to tear down the barriers between public and private spaces. By being at once personal and public, toys constitute a sort of missing link between the subject and the government, such that it becomes impossible to tell where the body of one ends and the body of the other begins. In a way, this conflation of bodies and spaces evokes the socialist measures dictated by Chávez and later reinforced by Maduro regarding the expropriation of private property and the building of public housing with walls displaying Chávez's magnified signature. Though these projects took opposite approaches—with the former being about taking away and the latter about giving back—the message in both cases was the same: owning something, no matter how personal or intimate, means being owned in return. With the toys that are jointly crafted and consumed by the government and the people, the expropriation of privacy, as we have seen, transcends the material sphere; not only are bodies not private, but times are not private either. To the intimacy that is built with a toy we must now add the public face of authority, miniaturized so it fits seamlessly in the gaps inevitably left by the imagination. Two timelines are thus woven together: the personal one, where creativity and imagination obliterate the body's fleeting nature, and the public one, where rehearsal and repetition ensure the survival of authority.

The Chávez doll that appears in the poster from the collection "Los amores de Chávez" (Chávez's loves) further strengthens the coming together of the public and the private. Unlike the other two toys, which did not reproduce Chávez in his entirety or interpellate their owner through any specific gender code, the Chávez doll has all its body parts and locates itself in the gendered space of the dollhouse. This is not to say that the toy is "only for girls"; in fact, a quick online search shows pictures of Chávez's father holding the doll, the father-son connection thus transferred to the plastic proxy. However, in the posters that in 2016 decorated the center of Caracas where Chavecito is held by a woman, the title appealing to Chávez's loves—"Los amores de Chávez"—turns the doll into a sort of socialist alternative to Ken, Barbie's famous companion. Memory and the role of the doll as an object of commemoration are thus interwoven with affects that circulate in two different but related dimensions: the childhood fantasy world where male dolls play Prince Charming and are a guarantee of safety and reciprocated love, and adulthood and the world of pleasure where toys are not just nostalgic treasures but also sources of intimacy and erotic playfulness. Holding the doll then involves welcoming it into the body's horizon by inserting it in the economy of fantasy and desire that governs both dimensions and that is invoked by the second phrase that appears on these posters: "Amor con amor se paga" (Love is paid with love). This phrase transforms the nature of the relationship with the body of power that has disappeared by making its remembrance about an affective debt that is anchored in the present and that looks to the future—a debt that can never be repaid, since it is contracted with the dead, and yet appears desirable as it promises emotional comfort and, perhaps, sensual pleasure. The body of power is thus not to be feared or just memorialized but to be desired, a desire that will never be satisfied—since Chávez is gone—but that, precisely for that reason, lingers stubbornly in the promise of free and endless play that Chavecito seems to make.

Toys like the ones discussed in this section thus point us to a way of understanding memory that relies on crafting, imagination, and desire. To the extent that they belong—at least initially—to a world of childhood where nothing has really taken shape, where bodies and objects serve as extensions of each other, and where temporal and spatial laws surrender to the whims of the imagination, they tempt us to mess with the past, to treat it lightly and irreverently, to toy with it until it ceases to be "back there"—sacred and cobwebbed—and materializes "right here," in the intimate space of the body whose labor the toy elicits and for which it offers in exchange the chance to repeatedly rehearse the body's most intimate fantasies and desires. It is in that subtle yet mighty displacement of the past from the realm of remembrance to the realm of imagination-driven desire where the narrative of memory that addresses the gap in political power materializes, a narrative whereby power's survival—in memory and in practice—depends on the futurity that people's desires provide. These people are not to be understood as the proverbial mass that, sheeplike, follows the leader in blind admiration, but rather as imaginative beings who shape and labor power into being, their agency simultaneously crafting and masking their own subjection.

The Stuff of the State

This chapter started out with a talking bird and ended with a doll. In the unlikely journey from one to the other, we encountered a parade of Chávez's doubles that render explicit how, in the afterglow of the Comandante's death, the past is not a matter of remembrance but of animation. Each double has illuminated a specific way the past can be animated, but, in all cases, animation has given rise to an overlapping of bodies and times that has turned Chávez into a bodily performance, turned remains into crafts, and turned memory into an act of imagination capable of propelling the past into the future and the present into the past. Many elements have contributed to the creation of the liminal space where this overlapping unfolds: the bursting of the auratic bubble of the state; an economic, social, and political crisis that has called the state's authority and legitimacy into question; and a political project that has coincided with and been fueled by new technologies and their promises of accessibility, immediacy, and participation. Together, these elements have encouraged people to become crafters, workers of imagination whose labor the state craves and seeks to absorb as it attempts to activate the spectral remains of a body of power that is not there.

Central to these operations that create this overlap between memory, imagination, the people, and the state is the state's stuff: the objects that render the state materially present in everyday life, that are often ordinary, and that are neither confined to the tedious realm of bureaucracy nor to the explicit display of state power through violence. These two forms—bureaucracy and state violence—tend to represent the public face of the state: what we believe the state "looks like" when it chooses to directly engage with the citizens circumscribed by its gaze. However, there is more to the state than long lines in front of public buildings and the aftermath of police repression. The state also has props: toys, memes, holograms, and butterflies that populate public and private spaces and that form relationships with people that might be fleeting or might last a lifetime. In the specific context of the afterglow following Chávez's death, these props—key components of the state's necromantic performance—are not only connected to Chávez in various ways, but they also display elements of playfulness, childish fascination, and amusement that allow for ways of imagining power and our relationship to it that are particularly compelling because they seem uniquely boundless. When I speak of childish fascination, I do not mean to tie the people who establish connections with these props to an understanding of children as vulnerable, weak, unaware, and uninformed. My understanding of children—and, more specifically, of childlike behavior—is that they are powerful sources of creativity, imagination, and irreverence, fearless creators for whom death is nothing more than a plaything. *That* is the child that the state appeals to, invokes, and seeks to mobilize through objects like Chavecito and the DIY Chávez, but also through tales of butterflies, luminous holograms, and funny memes: the childish part of every political subject that plays and toys around, that jokes and laughs, rehearsing multiple realities and futures where the dead—including Chávez—can keep on living.

This playfulness is without a doubt empowering; it confirms that for the state to be more than sheer force, for it to be a legitimate form of power, it *needs* people's imagination—it needs its legitimacy to be imagined and reimagined. Chiara Bottici in her work on imaginal politics argues as much when she remarks that "states would have never come about if, at some point, the free imagination of individuals had not led them to first depict them" (2014, 96). However, like all games, it is also confining because it operates in both directions: toying with something means being toyed with in return, imagining the state means being open to the knowledge that the imagined state imagines us back and, in the process, constitutes us. After all, the objects, images, and words we toy with—the ones discussed in this chapter—are the state's props: we might change them, modify them, draw on them, and mock them, but ultimately they are the state's, part of its rhetorical and mnemonic practice, and every act—no matter how creative or irreverent—that involves them bounces back into the state, not as a destabilizing challenge but as a form of animating magic.

We are thus left with a pressing question: What would it mean to imagine otherwise, *against* rather than with and for the state? And, most importantly, would we want to imagine otherwise if that meant giving up the persistent yearning for the masculine and salvific heroes that we, along with the state, keep bringing back from death?

Afterdeath

> When a ghost appears, it is making contact with you; all its forceful if perplexing enunciations are for you. Offer it a hospitable reception we must, but the victorious reckoning with the ghost always requires a partiality to the living.
>
> Avery Gordon, *Ghostly Matters*

Hidden inside a closet in Mérida, Venezuela, there is a sticker with the word "Sí" (figure Inter.1). The sticker is not new, nor is it a carefully preserved object or a cherished souvenir. Not anymore. In fact, it is not even a sticker but what remains of one after a fingernail unsuccessfully tried to remove it from the wall. The fingernail in question belonged to my grandmother, who had been an ardent supporter and admirer of Hugo Chávez in the early years of his presidency. The sticker itself had probably been distributed among voters during the 1998 presidential elections that brought Chávez to power in 1999. I say "probably" because I have no memory of the elections or of my grandmother's political position at the time; in fact, it was my mother who told me about the sticker and where it had come from. She also told me that, at some point after the elections, my grandmother had become angry with Chávez and, as a way of symbolically withdrawing her support for him, had tried to remove the sticker.

Inter.1 "Sí" sticker.

This gesture of trying to erase or banish something or someone from view and from memory and the visible evidence of the remnants that the act of erasure always leaves behind are representative of the politics of memory that have surrounded Chávez's figure since his death in 2013. The attempts to "erase" him can be most concretely seen in the several statues of him that have been taken down, cut to pieces, and set on fire in cities and towns all over Venezuela (Straka 2021), and, in a subtler way, in the many books that in promising to uncover the conspiracies and hidden truths of his death seem to insist on Chávez dying again, once and for all.

These acts of erasure have taken place as I write this book, a book that is in a way the inconvenient finger that repeatedly points to what the sticker in my grandmother's closet encapsulates: Chávez's remains, the stubbornness of an absence that remains present despite—or precisely because of—the many attempts to exorcise it. While my analysis has focused on how Chávez's spectral presence materializes in public space—and, in some cases, in private spaces and the digital world as well—and how it triggers, circumscribes, and draws from popular imagination, the force of his spectral lingering has also made itself evident in political surveys that show that popular support for Chávez remains high and exceeds that of his successor, Nicolás Maduro, and that of the opposition's leading figure, Juan Guaidó.[1] Underscoring his popularity ratings—and, more generally, tracing the various ways in which Chávez lingers in contemporary Venezuela—comes with the responsibility of addressing the questions that have been haunting this project since its very beginnings: What, then, should we do with Chávez? Should we ban him from our collective memory? Pretend he did not exist or, better yet, emphasize everything he—and, through him, the Bolivarian Revolution—did that led to a multidimensional crisis marked by starvation, hyperinflation, and ruins? Or, should we instead remember him more, honor him better, keep the fire of the revolutionary struggle he embodied burning so that Venezuela can finally achieve the dreams of independence it was promised in the nineteenth century and enter a new stage of its history that would be shaped by twenty-first-century socialism?

These questions have been central to the politically mediated and highly polarized acts of imagination that come from both pro-government groups and sectors of the opposition as they speculate on what would happen if Maduro stepped down and democratic elections finally took place. They have also been central throughout history and in different global contexts where the fate of a nation, a political project, and/or a people has been chained to the fate of a body and the memory narratives and practices created to commemorate it. Ernesto "Che" Guevara in Cuba (and across Latin America), Eva Perón in Argentina, Vladimir Lenin in the Soviet Union, Mustafa Kemal Atatürk in Turkey: the vast, ever-growing scholarship on these figures shows that the decisions made regarding the shape of their afterlives have impacted the formation of national and collective identities, inspired the elaboration and implementation of new and old ideological agendas, and, in some instances, triggered acts of extreme violence.

However important these questions might be—and however urgent they seem in moments of crisis, nostalgia, and anticipation such as the one that followed Chávez's death—answering them has not been the purpose of this book. This book is not about Chávez, even if Chávez is everywhere in it. This book is about Chávez's specter and, more generally, about haunting and imagination: about the political subject as a haunted subject, and about the limits that being haunted—*comfortably* haunted—places on our imagination. Each chapter has been an effort to denaturalize the haunting not only of Chávez but also of the epic, salvific male heroes that his political and theatrical performance invoked, whether consciously or unconsciously, favorably or critically. In the process, the ultimate goal has not been to banish the specter, but rather to wrestle with it: to understand how it is born and how much our imaginative labor fuels its afterlife, to recognize that haunting can become familiar—that not every specter is an unsettling ghost—and to face the fact that what at first glance might appear as irreconcilable binaries (us and them, government and opposition, the people and the state) are in fact two versions of the same (hi)story and two forms of supporting what so far has been its only protagonist. Put differently, and in the words of performance scholar Rebecca Schneider, the purpose of this project has been to "summon the ghosts, to bring them out of the shadows and into the scene where they always already exist, to make them apparent *as players*" (1997, 23; original emphasis).

To summon a specter that is *already there*, not really in the shadows as Schneider's quote suggests, but hypervisible, loud, and viral, is not the same as summoning the invisible ghosts banished by history and by the state's official narratives—the ghosts that Avery Gordon ([1997] 2008) finds in society's blind spots and that Juliana Martínez (2020) argues blur our vision, unsettle our understanding of space, and weaken our grasp of linear time. This is not a matter of forcing ourselves to be comfortable with uncanny echoes and ghostly matters, to embrace them so that we can finally clearly hear their demands for justice that state power often muffles. In fact, the goal is the opposite: to become uncomfortable with how comfortable we are living with the specter, how quickly we have accepted it as part of our lives and identities, voting for it over and over again to the point that the apparition and reproduction of thousands of disembodied eyes—Chávez's eyes, discussed in chapter 2—belonging to a dead man might seem annoying but not exceptional or particularly disturbing.

To activate this discomfort, it has been necessary, first, to linger on what is so often taken for granted, dismissed as one more eccentricity of the Venezuelan state's propaganda machine, or ignored in favor of more stable, permanent objects of collective memory, such as monuments, statues, and historical documents. This lingering—on Chávez's eyes, his signature, phone cards, and toys—has revealed how much these objects and images penetrate our daily life and give us the visual vocabulary we use to portray ourselves as political subjects and to articulate the narratives of resistance that mobilize us against the state and allow us to express political demands. Key to this penetration is the fact that these objects and images are both incomplete and needy: they want things from us—our imagination, desires, fantasies, and dreams—to "fill them up," give them meaning, and animate them, freeing them from the traps of the past and from the immobility of monumentality, and propelling them—and with them, Chávez and the salvific male heroes that come with him—into the future. Recognizing this neediness means recognizing our agency, the role we (the people *and* the state) have histori-cally played in the coming into being of the specter. Specters, after all, are not shadows, even though we have come to treat them as such; they do not quietly, passively, inevitably follow us around. Nor can they be reduced to (or trapped inside) monuments, plaques, and statues—all objects that stay still, offering us a view of history that relies on what is thought to be pol-ished and over and done with. Specters, this book has insisted, are social and political figures with whom we engage every day and in a multiplicity of ways. We make them and, in turn, they make us.

"Maduro, Chávez is watching you," Chávez watching Chávez, Chávez watching over his children, people watching Chávez, Bolívar watching Chávez, Bolívar against Bolívar, Chávez's Bolívar, Chávez's children, Chávez's *real* children, Chávez's eyes, the bones of Bolívar, Bolívar's hopes and dreams, "absolute loyalty to Chávez," "the enigmatic similarities between Juan Guaidó and Bolívar," "Bolívar's great-great-grandnephew Leopoldo López." An echo chamber inside a house of mirrors: familiar images and familiar figures that saturate and shape both top-down and from-below dy-namics. It is thus not enough to denounce this as a spectacle of the state—the "magnanimous sorcerer," Fernando Coronil (1997) talked about—that paralyzes people and turns them into a passive mass of spectators seduced by the ever-powerful Bolívar/Chávez. It is also not enough to underscore and praise subversive images coming "from below" that make Bolívar more "of the people" by transforming his appearance so he looks Black, Indigenous, or like a guerrilla fighter, or more like Chávez, or like the historically mar-ginalized and excluded. Both of these processes amount to the same thing: the perpetuation of the revolutionary male hero whose spectral gaze empowers *and* subjugates, and whose spectral figure liberates *and* confines, creating the paradox of a nation full of images and yet deprived of imagination, if imagination is understood as the creation of something truly new and thus truly discomforting.

To bring the specter out, to make spectrality the lens through which to read the practices and narratives of memory in contemporary Venezuela, is then to face what we have always known and how we have come to know it, and what we have already understood and the terms we have used to articulate that understanding, as well as to grapple with the difficulty of imagining beyond it. That difficulty haunts the vast scholarship developed around the cult of Bolívar and is explicitly articulated in Alicia Ríos's work on the topic: "What if, for just an instant, we forgot everything we have been taught about our past and tried to open ourselves up to a different present and future?" (2013, 178). Ríos's question inevitably leads to another one: How, exactly, can we do that? How can we forget everything that we have been taught about the past? And, more important, how do we guarantee that this forgetting lasts long enough for us to think of the present and the future differently? In this book, I have sketched out a possible answer to these questions that relies not on forgetting but instead on an uncomfortable way of remembering that starts with language: with trying out other ways of referring to the past and its lingering in the present that brings out what is excessive, disturbing, and oppressive about it and about the relationship we have developed with it.

I have thus not talked about the cult (of Chávez or of Bolívar) but about haunting, not transitions and continuations but afterglows, not a hero but a specter, not memory but afterlife, not mourning or commemoration but animation. None of these has been a metaphorical or poetic gesture; each term has been invoked with a commitment to explore and define the political, social, cultural, and mnemonic implications that come with it when we suspend our disbelief and take that term at face value. The assumption behind mobilizing and conceptualizing these terms is that creating new words or using old ones in new ways underscores an insufficiency in the vocabulary that is available to us and destabilizes our confidence and comfort in using that vocabulary to talk about ourselves and about our future in ways we believe are new and imaginative.

Both Chávez and Bolívar have been the subjects of illuminating academic studies, yet a number of those works use the vocabulary of the dynamics of the cult, and, in the case of Chávez, they have been heavily mediated by the political polarization that the Bolivarian Revolution has triggered not just in Venezuela but in political debates worldwide. In proposing that we talk about specters, I am proposing an approach to both figures that focuses on how they are connected to the way we, as a nation, develop our collective memory, all the while making uncomfortable—destabilizing—our relationship to and familiarity with that memory. Specters, after all, are odd: they are uncanny, unpredictable presences that shake our confidence in our ability to perceive and know the world that surrounds us. My use of the specter in the context of memory narratives and practices in Venezuela relies on the specter's destabilizing power to highlight the familiarity we have developed with both Chávez and Bolívar, and at the same time to challenge it, to create a critical distance that will allow us first to acknowledge that we are—and have always been—a haunted nation, then to consider not just who but what has been haunting us (what kind of political power, what kind of heroic figure, what kind of historical narrative), and finally, to embrace the right to ask what lies outside the circumscribing gaze of the specter.

This is now not so much a right but an obligation. The multidimensional crisis that has marked the years following Chávez's death has been studied extensively in terms of its political, economic, and social dimensions; however, it is a crisis of identity and of language as well. The burden of being the "gran pueblo heroico de Bolívar" (or "de Chávez") (the great heroic people of Bolívar, or of Chávez) has become unsustainable in light of the waves of migration, the widespread starvation, the ever-increasing number of deaths, and the overall disillusionment with those who have been protagonists of the revolutionary epic. Not even oil, with its magical properties, has been able to restore the glory of the nation. We are thus not only lacking basic goods but also the vocabulary to define ourselves. This void in language, however, is an opportunity for redefinition, for seeing beyond the epic and giving up the outdated loyalty to it and to its protagonists. Because it is only by doing that—by changing *how* we do memory before we think about *who* we remember—that new pasts and new characters can be welcomed into the present, on our terms, which will allow us to finally engage with them reciprocally, rather than spectrally, and to reboot political imagination in a way that reconfigures both the present and future, opening up the space for much-needed inclusive and nonalienated forms of sociality.

So, what next? Where do we go from here? How do we go about rebooting political imagination and developing new relationships with our stubborn dead now that we see them as specters? I propose we turn to discomfort: to the gross and the raw, to the unshaped and the sticky, to the messy matter of the past before it has been edited, polished, and sanitized to manufacture shiny icons and luminous heroes. I propose we abandon the comforting familiarity of the public plaza to linger in a space that oscillates between an artist's workshop and a catacomb, a space that invites acts of imagination born out of what Jennifer Doyle calls "difficult works": works that test the limits of our tolerance by asking us to engage with things that feel "like life and therefore cut too close" (2013, 4) and that force us to "keep company with vulnerability, intimacy, and desire" (20) while simultaneously undoing the ways we have come to understand those terms. Imagination, then, as working through and working with the difficult and the uncomfortable, the gross and the sticky. Imagination as the willingness to see the known not disappear from view, suddenly, as if exorcized, but rather slowly decompose in our hands.

In RAW, Venezuelan performance artist Deborah Castillo (2015) opens up the kind of space that invites us to witness and participate in this decomposition: the material undoing of the known, the familiar, and—key here—the spectral. In this exhibition—the artist's first solo exhibition in New York City—Castillo turns away from the luminosity of the specter and the power of its afterlife and fixes our attention on the movement of the raw materiality of the statues she makes, all built out of malleable clay and all featuring a military leader that could be Bolívar or Chávez or any of the presidents and dictators that have ruled Venezuela, but that could also be any of the hypermasculine military heroes that have ruled and continue to rule countries in Latin America and elsewhere. Her performances—combining video performance and live action—thus make the state-made and people-fueled specter materialize in a way that forces us to "handle" it rather than exorcising it or banning it from our memory. Handling in the most literal sense of the word: touching, feeling, holding, and moving with the hand. All dirty work, work that leaves stains on our palms, that assaults our senses, and that dissolves any attempt at commemoration or forgetting into the gray matter of a body that looks like a proto-statue and also, suspiciously and disturbingly, like a corpse. This is the kind of ghostbusting we are embarking on in the final section of this book: not in an effort to banish the specter and find a pure, unspectral, unhaunted, originary presence, but to embrace the specter—hold and squeeze it because now it is not only material but malleable—as it invites acts of imagination that have, as a point of arrival and as a point of departure, a partiality to the (nonepic, messy, complicated, unpredictable) living. As Gordon reminds us in her conclusion to *Ghostly Matters* ([1997] 2008), living with ghosts does not mean living *for* them: at the end of any scholarly ghost hunt, our commitment has to be to the living.

This commitment to the living, paradoxically, will be made among the dead, in what I am calling "afterdeath." The word inevitably conjures up that which appears to be its opposite: the afterlife. Rather than presenting the two concepts as mere opposites, one displacing or obliterating the other, I propose that we see the afterdeath and the afterlife as existing alongside each other, following parallel yet distinct paths. Before tackling the relationship between these two concepts and further developing the understanding of the afterdeath that will guide my reflection in the following section, let me clarify what I mean by afterlife.

In *The Dominion of the Dead*, Robert Pogue Harrison speaks of funerary rites as enabling "the release of the image," in which a dead person's corpse is separated from the dead person's image. He argues that, if the corpse holds on to the person's image at the moment of its demise, "funerary rites serve to disentangle that nexus and separate them into discrete entities with independent fates—the corpse consigned to earth or air, and the image assigned to its afterlife, whatever form that imaginary afterlife may take in this or that cultural framework" (2003, 148). For Harrison, then, the afterlife is the life that the dead—understood as the resemblance that corpses bear to their previously living selves—lead after death as "souls, images, voices, masks, heroes, ancestors, founders," and, we might add, specters (155). In the case of the specter, the afterlife Harrison talks about is characterized by temporal overlapping, acts of animation, affective exchanges, and—as we saw in the analysis of Chávez's spectral remains—the unfulfilled promise of a revolutionary project, all elements that enable the specter to become a politically active and socially relevant presence that incessantly haunts the present.

For the specter—and for all the other possible shapes that afterliving might take—to carry on with this posthumous existence, the corpse has to disappear from view. As Harrison points out, the afterlife becomes possible once the corpse has been "consigned to earth or air," implying it must become invisible either through incineration or burial deep in the ground, where hermetically sealed caskets ensure that its rotting matter remains safely contained. This argument opens Harrison's first chapter, where he notes that "to realize their fate and become truly dead [the dead] must first be made to disappear. It is because their bodies have a place to go that their souls or images or words may attain an afterlife of sorts among the living" (2003, 1). However, this need for places where bodies can go after their death is not only connected to the desire for them to stay among us and live the afterlife our imagination crafts for them; in creating these places, we are also protecting the sensorium of the living from the touch of death.

The many shapes of the afterlife Harrison talks about are, first and foremost, hygienic; the fact that different cultures make the dead stay among the living as souls, images, voices, heroes, and specters means that their bodies have been sterilely contained so they do not contaminate the living with sights, smells, and tastes that the living body rejects both consciously and viscerally. This act of sterilizing the dead adopts different forms, most obviously incineration and burial "six feet under" to ensure that body parts do not suddenly resurface and scare unsuspecting mourners or contaminate them with the bacteria that feed on rotting flesh. In some cases, the obtrusive familiarity of the dead is further counteracted by confining their bodies to strictly circumscribed places such as cemeteries that are located far from the most populated areas of cities, and by locking them in hermetically sealed caskets, which are themselves sealed inside steel or cement burial vaults. Sometimes, however, the bodies of the dead are kept close and even publicly displayed, as with the relics displayed in churches all over the world. Yet, even in those cases, the flesh and bones are there to be venerated but never touched, as guaranteed by the reliquaries in which they are exhibited. As Harrison argues, saints' bodies are not exhibited qua corpses but appear as "somehow 'alive' with expectation and animated by futurity"; that is, they are not there as reminders of the materiality of death but rather as evidence of things unseen—miracles, resurrection, the Kingdom of God—the promise of which then turns relics into "monuments of projected hope" (2003, 118).

Keeping bodies hidden—or keeping them out in the open but safely locked behind protective glass—not only shields us from their assault on our senses but also creates an illusion of ontological stability and finality that is essential for processes of mourning, remembering, and forgetting. These processes can only start after the body is "put to rest"; when that does not happen—when the body's whereabouts remain unknown—the event of death remains unfinished or unrealized, which means that mourning is displaced by the imperative to engage in a search that can only end with the burial of any kind of remains, no matter how small. This is why Harrison speaks of "an obligation to the corpse" that requires "disposing of it deliberately and ceremonially" and that ultimately translates into being able to tell exactly when a life ends and where the line that separates the dead and the living is (2003, 143). This "it" that Harrison uses to refer to the corpse is not insignificant; it evinces the kind of relationship we establish with the bodies of the dead, which is very different from the kind we have with the dead's afterliving image. While the latter's animated nature requires that we address the deceased using personal pronouns that imbue them with lively presence, the former's visible lack of livingness reduces the corpse to an it, to the realm of objects. Yet the corpse does not share the object's perceived stability; while on the outside it might seem immobile and unchanging, on the inside gases are produced and released, worms move around and reproduce, organs change color and shape, and so on—all processes that are nevertheless consistently hidden from view because they are only fully confronted in typically inaccessible or specialized places like the morgue or the medical school's amphitheater, because they are halted through the use of chemicals that delay decomposition, or because organs are removed and donated before they start to perish.

These processes are to a degree unacknowledged in Harrison's discussion of the dominion of the dead. While the journey that the dead's bodily matter embarks upon is certainly alluded to throughout the text and particularly in the opening chapter's discussion of graves and how the "human returns to the humus" (2003, 2), Harrison quickly draws our attention away from perishing—understood as matter's return to earth—and toward dying and the afterlives that are made possible through the distinctively human effort of turning the former into the latter. In fact, even when he looks right at the corpse, what he sees is a lifeless mass that becomes "the site of something that has disappeared, that has forsaken the sphere of presence, that has passed from the body into . . . into what? Death? The past? Another dimension?" (92). He argues that those who see the corpse gain access to the ethos of finitude and grapple with the absence of a presence and with absence rendered present. Harrison thus presents the corpse as the material representation of a void, and, in doing so, he does away with and does without its decomposing matter, going on to discuss the many ways in which death establishes and solidifies relations between the dead and the living.

In proposing the term "afterdeath" I am drawing our attention precisely to that decomposition: to the changes rotting flesh experiences, to the textures of putrefaction that we find intolerable, to the malleability of a corpse that threatens us with the accidental touch of the matter of death. As a concept, the afterdeath shares with the afterlife the imperative to go beyond what is considered "the end" but presents a different take on what that journey does and looks like. There is no transcendence in the afterdeath: death itself is neither ritualized nor overcome; instead, its mechanisms—the ways in which it transforms bodily matter—carry on alongside and in spite of what is rendered visible through remembrance or invisible through oblivion. Consequently, instead of the body afterliving and becoming ethereal—whether supernaturally or through memorialization—it becomes an uncontainable explosion of materiality.

Just as it acknowledges and brings into view the body's perishing, the afterdeath also makes us aware of a time that does not surround and frame the body but rather locates itself within the body, merging with the movements that occur as matter begins to rot. This time is not tied to eventfulness and abstraction but to the vibrations and micro-occurrences of putrefaction. Highlighting these organic movements, I call this time a "tempo" to draw a clear distinction between the time inside the corpse and the temporality outside it. This outside temporality, I propose, works around the body by inserting it in the framework of events and narratives that purport to give it social, political, cultural, and historical meaning. It is what enables the dead to become souls, heroes, images, ancestors, voices, and specters—to borrow Harrison's list—precisely because it allows them to afterlive by ensuring that they remain a part of the collective imaginaries and institutions that dictate what living is and looks like. Tempo, on the other hand, does not work on the body but from within its remains, registering the almost millimetric pace of their decomposition and thus guaranteeing the survival of uncontainable bodily matter that escapes signifying matrixes either because it is invisible to them or because it is always mutating and spilling over.

Though elsewhere I have discussed the afterdeath in relation to the material excess registered in works of contemporary Venezuelan fiction that zoom in and linger on the body's literal and explicit decomposition (see Troconis 2023b), in the following chapter I tie this act of decomposition to the raw state of the bodies Castillo creates using malleable clay. This rawness, I will argue, causes the "before" and the "after" of the idol to overlap and collapse. The "before" in this context is situated in the space of the artist's workshop: a space of crafting and incompleteness, of trying out and discarding, where the idol—the end result—is put on hold, its shape yet to be determined. The "after" is situated in the catacomb, specifically, *inside the grave*, where a form of intimacy is developed with the corpse itself: with its decomposing matter and with the matter of its undoing.

The result of this multitemporal intimacy is not the vanishing—or the banishing—of the specter, but rather the possibility of thinking about the dead, and about our relationship to them and to our collective past, differently. The materiality of the body discussed in the following chapter invites us to experience time outside the temporality of the national narratives that fuel the specter's afterlife; in other words, it frees us from the responsibility of chasing after the always postponed Bolivarian epic by showing us a time that means nothing, promises nothing, and asks for nothing. Moreover, this materiality brings about agency: a transformative power that does not come from the past but that acts on it and on its dead, that allows us to critically consider how much we owe to them and how much they owe to us, and that also leaves us free to walk away from them, if we want. Thus, while Castillo's performances, I argue, are indeed concerned with opening up a path for new ways of engaging with the past, they also set the stage for us to imagine other political futures where we and not our dead, no matter how heroic, are the protagonists.[2]

Let us then move away from the light radiating from the specter we now see, perhaps with different eyes, most likely with exhaustion, hopefully with the awareness of a haunted subject that recognizes themselves as haunted and that is ready—and a little afraid as well—to test the limits of the familiar and the comfortable in an effort to step outside the specter's gaze. Let us head into the shadows, not in search of new, better, and shinier images, but in search of a space of irreverent, unbounded imagination.

Let us, at last, commit to the living.

Raw and Rotten

5

Child, if you live long enough, you will learn the value of a set of eyes that do not watch you and a pair of lips that never speak.

Maria Romasco Moore, *Ghostographs*

Goodbye Kiss

Let us go back to where it all started, which is where it all ended. On the night of March 5, 2013, Venezuela's vice president, Nicolás Maduro, announced the death of Hugo Chávez to the nation and to the world. Following the news, millions in the country entered a state of mourning that manifested itself in a myriad of ways—tears and prayers, altars and insistent denial, flowers and graffiti, tattoos and red T-shirts—each a demonstration of love and a commitment to eternally remember the Comandante Eterno. While this multifaceted mourning unfolded, progressively mutating into the sort of animating force that births specters, Venezuelan artist Deborah Castillo was French-kissing Simón Bolívar. From February to April 2013 in Caracas's Centro Cultural Chacao, her video performance *The Emancipatory Kiss* (Castillo 2013b), which showed her kissing, licking, and sucking a golden statue of the Liberator for three and a half minutes, played as part of her exhibition *Action and Cult* (Castillo 2013a) (figure 5.1). The overlap

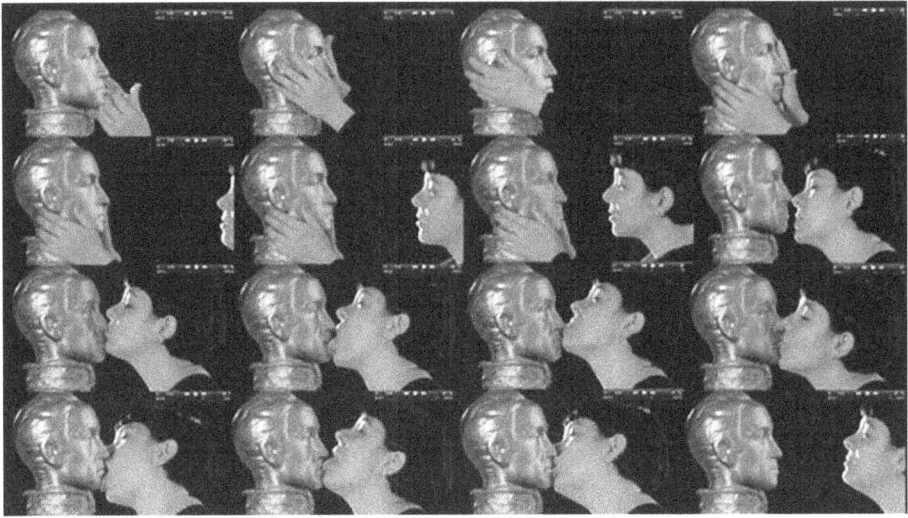

5.1 Deborah Castillo, sequence from *The Emancipatory Kiss* (2013). Photo: @deborah castillo studio. Courtesy of Deborah Castillo.

of Chávez's death and Castillo's kiss, of the national imperative to mourn and the irreverence of this erotic act, became intolerable, particularly (but not exclusively) for government supporters whose outrage ultimately won Castillo the title of "profaner of the fatherland" and drove her to leave Venezuela the following year.

Miguel Pérez Pirela, the host of the now defunct government-sponsored television show *Cayendo y corriendo*, verbalized this outrage in an episode broadcast in March 2013. In it, he showed the audience a still image of Castillo's performance that captured one of the moments when her tongue caresses Bolívar's chin and asked:

> Is this art? This is an unscrupulous act of disrespect against the memory and image of the father Liberator Simón Bolívar. . . . If there is anything that Chávez taught us, it is to love the figure of Bolívar. This, children . . . this, children, is a lack of respect . . . this is a lack of respect for our Liberator. This is not art, this is not art, this is a lack of respect for the figure of the Father of the Fatherland, for the Father of the Fatherland.[1]

Pérez Pirela also showed an image from Castillo's video performance *Sisyphus* (2013c), where she uses a chisel to simultaneously destroy and rebuild—though Pérez Pirela strategically ignored the rebuilding part in his description—a clay bust of Bolívar. More than his words, what stands out in Pérez Pirela's commentary is his anger, palpable in his brusque gestures and long, dramatic pauses. He is angry because Castillo's performances are considered art, angry because the children of the nation—he primarily addresses the children he imagines are watching him—have to witness her disrespecting their father, angry because she is ignoring Chávez's command to love Bolívar, and angry because the opposition, which he immediately associates with Castillo's exhibit, had at that time named one of their political groups after Bolívar. However, what is perhaps even more noteworthy is Pérez Pirela's choice to show *The Emancipatory Kiss* and *Sisyphus* together, treating them as if they were doing the same thing: kissing/disrespecting/destroying Bolívar. It was as if, in order to make sense of what Castillo's kiss meant—in order to pinpoint what made it so outrageous—he had to associate it with a performance where the destruction of the Liberator's face was unmistakable. However, kissing Bolívar is not the same as chiseling off his face, making it explode, or slapping it until it separates from his neck and falls to the ground.[2] Furthermore, inasmuch as kissing is often a sign of love, Castillo's kiss seems to follow *to the letter* Chávez's instructions to love Bolívar. Why, then, was Pérez Pirela so upset by Castillo's kiss? And, is it only him who is upset, or are we also disturbed by Castillo touching, kissing, sucking, and licking Bolívar's face?

Elsewhere I argued that what makes Castillo's kiss so intolerable not only to Pérez Pirela but to her audiences in general has to do with how she mobilizes obscenity as Roland Barthes understands it—that is, in terms of anachronism: "Whatever is anachronic is obscene. As a (modern) divinity, History is repressive. History forbids us to be out of time. Of the past we tolerate only the ruin, the monument, kitsch, what is *amusing*: we reduce this past to no more than its signature" ([1977] 2010, 177; see also Troconis 2023a). These "signatures" that Barthes mentions—ruins, monuments, kitsch—suck the "pastness" out of the past: an act of temporal exorcism that ensures that the past afterlives, that it lives *after* itself, and thus not *as* itself, that it inhabits the present as present (and also, optimistically, as future), hygienically self-contained, allowed to decay (as ruins do) but never to rot (as corpses do). Destroying a monument, tearing down a statue, removing the ruins: these actions might be disturbing, but they are not obscene. There is nothing obscene, nothing anachronic, about the present doing some decluttering, making space for new objects and the past that they commemorate, for shiny new mirrors where we can see our (updated) identity reflected—a perk of, or perhaps the main reason for, using glossy marble and polished bronze in statues, monuments, and plaques. A kiss that renounces veneration in favor of seduction, a kiss that acts, as Luce Irigaray puts it, as a "threshold unto *mucosity*" (quoted in Ives 2013, 62) where the solidity of the past and its narratives gets tested/tasted and where the icon is not an icon but a (metallic, gross) flavor . . . *that* is anachronism, an obscene encounter, a temporal faux pas. Castillo herself underscores this when she describes *The Emancipatory Kiss* as being "about impossibility. . . . Time in the erotic act dilates and contracts" (in Tiniacos and Alvarado 2013). In that act, the icon finally merges with the material structure supporting it, allowing us in the process to discover and feel—us too—its materiality.

Experiencing (and tasting) the materiality of the icon is at the center of what I have called "erotic iconoclash": an act that, unlike conventional forms of iconoclasm, leads to the spoiling rather than the destruction of the icon (see Troconis 2023a). The discomfort that follows this spoiling— and that places Castillo's work in the category of "difficult works" proposed by Jennifer Doyle (2013)—transcends national boundaries and invites us to ask ourselves, regardless of where we are and what our ideological position or political identity is, how far are we willing to go and how creative and provocative are we willing to be when it comes to handling the past and the figures that populate it.

Though always important and unsettling, this question appeared with particular urgency in *The Emancipatory Kiss*, where it became entangled with Chávez's legacy. Pérez Pirela alludes to this legacy when he reminds his audience of Chávez's lessons regarding the love owed to the father of the fatherland. He argued that kissing/destroying Bolívar was wrong because it insulted both Bolívar and Chávez, who had placed Bolívar at the center of the revolution and who loved him with a theatrical excess that shocked and bothered many but that never led to anything comparable with Castillo's lustful kiss. Her kiss trespassed a boundary that the seemingly infinite images and words that circulated in honor of Bolívar—during Chávez's presidency but also since the moment the Liberator's remains were repatriated in 1842—had occluded almost to the point of erasure. It brought to the fore and made uncomfortably unavoidable the national anxiety policing what can and cannot be done to our honorable dead and, perhaps more importantly, the gaping void that opens up in our collective imaginary when we kiss our salvific male heroes goodbye. It was, thus, a threat to what (and to those whom) we have always known and, because of that, it was also an invitation to dwell in the anxiety caused by the unknown in order to discover what sort of agency we can acquire there, and what sort of imaginative acts discomfort might breed.

This chapter accepts Castillo's invitation. It takes her sticky, clay-stained hand and lets it lead us into the space of the afterdeath that her 2015 exhibition *RAW* stages. In this space, we will not be welcomed by familiar faces, nor will we find solutions, resolutions, or completion. Uncomfortable, disturbed, and perhaps a little aroused, we will traverse that space—a workshop-turned-catacomb—and become implicated in all sorts of inappropriate handling of dead matter and of the matters of the dead. The result, I argue, will not be shiny new dead for us to animate and be haunted by—someone previously forgotten by history, a better hero or heroine—but a new form of relationality that could lead us to develop a more reciprocal relationship with the past and to engage in more irreverent acts of imagining the future.

Messing Up the Nation

Deborah Castillo's oeuvre—particularly the work she has developed since 2013—locates her among an ever-growing group of artists and performers who have messed with Venezuela's national symbols and iconic figures in an effort to unsettle the power they hold and the restrictive frameworks they have put into place when it comes to defining which bodies can be welcomed into the nation and which must be banned from it. In this group, we find artists such as Alexander Apóstol, Juan José Olavarría, and Iván Candeo, whose works—which include photography, drawing, and performance—serve as "*countermemories* or *counternarratives* of the national body, as they revise some of the broken promises of the Venezuelan national project (among others, the country's utopian transformation into a modern nation through the *oil boom*; the credo of progress as an egalitarian and emancipatory ideal; the inclusion of subaltern subjectivities in the republican project)" (Arroyo Poleo 2015, 215; original emphasis). For Fabiola Arroyo Poleo, these artists respond to what in the context of Chávez's presidency was presented as a "memory boom" (180) that was tied to a historiographical project meant to rescue those who have been forgotten by what in the context of the Bolivarian Revolution was called "bourgeois historiography" (187).

A key part of this project, she argues, has been the "rescuing" of unknown (or very little-known) figures such as the cacique Guaicaipuro, the Black soldier Pedro Camejo (known as Negro Primero), Matea and Hipólita Bolívar (known as Negra Matea and Negra Hipólita, both Black women who worked for Bolívar's family), the caudillo Ezequiel Zamora, and the leaders of antislavery insurrections José Leonardo Chirino and Juan Andrés López del Rosario (Arroyo Poleo 2015, 194). While the imagery created around these figures was powerful and omnipresent—some of their images were printed on the new banknotes that came out in 2008—their impact on the country's historical record is limited by the fact that they are all circumscribed by the narrative of the Bolivarian Revolution and thus have become one more political instrument to advance its ideological project. Through their work, Apóstol, Olivarría, and Candeo question this form of political instrumentalization and, in the case of Apóstol, the seemingly compulsive reliance on epic masculinity as the ultimate source of all political power.

However, the unsettling of Venezuela's national symbols is not limited to the artistic production that emerged during the years of the Bolivarian Revolution. The thirty years that preceded Chávez's rise to power were marked by the subversive works of Carlos Zerpa and Juan Loyola, who used art installations and performance to criticize patriotism, corrupt institutions, the ritualization of power, and violence perpetrated in the sacred name of the nation.[3] Furthermore, and a hundred years earlier, several women were already challenging the monopolizing presence of Bolívar as part of the national exhibition organized under President Antonio Guzmán Blanco to commemorate the Liberator's birth. Beatriz González-Stephan offers a brilliant analysis of this challenge in "Subversive Needlework," where she recounts how, the year before the exhibition opened its doors, an official announcement had stated that no group was to be excluded from this act of commemoration, and special care was put into inviting Venezuelan women to present their handicrafts and demonstrate their skill (2015, 59). Women's participation was overwhelming, with hundreds of pieces that included carpet- and mat-making, textiles, weaving, and "hair art." In this last category, an unknown Miss J. Paz Guevara submitted an image of the heroine of Colombian independence, Policarpa Salavarrieta, embroidered with human hair. In González-Stephan's analysis, this portrait—and the other works by women in which, she notes, Bolívar's face was significantly absent—challenged the monopoly of father figures and notable men populating the collective imagination and turned the exhibition into a starting point to rethink gender and gendering in the country. For women, she notes, "the Exhibition was a political act that allowed them to rethink the nation, as well as to think themselves part of it. In a certain way, it gave them a voice, if only a voice expressed through the chisel or through needle and thread" (72).

Castillo then is not the first artist to question the behaviors and rhetoric that allow Bolívar to haunt the nation and dictate the shape and tone authority must acquire to be deemed legitimate. Her performances, however, stand out because of how they invite us to confront what Rebecca Schneider calls the "explicit body" at the center of an ever-expanding corpus of feminist performance work that interrogates "social cultural understandings of the 'appropriate' and/or the appropriately transgressive" (Schneider 1997, 3).[4] This explicit body makes itself visible through an explosive literality that collapses symbolic space, making apparent "the fetishistic prerogatives of the symbol by which a thing, such as a body or a word, stands by convention for something else" (6), and literalizing "that which such symbolism excludes, secret(e)ing that which such symbolism secrets" (16). It is a body that often renders the work of art that made it explicitly "difficult" in the sense Doyle gives to the word—that is, unbearable, unpleasant, and even painful for an audience that, faced with things "that 'feel' like life and therefore cut too close" (4), must grapple with the slow collapse of the boundaries that define that which we deem tolerable, both in art and in life.

In the case of Castillo, the literalizing operations Schneider refers to take place through the artist's "inappropriate" engagement with materiality, both the materiality of her own dynamic, secreting body and the materiality of an "other" whose body—always male, often made of bronze or clay—symbolizes the sacred body of power in Venezuela and elsewhere. In *Lamezuela* (2011), for instance, Castillo knelt down to lick the shiny black boots of a soldier. This was a live public performance in Maracaibo, Venezuela, that she repeated eight years later with the boots of two soldiers in São Paulo, Brazil. In 2013, the shiny leather of the boots was replaced by the shiny face of a golden statue of Bolívar in *The Emancipatory Kiss*. Then, in 2015, the artist's first solo exhibit in New York, titled RAW, showed Castillo masturbating the nose of a nameless military man made of clay, using the severed limbs of another one to caress her naked body, and slapping a bust of yet another caudillo until the clay head fell to the ground. In all these performances, an amalgam of flesh, clay, saliva, leather, water, and dust materialized to make apparent the depth of the national anxiety that polices how we engage with symbols of authority: the conditions and modalities that dictate if and how we can touch them and that guarantee no boundaries are crossed that would inadvertently (or advertently) collapse "obscenity into sacrality and sacrality into obscenity" (Schneider 1997, 16).

That collapse is precisely what Castillo stages in RAW. The result, as we will see in the following section, is the material undoing of the figure of the caudillo. This undoing does not leave behind a clean space that would let us hope for a clean slate, nor does it produce something we can take with us: another caudillo; a new body of authority; Castillo's own female body as the long-awaited replacement for the hypermasculine, epic body of power. Instead, it leaves us with a call to action, ensuring that we no longer have the privilege of consuming anything in silence ever again, or of claiming we were unaware of or not accountable for the shape and shaping of power.

The Flesh of the Past

Placed atop a tower of bricks in the middle of a dimly lit gallery, a bust welcomed the public that on September 22, 2015, attended the opening night of Castillo's solo exhibition RAW at Mandragoras Art Space in Queens, New York (Castillo 2015a). Though the head's identity was never explicitly revealed, there was no mystery regarding what it represented; the frown, the beard, and the military epaulettes gave it the authoritative air of the caudillo and brought to mind the boundless power historically embedded in that figure and its many visual iterations in the Latin American urban and political landscape. There was, however, something odd about Castillo's caudillo, which particularly stands out when we consider it alongside the bronze and marble busts and statues placed in plazas and public buildings. Next to those arresting and seemingly eternal commemorative objects, Castillo's caudillo appeared frail, incomplete, and uncannily human; built with wet, still-malleable clay, he seemed to be made of *flesh*.

This "bodily" quality of the bust was also present in the other clay figures that appeared in the videos that were projected all around the gallery space. In *The Unnamable* (2015d), a pair of hands and forearms—also made of clay—caressed Castillo, who slowly moved them over her face and down her chest, giving them a sensual dynamism that represented them not as objects but as lively appendages (figure 5.2). In *Demagogue* (2015b), the head of another nameless military figure made of raw clay appeared against a plain black background, and Castillo held his phallus-shaped nose, moving her hand up and down in a masturbating motion that made the nose "grow," leaving gray stains on her palms (figure 5.3). The visitors moving from one screen to the other were enclosed in the gallery by six hundred pounds of wet clay hand-pressed onto the windows, preventing light from fully entering the space and thus creating an atmosphere of shadows that evoked simultaneously the oppression of those military regimes led by the figures represented in the sculptures, the intimacy of a sexual encounter, and the dread of finding oneself face-to-face with the dead. The climax of the night came when Castillo stood in front of the bust of the caudillo and started

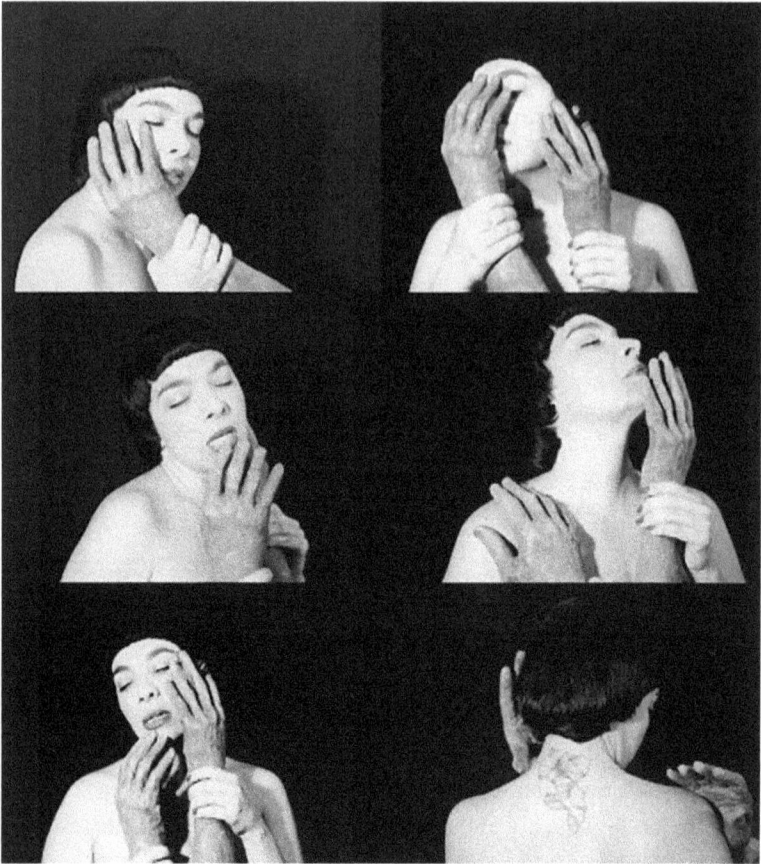

5.2   Deborah Castillo, *The Unnamable* (2015). Photo: Florencia Alvarado. Courtesy of Deborah Castillo.

slapping it, each slap disfiguring the head and separating it little by little from the neck until it finally gave way and fell to the ground.

This *live* performance—*Slapping Power* (2015c)—is part of a series of "affronts" that the artist has staged against the figure and body of the caudillo in an effort to call into question the structures of power that ground their authority in the feverish cult that this figure has historically awakened in Latin America (figure 5.4). Though this challenge to the power of the man in uniform resonates with the historical and political realities of countries all over the world, Castillo's performance work is also a response to a distinctively Venezuelan phenomenon that can be read as its own sort of performance: the cult of Bolívar. It is Bolívar and the parade of "Bolívar

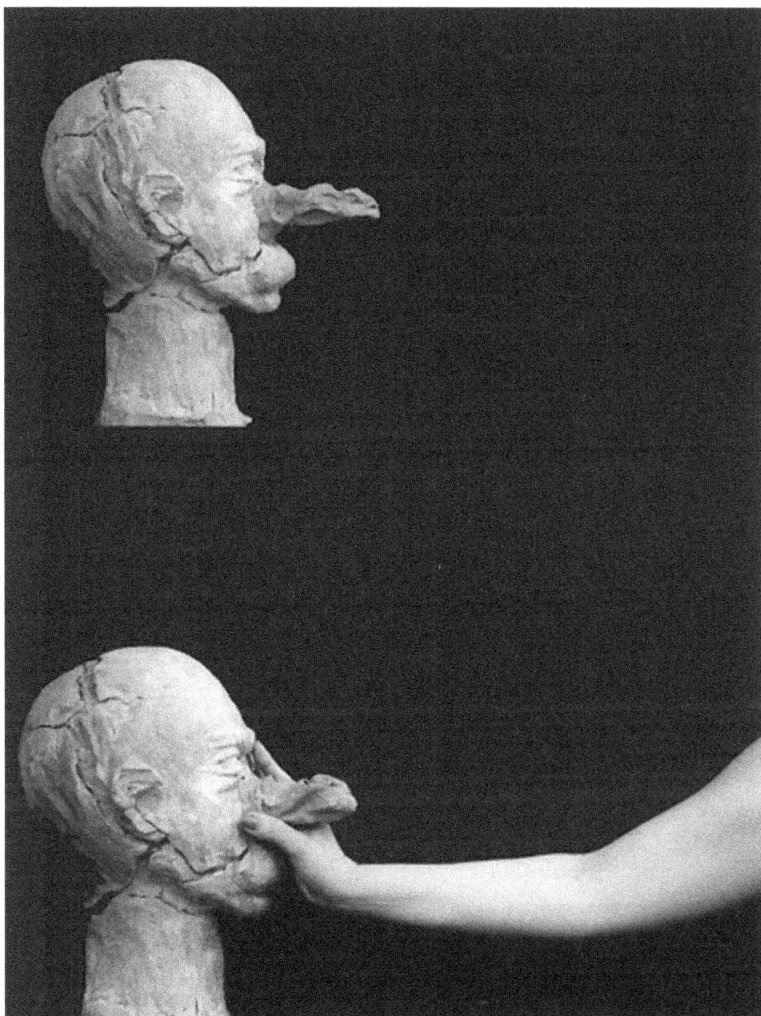

5.3 Deborah Castillo, *Demagogue* (2015). Photo: Florencia Alvarado. Courtesy of Deborah Castillo.

wannabes" that have governed the country since his death who have shown up in the artist's work since 2011—the year she performed *Lamezuela*. This piece—like Castillo's work since then—has been primarily discussed against the backdrop of the Bolivarian Revolution and the operations of power and subjugation that mediated the relationship between Chávez and the people. Castillo's work, however, goes beyond the political reality of contemporary Venezuela as it engages with the cult of Bolívar not only as a *chavista* phenomenon but as a national performance that, throughout history, has kept the country on its knees, burdened with the weight of Bolívar's unfulfilled dreams and always under the authority of his spectral gaze. In calling it a performance, I am emphasizing both the reiterated actions that are at the center of the cult—military parades, the construction of the many plazas named after Bolívar, the circulation of currency named after him, and so on—and the role that the body plays in perpetuating Bolívar's monopoly over the country's memory and identity: the kneeling in front of his image and the love expressed through submission or mimesis. These two elements—repetition and the body—are key in Castillo's work, where they are manipulated to take the cult to an extreme where what was once familiar becomes uncanny and repulsive. The magnitude and complexity of the artist's work make it impossible to discuss all of it in this chapter; thus, in what follows, the main focus will be on two of her actions performed for the camera: *The Unnamable* and *Demagogue*.

These two pieces—like all the other pieces exhibited as part of RAW— engage with the materiality and temporality of the statue and the role it has historically played not only in reproducing the body of the dead, but also in inserting it within the realm of the timeless and the sacred. As Katherine Verdery points out in *The Political Lives of Dead Bodies*:

> Statues are dead people cast in bronze or carved in stone. They symbolize a specific famous person while in a sense also *being* the body of that person. By arresting the process of that person's bodily decay, a statue alters the temporality associated with the person, bringing him into the realm of the timeless or the sacred, like an icon. For this reason, desecrating a statue partakes of the larger history of iconoclasm. Tearing it down not only removes that specific body from the landscape, as if to excise it from history, but also proves that because it can be torn down, no god protects it. (Verdery 1999, 5; original emphasis)

The two materials that Verdery mentions—bronze and stone—convey an impression of durability and completion that ensures that the body they create escapes processes of decay. Clay, particularly clay that is raw or unfired, does not have those properties; as the head of the man with the phallic nose in *Demagogue* reveals, sculptures made of raw clay can split, fall apart, and be easily manipulated or destroyed. Therefore, they seem to share the temporality of human flesh rather than the temporality of the gods, echoing the miraculous creation of man from clay that recurs throughout world religions

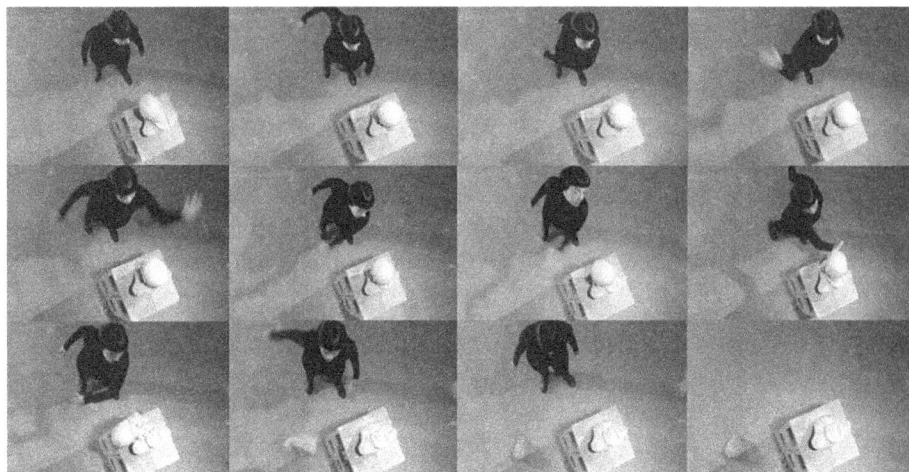

5.4 Deborah Castillo, sequence from *Slapping Power* (2015). Photo: Violette Bule. Courtesy of Deborah Castillo.

and mythologies. Castillo captures this "fleshiness" through the malleability of her sculpture and through the color and rough texture it acquires in pieces like *The Unnamable*, where the two hands appear unpolished, displaying the lines and folds of all human hands with a bluish-gray color that brings to mind the materiality of the corpse. Castillo thus intervenes in the temporality of an icon that has been rendered immortal through statues, not by removing one such statue from the urban landscape and, as Verdery puts it, "excising it from history," but rather by making her sculpture mortal from within, through a change in its materiality that allows it to remain as visible as it was before but that also renders it accessible to other (equally) mortal bodies such as Castillo's.

In fact, while in the actions performed for the camera the clay reproduces a sort of raw human flesh, that flesh is not and does not appear "alive." It is Castillo who gives it humanlike movement through her erotic engagement with the lips, nose, and hands, which then, at the mercy of the artist's body, end up acquiring a materiality that incorporates the slimy textures, fragile surfaces, and ashen coloring of the corpse.

In the hands of Castillo, that materiality becomes a site where concepts, temporalities, and affects that are typically at odds with each other intertwine: life and death, immortality and decay, the organic and the inorganic, love and rejection, seduction and repulsion all converge so as to trigger in the artist and in the audience equally conflicting reactions that invite an engagement with the dead that breaks with the dynamics of the cult. This engagement is central to the two aforementioned pieces and to Castillo's work overall; her sculptures and the dead they represent are not there as complete works demanding admiration or contemplation, but rather as (dead) bodies that pull live bodies in and out, in a sort of danse macabre that engages the three most intimate senses: taste, touch, and smell. As such, Castillo's sculptures are evocative of the kind of sculptures Georges Didi-Huberman, in *Being a Skull*, says are not "objects of space" but rather the transformation of "objects into subtle actions of a site, into *taking or having place*":

> In the first case, the completed object exhibits its closure by affirming its results, by rejecting the agent and the action (the process whereby it takes form) of a single past, according to a kind of forgetting of its own birth. In the second case, the sculpture tends to remain open and instead affirms the entanglement or lack of separation . . . it maintains between agent, action, and result. Each specific temporality of the work persisting within the others, enveloping them, and nourishing itself from them. (Didi-Huberman [2000] 2016, 45–46; original emphasis)

Castillo's sculptures do not succumb to the "forgetting of [their] own birth," nor are they immune to the threat of their own death; they are in a state of ongoing instability that is reinforced both by the artist's repetitive movements—which animate the otherwise still hands while wearing them away and bringing them closer to their destruction—and by the clay that is never solid enough to give the sculptures longevity. Thus, the sculptures stage the beginnings and endings that are erased from both the surface of statues and from the luminous immateriality of the specter. Consequently, Bolívar appears made of a kind of human material with the potential for decay that interferes with the magical aura that surrounds him when he is recreated in marble (a particularly long-lasting material) or bronze, which, in addition to being long lasting, also has the spellbinding effect of precious metals and the wealth they promise.

By transforming the iconic statue into a malleable sculpture, the specter into a body, and the body into a corpse, Castillo is not only inserting the icon in a different temporal framework—the fleeting one of raw clay—but she is also staging a sort of sensorial revolution, as suggested in the title of these two pieces. *The Unnamable* indeed forbids the act of naming and thus the conjuring that brings Bolívar's specter into being, and in doing so it hijacks the specter's capacity to address us and survey us, opening up a space for a different sense to take over: the sense of touch and, more specifically, the touch of Castillo's body. Something similar occurs in *Demagogue*; by denouncing in its title the manipulative oratory political leaders use to put their audience into a submissive trance, the piece drives attention away from the mouth—and its message—and toward the movements of the masturbating hand and the elongation of the nose.

Disturbing the balance among the senses can be read against the backdrop of a Western cultural tradition that conceptualizes sight as the principal category "by which the modern self has been understood to frame the world and separate it as an object of knowledge, understanding, and manipulation" (Smith 2007, 20). This is Mark Smith's argument in *Sensing the Past*, where he highlights the power dynamics embedded in the act of seeing, an act that "operates at a distance and with some power over the viewed" and that has the potential to fix and reify the objects and beings that exist in the field of vision (23). Along with hearing—which, Smith points out, has historically contributed to arranging and mediating forms of social organization and hierarchies (42)—sight has often been associated with order and rationality, while touch, taste, and smell have been relegated to the realm of the primitive and, if we follow Constance Classen's study of the European hierarchy of the senses, to the "female sensorium" (2005, 70).

This understanding of the senses—though it may skew toward an essentializing framework that does not encompass variations in the sensorial world across times, places, and cultures—highlights some of the ways in which the senses come into play in the context of the cult of figures such as Bolívar (and, more recently, Chávez) in Venezuela. The dynamics of this cult have been studied in depth by Venezuelan historian Germán Carrera Damas ([1969] 1973), who argued that the cult of Bolívar went from being a cult of the people and by the people to being a cult for the people—that is, a performance staged by those in power that made them the sole recipients of Bolívar's heritage and thus responsible for transmitting his will to the people. As a stately performance, the cult became a manipulative tactic serving the political interests of all Venezuelan dictators and presidents, who have consistently portrayed themselves as Bolivaroids leading the people to the glorious future where the nation would finally achieve Bolívar's dreams.

The process of deifying the hero occurred through the mobilization of the nation's eyes and ears, made to serve Bolívar and the fight he led for (always elusive) independence. As Carrera Damas, Elías Pino Iturrieta, and Ana Teresa Torres all point out, Bolívar's words broke free from their historical framework and spilled out into presents and futures, becoming a sort of timeless pattern or pious formula to be repeated carelessly and ad nauseam by those in power, who then appeared to be engaged in a compulsory act of ventriloquism that undergirded their authority and mobilized people's affective commitment to the Liberator. Citing fragments of Bolívar's speeches—in and out of context, faithfully and incorrectly—became compulsory in inaugural speeches, public events, military parades, and school activities. His words became a providential roar in Eduardo Blanco's *Venezuela heroica*—the epic tale of the wars of independence originally published in 1881 that is a staple in any Venezuelan home—and are on permanent display on official plaques and in murals and graffiti all over the country. With Chávez's government, listening to and repeating Bolívar's name became even more obligatory thanks to the president's decision to change the name of the country from República de Venezuela to República Bolivariana de Venezuela, and to use Bolívar's name as an adjective for everything from political parties and armed groups to social projects and food.

The frequency with which Bolívar's name is uttered is only matched by the frequency with which he is seen. Plazas, streets, avenues, schools, textbooks, stamps, figurines, coins, and banknotes: the country's visual landscape is shaped by his figure, one that the people also reproduce in a sort of collective dress rehearsal that begins with performing the "Padre de la Patria" in kindergarten and dressing like him for carnival, and that has ended in an act of sensuous mimesis whereby the president himself (Chávez) manages to look like him. In that sense, the demand to produce, reproduce, and re-reproduce Bolívar as an image seems to come, like the voice of the gods, both from behind (the past) and from above, a call to which every Venezuelan—including Castillo—must respond. The will-bending force of this demand is best summarized in the words that welcome those who visit the Museo Bolivariano in Caracas:

> The Liberator has commanded we erect monuments that remind future generations of the services rendered by those who were victorious at Ayacucho; but in their hearts is consecrated the monument that they have created to the son of glory. To the generous warrior who gave us a patria and turned us from slaves into soldiers of liberty and victory. On all of their hearts and in all of them is the statue of Bolívar. And we will leave it there for our children's children. So his memory may endure as long as the sun.

In this quote, Bolívar's statue occupies both public space and an intimate, affective one. Made of marble or bronze, he becomes a weight that must be passed on from generation to generation, all proudly claiming their title of "children of Bolívar," embracing the affective debt that comes with it, and participating in the endless re-creation of his figure so as to ensure that his memory "endures as long as the sun." This process of creation has an affective component that is encapsulated in filial love for a father figure, combining fear, admiration, and—most important—respect. This respect is a constant in the testimonies of the artisans whose figurines and paintings of Bolívar are exhibited in one of the rooms in the Museo Bolivariano. José Belandria, for instance, says: "Because when I was a little boy I learned that after God, Simón Bolívar. I do this work with the faith I put in him; it doesn't look much like the portraits that circulate around, but I give him my eyes, my nose, my hands . . . I give him my things that I make from the heart, I give him my respect." A carver named Goyito Bonilla shares a similar sentiment: "When I make Simón Bolívar, I do it with love and respect because that's how statues should be made, and if he is the Father of the Patria, all the more reason, because if ordinary fathers deserve respect, doesn't the father of a nation?"[5]

In highlighting the role respect plays in shaping their relationship with Bolívar, these accounts also call attention to the distance needed for that respect to materialize. Respect, which comes from the Latin verb "respicere," meaning "look back at, regard," operates in the realm of sight; thus, it relies on the power sight has to stabilize and assign boundaries and order to that which is seen.[6] To see something—and to see it clearly—means to leave the right amount of space between the person who sees and that which is seen; too close and the object of the gaze becomes blurry, too far and it becomes indistinguishable from the background. Thus, to see—and, consequently, to respect—means to ensure that the (seen/respected) other remains "over there." This does not mean that whoever sees and whomever/whatever is seen remain unaffected; both can be moved by the act, and in the context of Bolívar, all Venezuelans are required to feel something while looking at his image. Therefore, though the artisans cited in the museum exhibit work with their hands and thus engage with a sense that operates through the intimacy of surfaces coming into contact, the final product of their work—the figurine, painting, or carving—brings Bolívar close enough to be admired and respected, but not so close that the surfaces of his body/sculpture can be manipulated by others' transformative and sensuous touch. Creating an image thus involves maintaining a respectful distance that also allows for sounds—in the shape of words—to travel to and from Bolívar and his "offspring."

This brief journey through the different dynamics that are at the center of the cult of Bolívar in Venezuela is certainly incomplete. Nevertheless, the purpose behind exploring the behaviors that such a cult demands from the bodies of the nation is to foreground the cult's sensorial dimension. After all, cults are, first and foremost, interventions in the senses: the eyes looking up and down; the commands and prayers leaving the tongue and entering the ears; the bodies engaged in the synchronized standing up, bowing, kneeling, and reenacting. Power materializes in those movements, in the decision regarding who gets to look up and who gets to look down, who formulates the message and who obeys it. Narratives and memory practices also take shape on this sensorial level: the past that returns does so not just as a remembrance but as and through bodily sensations or interpellation by a pair of eyes that requires the body to stiffen and respectfully succumb to the authority of the figure behind them. To challenge such power and such narratives then, it becomes necessary to intervene in—to manipulate, hijack, short-circuit—the senses that preserve them and that enable their functioning and transmission. This is where Castillo's work comes in.

In RAW, the question that Castillo asks repeatedly is: What do we do with Bolívar (and his many proxies)? In the context of Venezuela and in light of the cult explored above, asking this question is already problematic. You do not do things to Bolívar, *Bolívar does things to you*: he frees you, commands you, guides you, protects you, possesses you, and loves you. This love is reciprocal and chaste; it is a platonic love that combines the respect due to Bolívar as a national hero and father with the unrestrained evocation of his name. Faced with such love and the possibilities that its abstract, platonic nature offers to those in power, Castillo responds with something that Venezuelan historian Tomás Straka in his analysis of *The Emancipatory Kiss* calls a literal representation of that love: "We have drawn close to Bolívar, indeed, for better and for worse. We have said so much of him, we have alleged so much about him, we have declared so much that we love him. We've slobbered all over Bolívar. Deborah Castillo is the first person to create a representation of that" (2013, 6). I would, however, propose that we read Castillo's work—particularly the works in RAW—as neither love nor a representation of love.

While the initial tenderness we see in Castillo's gestures and in the movement of her body as she approaches the head or the clay limbs might be taken for love, what follows is an act of carnal excess that resists naming and the legibility of clearly demarcated and identifiable emotions. This excess results from the contrast between colors, surfaces, materials, and times that find themselves in unlikely resonance. The term "resonance" carries different meanings across disciplinary boundaries and discursive contexts. As Susanna Paasonen (2011) points out, it has been used to refer to richness or significance, to the intensification and prolongation of sound, and to sympathetic vibrations, all of which she relates to the sort of engagement online users have with pornographic images and the technologies of transmission behind them. But Paasonen also highlights the material side of resonance, the visceral sensations and vibrations that are caused by the encounter between bodies and images: "The concept also points to the material factors of porn—the fleshy substance of the human body; the texture of images, screens, and signals; the technologies of transmission and the materialities of hardware, cables, and modems" (2011, 17).

This kind of material resonance is at play in the interaction that takes place in Castillo's videos as they bring together contrasting colors (Castillo's black outfit and red nails versus the sculpture's gray exterior), contrasting surfaces (Castillo's smooth skin versus the cracks in the clay), contrasting times (Castillo's present versus the sculpture as representation of the past, the video recording as simultaneously present and past), and contrasting matter (Castillo as organic/living matter, the sculpture as inorganic/cadaverous matter). When Castillo touches the phallic nose, it leaves stains on her hand; the sculpted hands leave an imprint on her skin. These material residues that the resonance between these contrasting elements leaves behind, along with the presence of the technology that projects them, the dust that accumulates on the gallery floor, and the clay falling from the windows, all insert the bodies that take part in the performances into a dynamic of textural perception that opens up a path for a different engagement with the past.

A key element in this engagement with the past that Castillo performs is a change in the way the past, represented in the sculpture of the caudillo, is perceived. The eyes' and ears' role enabling communication between past and present is shut down. Seeing and everything that goes into it—the open eyes, the distance, the power dynamics, the organizing and rationalizing—does not take place in either performance. In the case of *The Unnamable*, this is because Castillo's eyes remain closed throughout; she appears to be in a pleasurable state in which the limbs perceive each other blindly, relying only on the sensual rubbing of surfaces that include Castillo's skin and, briefly, the inside of her lower lip and right nostril, which introduce the possibility of tastes and smells that further intensify the intimacy between the two bodies. In the case of *Demagogue*, Castillo's eyes are not even in the frame, and the sculpture's eyes appear to be closed, the eyelids protruding and as misshapen as the rest of the features, which, by reproducing simultaneously facial features (eyes, nose, mouth) and external male genitalia (the penis and the testicles), further hinder the ability of the eyes (Castillo's, the audience's, and the sculpture's) to see, totalize, and organize. The sculpture's eyelids appear to be glued shut with the sticky fluid that drips down the chin/testicles and that seems to come from both the sculpture's nose/penis and from Castillo's wet hand. Similarly, hearing and speaking have been excluded from both performances. Neither has sound of any kind; in both, the ears are blocked either by Castillo's hair or by clay, and in both the mouth remains quiet either because Castillo does not open it (*The Unnamable*) or because it seems to be stuffed with the testicles hanging below the nose/penis (*Demagogue*).

With both hearing and sight disabled, perception becomes textural. Texture is "the visual and tactile surface characteristics and appearance of something," "basic scheme or structure," or "a pattern of musical sound created by tones or lines played or sung together."[7] As such, it involves more than just the sense of touch; it engages sight and hearing, the latter not only in the context of music but also when we hear the creaking of leather pants or the crunch of French fries. The word's etymology, however, points us to something much more sensual. It derives from the Latin word "textura" and from the verb "texere," which means "to weave" and brings to mind the movement of interlacing threads, one caressing the other as it goes first over it, then under it, each small action slowly driving time forward as it traces the journey that will later, when the work is complete, be known as "the making of."

Castillo's movement and the way it interacts with the surface of the clay head or the clay hands mirror this weaving; as flesh and clay come together and give pleasure to each other, what stands out is not the finished product but the *ongoingness* of the action and the energy that drives it forward and that marks the surfaces of the bodies it engages. In fact, finishing—understood both sexually and in the more general sense—is not part of either of these performances or of the other pieces that make up Castillo's exhibition. The title of the exhibition suggests as much: RAW refers to that which is unpolished, unfinished, or unprocessed, and also to sore surfaces on the body that have been exposed to harsh, continuous friction—both elements that are present in *The Unnamable* and in *Demagogue*, as well as in the slapping of the caudillo's clay head. In *The Unnamable*, in addition to the friction of the clay limbs that Castillo rubs against her naked body, there is the promise of ongoingness that materializes as the hands move downward and the image vanishes from the screen, thus leaving the following, more intimate action suspended but palpable and imaginable for the audience. In *Demagogue*, Castillo's rubbing of the nose/penis does not finish the sculpture, but rather keeps it going, making it grow and, when it cannot grow anymore, leaves it hanging with a crack in the tip, which makes those watching hold their breath as they wait for the nose to finally fall from the face—which it never does.

The energy that drives these performances is not the same kind of energy that gives Bolívar (and Chávez) his spectral afterlife; there is no transcendence, no luminosity, no mesmerizing spectacle, and no spiritual possession of a body that would allow power to carry on. Instead, the energy is physical. It jumps from body to body, from matter to matter, leaving marks and bumps that break, fracture, and undo, and that drive attention away from the result and to the whole experience of the "making of." Textures are key in this experience and in the relationship it establishes with the bodies from the past. Not only are textures evidence of the circulation of that physical energy—a sexual energy that focuses exclusively on pleasure—but they enable what Eve Kosofsky Sedgwick, when discussing Renu Bora's work on texture, calls an "active narrative hypothesizing, testing, and re-understanding of how physical properties act and are acted upon over time" (2003, 13). Bora, Sedgwick points out, distinguishes between two kinds or senses of texture, which he labels "texture" with one x and "texxture" with two. The latter is dense with information about how an object historically and materially came into being. It is the kind of texture one would find on a pot bearing the scars and uneven sheen of its making (14). The former, on the other hand, "defiantly or even invisibly blocks or refuses such information" (14); it is the kind of polished or glossy texture that signifies the willed erasure of its history and, I propose, the kind that is to be found on the bronze or marble statues of national heroes like Bolívar. These statues are representations of history; their surfaces are polished to perfection so that they can accurately replicate the features of the heroes. Thus, they are finished works that lend stability and legibility to history, a history that does not go inward—into the materiality and the making of the statue itself—but is projected outward, into the realm of the symbolic that is filled with powerful abstract concepts such as heroism, authority, freedom, and independence, all concepts that, like the smooth surfaces of the statues themselves, do not admit distracting bumps or sharp edges.

Unlike these statues, Castillo's sculptures display all kinds of texxtures. In *The Unnamable*, the hands that caress Castillo's face and body are covered in bumps and cracks, which, in conjunction with the various tonalities of gray, make the audience aware of the different steps and instruments that went into elaborating a sculpture that is not yet done but is still ongoing. In *Demagogue*, the variety of the textures becomes even more evident because Castillo plays with the consistency of the clay; while the clay used to mold the head appears to have solidified, the clay that makes up the nose is in a precarious state of rawness emphasized by the liquid dripping from it and by the gray stain it leaves on her palm. Watching the videos, then, is akin to having been granted access to the backstage of a show that never takes place or to the workshop of an artisan who never exhibits the finished piece. That is, to spaces of folding, cutting, and constructing; spaces filled with raw materials, residues, and tools; spaces where the question is never "What could it do to me/demand from me?" but rather "What could I do with it?" This last question is something that, Sedgwick argues, comes with perceiving texture:

> To perceive texture is never only to ask or know What is it like? Nor even just How does it impinge on me? Textural perception always explores two other questions as well: How did it get that way? And What could I do with it? . . . Even more immediately than other perceptual systems, it seems, the sense of touch makes nonsense out of any dualistic understanding of agency and passivity; to touch is always already to reach out, to fondle, to heft, to tap, or to enfold, and always also to understand other people or natural forces as having effectually done so before oneself, if only in the making of the textured object. (Sedgwick 2003, 13–14)

Perceiving textures thus means to be drawn *into* the object or body, to be inserted into its history—one that has nothing to do with events but rather with the twists and turns of the materiality shaped to represent and evoke them—and to be put in a sort of tactile dialogue with those who have left their fingerprints on the surface and who will continue to do so in the future. From this exchange emerges, I propose, a change in the relationship with the iconic dead figures that have haunted the nation. As the statues' polished surfaces and the specter's ethereality are replaced by rough surfaces, incomplete pieces, raw matter asking to be touched, shaped, and even destroyed, as Bolívar's haunting is challenged by the material history of texture and the ongoing making of the incomplete object, the weighty burden of the past becomes lighter. Rather than asking, What does the specter (of Bolívar, Chávez, the caudillo in general) want from us? What do we owe it? we can ask, What can (not "should") we do with its body and to it? And, perhaps, What does it owe us? Asking these questions means daring to imagine a relationship with the past whereby the dead do not choose for us, nor do they always have their way with us. Instead, we have our way with them, molding them and breaking them and slapping them at will, without shame and with no strings attached, an ongoing process of creation that, to quote Robert Pogue Harrison, keeps open a "'reciprocative rejoinder' that never simply denies but freely avows the will of the ancestors—and not only of the ancestors but also of those around us who, with sanctimonious piety, seek to make the historical present conform to an 'outstripped' past" (Harrison 2003, 102). With her body, Castillo performs this "reciprocative rejoinder," translating it into a bodily resonance where agency is not enabled by inheritance or the need to respond to a command, but rather exists in and is fueled by the realm (the presentness) of uncompliant pleasure.

The agency Castillo stages vis-à-vis a past that ceases to be spectral and becomes, thanks to the artist's energy and the touch of her body, malleable and challengeable, is a step toward developing a more reciprocal, constructive relationship with the dead that does not reproduce the dynamics of surveillance and obedience mediating haunting and the cult of heroes. The artist's work, however, takes the need to be freed from the allure of the specter one step further by putting the audience in a position where they must struggle with the visceral and excessive modality of the image they are made to see over and over again—an image that, I propose, is not just of the artist and her sensual intercourse with her clay sculptures, but also of her and her sensual intercourse *with a dead body*.

Though the sculptures' texxtures signal, as I have argued, their material history and the ongoingness of their "making of"—and, consequently, the making of the idol—they also evoke the appearance and consistency of a corpse. This is particularly true of *Demagogue* and *The Unnamable*, though the cadaverous aesthetic is not entirely absent from other pieces in the exhibition. In both of these performances, the clay figures' gray-and-blue coloring brings to mind ashen corpses, and their rough surfaces along with the involuntary mobility of the arms and the masturbated nose bring to mind decomposing flesh. The clay on the windows further contributes to this atmosphere of intimacy with the dead: blocking the entrance of natural light and slowly hardening until pieces fall onto the ground, the clay seems to lock the audience inside a crypt filled with decomposing bodies. Rather than putting these bodies to rest, Castillo engages in a sensual intercourse with them that brings together the pleasure that comes from witnessing the eroticism of the movements Castillo's naked body performs and the disgust that results from the realization that there is a corpse-like figure on the receiving end of that erotic performance. The audience then is not put in a position of passively watching Castillo but is pulled in and out—grabbed and pushed away—by the visceral interpellation of this combination of pleasure and disgust that invites at once proximity and recoil.

In "Absolutely Disgusting," Paasonen's conceptualization of disgust draws on the work of social historian William Ian Miller and phenomenologist Aurel Kolnai, who identify tight connections between disgust and "the embodied, biological, sexual, and material and associate the affect of disgust with particular material properties and textures" (Paasonen 2011, 211). Both see disgust as oriented toward the excessively carnal—things such as rotting flesh—and as necessitating turning away from and distancing oneself from the object of disgust. Furthermore, they argue that "disgust is immediate and sensory: it is experienced by smelling, touching, or seeing its cause in the rancid, filthy, sticky, excessively soft, or oozing object" (211). This understanding of what makes an object disgusting resonates with the kind of objects Castillo engages with. The sculptures in *The Unnamable* and *Demagogue* are falling apart or almost falling apart, the features distorted, the consistency visually unappealing, and, in the case of *Demagogue*, "excessively soft," oozing some substance that stains Castillo's hand. These characteristics alone make viewers pull back. Yet, as Sara Ahmed argues, before pulling back, the body has to come close, for it is only through such sensuous proximity that the object is experienced as disgusting in the first place:

> Disgust brings the body perilously close to an object only then to pull away from the object in the registering of the proximity as an offence. . . . Hence the proximity of the "disgusting object" may feel like an offence to bodily space, as if the object's invasion of that space was a necessary consequence of what seems disgusting about the object itself. Pulling back, bodies that are disgusted are also bodies that feel a certain rage, a rage that the object has gotten close enough to sicken and to be taken over or taken in. (Ahmed 2015, 86)

This double movement—coming closer and pulling back—is at the center of the audience's relationship with Castillo's performances: their condition as artistic performances pulls the audience in (to get a better look, to appreciate the piece), the revolting textures make them recoil; the allure of the familiar figure of the caudillo draws them back in, the similarity to a corpse pushes them away; the sensuality excites them and brings them back in, the sensuality *with the dead* makes them pull away. The rage that Ahmed mentions is also present, particularly when thinking about these two performances alongside *The Emancipatory Kiss*, discussed in the previous section. Pérez Pirela's rage over that piece had to do with Castillo herself, with what she was daring to do to Bolívar (and also to Chávez and his legacy), with the sickening (for him) proximity between her undeserving body and the glorious figure of the Liberator. Here, however, it is the caudillo who is gross, his decomposing body staining the surface of Castillo's skin, his material pastness contaminating the space of Castillo's—and the audience's—presentness: death thus inappropriately and grossly rubbing against life.

Recoiling from, being disgusted by, and distancing oneself from the father of the fatherland: all these actions—forbidden and thus subversive in the context of Venezuela's cult of Bolívar—are made possible thanks to Castillo's excessive proximity to the sculpture-corpse. These sculpture-corpses, like the spectral presence of Bolívar, are remains: what gets left behind, the past that stays anchored in the present, the evidence of an ongoing act of disappearance. Yet, while the specter operated in the realm of ethereality and of authoritative, hygienic commands and prayers, Castillo's sculptures allow the past to acquire the material weight of its pastness, the textures and decay of the history it is part of. Thus, they invite the development of a new historical sensibility whereby the figures of the past do not just appear or reappear but are "being made"; Castillo grants the audience access to the *making of the hero*, to the rawness of the body before it is captured by the epic, to its unstable materiality before it dries into an idol. This privileged access to the backstage of history represents a change in the sensorial dimension of the relationship we establish with the past; the ongoingness of the sculptures and the corresponding rawness of the clay they are made of quiet and blind that past so that what is left is a textural perception that ultimately allows us to ask: What can we do to the past? Simple as this question might be, it represents a shift in the power relations that otherwise enable haunting to become a practice of national memory and to serve as a mechanism to ground and legitimize political authority.

This call to acknowledge and accept the transformative power of this agency over the rawness of the past is accompanied by a cadaverous aesthetic that prompts recoiling from that past; dripping, ashen, and uncannily soft, the body of the caudillo triggers disgust as it evokes the materiality of a corpse, which, thanks to Castillo's bold movements, gets too close, too intimate. Taken together, these two actions—getting close so as to do something to the past, stepping back in reaction to its grossness—inject dynamism into the relationship with the (no-longer-so-glorious) dead that brings to mind Harrison's central argument regarding intercourse with the dead, which must be, he argues, "frank and ongoing" (2003, 102). The frankness of this intercourse depends, I propose, on acknowledging its complexity; the dead never "just" appear, they cannot "just" be invoked, they cannot "just" be emulated or resuscitated. As Castillo's work shows, the dead are raw and textured, they are dirty and gross, and it is precisely this complex materiality that allows us ultimately to make them our own, with the meaning of "making them our own" left open to interpretation and, most important, to change.

I speak of an "us" because Castillo's performances never involve just her; the engagement with the past she stages in the works that form RAW incorporates the audience as well. In fact, as audience members navigate a space that is more workshop than gallery, they find themselves surrounded by surfaces that beg to be touched, that appear to vibrate with anticipation as they wait for the unexpected-yet-desired encounter with somebody's (anybody's) wandering hand. Hence the pounds of clay on the windows and the wet bust occupying the center of the space. In their raw, unprotected, and incomplete state, they emit a silent but powerful invitation to the audience themselves to unmake a figure that is, through the endless possibilities opened up by the potentiality of a new touch, rendered powerless because it is not done yet (and perhaps never will be).

This invitation to touch becomes louder and more compelling thanks to the erotic nature of Castillo's performances and their effect on those who are encouraged to linger and watch her touch herself and masturbate the caudillo's clay nose. Her sensual movements, as I have mentioned, pull us in, but they do more than that: they activate our bodies so bodies (ours) and image (Castillo's) touch. Both pornography studies and media studies offer us productive ways of understanding this touching. Vivian Sobchack's *Carnal Thoughts*, for instance, speaks of the body sensually grasping what it sees on-screen, reverberating to all sounds, vibrating to all colors, to a point at which body and image cease to be two separate, discrete units and become surfaces in contact, "engaged in a constant activity of reciprocal re-alignment and inflection" (2004, 53). Elizabeth Grosz conceptualizes perception as "the flesh's reversibility, the flesh touching, seeing, perceiving itself, one fold (provisionally) catching the other in its own self embrace" (1993, 46). Paasonen (2011), as discussed above, uses the term "carnal resonance" to unravel the material and visceral sensations and vibrations that are caused by encounters with pornography. Finally, Linda Williams, following Walter Benjamin, proposes "innervation" to underscore the experience of not only taking in and being moved by the images that surround us but also transmitting energy from the inside of our bodies back to the outside world (2008, 17).

Tying all these concepts together is the understanding that exposure to images/performances like the ones in RAW—a sensual crafting where surfaces rub against each other, where flesh shapes and unshapes flesh-like clay—charges us with vitality. As the bodies on-screen move, *we too are moved*, we feel our skin vibrate with self-awareness, with self-mastery, and with an energy that cannot be contained by the malleable body that, vulnerable to touch (Castillo's and ours), has lost its hold on power, ideology, authority, and signification. The nature of this intimacy is of course undetermined; it might be desirable, surprising, unwanted, disturbing, and even repulsive— the clay bodies are, after all, also dead bodies. Yet what is undeniable is its existence; the power it gives us, whether we want it, or need it, or not.

In RAW, that power finds an actual outlet in the performance *Slapping Power*, where Castillo slaps the bust that, throughout the night, she had been reshaping and perfecting through caresses. The slapping, however, is not just hers; it is the audience's too. Stimulated, energetic, and determined, the bodies in the audience cheer, scream, clap, and encourage Castillo to hit the head harder and faster.[8] Whom is she actually slapping? As each slap disfigures the face little by little, it is the audience that must provide the answer to that question. It could be Bolívar, it could be Chávez, it could be Maduro, it could be any salvific male hero among the many populating Venezuela's (and Latin America's) history. The name does not matter; what matters is the power of changing the face of power, of being disloyal to tradition, of being careless with masculinity, and of knowing that that power stays with us, in the tingling of our hands, even after the head has finally fallen to the ground.

A Call for Discomfort

I was there, in the audience, the opening night of Castillo's RAW. A friend had invited me to accompany him, and I had accepted not because I was familiar with her work, but because I was curious to see if and how she would engage with Chávez and the Bolivarian Revolution. It was, after all, 2015: two years after Chávez's death and one year after the economic collapse and the protests that took place all around the country in 2014. The reverberating echoes of these events had intensified the polarization that mediated every academic exchange about Venezuela, and both social media and art had been mobilized by *chavistas* defending Maduro's government and Chávez's legacy and *opositores* denouncing the economic crisis and the deaths caused by political repression. I thus walked into the gallery expecting to see Chávez everywhere and was surprised to find him nowhere.

Well, not exactly "nowhere." He was there as one of the many epic male heroes Castillo's nameless caudillo embodied. He was also there because *I projected him there*; he was whom I saw in the clay figures Castillo caressed, masturbated, and slapped. Others, I am sure, saw him too—particularly those who, like me, were from Venezuela. And yet, just like I knew I was not the only one who saw Chávez in Castillo's caudillo, I also knew that other people in the audience were seeing someone else. Who? I did not ask. Another hero from Latin America perhaps, or a similar figure from somewhere else; these figures, we know all too well, abound. Thus, while my first thought was of Chávez, as I walked around and listened to people discuss the performances, he was soon joined in my mind by Maduro, then Bolívar—who was actually there, in the video performance *Sisyphus*—and then all the military figures that populated plazas, national holidays, and textbooks while I was growing up in Venezuela. They were all there, in their uniforms and also without them, for in Castillo's caudillo I also saw other male political leaders whose incendiary rhetoric and relentless appeal to Venezuela's glorious past and the dreams of Bolívar imbued them with the same epic allure of the men in uniform. With all of them parading in my mind, I grew more and more eager to see what Castillo would do to them, how she would make them disappear and propose someone else who would finally challenge the epic hypermasculinity that had monopolized political power in Venezuela since its beginnings as an independent nation. In other words, I wanted the specter of the caudillo to be exorcized and an act of conjuring to be performed that would allow a new spectral figure to reveal itself.

But the caudillo did not fully disappear, nor did Castillo give power a new face; no new hero or heroine walked in or materialized to take the caudillo's place, and the slapping—the climax of the night—left behind not a clean void but a mess: pieces of clay everywhere, a decapitated bust, and a disfigured head on the floor. Furthermore, whatever feeling of catharsis I was seeking was quickly replaced by unease, anxiety, and embarrassment.

Castillo's actions made me *uncomfortable*. I wanted a clean resolution and, then, a solution, an alternative, something new we could all look at and take with us. Instead, what Castillo gave me—what she gave everyone—was clay. Malleable, wet clay that stuck to everything, that dirtied things and "talked dirty" to the audience, and that referred only to itself as a sort of "expectant matter": the rawness of the present that refused to be willed away by either appealing to the past (there was no past, only clay) or to the future (there was no future, only clay). The collapse of the images did not lead to more images; it led to action, to working with clay—with the not-yet and with the could-be—and reacquainting ourselves with the discomfort that comes from encountering and taking part in indetermination and from embracing the possibility of an act of imaginative, unbounded making.

This discomfort is simultaneously unpleasant and illuminating. A hand masturbating the nose of a figure that, in the Venezuelan context, has been the revered object of a cult for over two hundred years is unpleasant because of the explicitness and obscenity of the gesture, and because of the almost visceral resistance that arises when a habit—of adoration, of respect, of submission—is interrupted. *Slapping Power* is unpleasant because it takes too long: the head does not fall immediately, but stays there, slowly detaching itself from its own neck, forcing us to acknowledge that this sort of reckoning with the heroes of the past is painfully slow and rarely wholly satisfying. Even the gallery space for RAW was unpleasant because it smelled weird (like clay), pieces of clay stuck to the audience's clothes, and there was not enough light—it was too somber, too catacomb-like. And all of it—the masturbation, the slapping, the darkness, the dirt—is also illuminating because it gives materiality and weight to the realization that we did not just "get" founding fathers and heroes through an act of divine will or because it was our collective and glorious destiny. *We made them,* we created their heroism and froze it in poems and sculptures, and that means we can unmake them and use the raw matter to make something else, to imagine otherwise because we are uncomfortable and forced, by Castillo, to linger in that discomfort and create something with it rather than outside it. This call to action, creation, and imagination is connected not only to the malleability of the clay and the way it repeatedly offers itself to the touch of the audience, but also to the lived and lively energy that results from the convergence of performance and intimacy in RAW. Being in a space where everything looks like it is about to unravel, where every bust and every statue has loosened up, where intimate gestures with the dead arouse uncomfortable affective energies, means feeling uniquely engaged: feeling like, by virtue of simply being and staying there, we are part of the making of something that vibrates with the potential of the unexpected.

This feeling, born in the present and in the *live* of performance yet oriented toward a future on the verge of being imagined, is why I have chosen Castillo's work to conclude this book. It could have ended in ruins—the ruins that so often appear in contemporary works of Venezuelan fiction as reminders of the terrible state of the social, political, and economic fabric of the nation. Ruins, however, only look back, at what was and could have been, or around, at the trash, the devastation, and the destruction that will keep producing more and more, seemingly infinite, ruins. Whatever future ruins promise, then, is foreclosed: ahead of the ruins is ruination, a slow journey toward erasure at worse, or preservation at best. Ruins thus are an excellent referent if what we are going for is denunciation and everything that follows it: anger, sadness, nostalgia. Here, however, I would like to go after something different, not because denouncing Venezuela's multidimensional crisis is not necessary and urgent—it obviously is—but because there must be something else, something *after*: the cautious hope that things might still be otherwise. I thus choose clay over ruins, "something to be done" over "something over and done with."

I also choose discomfort—a feeling that could be classified as one of what Sianne Ngai (2005) calls "ugly feelings"—over more cathartic, defined, satisfactory, and object-oriented feelings like anger, sadness, or nostalgia. These three feelings—like ruins, so palpably present in narratives about contemporary Venezuela—have a certainty to them that discomfort does not.[9] They all come with a clear image, be it of the past one craves (nostalgia), or of the object of the emotion (anger and sadness). In other words, they are about what is, what was, and what should be or should have been, which means they are about what is known, what one is passionately sure about. Discomfort is none of these things: it is the gut feeling that something is not right, that we are amid the unfamiliar, in an unknown (or known but uncanny) territory that bothers and unsettles. Discomfort is a sign that we are unprepared, that what we once thought we cannot think anymore, not without a sense of dread or doubt. Unlike pain, it will not make us close our eyes, though we might certainly cringe; unlike joy it is not eventful or exceptional, and it will not make us wish things would never change. Discomfort is easily solvable: we need only to seek what makes us comfortable again, what we know and love. But if we stay with it—as I have argued we are encouraged to do in RAW—we will get a front-row seat to the loosening up and undoing of what we used to know and thus the opportunity to think about what else could be that is *not* simply what is comfortable. This is why I propose that truly new acts of imagination can only take place in discomfort: in the counterintuitive decision to stay with the irritation, the annoyance, and the embarrassment that bind us to others in ways anger, sadness, or nostalgia cannot, and that can bring about something we might not fully recognize or even fully understand and that, precisely for that reason, might be the first step toward a new, unexplored, unimagined, and much-needed future, political and otherwise.

Concluding this book with Castillo's RAW is thus to conclude it with an invitation to seek out other discomforting spaces where we can be uncomfortable together and ask each other why, exactly, we feel that way, which of our assumptions and certainties are being called into question, and what we can do—what we can create or imagine—while we see power as we have always known it crumble and are asked to hold the malleable remnants in our hands. Finding these spaces and willing ourselves to linger in them is an urgent task, not only because it is there, as I have argued in this chapter, that new, more equitable relationships with the past and its heroes might materialize, but also because new ways of being together might materialize as well, ways that do not immediately reproduce Venezuela's political polarization nor appeal to easily legible and predefined political identities. That is, after all, the beauty of discomfort; like disgust—as conceptualized by Ngai in the afterword of *Ugly Feelings* (2005, 332–56)—it does not belong to one group or another. It can affect both at the same time. Castillo's work is proof of that; no one can watch her French-kissing Bolívar or masturbate the nameless caudillo's nose and remain undisturbed. *We all cringe*, which means that there is something we have in common, and that realization—however seemingly insignificant—is, if not the first draft of a new way of being together, then at the very least the starting point of what up until then was an impossible conversation. And that, for now, is more than enough.

Coda

An Impulse toward Potentiality

"An impulse towards potentiality." The words are Kathleen Stewart's, and they belong to the last pages of *Ordinary Affects*, where she states that the book "does not mean to come to a finish, it wants to spread out into too many possible scenes with too many real links between them" (2007, 128). Stewart's work and the work of many scholars of performance and affect theory were central to the conception of this book, not only informing its conceptual approach but also the way it is structured and how it, too, refuses to end. This refusal is, in a way, unavoidable: as I write this, no major political or social event has created the sort of transformation or rupture that would interrupt the afterglow in which this book was born and that would allow us to see its object of study reflected in a new rearview mirror. Nothing has changed in Venezuela in the decade following Chávez's death, or, more accurately, whatever has changed has been less of a change and more of an accumulation and intensification of the same, partly facilitated by the impasse and health crisis the COVID-19 pandemic triggered in 2020. The book thus remains without a significant historical ending to cling on to.

It also does not *want* to end, not after entering Deborah Castillo's RAW exhibition and exiting it covered in clay and with a tingling sensation that alerts us to the fact that there is a "something to be done," an "imagining otherwise" that is pending. This imagining otherwise is not a one-person act; it cannot be, not when what is at stake is relationality itself, as I argued in chapter 5. Thus, I propose to approach it with others, with people whose work in various fields has accompanied me on the journey this project has taken me on, as a reminder that, even in a comfortably haunted nation like Venezuela, something always escapes that is not another familiar or ghostly past or another already imagined future, but a stubborn, nonheroic, tentative yet overwhelmingly alive present. Rather than attempting to make them all cohere into a single narrative, answer, or image, I present these works below in the form in which I think they are the most powerful: as a constellation of vignettes, each outlining a present bursting with futurity, and each open to affecting and being affected by the other presents that materialize around it. They are not solutions looking to foreclose a conversation; instead, they are gestures—in the way Georges Didi-Huberman (2018) speaks of them—of people both inside and outside Venezuela who are trying to do something different, out of curiosity, out of necessity, out of frustration, or out of love.[1] Each is an invitation to dwell on the imagining otherwise of the reality we know, an invitation that is fleeting and that yet remains hopeful of potentially lingering for much longer than expected.

1. Benita Mendoza Soup Kitchen

Sujatha Fernandes, "Barrio Women and Popular Politics in Chávez's Venezuela" (2013)[2]

> Why should we name our soup kitchen after Simón Bolívar or Sucre? It's always the same old heroes of the republic. We have to think with our heads. Until when will we be stuck in the same old schema? Why can't we name the soup kitchen after Benita Mendoza, a working woman here in the barrio who has raised three kids, been left by three husbands, studied in spite of all the difficulties, and retired to work here as a volunteer?

2. Neck Deep in El Guiso

Violette Bule, *Echo Chamber* (2020)[3]

Fifteen cooking pots placed in a circle on top of a wooden table painted black (figure C.1). Inside each of them, there is a sound and an image. The sound comes from the depths of the country's entrails. Depending on which lid is lifted, it is the sound of Bill Clinton's visit to Venezuela in 1997 and the mixed reactions it generated among the people, or of denunciations of corruption in the country's electoral system, or of US journalist Barbara Walters interviewing

C.1   Violette Bule, *El Guiso* (2020). Courtesy of Violette Bule.

Hugo Chávez in 2007, or of Donald Trump calling Juan Guaidó Venezuela's "true president," or of Vladimir Putin reiterating his support of Nicolás Maduro, or of the day Bassil Alejandro Da Costa Frías (1990–2014)—marketing student at Universidad Alejandro de Humboldt—was murdered during the Caracas protests against Maduro on February 12, 2014, or of the loud banging of pots and pans known as "cacerolazos." A disorganized archive that has been extracted from "the cesspool of the Venezuelan media world" and thus one that combines pasts that did not pass and frustrated futures; in other words, dreams, hope, and crap.[4]

The image inside the pot, stewing in the sounds coming from it, is the image of your face—if you lifted the lid—for inside the pots there is nothing to be consumed: only a void and, at the bottom, a shiny, unforgiving mirror.

3. Oil, Intervened

Ana Alenso, *Oil Intervention # 7* (2019)[5]

Scaffolding parts, hoses, steel, nickel, diesel nozzle, and bottled water (figure C.2). Surrounding them, nature: leaves, wood, air, and dirt. Is this an image coming from the present—Venezuela's well-known present (and

C.2   Ana Alenso, *Oil Intervention #7* (2019). Photo: Joe Clark. Courtesy of
       Ana Alenso.

past) of extractivism and oil dependency? Or is it coming from the future—a
future where these objects have been left behind, abandoned, because at
some point another path was chosen that changed the country's relationship to its natural resources? Are these objects working? Is oil moving inside the hoses, slowly making its way to the bottle of water to be better and
more easily consumed? Or are they nonfunctional ruins on their way to
blend in with the natural landscape, creating an odd overlap that, though
not entirely harmless, holds within itself the cautious hope that something

different might still be possible? There is no answer; only, in the middle of it all, a mirror.

4. I Believe You (Finally)

"'Yo te creo': La era del #MeToo llegó a Venezuela," *Semana* (2021)[6]

> "Tranqui, yo perreo sola" (No worries, I'll dance alone)
> "No soy tu negra" (I'm not your *negra*)
> "Aborto legal" (Legal abortion)
> "El machismo mata + que el covid-19" (Machismo kills more than COVID-19)
> "No somos histéricas somos históricas" (We're not hysterical we're historical)
> "Educación sexual para decidir" (Sex education to make a choice)

5. Braiding to Care

Adriana Rondón-Rivero, *Trenzar una a una nuestras historias* (2014a)[7]

A group of women of different ages and nationalities—Venezuelan included—sit, one behind the other, in a circle in a park in Denver (figure C.3). Near them is a basket with red flowers, mirrors, brushes, and hairpins. They start brushing and braiding each other's hair, decorating it with the flowers and laughing and joking as they hold the mirror and check the result. Do they know each other? Some do, some do not, but it does not matter, for they will still tell each other stories and they will still carefully and lovingly braid the hair of whoever is in front of them. When it is all over, they will walk away and take with them a flower, a new hairstyle, and the lingering warmth of the memory of having been cared for—of having been *consentida*—and of having cared for someone in return.

Each of these vignettes is a hand reaching out. Evidence not of things going well or as planned, but of things going somewhere undetermined, simultaneously exciting and unsettling. They capture the affects and potentialities of scenes that rarely make it into historical narratives that demand clear beginnings, clearer endings, and tangible results. These are scenes of people trying things out without knowing whether they are going to last or work out. Lingering in and thinking with and through them can be frustrating

C.3   Adriana Rondón-Rivero, *Trenzar una a una nuestras historias* (2014).
Courtesy of Adriana Rondón-Rivero.

because of the discomfort triggered by that which is fleeting or undetermined, or because it could be argued that these scenes "miss the point"—the point being the urgency of resolving Venezuela's multidimensional crisis, the need for people to be held accountable for crimes committed in the decades of the Bolivarian Revolution, and the deeply rooted resentment and social divisions that come from so many injustices and unfulfilled promises. These scenes do not offer solutions to any of these issues, but they do offer spaces of imagination and of "being with" one another that could turn into new ways of defining what constitutes the social and political bonds that bring Venezuelan people together and in dialogue with other continental and global communities and struggles. Hence why in all of them there seems to be, explicitly or implicitly, a mirror. This is not the kind of mirror that shapes and fixes individual identity but the kind that makes us aware of our surroundings: of who/what is there with us and how they/it might affect and be affected by us.[8] Holding up that mirror is thus, also, an impulse toward potentiality.

These vignettes are no utopia: they are not an ideal to be realized, the future as it should have always been, or a promising impossibility. Neither are they dystopian: records of ruins piling up on top of other ruins, confirming that all that is left in and of Venezuela is chaos, corruption, and tragedy. They are, in Stewart's terms, "a mode of attunement, a continuous responding to something not quite already given and yet somehow happening" (2007, 127). Thus, they allow me to un-end this book, not with the sigh of relief that would follow an act of completion, but with the palpable mix of pleasure and apprehension that comes with being in a state of trying.

Ithaca, July 2024

Introduction

1   Twitter was rebranded as X in July 2023. In this book, I have chosen to refer to it as "Twitter," as that was the name the platform had when the events I discuss were taking place.

2   The UN Refugee Agency estimates that, as of 2022, there were over six million Venezuelan refugees and migrants worldwide, the vast majority in countries within Latin America and the Caribbean. In addition to the migration crisis, the majority of Venezuelans in the country are affected by severe food shortages, skyrocketing poverty, rampant violence, a public health sector collapse, and economic and infrastructural issues resulting from the plummeting of oil production to pre–World War II levels.

3   The scholarly publications on Hugo Chávez and Venezuela's Bolivarian Revolution are too many to list in full. I would, however, highlight Alejandro Velasco's article "The Many Faces of Chavismo" (2022) and the issue of the *NACLA Report*, titled "Chavismo Revisited" (2022), as the most recent sources to engage with Chavismo from a multidisciplinary and critical perspective.

4   My proposal to conceptualize the Venezuelan state as a performer follows the path established by Lisa Blackmore's *Spectacular Modernity* (2017), Fernando Coronil's *The Magical State* (1997), Rafael Sánchez's *Dancing Jacobins* (2016), and Michael Taussig's *The Magic of the State* (1997).

5   These works include Javier Corrales and Michael Penfold's acclaimed *Dragon in the Tropics* ([2011] 2015), Richard Gott's *Hugo Chávez and the Bolivarian Revolution* (2005), Fermín Lares's *El expediente del chavismo* (2014), Cristina Markano and Alberto Barrera Tyszka's *Hugo Chávez* (2007), and David Smilde, Verónica Zubillaga, and Rebecca Hanson's edited volume *The Paradox of Violence in Venezuela* (2022), among others.

6   These works include Luis Fernando Angosto-Ferrández's *Venezuela Reframed* (2015), George Ciccariello-Maher's *We Created Chávez* (2013), Sujatha Fernandes's *Who Can Stop the Drums?* (2010), Naomi Schiller's *Channeling the State* (2018), and Alejandro Velasco's *Barrio Rising* (2015), among others.

7   For an analysis of the exhumation and the overall significance of Bolívar's bones for the founding of the nation, see Luis Duno-Gottberg's "Embodiments and Disembodiments of the Nation, the People, and the State" (2016).

8   "He is not God, but only because it would have been heresy to proclaim that he was. But he is a god, and for his emerging cult, it will be necessary to construct an entire religion, the second religion, called upon to complement in the civil realm the role that the other one carries out in the spiritual and moral realm. A religion that will, above all, have the virtue of responding to the very concrete, urgent demands of a political conflict at the moment when it emerges, but that will preserve this therapeutic quality and will as a result provide more than one useful service to more than one useless cause" (Carrera Damas [1969] 1973, 61).

9   Alicia Ríos argues that, though groundbreaking, Carrera Damas's text ultimately cannot avoid casting Bolívar in a positive light. According to Ríos, Carrera Damas critiqued "how Bolívar, his figure, and his ideas have been used" and not "the problems his own governance and vision might contain" (2013, 48).

10   The cult of María Lionza brings together African, Indigenous, and Catholic beliefs, and it is practiced by members of all Venezuelan social classes. The rites take place on Venezuela's Sorte Mountain, in the state of Yaracuy, and involve invoking a wide variety of spirits—including that of María Lionza herself—who possess the bodies of mediums to provide advice, help, and healing. See Michaelle Ascencio's *De que vuelan, vuelan* (2012).

11   The MBR–200, or Revolutionary Bolivarian Movement-200, was a political and social movement founded by Chávez in 1982. The members of this movement were responsible for the failed 1992 coup against President Carlos Andrés Pérez. The evolution of the relationship between Chávez and Bolívar is most clearly seen if one compares his interview with Agustín Blanco Muñoz in *Venezuela del 04F al 06D-98* (Chávez Frías and Blanco

Muñoz 1998) and his interview with Ignacio Ramonet in *Hugo Chávez* (Ramonet 2013). Muñoz repeatedly goes back to the question of the cult of Bolívar and how it has been manipulated by all the presidents that preceded Chávez; Chávez responds by emphasizing that, while Bolívar is an important referent for him, he is not the only one, nor will his political movement "tie national identity or national consciousness to Bolívar" (Chávez Frías and Blanco Muñoz 1998, 109). His interview with Ramonet goes in the opposite direction. Bolívar and Chávez are elevated, together, to the same mythical realm marked by "eternal returns" (Ramonet 2013, 58) and the intimate connection between the two figures. This bond is exemplified by, among other things, the anecdote of Chávez writing a short story called "Mauricio" about the need for Bolívar's return (422) and the anecdote of the fake bills that were circulating when Chávez was arrested after the 1992 coup decorated with Chávez's face instead of Bolívar's (557).

12   Regarding this fusion, in a speech at the inauguration of Bolívar's new mausoleum on May 14, 2013, Maduro said: "To speak of Bolívar in the twenty-first century is to speak of Hugo Chávez Frías, his great defender . . . Hugo Chávez, the Bolívar of the twenty-first century, the Liberator of the twenty-first century" (Norman 2017, 201). Meanwhile, the sentiment of "losing Bolívar" was further strengthened by Chávez's (and then Maduro's) use of the word *apátrida* to refer to the opposition. More than a reference to the legal status of being stateless, the word—used as an insult—signaled the loss of the *patria/pater*, and thus the impossibility of belonging to Venezuela or identifying with Bolívar anymore. In "Magical History," Fernando Coronil argues that the virulence of the opposition against Chávez cannot simply be explained by their exclusion from positions of privilege; rather, it is a result of "a loss of identity, of a sense of place in society, the fear that the future won't belong to them," and the fact that, in the logic of divisions that dictates the history that Chávez created for the nation, "if they are not with Chávez, they are not only [out] of the government, but [out] of history" (2008, 11).

13   For a discussion of the relationship between oil and the magical state, see Fernando Coronil's *The Magical State* (1997).

14   Most studies of necromancy focus on Europe's medieval and early modern periods. In terms of political theory, necromancy is indirectly invoked in Achille Mbembe's *Necropolitics* (2019) and more explicitly developed in Ágnes Horváth's *Political Alchemy* (2021) as well as works on postsocialist countries inspired by Katherine Verdery's *The Political Lives of Dead Bodies* (1999), such as Vladimír Naxera and Petr Krčál's "Post-Socialist Political Necromancy" (2022).

15   *Britannica*, s.v. "necromancy," September 15, 2023, https://www.britannica.com/topic/necromancy.

16 This chain of equivalence was rendered explicit during the official speech Chávez gave in the state of Anzoátegui on July 12, 2012, as part of his presidential campaign, where he claimed: "Chávez became the pueblo . . . that is how I feel, I feel I am incarnated in all of you, as I said and I will repeat it: you too are Chávez, you Venezuelan women; you too are Chávez, Venezuelan men; you too are Chávez, workers, grandmothers, grandfathers; you too are Chávez, little Venezuelan girls and boys; Chávez truly became the people" (Comando Carabobo 2012).

17 The day the hologram appeared, December 8, is the day Maduro's government has officially named "Day of Loyalty and Love for Supreme Commander Hugo Chávez and the Fatherland."

18 The most literal rendition of Chávez's specter would actually be Chávez's spirit invoked in the chapel and on private altars all over the country. A popular prayer repeated to invoke him is the Lord's Prayer, adapted to feature Chávez as the main deity. María Estrella Uribe, a PSUV delegate, recited this prayer on September 1, 2014, at the closing ceremony of the party congress.

19 In "Four Exoskeletons and No Funeral," Jonathan Gil Harris asks: "Is there a specter haunting the discourse of spectrality? And what might this specter be? I would suggest it is matter itself, and more specifically a surplus mineral matter that 'haunts'—though that is perhaps too immaterial a term for what is thoroughly material—the very phrase 'the time is out of joint'" (2011, 619). He proposes to focus not on the temporality of spectrality but on its materiality, and on how the material accumulation and layering of different times in the present creates material specters he calls "exoskeletons." Though his approach centers on mineral matter and mineral duration, I find his insistence on analyzing the matter of haunting central to understanding the specter as a social and material force shaping the present.

20 Ribas-Casasayas and Petersen's edited volume *Espectros* (2017b) offers a wide variety of theoretical approaches to ghostly matters in Latin America. Addressing ghosts of the Spanish Civil War, Jo Labanyi's essays "History and Hauntology" (2000) and "Engaging with Ghosts" (2002) and the work of José Colmeiro ("Nation of Ghosts?" [2011]), Patricia Keller (*Ghostly Landscapes* [2015]), and Joan Ramon Resina (*The Ghost in the Constitution* [2017]) have been central to conceptualizing the ghostly in connection to historical memory and Spanish cultural production.

21 On January 23, 2019, in front of thousands of protesters in Caracas, Juan Guaidó—the thirty-five-year-old leader of Venezuela's then opposition-controlled Asamblea Nacional—declared himself interim president, challenging the results of the May 2018 presidential elections, widely denounced as fraudulent, which led Maduro to begin his second term in office.

22   Chávez's voice also opened Maduro's campaign rallies, which started with a recording of Chávez singing the national anthem or his well-known rendition of the song "Patria querida."

23   The photograph of Chávez in the rain at the closing of his 2012 presidential campaign (figure I.4) appeared in a promotional 2013 calendar (for the month of March) distributed by the PSUV and sponsored by the government and by Venezuela's oil company Petróleos de Venezuela.

24   The Museo Bolivariano is dedicated to Simón Bolívar and holds collections of objects related to his life and to Venezuela's independence battles. The PSUV emerged after Chávez won the 2006 presidential elections. It was the result of the merging of most of the unidentified parties that supported the Bolivarian Revolution. It held its founding congress in early 2008, and Chávez was proclaimed president of the new party on March 14 of that year. The party's website (www.psuv.org.ve/) includes a section dedicated to Chávez's speeches and a gallery featuring several photographs of Chávez. The party's logo, which appears at the top of the home page, features the graffiti of Chávez's eyes. Chávez remains the head of the party, which named him *Comandante Eterno* (Eternal Commander) after his death.

25   I use the term "nonarchive" to signal that Chávez's spectral remains do not exist, stored and cataloged, in an official archive, nor could they and their various iterations be gathered and archived in full, precisely because of their ongoing production and circulation in public, private, and virtual spaces. However, they do appear in archives such as the exhibits put together and displayed in Caracas's Biblioteca Nacional and in the PSUV headquarters in Mérida—both sites that I visited in the summer of 2016 and that held collections of posters and memorabilia featuring Chávez. Moreover, inasmuch as Chávez's spectral remains also include performances such as the acts of doubling, impersonation, and mimesis analyzed in chapter 4, they straddle the (always porous) line separating archives from what performance scholar Diana Taylor calls "repertoire": "embodied and performed acts [that] generate, record, and transmit knowledge" and that, in this particular context, promise to also establish a direct line of communication between the living and the living dead (2005, 21). These remains then complicate any stabilizing conceptualizations of archives and also challenge the archival impulse of this book, which is tasked with both "collecting" them in order to analyze them and acknowledging that the resulting "archive" will always be incomplete.

26   My use of "actant" reflects Latour's definition of the term as "something that acts or to which activity is granted by others" (1996, 373).

27   I am referring specifically to Benjamin's *The Arcades Project* ([1982] 1999), Barthes's *A Lover's Discourse* ([1977] 2010), and Stewart's *Ordinary Affects* (2007).

Chapter 1. Chronicle of a Death Postponed

1   For a video of Chávez's speech, see Ministerio del Poder Popular para la Comunicación y la Información's "Mensaje del Presidente Chávez" (2011).

2   Chávez often drew a connection between his life and Friedrich Nietzsche's idea of the eternal return, which he understood as coming back from (and thus surviving) many deaths. In one of the speeches he gave during the 2012 presidential campaign, he stated: "I am like Nietzsche's eternal return because I in fact have come back from various deaths" (Ramonet 2013, 58). Those "deaths" refer both to the death threats he allegedly received throughout his time as president—and that he discusses in detail in his conversations with Ignacio Ramonet—as well as the symbolic deaths represented by his imprisonment after the 1992 coup and by his temporary exile on La Orchila after the failed 2002 coup against him. In his biographical text on Chávez, Ramonet embraces the idea of Chávez returning from many deaths and living many lives, as demonstrated by, among other things, the book's title: *Hugo Chávez: Mi primera vida*. We can understand this repeated rhetorical resurrection as contributing to the creation of the sort of pre-posthumous spectrality that, as I argue in chapter 2, was central for setting the stage for Chávez's posthumous haunting.

3   Olivares's and Zapata's accounts regarding the events leading up to Chávez's death point to complots that implicate the Cuban government and underscore supernatural events that allegedly took place in the Hospital Militar where he was admitted after returning from Cuba. Olivares's work also suggests that there might have been two caskets used in the funerary rites, one filled with stones that was paraded among the people and the one that was exhibited in the Academia Militar that held Chávez's body (2020, 144).

4   Adán Chávez, Hugo Chávez's brother, has repeatedly stated that Chávez was infected with cancer by the United States with the support of the Venezuelan opposition, as part of a "violent imperial plot" meant to stop Venezuela's socialist revolution (*Cubanet* 2018).

5   Chávez himself alluded to this refusal to share medical reports during the 2011 healing ceremony that took place in Miraflores in his honor: "Whoever wants to ask my doctor, go and talk to Jesus, and ask him, eh, and the second one is Fidel, that's my second doctor, go ask Fidel, and the third, well, the doctors, the whole medical team, Doctor Sader, the minister of health, since she is a pediatrician, then I'm a little boy, a baby, see, reborn. . . . Now, since these *escuálidos* [a term that means 'sickly looking' or 'scrawny' but that in Venezuela is used by the government and its supporters to refer to and insult the opposition] are crazy to know who my doctors are, I'm not going to expose my doctors to the insults of these

low-down people filled with hate who would be capable of anything, no, and so it's down to me, and I'll keep doing it, to share my medical reports, I share them, it's not very hard, I study them, Aristóbulo, and then I explain it [laughter], I'm learning quite a bit" (Todo Chávez 2011).

6   For an analysis of conspiracy theories and their effects on Venezuela's political life since Chávez's arrival in power, see Gabriel Andrade's "Conspiracy Mongering in Venezuela" (2020b).

7   It is important to recognize that Sontag's study begins and ends with a warning against turning illnesses into metaphors: "My point is that illness is not a metaphor, and that the most truthful way of regarding illness— and the healthiest way of being ill—is one most purified of, most resistant to, metaphoric thinking" (2001, 3). If we are to resist that thinking, she proposes, metaphors have to be "exposed, criticized, belabored, used up" (182).

8   As Beatriz Lecumberri points out in *La revolución sentimental* (2012), death, as an abstract, poetic, and heroic concept, was a constant in Chávez's rhetoric. Not only did he finish his speeches referring to death as the ultimate sacrifice that the revolution required of him and his supporters, but his fixation on Bolívar and the nineteenth-century wars of independence turned every decision he and his cabinet made into an epic battle that, if lost, threatened to bring about death on a national scale.

9   In addition to staging Chávez's political performance—which often translated into his passing new laws and publicly firing members of his cabinet— *Aló Presidente* also explicitly drew attention to Chávez's body through the musical performances he would participate in, his self-referential anecdotes, and his hyperbolic gestures.

10 For a discussion of disputes between the two groups regarding the use of Venezuelan national symbols on items of clothing and in other political and social contexts, see Gabriel Andrade's "Banal Nationalism" (2020a).

11 For a video of the song, titled "Chávez, corazón del pueblo" and sung by Hani Kauam, Los Cadillacs, and Omar Enrique, see CRM 2012.

12 For a transcript of the ceremony, see Todo Chávez 2011. For a video of the ceremony, see ViVe 2011.

13 The general coordinator of Paz Dominicana, Rafael Guillén, explained the group's presence at the ceremony by alluding to Chávez as the embodiment itself of the unity between the peoples of Latin America and the Caribbean: "Hugo Chávez went beyond the borders of Venezuela to become a symbol of the unity of our pueblos. Hugo Chávez is the patrimony of humanity, Hugo Chávez is the full realization of a world that is possible, with Comandante Fidel Castro as the pillar, realizing the dreams of Bolívar, of Martí, of Christ the Redeemer of all of humanity" (Todo Chávez 2011).

His words must also be understood in the context of the strengthening of the diplomatic relations between Venezuela and the Dominican Republic in light of the agreements signed by the two countries in 2010, which included Venezuela's purchase of 49 percent of the shares of the Refidomsa oil refinery and the broadcasting of the TeleSUR network in the Dominican Republic.

14   For a video of Chávez taking part in this ceremony, see VTV's "Hugo Chávez: 'Christ!!!'" (2012).

15   Vásquez Lezama develops her analysis of somatic culture through the case study of Franklin Brito, whose death was the first by hunger strike in Venezuelan history. She argues that Brito's use of his body in protest of the invasion of his farm—one of the many conflicts that arose when the Bolivarian Revolution's agrarian reform was set in motion—"had universal transcendence because it condensed a series of institutional ills and incarnated them—literally—in public space" (2019, 107).

16   For a critical analysis of the different metaphors historically used to refer to oil in the context of Venezuela and their social and political impact, see María Sol Pérez Schael's *Petróleo, cultura y poder en Venezuela* (1993).

17   For an analysis of the relationship between spectacularity and modernity in Venezuela under the dictatorship of Marcos Pérez Jiménez, see Lisa Blackmore's *Spectacular Modernity* (2017). For a discussion of the various meanings attributed to Chávez's vision of twenty-first-century socialism, its promises, and its shortcomings, see Smilde's "From Populist to Socialist to Authoritarian Chavismo" (2021) and Troconis's "Unfinished Business" (2022).

18   "Already in the twentieth century, Eleazar López Contreras had sought to involve Bolívar in his plans, without aiming for excessive intimacy. . . . He was close to his inspirational figure, but not too close. He only animated a fleeting descent. In Chávez's case, we are looking at a stable phenomenon that deserves careful consideration" (Pino Iturrieta [2003] 2006, 191–92).

19   Pino Iturrieta argues that leaders invoking Bolívar because they deem it politically efficacious is one thing; however, "the chapter of the empty chair is divorced from normalcy, that is, from an operation carried out by political activists on purpose with the aim of brushing up against spiritism" ([2003] 2006, 194).

20   Pedro Pérez Delgado, popularly known as Maisanta, was a minor leader who, between 1898 and 1921, took part in the last *llanero* uprisings— uprisings in the Venezuelan plains or *llanos*—against Cipriano Castro (in power from 1899 to 1908) and then against Juan Vicente Gómez (in power from 1908 to 1935). He was also Chávez's ancestor, a link that Chávez underscored by publicly wearing Maisanta's scapulary of Our Lady of Perpetual Help. According to Juan Pablo Dabove, this link legitimized Chávez's

revolutionary credentials by making him part of an insurgent *llanero* family. See Dabove's "Hugo Chávez and Maisanta" (2011).

21 Cristina Marksman's sister, the historian Herma Marksman, was Chávez's partner and important political collaborator in the decade preceding the 1992 coup d'état against Carlos Andrés Pérez. Her memories of those years and her highly critical view of Chávez and his political trajectory are the subject of *Habla Herma Marksman: Chávez me utilizó* (Marksman and Blanco Muñoz 2004), a book that compiles the eight interviews Agustín Blanco Muñoz conducted with Marksman between 2003 and 2004.

22 Chávez is far from the only political leader in Latin America whose life, governance, and death were understood in terms of black magic and supernatural powers. Lauren Derby's "The Dictator's Two Bodies" (1999) is a fascinating study of Dominican dictator Rafael Trujillo and the widely shared belief that the source of his power (economic, political, and otherwise) was a mythical figure called *muchachito*, a figure that, the author concludes, was the spiritual manifestation of the everyday behind-the-scenes machinations of power, rendered inaccessible and unknowable to the population.

23 I am grateful to Javier Guerrero for bringing this article to my attention.

24 Before Chávez left to receive treatment for his cancer in Cuba in July 2011, he activated his electronic signature, which was given the same legal validity as his handwritten signature and was used to sign the Gaceta Oficial decrees in 2013 that named Nicolás Maduro provisional president and Jorge Arreaza (Chávez's son-in-law) vice president.

25 Two videos were posted on YouTube discussing the mistakes made in the digital alteration of this photograph and the "staged" nature of the image, which meant that the photograph and, most importantly, Chávez's alleged recovery were false. This analysis was conducted by photographer Luis Perea (NTN24 2013b) and animation expert Ibrahim Chaffardet in conversation with the news channel NTN24 (NTN24 2013a). Mario Silva—host of the pro-government television show *La hojilla*—then proceeded to refute the allegation that the newspaper Chávez appears to be holding was photoshopped into the picture through an analysis of pixels based on his own experience using Photoshop. Lastly, an article appeared on CNN en Español where Dartmouth College professor Hany Farid argues that, while there is no way to prove that the photograph is authentic, the evidence presented by Chaffardet is not enough to prove that it is false (CNN 2013).

26 For examples of the visual corpus, see Juan Carlos Desanzo's 1996 film *Eva Perón*, Tristán Bauer's 1997 documentary *Evita, la tumba sin paz*, and Pablo Agüero's 2015 film *Eva no duerme*.

27   I am grateful to André Nascimento for bringing this reference to my attention.

28   After the exhumation of Bolívar's remains in 2011, Chávez ordered the remodeling of the Panteón Nacional, which was reopened in 2014 and where Bolívar now appears resting in his own mausoleum, separated from the other national heroes whose bodies remain in the old structure of the Panteón.

29   When I visited the Cuartel de la Montaña in the summer of 2016, a number of visitors who were part of my tour group cried when approaching Chávez's coffin. Luis Fernando Angosto-Ferrández also writes that, during his visit in late 2013, he was "struck by the mourning expressions and teary eyes of several people leaving the mausoleum. The whole visit to the mausoleum is an emotionally charged one, from beginning to end, and the sequence structuring the visit facilitates people's expressions of emotion" (2016, 11).

30   These messages have been compiled and restructured as poems in Márquez et al., *Chávez te amo* (2015).

31   For a compilation of testimonies from people who got a tattoo of Chávez's signature, see Linares's "Testimonios" (2014).

32   In an interview with Luis Vicente León published in September 2020, the president of the polling company Datanálisis pointed out that while Maduro only had 13 percent popular support, 51 percent of Venezuelans still supported Chávez's political agenda. See Stefanoni's "Los dilemas de la oposición venezolana" (2020).

33   For an analysis of foreign intervention in contemporary Venezuela, see Buxton's "Venezuela: Deeper into the Abyss" (2018).

Chapter 2. Under the Specter's Gaze

1   The *k* can also be read as a reference to Venezuelan director Diego Rísquez's *Amérika* trilogy: *Bolívar, sinfonía tropical* (1979), *Orinoko, nuevo mundo* (1984), and *Amérika, terra incognita* (1988). Like *FANtasmo*, Rísquez's trilogy explores the intermeshing of history and myth, the poetic and the political, in Venezuelan history, particularly during the preconquest and the wars of independence. One of Rísquez's main goals in creating the trilogy was to destroy the colonial and mythical imagery that has permeated and defined the nation's identity. *FANtasmo*, we could argue, shares that goal and executes it through a grainy aesthetic—another element it has in common with Rísquez's films—that highlights and calls into question the grip epic images have on the Venezuelan collective imaginary. For a discussion of Rísquez's trilogy, see Will's "Interview with Diego Rísquez" (1985).

2   The term "spectacular modernity" "raises questions about what type of spatial and visual technics were deployed to stage dazzling displays of progress under military rule. In turn, it compels an analysis of how modes of seeing, displaying, and viewing buttressed the dictatorship's attempt to redistribute political representation" (Blackmore 2017, 20).

3   Blackmore offers a compelling analysis of the consumption of everyday commodities—clothes, cars, powdered milk—during Pérez Jiménez's dictatorship and the role that such consumption plays in naturalizing specific forms of social order that are often overlooked. See the chapter "Bringing Progress Home" in *Spectacular Modernity* (2017).

4   In this book I have chosen to discuss Chávez's presence in the urban landscape of two cities: Caracas and Mérida. As the capital, Caracas has often been at the center of academic studies regarding Chávez and the revolutionary work done by people in the city's barrios. However, Mérida, like other Venezuelan cities considered "peripheral," has rarely been studied in works engaging with the social, political, economic, and cultural reality of contemporary Venezuela. In including it in this book and in the analysis of Chávez's spectral afterlife, I hope to show how that afterlife extends beyond the geographical boundaries of Caracas and is also staged in cities like Mérida, known for being primarily *de oposición*. As Donald V. Kingsbury notes, "Mérida has been a center of opposition to the Bolivarian Revolution and has seen intense battles between government supporters—predominantly made up of the poor and nonwhite majority of the population—and the more affluent and whiter opposition" (2018, 1).

5   Thomas Kestler and Miguel Latouche argue that Chávez "remained the main symbolic figure of his regime and his political project. He embodied the entirety of the ideas associated with the regime and constantly produced meaning in a kind of performative symbolism" (2019, 11). Coronil, in "Magical History," argues that an intensified personalization of the state occurred under Chávez's government (2008, 11–12). Chávez's centrality also stands out in the accounts of the people Ciccariello-Maher interviews, a number of which insist on distinguishing between Chávez, the "maximum leader," and the ministers who surround him and who, "don't smell like revolution" (2013, 84).

6   In Venezuela—and in other Latin American countries—the word *cadenas* refers to joint broadcasts, typically of a political nature, over various media (usually radio and television), directed at the general population. In Venezuela, after the passing of the Law on Social Responsibility on Radio and Television (Ley Resorte) in 2004, it was established that *cadenas* must be carried not only by radio and television broadcasters but by cable networks with less than 60 percent international production. *Cadenas* have no time limit, and Chávez's were famous for being extraordinarily long.

7   While in this book I focus on the space of the city, particularly Caracas and Mérida, posters and billboards featuring Chávez also appeared in rural areas and at oil refineries. Chávez's *Aló Presidente* show also allowed him to travel to areas of the country traditionally considered peripheral or difficult to reach, like the Venezuelan Amazon, expanding his presence to occupy those areas as well.

8   Additionally, Romero García's film was part of the official selection of the 2009 Documenta Madrid Film Festival and the 2011 Toulouse Film Festival.

9   "I'm not going to say there was censorship, that they're after me, but they took it to a selection committee, they took it to the director of the Cinemateca, and he said that it was very ambiguous and that there were people in the film who called the president crazy, or something like that, and so it wasn't possible. So we said: 'It doesn't matter, we're going to carry on and we're going to take it to the Centro Cultural Chacao, to see what happens.' I took it there, and they said they couldn't, because the film was very ambiguous" (Romero García, quoted in Gamba 2013).

10   Chávez also shares this anecdote in his conversations with Ignacio Ramonet about "the Chávez myth." The carnival celebrations he mentions are the ones that took place after he was imprisoned following the 1992 coup. In addition to the kids dressing up like "Chavito"—and in addition to the men and women who, Chávez said, also dressed up like him—he also shared with Ramonet an anecdote about a group of people who, during that year's popular celebrations known as *fiestas de Elorza*, had a white horse that no one was riding leading a parade, the absence of the rider referring to the absence of Chávez, the "new" Bolívar. See Ramonet (2013, 545).

11   Marcos Pérez Jiménez's military dictatorship (which lasted from 1950 to 1958) ended with the signing of the Puntofijo Pact, which launched the country toward a stable democracy fueled by a booming oil economy that would make Venezuela stand out as exceptional among its neighbors, the majority of which found themselves governed by repressive military regimes and/or struggling with economic problems and social unrest. Venezuela's exceptionalism—which for many was more an illusion or a myth than a reality—ended with the 1989 riots that came to be known as "El Caracazo," to which Carlos Andrés Pérez's government responded with massive repression, sending in troops and firing indiscriminately at people on the streets. It was only after suspending constitutional guarantees, arresting thousands of people, and imposing a state of siege, that the government managed to regain control. While the government insisted that fewer than three hundred people were killed, COFAVIC—a human rights organization created to defend the victims of the massacre—and other NGOs have pointed out that no real investigation has been conducted to determine the exact number of victims. See COFAVIC's "34 años del

Caracazo" (2023). For an analysis of the political narratives constructed around "El Caracazo" during the years of the Bolivarian Revolution under Chávez, see Vásquez Lezama's "El Caracazo (1989) y la tragedia (1999)" (2012).

12 One of the men interviewed angrily lectures the film crew, arguing that those questions are not "clear or concise," and thus refuses to answer them. This response reveals the clarity the country's polarization demands. Asking whether someone knows Chávez is not immediately legible as a question associated with *chavismo* or *oposición*, hence why, I would argue, the man finds it bothersome.

13 In highlighting the relevance of the emotional discourse underlying the revolutionary process in Venezuela, I challenge the association between emotion and passivity, which sees emotion as below thought and reason. As Sara Ahmed notes, throughout history, to be emotional has meant "to have one's judgement affected: it is to be reactive rather than active, dependent rather than autonomous" (2015, 3). I do not see the emotions that Chávez triggers and that *FANtasmo* captures as turning the interviewees into dependent or passive bodies; if anything, their emotions signal acts of creativity and imagination about Chávez that allow him to appear in different modes and roles. These acts do not make Chávez active and the people passive, but they do establish a relationship that shapes the bodies of both Chávez and the people.

14 Although the government has not employed Chávez's eyes in the manner the woman suspected, it has developed other ways of violating the secrecy of the voting process. The secrecy of the electoral vote in Venezuela has been repeatedly called into question since the infamous Lista Tascón, which was published online in 2004 by Luis Tascón, a member of the Asamblea Nacional, after the 2003 recall referendum that took place under Chávez's presidency. The list included the names and national identity card numbers of over two million Venezuelans who voted against Chávez in the referendum. The list was then allegedly used to deny jobs, benefits, and documents to those who appeared on it and was ultimately taken down from the internet. The internet has become a platform of political control in many other ways. For an analysis of policies and practices deployed by the Venezuelan government between 2009 and 2020 to control contested online spaces, see Puyosa's "Asymmetrical Information Warfare in the Venezuelan Contested Media Spaces" (2021).

15 Chiara Bottici underscores the central role images play in contemporary electoral battles, where "only those images that can capture people's attention so as to prevent them from turning to something else are selected" (2014, 112). We could argue that the image of Chávez's eyes successfully performed that role, as they captured people's attention not only because

of their virality but also because the design itself made people feel "looked at" and thus interpellated by Chávez's gaze.

16   Comando Carabobo is the name of the headquarters of Chávez's 2012 presidential campaign.

17   For a discussion of the eyes' reproduction on the walls of the housing and apartment complexes built by the Gran Misión Vivienda Venezuela, see Wilson Wetter's "The Eyes of Chávez: Social Housing as Monument and Image" (2021).

18   For a discussion of the role the monumentalization of Bolívar played throughout Venezuela's history as an independent nation in the government's efforts to turn crowds into homogeneous and thus "rulable" people, see Rafael Sánchez's chapter "Monumental Governmentality" in *Dancing Jacobins* (2016).

19   Che's eyes feature in Octavio Getino and Fernando Solanas's 1968 film *La hora de los hornos*, among other literary and cultural materials. They were also reproduced in a stencil that has been stamped on clothing items and accessories sold all over the world, using a design based on Alberto Korda's 1960 photograph of him, titled *Guerrillero Heroico*. Beyond the ideological affinities between the two figures and the close political and economic relationship between Cuba and Venezuela during the years of the Bolivarian Revolution, the visual link between Chávez's eyes and Che Guevara's eyes can also be read as an attempt to link Chávez's struggle with cancer with Guevara's revolutionary struggle against imperialism, so that, if and when Chávez died, his death—ordinary as it was—could be understood within the same heroic narrative that framed Guevara's death in combat, as shown in *La hora de los hornos*.

20   "Our Chávez who art in heaven, on earth, in the sea, and in us, your delegates. Hallowed be thy name, thy legacy come to us to carry to the people near and far. Give us this day your light so it may guide us every day. Lead us not into the temptation of capitalism, but deliver us from the evil of the oligarchy, the crime of contraband, because ours is the patria, the peace, and the life. Forever and ever, amen. Viva Chávez!" (Placer 2015, 255).

21   In addition to Bolívar, Chávez often appeared on posters, murals, and graffiti next to images of Jesus Christ, whom Chávez called "the first socialist." See, for example, the image in Navarrete's "Los ojos de Chávez" (2015, 68).

22   Chávez's role as a member of the Venezuelan family unit is something the people interviewed in *FANtasmo* repeatedly allude to, and I will discuss it in the following chapters. A noteworthy example of the lingering power of that role appears in an image featured in Jessica Velásquez Urribarrí's article "Resemiotisations across Time, Space, Materials and Modes" (2023). The image, taken by @andrernandez, shows a young pregnant woman with

Chávez's eyes drawn on her belly along with the phrase "Yo soy Chávez," commemorating the second anniversary of Chávez's death in 2015.

23   Yael Navaro-Yashin develops a brilliant analysis of the ways in which, through their everyday practices, Turkish people have been reifying and reinstating the Turkish state. In her words: "Statist rituals organized by the state for itself are no longer as convincing or as moving as informal ones organized by the people for the state. In Turkey, it has recently proven more effective for state power to reproduce itself, not by enforcing narcissistic rituals, but by enabling certain groups, outside the center of state practice, to produce in-and-of-themselves, in Foucault's sense of the term, rituals of thralldom for the state" (2002, 119). Navaro-Yashin's analysis of the operations of state power strongly resonates with the contemporary Venezuelan context and the operations of what I have called Venezuela's "necromantic state." Furthermore, her chapter "The Cult of Atatürk" discusses the invocation of Mustafa Kemal Atatürk and offers a productive comparison with Chávez's spectral afterlife. I thank Begüm Adalet for referring me to Navaro-Yashin's work.

24   The connection between Chávez's enduring symbolic presence and the continuity of Maduro's regime is discussed in Kestler and Latouche's "The Ideational Foundations of Authoritarianism in Venezuela" (2019) and Michelutti's "'We Are All Chávez'" (2017). For a discussion of other factors that have contributed to keeping Maduro in power, see Corrales's "Authoritarian Survival" (2020).

25   "Presence opens out into presentation of presence. Facing the spectator, the obtuse power of the image as being-there-without-reason becomes the radiance of a face, conceived on the model of the icon, as the gaze of divine transcendence" (Rancière [2007] 2009, 23).

26   The image appears on page 50 in Elkins's text, without any information regarding the artist or the work's title.

27   Derrida reads the visor effect in relation to questions of inheritance and as the basis of a form of ethics regarding an "other" whose spectral gaze undoes the possibility of absolute autonomy: "The predecessor has come before me, . . . I who am before him, I who am because of him, owing to him, . . . owing him everything . . . And I cannot settle my debt, I can neither give back nor exchange because of this absence of the other, which I can't look in the eye" (Derrida and Stiegler 2002, 122). In the case of Chávez's eyes, this sense of debt and responsibility Derrida identifies is echoed in the official narrative constructed around Chávez, he to whom eternal loyalty and love is owed, as Navarrete argues.

28   As I develop an interpretation of the encounter with Chávez's eyes that underscores what they, in W. J. T. Mitchell's terms, "want," I am building

on Althusser's notion of interpellation or "hailing" as the primal scene of ideology and Lacan's conceptualization of the gaze as the moment one experiences being seen by the other. See Althusser's *On The Reproduction Of Capitalism* (2014) and Lacan's *The Four Fundamental Concepts of Psycho-Analysis* (2019).

29   For his expanded reading of Chávez's eyes, see Sánchez's "Los ojos de Chávez: Post-verdad y populismo en Venezuela" (2019).

30   "The 'becoming crowds' of the Venezuelan middle classes [have], in the past few years again and again fill[ed] the streets and squares of Caracas as monstrous agglomerations of individuals gathering for the sole purpose of forcing Chávez out of power. The fact that so far the Venezuelan opposition has not been able to capitalize on these crowds to articulate itself as a viable alternative to the Chavista regime is a sure indication of the extent to which the theologico-political is a spent force in Venezuela" (Sánchez 2016, 328).

31   Though often supported by the Venezuelan government, which has used their artistic and cultural works in creating the visual language of the Bolivarian Revolution and of the twenty-first-century socialism advertised by Chávez in 2006, these groups are driven by their own commitment to popular representation and communication. The Ejército Comunicacional de Liberación, for instance, defines itself as "a force in constant formation and reformulation; a handful of young people who have taken up arms of paper and who, through communication with the people, believe in the development of a new conscious, responsible aesthetic based on the clear, effective promotion of messages that contribute to delving more deeply into socialism. Our actions and products follow three basic lines: agitation, formation, and sustainability" (Issuu n.d.).

32   The eyes do, however, appear in materials stored in official archives, such as the collection of posters made and circulated during Chávez's 2012 presidential campaign, which, as of 2016, were archived in Caracas's Biblioteca Nacional.

33   Leopoldo López is a Venezuelan opposition leader, cofounder of the political party Primero Justicia, founder of the political party Voluntad Popular, and former mayor of Chacao. He was arrested and charged with arson and conspiracy after he called for protests in February 2014 and was imprisoned in Ramo Verde. His arrest has been denounced as politically motivated by the European Union, Amnesty International, Human Rights Watch, and several other human rights organizations. He was transferred to house arrest in 2017, imprisoned once again in Ramo Verde, and then put back under house arrest that same year. He was released in 2019 and left Venezuela in 2020.

34   Barrios's solo show was held at Brooklyn's Superchief Gallery in February 2016. While I read his work in connection with Chávez's eyes, the

exhibit's provocative representations of violence and of the ways in which violence is observed and enjoyed exceed the Venezuelan context. See Superchief TV 2016.

35   For a discussion of the role of the gaze in Méndez Guédez's *Y recuerda que te espero*, see Lander's "*Y recuerda que te espero* by Juan Carlos Méndez Guédez"(2021).

36   Zapata dedicates several sections of his book to a speculative discussion of Cuba's—and Fidel Castro's—influence on Venezuela's internal affairs since Chávez was elected president. See "La maquinación de Fidel Castro," "Asaltantes del poder," and "Maduro en marcha" in Zapata's *Chávez a la hora y en la hora de su muerte* (2021).

Chapter 3. (Re)Collecting Chávez

Part of chapter 3 first appeared in "Unfinished Business: Visuality, Space, and the State in (Post) Socialist Venezuela," *Comparative Literature Studies* 59, no. 3 (2022): 527–48.

1   Though I could clearly see both posters described here from the car, I was unable to properly photograph them.

2   My understanding of porosity draws on Susan Buck-Morss's discussion of the term in *The Dialectics of Seeing* (1989). The term was proposed by Asja Lācis, as she and Walter Benjamin sat down to write an article about the historical disintegration visible in Italy's classical ruins. It captures the fact that "the structuring boundaries of modern capitalism—between public and private, labor and leisure, personal and communal—have not yet been established" (Buck-Morss 1989, 26), leading to spatial anarchy, social intermingling, and impermanence.

3   Ninette Lina Ron Pereira (1959–2011) was a Venezuelan political leader and the founder and president of the Unidad Popular Venezolana party. She was a strong, vocal supporter of Hugo Chávez and the Bolivarian Revolution, popularizing the phrase "Con Chávez, todo; sin Chávez, plomo" (With Chávez, everything; without Chávez, bullets). After her death in 2011, people started referring to Plaza Andrés Eloy Blanco as Plaza Lina Ron, to honor her memory and underscore the plaza's role as the stage for several of her political rallies.

4   On December 17, 2019, Nicolás Maduro reminded the Venezuelan people of the oath Chávez and the founding members of the MBR-200 swore under the Samán de Güere in 1982, an oath that committed them to freeing the people from the corruption, poverty, and oppression inflicted by the country's political system and the oligarchy, and that ultimately led to the 1992 coup against Carlos Andrés Pérez. The oath was inspired by and

reproduces the wording of the Monte Sacro oath Simón Bolívar swore as he committed himself to Hispanic American independence. This is one example of Chávez's bodily citation of Bolívar; others can be found in Elías Pino Iturrieta's *El divino Bolívar* ([2003] 2006) and Ana Teresa Torres's *La herencia de la tribu* (2009).

5 Lucia Michelutti, in her analysis of what she calls "mini-Chávezes," points out that, from the moment Chávez's death was announced in March 2013, to 2017, Maduro referred to Chávez 7,041 times (2017, 244). Additionally, the two leaders often appeared (and continue to appear) together in pictures, on banners, and on election posters.

6 Created in February 2012, the art collective Trinchera Creativa brings together graphic designers, artists, and content creators who have shown their support for Chávez and the Bolivarian Revolution through the production of graffiti, posters, murals, and other iconographic objects such as the TC Chavez Pro app. For a discussion of the role of popular art in the context of the Bolivarian Revolution, see Pascual Marquina's "Cultural Production in Revolutionary Venezuela" (2019).

7 *Tal Cual* republished Márquez's article as part of their eighteenth-anniversary celebrations. For the article, along with a brief commentary on the fine the journal had to pay for it, see Márquez's "Querida Rosinés" (2018).

8 For an analysis of the changes made during Chávez's presidency to the Venezuelan flag, coat of arms, and banknotes, see Andrade's "Banal Nationalism: Disputes in Venezuela"(2020). For an analysis of the changes made to the horse, see Angela Marino's chapter "The Symbol Keeps Performing" in *Populism and Performance in the Bolivarian Revolution of Venezuela* (2018).

9 For this episode, see Noticias Venezuela's "Chávez y el niño de la galleta" (2022).

10 For a detailed analysis of the complicated relationship between gender, labor, and the Bolivarian Revolution, see Rachel Elfenbein's *Engendering Revolution* (2019).

11 Tito Oviedo, Venezuelan student leader and politician, used the phrase "Los verdaderos hijos de Chávez" in his 2021 political campaign for governor of Ciudad Guayana. See Oviedo 2021.

12 In *El ocaso del Comandante* (2015), Ludmila Vinogradoff discusses Chávez's (biological) afterlife in connection with the children he had but never publicly recognized. In the chapter titled "La pasión de la aeromoza," Vinogradoff tells the story of the two daughters he had outside his marriages to Nancy Colmenares and Marisabel Rodríguez: Génesis María and Sara Manuela. Nicolás Maduro recognized the existence of these two daughters in 2014, which triggered questions regarding inheritance and the possibility of the existence of other unrecognized children fathered by Chávez.

13   Misión Milagro is a social program developed in conjunction with the government of Cuba to help people from the poorest sectors of the population get surgeries and treatment for various eye problems.

14   For an account of the close relationship between Omar Cruz and Chávez, and the role the former's artwork played in the context of the revolution, see VTV's "ENTREVISTA AL CARICATURISTA OMAR CRUZ POR EXPOSICIÓN 'CAMPOS DE LIBERTAD' EN EL MUSEO CRUZ DIEZ." (2021a).

15   For the latest report on unlawful executions, forced disappearances, arbitrary detentions, and torture in the country since 2014, see the report published by the United Nations–backed fact-finding mission on Venezuela on September 15, 2020 (CDH 2020).

16   In *A Hero's Curse*, Kajsa Norman notes that, in the months leading up to the 2012 presidential elections, the mission Mi Casa Bien Equipada distributed 1.3 million subsidized washing machines, dishwashers, stoves, and flat-screen TVs made in China with Chávez's name and face printed on the boxes (2017, 165). After his death, two huge billboards were placed by the entrance to Petróleos de Venezuela (PDVSA), the Venezuelan state-owned oil and natural gas company, featuring Chávez, with his fist in the air "behind a sea of jubilant PDVSA workers dressed in red and waving their helmets" (168). The entrance hall also housed a photography exhibit portraying the role of oil in the revolution since the 1990s with Chávez as the protagonist of the various stages of this process.

17   For a discussion of the role of television and media communication in the context of the Bolivarian Revolution, see Schiller's *Channeling the State* (2018) and Silva-Ferrer's *El cuerpo dócil de la cultura* (2014).

18   For a discussion of the government's understanding of this form of unconventional war, see the 2018 BBC interview with the minister of communication and information, Jorge Rodríguez (Paullier 2018), and the document released in 2013 by the Ministerio del Poder Popular para la Comunicación e Información, *Venezuela contra la guerra económica* (GBV 2013).

19   For a discussion of the memory market in connection with the Mothers of the Plaza de Mayo—the Argentine human rights organization and social movement that was founded in 1977 by women whose children were kidnapped by the military dictatorship that ruled Argentina from 1976 to 1983— see Susana Kaiser's "Memory Inventory" (2011). Regarding other conceptual approaches to commodities and memory markets, Celeste Olalquiaga in *The Artificial Kingdom* (1998) develops an understanding of kitsch and the memory market that draws a distinction between melancholic kitsch and nostalgic kitsch, and that explores the afterlives of souvenirs and cultural fossils.

20   For a discussion of the ways in which the neoliberal market in the context of postdictatorship in the Southern Cone obliterates, hides, or insists

on a clean break with the past, see Nelly Richard's critical analysis of the Chilean transition in *Fracturas de la memoria* (2007) and Idelber Avelar's introduction to *The Untimely Present* (1999).

21 A similar operation of miniaturization occurs with the prayer cards of Chávez that decorate improvised altars built in his honor, where he occasionally appears next to religious figures. The creation and circulation of such cards has not been without controversy. The card showing Chávez next to Jesus with the caption "Camarada, no temas ni desmayes que yo estaré contigo cada instante de tu vida," (Comrade, do not fear, do not be dismayed, for I will be with you every moment of your life), which appeared during Easter the year of Chávez's death, was heavily criticized by leaders of the Catholic Church in Venezuela, who rejected Chávez's designation as "the redeemer of the poor." For an image of the card, see 20 Minutos's "Chávez, convertido en estampa junto al cristo Nazareno" (2022).

22 For an in-depth analysis of the relationship between Chávez and Maisanta, and how Chávez drew on it to insert himself in the nation's history of rebellion, see Dabove's "Hugo Chávez and Maisanta" (2011).

23 There is a growing corpus of literature that examines the state of internet service in Venezuela and the central role it plays as a form of state surveillance and information control, as well as being an indispensable tool for the organization of protests, marches, and other challenges to Maduro's regime. For an analysis of the information communities that take shape during the country's daily power outages, see Thomas, Saldanha, and Volkova's "Studying Information Recurrence, Gatekeeping, and the Role of Communities during Internet Outages in Venezuela" (2021). For a discussion of misinformation on digital platforms, see Burgos and Hernández Díaz's "Desinformación digital en Venezuela" (2021). For an analysis of the state's use of Twitter as a form of censorship, see Puyosa's "Asymmetrical Information Warfare in the Venezuelan Contested Media Spaces" (2021).

24 On January 30, 2005, in front of a roaring crowd that had gathered at the Gigantinho stadium in Porto Alegre, Brazil, for the fifth annual meeting of the World Social Forum, Chávez gave a speech that encouraged a continental turn to "twenty-first-century socialism." In his speech, Chávez proposed that, unlike the kind of socialism that had developed in the context of the Soviet Union, this reinvented, "true socialism" would be anchored in equality and justice and would emerge through the development of new systems built on cooperation, not competition. The merits and blind spots of Chávez's socialist agenda have been the subject of numerous works and controversial debates. See Azzellini's *Communes and Workers' Control in Venezuela* (2018), Bruce's *Real Venezuela* (2008), Guerra's *El mito del socialismo bolivariano* (2019), Hetland's "Emergent Socialist Hegemony in

Bolivarian Venezuela" (2015), and Smilde's "From Populist to Socialist to Authoritarian Chavismo" (2021).

25   Yaneira Wilson Wetter in "Le logement social au XXIe siècle au Venezuela" (2020) offers a compelling analysis of the architectural aesthetic of the houses and apartment buildings constructed by the GMVV, and how it is perceived by the inhabitants of the buildings, who are typically excluded from the conversation regarding their design—which makes many of them feel like they are living inside a refrigerator—and often from the process of construction as well. She explores the contradictions and shortcomings of the housing program, related to the state's demand to build the houses fast—which is not always possible or beneficial for the workers. She also highlights difficulties that emerge from the tension between political rhetoric and bureaucratic practice, and between community leaders and those within the organizational structure of the program.

26   For the video, see VTV's "Entregan 90 viviendas" (2020).

27   For the video of Chávez activating his electronic signature, see Bracci Roa's "Generan firma electrónica del Presidente Chávez" (2011).

28   Creating the illusion—and, sometimes, the reality—of immediacy was one of the central operations of the Bolivarian Revolution during Chávez's presidency. Two platforms served as a stage that facilitated and displayed the political, social, and material effects of this immediacy: Chávez's television show *Aló Presidente* and his Twitter account @chavezcandanga. The former allowed Chávez to pass laws, expropriate buildings, and fire members of his cabinet right away, outside the temporal and official boundaries of legal procedures. The latter allowed him—or rather, the team in charge of managing the account—to respond to people's demands as soon as they were posted, with tweets that promised a prompt resolution of any problems.

29   Neef, quoting Derrida, underscores the role of the signature as that which is "added to a thing that counts as complete for its completion" (2011, 284).

30   Based on interviews with a number of inhabitants of these apartment buildings and houses, Wilson Wetter concludes that, in spite of the quotidian difficulties they face (lack of public transportation, water, and electricity, for example), "people receive these houses or apartments as if they were a gift from the president, although, symbolically, he remains 'the owner'" (2020, 14).

31   Though Mauss's theory of the gift has been widely cited outside the specific cultural context he examines in his work, it is still relevant to note that, in the case of the quote I include in the text, he is referring to the customs of the Māori, the Indigenous Polynesian people of mainland New Zealand.

32   The phrase "Hasta la victoria siempre" was popularized by Che Guevara but frequently repeated by Chávez.

33   See, for instance, William John Hardy's *The Handwriting of the Kings and Queens of England* (1893).

34   My definition of citation draws on work on the semiotics of citation by Constantine V. Nakassis, in "Citation and Citationality": "citational acts re-present and bracket that which they cite and, in doing so, open up new social horizons of possibility, signification, and, in some cases, performative power. The citation is a play of sameness and difference, identity and alterity, an interdiscursive calibration of an event of citing and a cited event, and is reflexive about that very fact" (2013, 76).

35   While addressing the Venezuelan audience and his fellow soldiers on live television during the 1992 coup attempt, Chávez said, "for now, the objectives we had set have not been accomplished in the country's capital." Those two words, "for now," have since been interpreted as triggering a feeling of hope in a population that felt disenchanted with the country's political system and that would then turn to Chávez, who portrayed himself as outside that system, as a candidate that would offer a better, more just, and more inclusive political future.

36   For an example of the letters Chávez sent while imprisoned in Yare, see the "Carta del Comandante Presidente Hugo Chávez a su paisano y amigo Armando Rivas" (Chávez 2022).

Chapter 4. Toying with the Comandante

1   For a video of this conversation, see *El Heraldo*'s "Chávez se me apareció en forma de pajarito" (2013).

2   Dr. José Gregorio Hernández was a Venezuelan physician known for treating the poor for free and bringing them medicines sometimes purchased with his own money. After his death in 1919, people around the country claimed to receive miracles after praying to him. Several attempts have since been made to get the Vatican to recognize him as a saint.

3   In 2013, a number of international newspapers reported on Maduro's alleged devotion to controversial Indian guru Sathya Sai Baba, whose portrait—it was rumored—adorned one of the president's offices. Among other feats, Sathya Sai Baba was known for his ability to perform miracles including resurrections and purported materializations of gold objects. While there is no direct connection between this spiritual devotion as it was reported at the time and the birds and butterflies Maduro claimed were the reincarnation of Chávez, taken together they fueled both the state's specter-making performance and suspicions that, as I mentioned in chapter 1, grounded the widespread belief that "foreign forces" were dictating Venezuela's fate after Chávez's death.

4   To view the ad, posted by the cell phone company Wom, see VTVN's "Este es el comercial chileno" (2015).

5   For a description of the oath and the similarities between Chávez's oath and Bolívar's oath, see GBV's "17 de diciembre de 1982" (2022).

6   The practice of tying claims to authority to the spirit of Bolívar goes back to Antonio Guzmán Blanco's presidency and his order to repatriate Bolívar's remains in 1876, an act that triggered the national practices of commemoration around the figure of the Liberator that would establish his cult in the following years.

7   While my interest is in calling attention to the ordinary ways in which the people and the state come together to support and perpetuate certain political and visual vocabularies that, while guaranteeing the survival of a state in crisis, run the risk of circumscribing political imagination and foreclosing futures grounded in nonpatriarchal, nonepic understandings of authority, popular agency also operates in Venezuela in ways that go beyond this specific dynamic. Alejandro Velasco's work on the 23 de Enero slum in *Barrio Rising* (2015), Rachel Elfenbein's analysis of women's labor and maternalism in the Bolivarian Revolution in *Engendering Revolution* (2019), Dario Azzellini's study of communes in the discourse of twenty-first-century socialism in *Communes and Workers' Control in Venezuela* (2018), and Naomi Schiller's work on the community television station Catia TVe in *Channeling the State* (2018) are a few of the most notable examples of scholarship that highlights the potentialities and the limits of forms of popular agency that were empowered by the Bolivarian state but that also went beyond and developed outside it. My understanding of popular agency acknowledges these complexities; however, it also recognizes how, through everyday practices of meaning-making that appropriate the political, social actors reify and reinstate the state, often recycling rather than transforming exclusionary structures of power and terms of subjugation and domination.

8   For the video, see *El País*'s "A Maduro se le posa una mariposa" (2017).

9   The word "mariposón" literally means "big butterfly" but colloquially refers to a man who has frequent but fleeting romantic relationships.

10   Velasco explores the contradictions within *chavismo* from Chávez's arrival in power to Maduro's current regime in his article "The Many Faces of Chavismo" (2022).

11   Maduro and his salsa dancing are a compelling yet complicated example of what Rafael Sánchez calls "dancing Jacobins": the sensuous, lascivious, irreverent gestures Venezuela's "founding fathers" (including Bolívar, who in the historiography and popular representations of him appears as a lover of dancing) perform, breaking free momentarily from their monumentalized

persona and creating a tension between the two—monument and "the man of flesh and blood"—that is central for preventing the people from becoming an unruly crowd during both stability and crises. This tension, rather than being resolved, relies on the oscillation between *relajo* (commotion, disorder, party) and monumentality: in Sánchez's words, "even if the notable himself is in some ways a *tipo de relajo*, not even in an extreme situation does he ever completely let go. A quaint rhetorical flourish will always be there to save the day, reminding everyone of the notable's lofty, ethereal being amidst the most earthly excesses" (2016, 198). It is that return to monumentality that may be missing from Maduro's performance, which seems to get stuck in a *relajo* that also falls short when it comes to capturing people's attention and appreciation, as Bellaviti's "*La hora de la salsa*" (2021) shows.

12 For an exploration of the technological sublime and its connection to space and the nation, see Nye's *American Technological Sublime* (1994).

13 Fantasy, Brading argues, "provides political practices with energy and direction" and thus acts as the fuel that keeps the fight going and the glue that, in populist practices, holds people together amid a variety of social grievances (2013, 34). In the case of Chávez's political project, the energy and direction were tied to Bolívar's ghostly energy—as Brading points out when he refers to Bolívar as the "vector" of Chávez's revolution (50). See the chapter "Populism, Theories, and Logics," in Brading's *Populism in Venezuela* (2013).

14 Misión Ribas is a Bolivarian *misión* that provides remedial classes for Venezuelan students who drop out of high school.

15 For a video of the discussion regarding the image of Chávez's female double, see Univision Noticias's "Una foto de una mujer" (2014).

16 Examples of this parodic use of the meme of Chávez's double include one in which the picture of another woman, seemingly in distress and dressed entirely in red, looks at the female Chávez and, with what is framed as hopeful desperation, asks, "Comandante, is that you?" In another meme, the double says: "I am not dead. It's an imperialist lie."

17 With "thing," I am loosely drawing from W. J. T. Mitchell's dialectical conceptualization of things and objects, whereby objects are stable, with a name, identity, history, use, and function, and things are nebulous yet obdurate, sensuously concrete and vague, a "hybrid thing . . . that requires more than one name, more than one identity" (2005, 156). Things, thus, are open to transformation and instability, to the possibility of endless nonidentical reproductions, which is what, in my analysis, characterizes Chávez's "memeification."

18 Diosdado Cabello is a Venezuelan politician, a member of the Asamblea Nacional, and an active member of the Venezuelan armed forces, holding the rank of captain.

19   One of the videos that has circulated on WhatsApp, for instance, shows a montage of black-and-white images of scenes of violence and poverty from contemporary Venezuela, which, in the video's logic, mirror the economic crisis and repression that took place during the 1989 wave of protests known as El Caracazo. Chávez's voice appears in the background, condemning the hunger and poverty that led to El Caracazo and thus seeming to posthumously condemn the actions of his own government. For the video, see Castillo's "Chávez habla del Caracazo" (2014).

20   I refer to this as "grotesque" not only because of the odd proportions of the doll's head and features, but also because, as Susan Stewart argues, following Mikhail Bakhtin, the grotesque body is a body in the act of becoming and "a body of parts" (1993, 105). The bodily parts Stewart focuses on are primarily bowels and genitals, which are not the parts that make up the DIY Chávez. However, the idea of the body in a state of becoming, made of scattered parts, accurately captures the state of Chávez's DIY body before one puts it together. Other grotesque dolls, more closely aligned with the kind of body Stewart discusses, are the ones created by Venezuelan painter and sculptor Armando Reverón. For a discussion of the role of these dolls in Reverón's work and life as well as the ways in which the grotesque unsettles boundaries that police and shape national bodies and artistic traditions, see Javier Guerrero's chapter "Las muñecas de Armando Reverón" in *Tecnologías del cuerpo* (2014).

21   The Chavecito doll reappeared on social media platforms (Instagram, Facebook, Twitter) as "Chavela Frías," Hugo Chávez's "intersex twin," who challenges through parody and humor Chávez's epic masculinity as well as the political and social discourses coming from both the Right and the Left in Venezuela. For Chavela's fictional biography, see Stolk's "A Date with Chavela Frías" (2016).

22   In *Toying with God* (2010), Nikki Bado-Fralick and Rebecca Sachs Norris develop a brilliant analysis of the ways toys intervene in and shape political subjectivities and religious beliefs and practices. Their archive includes religion-themed board games as well as toys and dolls that represent various religious figures.

23   Examples of these movies include *Child's Play* (1988), *The Dummy* (2000), *Dead Silence* (2007), *Annabelle* (2014), and *The Boy* (2016). Historically, dolls have not been limited to being toys for children. As Bado-Fralick and Sachs Norris point out, dolls "around the world have been adored as figures or idols of goddesses and gods and have acted as ancestors, offerings, fetishes, amulets, talismans, and scapegoats" (2010, 33). This history, they note, evinces dolls' ability to "evoke within us a deep psychological ambivalence rooted in the fundamental worry that our control over the magic in dolls just might be slipping" (31–32).

24   It is worth mentioning, however, that the origin of the teddy bear ties it
        to the body of another man in power: Theodore Roosevelt. According to
        the official narrative posted by the Theodore Roosevelt Association on its
        website under the heading "The Real Teddy Bear Story," the teddy bear was
        created because of a cartoon that showed the president refusing to shoot a
        bear during a hunting trip in Mississippi in 1902. The cartoon showed the
        black bear as a frightened cub, which then served as the model for a candy
        shop owner, Morris Michtom, who asked President Roosevelt for permission
        to name the two stuffed bears he put on display "Teddy's bears" (Theodore
        Roosevelt Association). Though this story does not play a role in Sturken's
        analysis, and though the international popularity of the teddy bear has
        made the toy transcend its association with this specific historical context,
        we could argue that in a way it is also an example of the image of political
        innocence that Sturken discusses—for it made Roosevelt into a caring
        man refusing to hurt an innocent animal. It also speaks to the interplay
        between political power, playfulness, and imagination, which reflects the
        affective engagement that, I have argued, Chávez-themed toys demand.

Interlude. Afterdeath

1   In 2020, Luis Vicente León, president of Datanálisis—one of Venezuela's
        most respected polling companies—placed popular support for Maduro
        at 13 percent and for Juan Guaidó at 26 percent (Stefanoni 2020). He also
        mentioned that, at the time, 51 percent of Venezuelans continued to sup-
        port the administration of the deceased former president Hugo Chávez.
        Another poll conducted in May 2022 by More Consulting included, under
        the section "Futuro de Venezuela," the following question: "Let us imag-
        ine for a moment that next Sunday there were a presidential election in
        Venezuela and that Hugo Chávez were alive. Would you vote for him?" Of
        those interviewed, 48.4 percent answered yes. Beyond the percentage itself,
        it is interesting that, nine years after Chávez's death, he is still included in
        these polls as a potential candidate against whom all living political lead-
        ers must be measured.

2   Regarding this civil "we" that the epic excludes, Ana Teresa Torres notes:
        "The cult of the hero is always a cult of death, a cult for someone who has
        given their life for the fatherland. . . . Who, then, is everyone else? Appen-
        dices to history? Mere passersby in the landscape? What do we belong to,
        those Venezuelans who have not died (nor wish to die), we who have not
        suffered in prison (nor wish to), who have not been (nor wish to be) he-
        roic resistors against a dictator or valiant warriors in a great feat? Are we,
        perhaps, beings outside the fatherland, admirers who witness capital-H
        History from the wings? What includes us, then, if history seems to exist
        without us?" (Torres 2009, 16).

Chapter 5. Raw and Rotten

An earlier version of chapter 5 was published as "RAW: The Flesh of the Past," in *Deborah Castillo: Radical Disobedience*, edited by Alejandro Castro and Irina R. Troconis (New York: HemiPress, 2019).

1   Castillo reproduced the video of Pérez Pirela's critique of her performances in her video *Censura/censorship* (2015e).

2   Castillo performs these actions in *Slapping Power* (2015c) and *Parricidio* (2017).

3   See, e.g., Zerpa's *Señora Patria, sea usted bienvenida* (1979b) and *Yo soy la Patria* (1979a), and Loyola's *Intervención urbana en chatarra* (1982). For a comprehensive overview of Loyola's work, see Esteva-Grillet's essay "Juan Loyola" (2019).

4   The "explicit body" Schneider theorizes has been central to a group of Latin American female artists who, like Castillo and since the 1960s, have confronted patriarchy, racism, and repressive government regimes as well as challenged brutality and corruption through acts of desecration drawing on the unsettling power of bodily secretions. The work of a number of these artists was featured in the exhibition *Radical Women: Latin American Art, 1960–1985,* curated by Cecilia Fajardo-Hill and Andrea Giunta, which debuted at the Hammer Museum in Los Angeles in 2017. It is also the subject of the volume *Holy Terrors: Latin American Women Perform* (2003), edited by Diana Taylor and Roselyn Costantino.

5   These quotes are included in the explanatory text that introduces visitors to the artwork displayed in the museum: paintings, figurines, drawings, and photographs by numerous Venezuelan artists and artisans, among whom we find the aforementioned José Belandria and Goyito Bonilla.

6   *Online Etymology Dictionary,* s.v. "respect (v)," accessed October 24, 2023, https://www.etymonline.com/search?q=respect.

7   *Merriam-Webster,* s.v. "texture," accessed October 18, 2023, www.merriam-webster.com/dictionary/texture.

8   The impact the audience's reaction had on Castillo's execution of her performance is best seen in the second iteration of *Slapping Power,* which took place at Los Angeles's Broad Museum, October 11, 2018. In this performance, the audience's encouragement and enthusiasm ultimately led Castillo to use her nails to scratch the face of the bust to better reflect the collective anger toward the military figure that she felt the audience was experiencing (see Castillo 2019).

9   On nostalgia in contemporary Venezuelan fiction, see López 2019, 2020.

Coda

1   I am here referring to Didi-Huberman's understanding of gestures as "the body that resists, searches for another hand, to grab onto its hand, and to prolong its action" (2018, 18). Thus, a gesture as both marking a fissure, a moment of rupture (however small or seemingly inconsequential) and signaling the need for a connection that extends across times and spaces and that, precisely because of its ongoingness, is imbued with infinite potency.

2   In "Barrio Women and Popular Politics in Chávez's Venezuela," sociologist Sujatha Fernandes gives an account of the local participatory spaces built by women in the barrios of Caracas and the way they challenge "gender roles, collectivize private tasks, and create alternatives to male-centric politics" (2013, 117). In her discussion of the daily work that goes into organizing a soup kitchen in the parish known as Carretera Negra of La Vega, she includes an issue raised by one of her interviewees, Orlando, who said that "militants from the Chavista vanguard youth organization Frente Francisco de Miranda had stopped by the soup kitchen and demanded that the community activists put a banner outside the kitchen with the insignia of the Chavista mayor and a name taken from one of the founding heroes, such as Bolívar or Sucre" (139). The vignette is a transcript of the answer another interviewee, Freddy, gave after listening to Orlando's comment.

3   Venezuelan artist Violette Bule's exhibit *Echo Chamber* opened to the public at the Transart Foundation for Art and Anthropology in Houston, August 2020 (Bule 2020a). It included three pieces—*REQUIEM200≤*, *El Guiso*, and *El Helicoide*—as well as a selection of Bule's photographs. Combining digital technologies with wood and metal, Bule's work as staged in *Echo Chamber* offers a poignant critique of social issues, power structures, and the politics of memory that, throughout Venezuela's history, have permeated discourses of progress and modernity as well as revolutionary projects promising political change. She invites the audience to sort through the remnants of many uncomfortable or forgotten pasts that have accumulated in the present and work through them in efforts to develop a more critical relationship to history and thus a more open and creative engagement with the future. The vignette features the piece titled *El Guiso* (Bule 2020b). In Venezuela, the word "guiso" denotes both a stew that can be made with a wide variety of ingredients and an act of fraud, corruption, or deception that breaks the law for personal gain. Other works by Bule can be accessed on her web page: https://www.violettebule.com/.

4   The quotation is from a personal communication by email with Bule, April 2020.

5   Ana Alenso's installation is one of several that the Venezuelan artist has created to denounce the country's oil dependency and extractivist practices. The

piece was staged at the Garden Bridge in Berlin's Brücke Museum in 2019. Other works by Alenso are available on her web page: http://anaalenso.com/.

6   This vignette includes some of the slogans featured on posters women carried during protests that took place as part of Venezuela's Yo te creo movement (#YoTeCreoVzla). The movement started in May 2021 on social media, with the testimonies of women who denounced the sexual abuse they had suffered at the hands of well-known Venezuelan artists, writers, and musicians. As it developed, it went beyond the specificities of the cases related to the entertainment industry to become a collective movement that advocated for women's rights and that joined other Latin American fourth-wave grassroots feminist movements such as Argentina's Ni una menos. See *Semana*'s "'Yo te creo'" (2021).

7   *Trenzar una a una nuestras historias* is a poetic action organized by Venezuelan artist Adriana Rondón-Rivero in September 2014 in Denver (see Rondón-Rivero 2014a, 2014b). She described it as "an instance of ephemeral live art, of a public-performance nature, conceived of as a brief moment of intimacy and communion among women, in which the ancestral activity of women braiding one another's hair creates an environment of trust and calm that is conducive to sharing stories, anecdotes, or personal experiences" (González-Flores 2018). A new version of the action titled *Trenzando una a una nuestras historias de mujeres migrantes* took place via Zoom in 2020. In it, thirty-three migrant Venezuelan women appeared on their respective screens holding a thread and sharing with the group their names, their stories, and the objects that reminded them of home and that they had taken with them when they left Venezuela in search of a better life and better opportunities. For a video of the 2020 poetic action, see Rondón-Rivero's "Video completo 'Trenzando una a una nuestras historias de mujeres migrantes'" (2020). For a video of the 2014 poetic action, see Rondón-Rivero's "Trenzar una a una nuestras historias" (2014).

8   In *Dancing Jacobins*, Rafael Sánchez speaks of representations of Simón Bolívar in the public space of the nation as mirrors: "The ongoing goal is the saturation of Venezuela's public spaces with as many Bolívar-mirrors— busts, equestrian monuments, oversized portraits—as possible, so that, whenever the need arises, the nation's heterogeneous majorities may be wrested from their dangerous wanderings and, through reflection, made to coalesce in front of those mirrors as a mobilized Bolivarian people" (2016, 294). This kind of mirror shapes reflections into one specific identity. The mirrors in these vignettes, I propose, do the opposite; their goal is not to fix an identity in place, but to gesture toward forms of relationality that can lead to communities of care (as in Rondón-Rivero's poetic action) or to discomforting critical approaches to state archives and national history (as in Bule's installation).

REFERENCES

ABC. 2013. "Día del tatuaje gratis con la firma sempiterna de Hugo Chávez." ABC Internacional, April 1. https://www.abc.es/internacional/20130401/abci-tatuajes -chavez-hugo-201304011705.html.

ABC. 2014. "Crean un procesador de texto que imita la letra de Hugo Chávez." ABC Internacional, July 29. https://www.abc.es/internacional/20140729/abci -chavez-escritura-201407281931.html.

Acedo, Omar. 2013. "Chávez seguirá contigo." YouTube video, 4:54. Accessed April 16, 2024. https://www.youtube.com/watch?v=7yokHgFi_BU.

Agamben, Giorgio. 2013. "On the Uses and Disadvantages of Living among Specters." In *The Spectralities Reader: Ghosts and Haunting in Contemporary Cultural Theory*, edited by María del Pilar Blanco and Esther Peeren, 473–77. New York: Bloomsbury Academic.

Agüero, Pablo, dir. 2015. *Eva no duerme*. JBA Production. 1 hr., 25 min.

Ahmed, Sara. 2010. "Happy Objects." In *The Affect Theory Reader*, edited by Melissa Gregg and Gregory J. Seigworth, 29–51. Durham, NC: Duke University Press.

Ahmed, Sara. 2014. *The Cultural Politics of Emotion*. New York: Routledge.

Alba, Álvaro. 2011. "Enfermedad de Chávez aviva el mito de la 'maldición del panteón de Bolívar.'" Radio y Televisión Martí, July 7. https://www.martinoticias .com/a/enfermedad-de-chavez-aviva-el-mito/9009.html.

Alenso, Ana. 2019. *Oil Intervention #7*. Installation, Brücke Museum, Berlin, August 11–October 13, 2019.

Althusser, Louis. (1995) 2014. *On the Reproduction of Capitalism: Ideology and Ideological State Apparatuses*. Translated by G. M. Goshgarian. New York: Verso.

Andrade, Gabriel. 2020a. "Banal Nationalism: Disputes in Venezuela, 1999–2019." *Journal of Nationalism, Memory, and Language Politics* 14, no. 2: 177–95.

Andrade, Gabriel. 2020b. "Conspiracy Mongering in Venezuela: The *Chavismo* Period (1998–2018)." *Bulletin of Latin American Research* 39, no. 4: 500–512.

Angosto-Ferrández, Luis Fernando. 2015. *Venezuela Reframed: Bolivarianism, Indigenous Peoples and Socialisms of the Twenty-First Century.* London: Zed Books.

Angosto-Ferrández, Luis Fernando. 2016. "The Afterlives of Hugo Chávez as Political Symbol." *Anthropology Today* 32, no. 5: 8–12.

Apolinar Rea. 2010. "Mostrados los restos del libertador exhumación Simón Bolívar." YouTube video, 6:11. https://www.youtube.com/watch?v=GvBociElsYk.

Aporrea. 2007. "(VIDEO) Chávez: 'El muñeco.'" Aporrea. Accessed September 20, 2020. https://www.aporrea.org/actualidad/n94072.html.

Aporrea. 2013. "11 Abr 2013 7 avenidas colmadas en Caracas en cierre de campaña de Nicolás Maduro Presidente 2013." YouTube video, 5:50:06. Accessed September 20, 2020. https://www.youtube.com/watch?v=R84VxhG15QE.

Aporrea. 2014. "Lanzan en Venezuela primera tipografía digital con la letra de Chávez." Aporrea, July 28. https://www.aporrea.org/tecno/n255154.html.

Arispe, Ricardo. 2017. *#Somos#Resilientes.* Caracas: Self-published.

Arroyo Poleo, Fabiola. 2015. "Reescrituras visuales del cuerpo nacional: Políticas y poéticas de la memoria histórica en la Venezuela actual." In *La política encarnada: Biopolítica y cultura en la Venezuela bolivariana*, edited by Luis Duno-Gottberg, 179–216. Caracas: Equinoccio.

Ascencio, Michaelle. 2012. *De que vuelan, vuelan: Imaginarios religiosos venezolanos.* Caracas: Editorial Alfa.

Assmann, Jan. 2006. *Religion and Cultural Memory: Ten Studies.* Stanford, CA: Stanford University Press.

Avelar, Idelber. 1999. *The Untimely Present: Postdictatorial Latin American Fiction and the Task of Mourning.* Durham, NC: Duke University Press.

Azzellini, Dario. 2018. *Communes and Workers' Control in Venezuela.* Chicago: Haymarket Books.

Bado-Fralick, Nikki, and Rebecca Sachs Norris. 2010. *Toying with God: The World of Religious Games and Dolls.* Waco, TX: Baylor University Press.

Barráez, Sebastiana. 2017. "Los verdaderos hijos de Chávez." *El Estímulo* (Caracas), November 21. https://elestimulo.com/los-verdaderos-hijos-de-chavez/.

Barrera Tyszka, Alberto. 2015. *Patria o muerte.* Barcelona: Tusquets Editores.

Barthes, Roland. (1977) 2010. *A Lover's Discourse: Fragments.* Translated by Richard Howard. New York: Hill and Wang.

Barthes, Roland. (1980) 1981. *Camera Lucida: Reflections on Photography.* Translated by Richard Howard. New York: Hill and Wang.

Bastidasa, Alejandra. 2022. "Legado del Comandante Eterno Hugo Chávez continúa más vivo que nunca en el corazón del pueblo." Ministerio del Poder Popular de Economía, Finanzas y Comercio Exterior, March 5. http://www

.mppef.gob.ve/especial-legado-del-comandante-eterno-hugo-chavez-continua
-mas-vivo-que-nunca-en-el-corazon-del-pueblo/.

Baudrillard, Jean. (2007) 2009. *Why Hasn't Everything Already Disappeared?*
Translated by Chris Turner. London: Seagull Books.

Bauer, Tristán, dir. 1997. *Evita, la tumba sin paz*. YouTube video, 55:21. Accessed
June 25, 2023. https://www.youtube.com/watch?v=hcL_cybH340.

Beasley-Murray, Jon. 2010. *Posthegemony: Political Theory and Latin America.*
Minneapolis: University of Minnesota Press.

Bellaviti, Sean. 2021. "*La hora de la salsa*: Nicolás Maduro and the Political Dimensions of Salsa in Venezuela." *Journal of Latin American Studies* 53, no. 2: 373–96.

Benjamin, Walter. 1999. *The Arcades Project*. Translated by Howard Eiland and
Kevin McLaughlin. Cambridge, MA: Belknap Press.

Benjamin, Walter. 2006. "On the Concept of History." In *Selected Writings 4:
1938–1940*. Edited by Howard Eiland and Michael W. Jennings, 389–400. Cambridge, MA: Belknap Press.

Bilbija, Ksenija, and Leigh A. Payne. 2011. "Time Is Money: The Memory Market
in Latin America." In *Accounting for Violence: Marketing Memory in Latin
America*, edited by Ksenija Bilbija and Leigh A. Payne, 1–40. Durham, NC:
Duke University Press.

Billig, Michael. 1995. *Banal Nationalism*. London: Sage Publications.

Blackmore, Lisa. 2014. "Capture Life: The 'Document Monument' in Recent Com-
memorations of Hugo Chávez." *Journal of Latin American Cultural Studies* 23,
no. 3: 235–50.

Blackmore, Lisa. 2017. *Spectacular Modernity: Dictatorship, Space, and Visuality in
Venezuela, 1948–1958*. Pittsburgh, PA: University of Pittsburgh Press.

Blanco, Eduardo. 1979. *Venezuela heroica: Cuadros históricos*. Caracas: Monte
Ávila Editores.

Blanco, María del Pilar, and Esther Peeren. 2013. "Introduction: Conceptualizing Spectralities." In *The Spectralities Reader: Ghosts and Haunting in Contemporary Cultural Theory*, edited by María del Pilar Blanco and Esther Peeren,
1–27. New York: Bloomsbury Academic.

Bottici, Chiara. 2014. *Imaginal Politics: Images beyond Imagination and the Imaginary*. New York: Columbia University Press.

Boym, Svetlana. 2001. *The Future of Nostalgia*. New York: Basic Books.

Bracci Roa, Luigino. 2011. "Generan firma electrónica del Presidente Chávez."
YouTube video, 6:03. Accessed January 30, 2022. https://www.youtube.com
/watch?v=oG5OhsEWT2s.

Brading, Ryan. 2013. *Populism in Venezuela*. New York: Routledge.

Brennan, Teresa. 2004. *The Transmission of Affect*. Ithaca, NY: Cornell University Press.

Brown, Bill. 2004. "Thing Theory." In *Things*, edited by Bill Brown, 1–22. Chicago:
University of Chicago Press.

Bruce, Iain. 2008. *Real Venezuela: Making Socialism in the 21st Century*. London: Pluto Press.

Buck-Morss, Susan. 1989. *The Dialectics of Seeing: Walter Benjamin and the Arcades Project*. Cambridge, MA: MIT Press.

Bule, Violette. 2020a. *Echo Chamber*. Exhibition, Transart Foundation for Art and Anthropology, Houston, TX, August 1–October 18, 2020.

Bule, Violette. 2020b. *El Guiso*. Installation. Transart Foundation for Art and Anthropology, Houston, TX.

Burgos, Edixela, and Gustavo Hernández Díaz. 2021. "Desinformación digital en Venezuela: *Trolls, Bots* y *Cyborgs*." *Estudios Venezolanos de Comunicación* 196:121–33.

Burke, Clare, and Suzanne M. Spencer-Wood. 2018. "Introduction." In *Crafting in the World: Materiality in the Making*, edited by Clare Burke and Suzanne M. Spencer-Wood, 1–18. Berlin: Springer.

Buxton, Julia. 2018. "Venezuela: Deeper into the Abyss." *Revista de Ciencia Política* 38, no. 2: 409–28.

Carrera Damas, Germán. (1969) 1973. *El culto a Bolívar: Esbozo para un estudio de la historia de las ideas en Venezuela*. Caracas: Ediciones de la Biblioteca de la Universidad Central de Venezuela.

Castillo, Deborah. 2011. *Lamezuela*. Street performance, Maracaibo, Venezuela.

Castillo, Deborah. 2013a. *Action and Cult*. Exhibition, Centro Cultural Chacao, Caracas, Venezuela, February 27–April 14, 2013.

Castillo, Deborah. 2013b. *The Emancipatory Kiss*. Video performance. Centro Cultural Chacao, Caracas, Venezuela.

Castillo, Deborah. 2013c. *Sisyphus*. Video performance. Centro Cultural Chacao, Caracas, Venezuela.

Castillo, Deborah. 2015a. *RAW*. Exhibition, Mandragoras Art Space, New York, September 22–October 15, 2015.

Castillo, Deborah. 2015b. *Demagogue*. Video performance. Mandragoras Art Space, New York.

Castillo, Deborah. 2015c. *Slapping Power*. Live performance. Mandragoras Art Space, New York.

Castillo, Deborah. 2015d. *The Unnamable*. Video performance. Mandragoras Art Space, New York.

Castillo, Deborah. 2015e. *Censura/Censorship*. Vimeo video, 3:20. Accessed April 6, 2019. https://vimeo.com/145309381.

Castillo, Deborah. 2017. *Parricidio*. Video performance. Galería Carmen Araujo Arte, Caracas, Venezuela.

Castillo, Deborah. 2019. "The Broad Museum—Live Performance." Vimeo video, 00:56. Accessed October 30, 2022. https://vimeo.com/318072335.

Castillo, Fred. 2014. "Chávez habla del Caracazo." YouTube video, 1:37. Accessed October 30, 2022. https://www.youtube.com/watch?v=NI5AvEO5N1Q.

Castro, Juan Cristóbal. 2020. *Arqueología sonámbula*. Bogotá: Anfibia.

Castro Leiva, Luis. 2005. "De la patria boba a la teología bolivariana." In *Luis Castro Leiva: Obras, volumen I*, 174–400. Caracas: Fundación Polar.

CDH (Consejo de Derechos Humanos). 2020. *Conclusiones detalladas de la misión internacional independiente de determinación de los hechos sobre la República Bolivariana de Venezuela*. https://cepaz.org/wp-content/uploads/2020/09/A _HRC_45_CRP.11_SP.pdf.

Chávez, Hugo (@chavezcandanga). 2010. "Epa que tal? Aparecí como lo dije: a la medianoche. Pa Brasil me voy. Y muy contento a trabajar por Venezuela. Venceremos!!" Twitter, April 28. https://twitter.com/chavezcandanga/status /12988160900?lang=en.

Chávez, Hugo. 2012. *Cuentos del arañero*. Caracas: Txalaparta.

Chávez, Hugo. 2022. "Carta del Comandante Presidente Hugo Chávez a su paisano y amigo Armando Rivas." Todo Chávez. Accessed July 7, 2022. http:// todochavez.gob.ve/todochavez/6274-carta-del-comandante-presidente-hugo -chavez-a-su-paisano-y-amigo-armando-rivas.

Chávez Frías, Hugo, and Agustín Blanco Muñoz. 1998. *Venezuela del 04F–92 al 06D–98: Habla el Comandante Hugo Chávez Frías*. Caracas: Catedra Pio Tamayo, CEHA/IIES/FACES/UCV.

Ciccariello-Maher, George. 2013. *We Created Chávez: A People's History of the Venezuelan Revolution*. Durham, NC: Duke University Press.

Clarín. 2016. "Un holograma de Hugo Chávez camina por las calles de Caracas." *Clarín* (Buenos Aires), December 12. https://www.clarin.com/mundo /holograma-hugo-chavez-camina-caracas_0_BkahkV2ml.html.

Classen, Constance. 2005. "The Witch's Senses: Sensory Ideologies and Transgressive Femininities from the Renaissance to Modernity." In *Empire of the Senses*, edited by David Howes, 70–84. Oxford: Berg Publishers.

CNN. 2013. "Forense digital no ve manipulación en fotos de Chávez con sus hijas." CNN Español, February 18. https://cnnespanol.cnn.com/2013/02/18/videos -denuncian-presunto-montaje-en-foto-de-hugo-chavez/.

COFAVIC. 2023. "34 años del Caracazo: Hacerse nuevas preguntas." COFAVIC, February 24. https://cofavic.org/2023/02/24/34-anos-del-caracazo-hacerse -nuevas-preguntas/.

Colmeiro, José. 2011. "Nation of Ghosts? Haunting, Historical Memory and Forgetting in Post-Franco Spain." *452ºF. Electronic Journal of Theory of Literature and Comparative Literature* 4:17–34.

Colombeia TV. 2016. "Chávez caminante 8D." Facebook Watch video, 1:15. Accessed February 20, 2022. https://m.facebook.com/Colombeiatv/videos /ch%C3%A1vez-caminante-8dun-holograma-del-l%C3%ADder-de-la -revoluci%C3%B3n-venezolana-hugo-ch%C3%A1ve/1040645429377937/ ?_rdr.

"Comandante Chávez: ¡Amor con amor se paga!" 2017. YouTube video, 1:16. Accessed January 20, 2022. https://www.youtube.com/watch?v=-DGtA1St68I.

Comando Carabobo. 2012. "¡Chávez es Pueblo! ¡Chávez somos millones, tú también eres Chávez!" YouTube video, 00:40. Accessed June 6, 2022. https://www.youtube.com/watch?v=n4sdk7Zyaa8.

Coronil, Fernando. 1997. *The Magical State: Nature, Money, and Modernity in Venezuela*. Chicago: University of Chicago Press.

Coronil, Fernando. 2008. "Magical History: What's Left of Chavez?" Unpublished. Accessed October 23, 2023. http://lanic.utexas.edu/project/etext/llilas/vrp/coronil.pdf.

Corrales, Javier. 2020. "Authoritarian Survival: Why Maduro Hasn't Fallen." *Journal of Democracy* 31, no. 3: 39–53.

Corrales, Javier, and Michael Penfold. (2011) 2015. *Dragon in the Tropics: The Legacy of Hugo Chávez*. Washington, DC: Brookings Institution Press.

CRM (Colectivo Revolucionario Mérida). 2012. "VIDEO 'Chávez corazón del pueblo' Hany Kauam, Los Cadillacs y Omar Enrique Campaña Carabobo 2012." YouTube video, 4:21. Accessed January 30, 2021. https://www.youtube.com/watch?v=IOxj9MLP_u8.

Cubanet. 2018. "'A Chávez lo mataron,' asegura su hermano Adán." *Cubanet* (Coral Gables), June 7. https://www.cubanet.org/venezuela/chavez-lo-mataron-asegura-hermano-adan/.

Dabove, Juan Pablo. 2011. "Hugo Chávez and Maisanta: Orality, Literacy and the Construction of Legitimacy Outside the Law." *Vanderbilt e-Journal of Luso-Hispanic Studies* 7. https://ejournals.library.vanderbilt.edu/index.php/lusohispanic/article/view/3269/1491.

Dawkins, Richard. 1976. *The Selfish Gene*. New York: Oxford University Press.

Derby, Lauren. 1999. "The Dictator's Two Bodies: Hidden Powers of State in the Dominican Imagination." *Etnofoor* 12, no. 2: 92–116.

Derrida, Jacques. 1988. *Limited Inc*. Translated by Samuel Weber. Evanston, IL: Northwestern University Press.

Derrida, Jacques. 1993. *Specters of Marx: The State of the Debt, the Work of Mourning and the New International*. Translated by Peggy Kamuf. New York: Routledge.

Derrida, Jacques. 1995. "Archive Fever: A Freudian Impression." Translated by Eric Prenowitz. *Diacritics* 25, no. 2: 9–63.

Derrida, Jacques, and Bernard Stiegler. 2002. *Echographies of Television: Filmed Interviews*. Cambridge: Polity Press.

Desanzo, Juan Carlos, dir. 1996. *Eva Perón*. Facets, 1 hr., 54 min.

Diario Extra. 2014. "Chávez sigue escribiendo . . . en Word." *Diario Extra* (San José), July 28. https://www.diarioextra.com/Noticia/detalle/237425/ch-vez-sigue-escribiendo-en-word.

Didi-Huberman, Georges. (2000) 2016. *Being a Skull: Site, Contact, Thought, Sculpture*. Translated by Drew Burk. Minneapolis: Univocal.

Didi-Huberman, Georges. 2018. "Conflicts of Gestures, Conflicts of Images." *Nordic Journal of Aesthetics*, no. 55/56, 8–22.

Doyle, Jennifer. 2013. *Hold It Against Me: Difficulty and Emotion in Contemporary Art*. Durham, NC: Duke University Press.

Duno-Gottberg, Luis. 2015. "Narrativas somáticas y cambio social: Notas para el cuadro venezolano." In *La política encarnada: Biopolítica y cultura en la Venezuela bolivariana*, edited by Duno-Gottberg, 263–97. Caracas: Equinoccio.

Duno-Gottberg, Luis. 2016. "Embodiments and Disembodiments of the Nation, the People, and the State." In *Simón Bolívar: Travel and Transformations of a Cultural Icon*, edited by Maureen G. Shanahan and Ana María Reyes, 230–45. Gainesville: University Press of Florida.

800 Noticias. 2016. "Villegas: Holograma de Chávez levantó roncha en Miami." *800 Noticias* (Caracas), December 10. http://800noticias.com/villegas-holograma -de-chavez-levanto-roncha-en-miami.

El Comercio. 2013. "Sujeto mató a su madre como sacrificio por salud de Hugo Chávez." *El Comercio* (Lima), January 18. https://elcomercio.pe/mundo/actualidad /sujeto-mato-su-madre-como-sacrificio-salud-hugo-chavez-noticia-1524710/.

Elfenbein, Rachel. 2019. *Engendering Revolution: Women, Unpaid Labor, and Maternalism in Bolivarian Venezuela*. Austin: University of Texas Press.

El Heraldo. 2013. "Chávez se me apareció en forma de pajarito: Maduro." YouTube video, 1:10. Accessed September 20, 2020. https://www.youtube.com/watch?v =qv5dAqSSoXU.

Elkins, James. 1996. *The Object Stares Back: On the Nature of Seeing*. San Diego, CA: Harcourt Brace.

El Mundo. 2006. "'Chavecito' hace campaña en Venezuela." *El Mundo* (Madrid), November 28. https://www.elmundo.es/elmundo/2006/11/27/internacional /1164627428.html.

El Mundo. 2011. "Magia negra contra la enfermedad de Chávez." *El Mundo* (Madrid), September 13. https://www.elmundo.es/america/2011/09/11/venezuela /1315755012.html.

El Mundo. 2013. "'El País' retira de los quioscos el periódico tras publicar una foto falsa de Chávez." *El Mundo* (Madrid), January 24. https://www.elmundo .es/elmundo/2013/01/24/comunicacion/1359010453.html.

El País. 2017. "A Maduro se le posa una mariposa y la reconoce como el 'espíritu inmortal de Chávez.'" *El País* (Madrid), April 8. https://elpais.com/elpais/2017 /04/08/videos/1491665755_866265.html.

El Universo. 2005. "El 'Chavecito,' el muñeco de Hugo Chávez para las navidades en Venezuela." *El Universo* (Quito), November 10. https://www.eluniverso.com /2005/11/10/0001/14/50F1352047594A8F9882DA2B2B7CE78C.html/.

El Universo. 2017. "Campaña de Diosdado Cabello: 'Aquí no se habla mal de Hugo Chávez.'" *El Universo* (Quito), January 26. https://www.eluniverso.com/noticias /2017/01/27/nota/6017368/campana-cabello-aqui-no-se-habla-mal-chavez/.

EsCaracas. 2019. "Las enigmáticas similitudes de Juan Guaidó con Simón Bolívar." *EsCaracas* (Caracas), January 15. https://escaracas.com/ccsnews/2019/01/15 /similitudes-guaido-simon-bolivar/.

Esteva-Grillet, Roldán. 2019. "Juan Loyola: el artista que previó al país vuelto chatarra." *Trópico absoluto*, August 25. https://tropicoabsoluto.com/2019/08 /25/juan-loyola-el-artista-que-previo-al-pais-vuelto-chatarra/.

Evnine, Simon J. 2018. "The Anonymity of a Murmur: Internet (and Other) Memes." *British Journal of Aesthetics* 58, no. 3: 303–18.

Fajardo-Hill, Cecilia, and Andrea Giunta, eds. *Radical Women: Latin American Art, 1960–1985*. New York: Prestel, 2017. Exhibition catalog.

Fechner-Smarsly, Thomas. 2006. "Blood Samples and Fingerprint Files: Blood as Artificial Matter, Artistic Material, and Means of the Signature." In *Sign Here! Handwriting in the Age of New Media*, edited by Sonja Neef, José van Dijck, and Eric Ketelaar, 196–205. Amsterdam: Amsterdam University Press.

Fernandes, Sujatha. 2010. *Who Can Stop the Drums? Urban Social Movements in Chávez's Venezuela*. Durham, NC: Duke University Press.

Fernandes, Sujatha. 2013. "Barrio Women and Popular Politics in Chávez's Venezuela." In *The New Latin American Left*, edited by Jeffery R. Webber and Barry Carr, 117–46. Lanham, MD: Rowman and Littlefield.

Foucault, Michel. 1995. *Discipline and Punish: The Birth of the Prison*. Translated by A. Sheridan. New York: Vintage Books.

Gamba, Pablo. 2013. "Un iconoclasta en la Venezuela de Chávez." *El Espectador Imaginario* (Barcelona), July. https://www.elespectadorimaginario.com /iconoclasta-en-la-venezuela-de-chavez/.

GBV (Gobierno Bolivariano de Venezuela). 2013. *Venezuela contra la guerra económica*. Caracas: Ministerio del Poder Popular para la Comunicación y la Información.

GBV. 2022. "17 de diciembre de 1982: El Comandante Eterno Hugo Chávez juró ante El Samán de Güere." 2022. Gobierno Bolivariano de Venezuela, Vicepresidencia de la República Bolivariana de Venezuela. Accessed July 8, 2022. http://vicepresidencia.gob.ve/17-de-diciembre-de-1982-el-comandante-eterno -hugo-chavez-juro-ante-el-saman-de-guere/.

González-Flores, Germán. 2018. "'Trenzar una a una Nuestras Historias.'" *La Prensa de Colorado* (Brighton), March 30. https://laprensadecolorado.com /trenzar-una-a-una-nuestras-historias/.

González-Stephan, Beatriz. 2015. "Subversive Needlework: Gender, Class and History at Venezuela's National Exhibition, 1883." In *Images of Power*, edited by Jens Andermann and William Rowe, 51–77. New York: Berghahn Books.

Gordon, Avery F. (1997) 2008. *Ghostly Matters: Haunting and the Sociological Imagination*. Minneapolis: University of Minnesota Press.

Gott, Richard. 2005. *Hugo Chávez and the Bolivarian Revolution*. London: Verso.

Gratch, Lyndsay Michalik. 2017. *Adaptation Online: Creating Memes, Sweding Movies, and Other Digital Performances*. Lanham, MD: Lexington Books.

Gregg, Melissa, and Gregory J. Seigworth. 2010. "An Inventory of Shimmers." In *The Affect Theory Reader*, edited by Melissa Gregg and Gregory J. Seigworth, 1–25. Durham, NC: Duke University Press.

Grosz, Elizabeth. 1993. "Merleau-Ponty and Irigaray in the Flesh." *Thesis Eleven* 36, no. 1: 37–59.

Guaglianone, José Leonardo. 2015. "Memoria visual en la pista: Artes y culturas urbanas políticas de Caracas (1998–2013)." In *Rostros y rastros de un líder: Hugo Chávez; memoria de un pueblo*, 76–113. Caracas: Archivo General de la Nación, Centro Nacional de Historia. Grupo UN.

Guerra, José. 2019. *El mito del socialismo bolivariano*. Caracas: Editorial Dahbar.

Guerrero, Gustavo. 2020. "Cinco poetas venezolanos ante el nuevo siglo." *Guaraguao* 24, no. 64: 39–63.

Guerrero, Javier. 2012a. "Cultures of the Body: Venezuela's *Holy* Family." *452°F. Electronic Journal of Theory of Literature and Comparative Literature* 6:17–38.

Guerrero, Javier. 2012b. "El muñeco Chávez." *Tal Cual Digital* (Caracas), June 16.

Guerrero, Javier. 2014. *Tecnologías del cuerpo: Exhibicionismo y visualidad en América Latina*. Madrid: Iberoamericana Editorial Vervuert.

Hardy, William John. 1893. *The Handwriting of the Kings and Queens of England*. London: Religious Tract Society.

Harris, Jonathan Gil. 2011. "Four Exoskeletons and No Funeral." *New Literary History* 42, no. 4: 615–39.

Harrison, Robert Pogue. 2003. *The Dominion of the Dead*. Chicago: University of Chicago Press.

Hetland, Gabriel. 2015. "Emergent Socialist Hegemony in Bolivarian Venezuela: The Role of the Party." In *Crisis and Contradiction: Marxist Perspectives on Latin America in the Global Political Economy*, edited by Susan J. Spronk and Jeffery Webber, 120–37. Leiden: Brill.

Hirsch, Marianne. (1997) 2012. *Family Frames: Photography, Narrative, and Postmemory*. Cambridge, MA: Harvard University Press.

Horváth, Ágnes. 2021. *Political Alchemy: Technology Unbounded*. Abingdon, UK: Routledge.

Huyssen, Andreas. 2003. *Present Pasts: Urban Palimpsests and the Politics of Memory*. Stanford, CA: Stanford University Press.

Issuu. n.d. "Ejército comunicacional." Issuu. Accessed June 29, 2022. https://issuu.com/ejercito.comunicacional.

Ives, Kelly. 2013. *Luce Irigaray: Lips, Kissing, and the Politics of Sexual Difference*. Maidstone, UK: Crescent Moon Publishing.

Johnston, Sean F. 2016. *Holograms: A Cultural History*. Oxford: Oxford University Press.

Jusino Díaz, Cristel. 2015. "'Balance prepóstumo': Temporalidad queer y literatura latinoamericana, 1983–1993." PhD diss., New York University.

Kaiser, Susana. 2011. "Memory Inventory: The Production and Consumption of Memory Goods in Argentina." In *Accounting for Violence: Marketing Memory in Latin America*, edited by Ksenija Bilbija and Leigh A. Payne, 313–37. Durham, NC: Duke University Press.

Kantorowicz, Ernst. (1957) 2016. *The King's Two Bodies: A Study in Medieval Political Theology*. Princeton, NJ: Princeton University Press.

Keller, Patricia M. 2016. *Ghostly Landscapes: Film, Photography, and the Aesthetics of Haunting in Contemporary Spanish Culture*. Toronto: University of Toronto Press.

Kestler, Thomas, and Miguel Latouche. 2019. "The Ideational Foundations of Authoritarianism in Venezuela: Institutionalizing the Charismatic Legacy of Hugo Chávez." Unpublished. https://www.academia.edu/42968809/The_Ideational _Foundations_of_Authoritarianism_in_Venezuela_Institutionalizing_the _Charismatic_Legacy_of_Hugo_Ch%C3%A1vez?sm=b.

Key, Ramón, and Claudina Villarroel. 2018. "El petróleo será insuficiente: El colapso de la industria petrolera y la crisis venezolana." *Debates IESA* 23, no. 2: 18–25.

Khan, Omar. 2014. "'Los maletines' narra la violencia y corrupción de la Venezuela chavista." *El País* (Madrid), July 13. https://elpais.com/cultura/2014/07/13 /actualidad/1405259864_318771.html.

Kingsbury, Donald V. 2018. *Only the People Can Save the People: Constituent Power, Revolution, and Counterrevolution in Venezuela*. Albany: State University of New York Press.

La Nación. 2014. "Se le apareció otro 'pajarito' a Nicolás Maduro y le dijo que Hugo Chávez 'está feliz.'" *La Nación* (Vicente López, Argentina), July 29. https://www .lanacion.com.ar/el-mundo/se-le-aparecio-otro-pajarito-a-nicolas-maduro-y -le-dijo-que-hugo-chavez-esta-feliz-nid1713948/.

La Tercera. 2013. "El misterioso doble de Chávez." *La Tercera* (Santiago, Chile), April 20. https://www.latercera.com/diario-impreso/el-misterioso-doble-de -chavez/.

Labanyi, Jo. 2000. "History and Hauntology; or, What Does One Do with the Ghosts of the Past? Reflections on Spanish Film and Fiction of the Post-Franco Period." In *Disremembering the Dictatorship*, edited by Joan Ramon Resina, 65–82. Leiden: Brill.

Labanyi, Jo. 2002. "Engaging with Ghosts; or, Theorizing Culture in Modern Spain." In *Constructing Identity in Twentieth-Century Spain: Theoretical Debates and Cultural Practice*, edited by Jo Labanyi, 1–14. Oxford: Oxford University Press.

Lacan, Jacques. (1977) 2019. *The Four Fundamental Concepts of Psycho-Analysis*. London: Routledge.

Lander, María Fernanda. 2021. "*Y recuerda que te espero* by Juan Carlos Méndez Guédez: Seeing and Being Seen in Revolutionary Venezuela." In *Wall to Wall: Law as Culture in Latin America and Spain*, edited by Cristina Pérez-Arranz, Carlos Varón González, David Yagüe González, and Ana Yáñez Rodríguez, 67–80. Wilmington, DE: Vernon Press.

Lapatilla Patillavideo. 2015. "Nicolás Maduro se coloca unos lentes con los ojos de Chávez." YouTube video, 1:05. Accessed February 3, 2022. https://www.youtube .com/watch?v=twrSunOtq_Y.

Lares, Fermín. 2014. *El expediente del chavismo: El rojo balance del socialismo del siglo XXI (1999–2014)*. Caracas: La Hoja del Norte.

Latour, Bruno. 1996. "On Actor-Network Theory: A Few Clarifications Plus More Than a Few Complications." *Soziale Welt* 47:369–81.

LBRV (Luigino Bracci Roa desde Venezuela). 2021. "Retratos de Simón Bolívar y Hugo Chávez retornaron al Palacio Federal Legislativo." YouTube video, 31:58. Accessed February 3, 2022. https://www.youtube.com/watch?app=desktop&v=xNSOafo3Lxk.

Lecumberri, Beatriz. 2012. *La revolución sentimental: Viaje periodístico por la Venezuela de Chávez*. Caracas: Ediciones Puntocero.

Lefebvre, Henri. 2003. "Space and the State." In *State/Space: A Reader*, edited by Neil Brenner, Bob Jessop, Martin Jones, and Gordon MacLeod, 84–100. Oxford: Blackwell Publishing.

Libertad Digital. 2013. "Maduro presenta al doble de Chávez: 'Aquí está. ¡Vive!'" *Libertad Digital* (Madrid), April 10. www.libertaddigital.com/internacional/latinoamerica/2013–04–10/maduro-presenta-al-doble-de-chavez-aqui-esta-chavez-vive-1276487148/.

Linares, Albinson. 2014. "Testimonios: ¿Por qué la gente se tatúa la firma de Chávez?" *Prodavinci*, August 1. https://historico.prodavinci.com/2014/08/01/actualidad/cronica-audios-testimonios-por-que-la-gente-se-tatua-la-firma-de-chavez-por-albinson-linares/.

López, Jaime. 2010. "Exhuman el cadáver de Simón Bolívar para investigar si fue envenenado con arsénico." *El Mundo* (Madrid), July 17. https://www.elmundo.es/america/2010/07/16/venezuela/1279300516.html.

López, Magdalena. 2019. "Fleeing (Post-)Chávez Memories: The 1990s and the Black Friday Generation." In *A Post-Neoliberal Era in Latin America?*, edited by Daniel Nehring, Gerardo Gómez Michel, and Magdalena López, 177–94. Bristol: Bristol University Press.

López, Magdalena. 2020. "Los usos del pasado y el campo cultural venezolano: Cinco novelas (2016–2020)." *Akademos* 22, nos. 1/2: 129–54.

Loyola, Juan. 1982. *Intervención urbana en chatarra*. Street art intervention. Isla de Margarita, Venezuela.

Makhortykh, Mykola, and Juan Manuel González Aguilar. 2020. "Memory, Politics and Emotions: Internet Memes and Protests in Venezuela and Ukraine." *Journal of Media and Cultural Studies* 34, no. 3: 342–62.

Marcano, Cristina, and Alberto Barrera Tyszka. 2007. *Hugo Chávez: The Definitive Biography of Venezuela's Controversial President*. New York: Random House.

Marino, Angela. 2018. *Populism and Performance in the Bolivarian Revolution of Venezuela*. Evanston, IL: Northwestern University Press.

Marksman, Herma, and Agustín Blanco Muñoz. 2004. *Habla Herma Marksman: Hugo Chávez me utilizó*, 2nd ed. Caracas: Catedra Pio Tamayo.

Márquez, Laureano. 2018. "Querida Rosinés." *Tal Cual* (Caracas), April 11. https://talcualdigital.com/querida-rosines-por-laureano-marquez/.

Márquez, Vanessa, Carmen Valencia, Ronald Erazo, Gregorio Suárez, Jorge Agudelo Álvarez, and Xiomara Godoy, eds. 2015. *Chávez te amo: El pueblo merideño. Ahora más que nunca soy Chávez*. Mérida, Venezuela: Museo de Ciencia y Tecnología.

Martínez, Juliana. 2020. *Haunting without Ghosts: Spectral Realism in Colombian Literature, Film, and Art*. Austin: University of Texas Press.

Martínez, Tomás Eloy. (1995) 2022. *Santa Evita*. Miami: Penguin Random House Grupo Editorial.

Mauss, Marcel. (1925) 2011. *The Gift: Forms and Functions of Exchange in Archaic Societies*. Translated by Ian Cunnison. Mansfield Centre, CT: Martino Fine Books.

Mbembe, Achille. 2006. "The Banality of Power and the Aesthetics of Vulgarity in the Postcolony." In *The Anthropology of the State: A Reader*, edited by Aradhana Sharma and Akhil Gupta, 381–400. Oxford: Wiley Blackwell.

Mbembe, Achille. 2019. *Necropolitics*. Translated by Steve Corcoran. Durham, NC: Duke University Press.

McCarthy, Michael. 2017. "Venezuela's Crisis: Beyond Economic Explanations: An Interview with Michael McCarthy." *Georgetown Journal of International Affairs* 18, no. 2: 129–36.

Méndez Guédez, Juan Carlos. 2014. *Los maletines*. Madrid: Siruela.

Méndez Guédez, Juan Carlos. 2015. *Y recuerda que te espero*. Caracas: Editorial Madera Fina.

"Mensaje del Presidente Chávez de su enfermedad desde Cuba 30-06-11." 2011. YouTube video. Uploaded by Julio Nova, July 1, 2011. https://www.youtube.com/watch?v=orzoI1Zp_5E.

Merleau-Ponty, Maurice. (1968) 2004. "The Intertwining—The Chiasm." In *Maurice Merleau-Ponty: Basic Writings*, edited by Thomas Baldwin, 247–71. London: Routledge.

Michelutti, Lucia. 2017. "'We Are All Chávez': Charisma as an Embodied Experience." *Latin American Perspectives* 44, no. 1: 232–50.

Miller, Daniel. 2010. *Stuff*. Cambridge: Polity Press.

Ministerio del Poder Popular para la Comunicación y la Información. 2011. "Mensaje del Presidente Chávez de su enfermedad desde Cuba 30-06-11." YouTube video, 15:00. Accessed April 11, 2024. https://www.youtube.com/watch?v=orzoI1Zp_5E.

Mitchell, W. J. T. 2005. *What Do Pictures Want? The Lives and Loves of Images*. Chicago: University of Chicago Press.

Montejo, Eugenio. (1976) 1988. "Nostalgia de Bolívar." In *Alfabeto del mundo*, 89–90. Mexico City: Fondo de Cultura Económica.

Morales, Alfredo, Javier Borondo, Juan Carlos Losada González, and Rosa M. Benito. 2015. "Measuring Political Polarization: Twitter Shows the Two Sides of Venezuela." *Chaos: An Interdisciplinary Journal of Nonlinear Science* 25, no. 3: 033114. https://doi.org/10.1063/1.4913758.

Morgan, David. 2018. *Images at Work: The Material Culture of Enchantment*. Oxford: Oxford University Press.

Morsbach, Greg. 2005. "Muñeco de Chávez causa furor." *BBC NEWS*, December 23. http://news.bbc.co.uk/hi/spanish/misc/newsid_4555000/4555970.stm.

Naím, Moisés. 2019. *Dos espías en Caracas*. Barcelona: Ediciones B.

Nakassis, Constantine V. 2013. "Citation and Citationality." *Signs and Society* 1, no. 1: 51–78.

Nancy, Jean-Luc. 2008. *Corpus*. Translated by Richard A. Rand. New York: Fordham University Press.

Navaro-Yashin, Yael. 2002. *Faces of the State: Secularism and Public Life in Turkey*. Princeton, NJ: Princeton University Press.

Navarrete, Rodrigo. 2015. "Los ojos de Chávez." In *Rostros y rastros de un líder: Hugo Chávez—memoria de un pueblo*, 54–75. Caracas: Archivo General de la Nación, Centro Nacional de Historia. Grupo UN.

Naxera, Vladimír, and Petr Krčál. 2024. "Post-Socialist Political Necromancy: Weaponization of Dead Bodies in Czech Culture Wars." *Nationalities Papers* 52, no. 2: 321–36.

Neef, Sonja. 2011. *Imprint and Trace: Handwriting in the Age of Technology*. London: Reaktion Books.

Ngai, Sianne. 2005. *Ugly Feelings*. Cambridge, MA: Harvard University Press.

Norman, Kajsa. 2017. *A Hero's Curse: The Perpetual Liberation of Venezuela*. London: Hurst Publishers.

Noticias Venezuela. 2022. "Chávez y el niño de la galleta." YouTube video, 1:32. Accessed January 30, 2022. https://www.youtube.com/watch?v=BcKEYAulRfo.

NTN24. 2013a. "Experto en animación 3D asegura que las fotografías del presidente Chávez son un montaje." YouTube video, 12:27. Accessed January 30, 2022. https://www.youtube.com/watch?app=desktop&v=r40YKzO-Gkg.

NTN24. 2013b. "Fotógrafo profesional asegura que imagen publicada de Hugo Chávez ha sido 'alterada.'" YouTube video, 7:59. Accessed January 30, 2022. https://www.youtube.com/watch?v=HoTa3RyoDHA.

Nye, David E. 1994. *American Technological Sublime*. Cambridge, MA: MIT Press.

Olalquiaga, Celeste. 1998. *The Artificial Kingdom: On the Kitsch Experience*. Minneapolis: University of Minnesota Press.

Olivares, Francisco. 2020. *Los últimos días de Hugo Chávez: El alucinante encubrimiento de la enfermedad y muerte del líder del socialismo del siglo XXI*. Self-published.

Orwell, George. (1949) 1950. *1984*. New York: Signet Classics.

Oviedo, Tito (@oviedoPSUV). 2021. "Los verdaderos hijos de Chávez, tenemos una cita hoy #15Jul con la revolución y con la democracia; así que nos vemos en Dalla Costa a las 2 de la tarde." Twitter, July 15. https://twitter.com/oviedopsuv/status/1415687872825397248.

Paasonen, Susanna. 2011. *Carnal Resonance: Affect and Online Pornography*. Cambridge, MA: MIT Press.

Pascual Marquina, Cira. 2019. "Cultural Production in Revolutionary Venezuela: A Conversation with Kael Abello." *MR Online* (New York), September 30. https://mronline.org/2019/09/30/cultural-production-in-revolutionary-venezuela-a-conversation-with-kael-abello/.

Paullier, Juan. 2018. "'Hay una guerra mediática, psicológica, casi que de linchamiento en contra de Venezuela': Jorge Rodríguez, ministro de Comunicación." *BBC News*, March 27. https://www.bbc.com/mundo/noticias-america-latina-43544726.

Pedota, Flavio, dir. 2019. *Infección*. Luz Creativa Productions/Desenlace Films, 1 hr., 37 min.

Pérez Daza, Johanna. 2018. "Sobre el fotolibro #Somos #Resilientes." *Prodavinci*, May 8. https://prodavinci.com/sobre-el-fotolibro-somos-resilientes/.

Pérez Schael, María Sol. 1993. *Petróleo, cultura y poder en Venezuela*. Caracas: Monte Ávila Editores.

Pino Iturrieta, Elías. (2003) 2006. *El divino Bolívar*. Caracas: Alfadil Ediciones.

Placer, David. 2015. *Los brujos de Chávez*. Caracas: Sarrapia Ediciones.

Plaza Azuaje, Penélope. 2018. *Culture as Renewable Oil: How Territory, Bureaucratic Power and Culture Coalesce in the Venezuelan Petrostate*. Abingdon, UK: Routledge.

Puyosa, Iria. 2018. "Venezuelan Government Strategies for Information War on Twitter." *SSRN*, September 9. http://dx.doi.org/10.2139/ssrn.3459724.

Puyosa, Iria. 2021. "Asymmetrical Information Warfare in the Venezuelan Contested Media Spaces." In *When Media Succumbs to Rising Authoritarianism: Cautionary Tales from Venezuela's Recent History*, edited by Ezequiel Korin and Paromita Pain, 51–67. Abingdon, UK: Routledge.

Ramírez, Leo. 2014. "Los ojos que te ven." *AFP Focus*, March 10. https://focus.afp.com/los-ojos-que-te-ven.

Ramonet, Ignacio. 2013. *Hugo Chávez: Mi primera vida. Conversaciones con Ignacio Ramonet*. Caracas: Vadell Hermanos Editores.

Rancière, Jacques. (2007) 2009. *The Future of the Image*. Translated by Gregory Elliott. London: Verso.

Recina, Joan Ramon. 2017. *The Ghost in the Constitution: Historical Memory and Denial in Spanish Society*. Liverpool: Liverpool University Press.

Red Ética FNPI. 2013a. "Foto de Chávez caminando en La Habana fue tomada en 2011." *Red Ética* (Cartagena). Accessed April 6, 2019. https://fundaciongabo.org/es/etica-periodistica/etica-de-la-imagen/foto-de-chavez-caminando-en-la-habana-fue-tomada-en-2011.

Red Ética FNPI. 2013b. "Foto de Chávez muerto es falsa." *Red Ética* (Cartagena). Accessed April 6, 2019. https://fundaciongabo.org/es/etica-periodistica/etica-de-la-imagen/foto-de-chavez-muerto-es-falsa.

Rendon, Moises, and Arianna Kohan. 2019. "The Internet: Venezuela's Lifeline." Center for Strategic and International Studies, December 4. https://www.csis.org/analysis/internet-venezuelas-lifeline.

Reuters. 2011. "Discurso presidente venezolano Hugo Chávez sobre salud." *Reuters*, July 1. https://www.reuters.com/article/latinoamerica-venezuela-chavez -discurso-idLTASIE76O0C420110701.

Ribas-Casasayas, Alberto, and Amanda L. Petersen. 2017a. "Introduction: Theories of the Ghost in a Transhispanic Context." In *Espectros: Ghostly Hauntings in Contemporary Transhispanic Narratives*, edited by Alberto Ribas-Casasayas and Amanda L. Petersen, 1–13. Lewisburg, PA: Bucknell University Press.

Ribas-Casasayas, Alberto, and Amanda L. Petersen, eds. 2017b. *Espectros: Ghostly Hauntings in Contemporary Transhispanic Narratives*. Lewisburg, PA: Bucknell University Press.

Richard, Nelly. 2007. *Fracturas de la memoria: Arte y pensamiento crítico*. Buenos Aires: Siglo XXI de España Editores.

Riera, Carme, and Gonzalo Jiménez. 2014. *Las 50 fotografías inolvidables de Hugo Chávez*. Caracas: Últimas Noticias.

Ríos, Alicia. 2013. *Nacionalismos banales: El culto a Bolívar; literatura, cine, arte y política en América latina*. Pittsburgh, PA: Instituto Internacional de Literatura Iberoamericana.

Rísquez, Diego, dir. 1979. *Bolívar, sinfonía tropical*. Producciones Guakamaya, 1 hr., 43 min.

Rísquez, Diego, dir. 1984. *Orinoko, nuevo mundo*. Producciones Guakamaya, 1 hr., 43 min.

Rísquez, Diego, dir. 1988. *Amérika, terra incógnita*. Producciones Guakamaya, 1 hr., 30 min.

Roach, Joseph. 2007. *It*. Ann Arbor: University of Michigan Press.

Romasco Moore, Maria. 2018. *Ghostographs: An Album*. Brookline, MA: Rose Metal Press.

Römer-Pieretti, Max. 2021. "Chávez's Eyes: An Iconic Presence in the Venezuelan Political Communication." In *When Media Succumbs to Rising Authoritarianism: Cautionary Tales from Venezuela's Recent History*, edited by Ezequiel Korin and Paromita Pain, 106–19. Abingdon, UK: Routledge.

Romero García, Jonás, dir. 2009. *FANtasmo*. Vimeo, 30 min. https://vimeo.com /13777745.

Rondón-Rivero, Adriana del Mar. 2014a. *Trenzar una a una nuestras historias*. Denver: La Prensa de Colorado.

Rondón-Rivero, Adriana del Mar. 2014b. "Trenzar una a una nuestras historias: Una acción poética de Adriana Rondón." Vimeo video, 4:23. Accessed July 1, 2022. https://vimeo.com/106403431.

Rondón-Rivero, Adriana del Mar. 2020. "VIDEO COMPLETO 'Trenzando una a una nuestras historias de mujeres migrantes.' Adriana Rondón-Rivero." YouTube video, 39:10. Accessed July 1, 2022. https://www.youtube.com/watch?v =Ruy7ixS4YEg.

Rueda, Manuel. 2013. "Chavez Tattoos Express Love for Socialism and Possible Cult of Personality." *ABC News*, April 12. https://abcnews.go.com/ABC

_Univision/News/chavez-tattoos-express-love-socialism-cult-personality/story?id=18939466.

Salas de Lecuna, Yolanda. 1987. *Bolívar y la historia en la conciencia popular*. Caracas: Instituto de Altos Estudios de América Latina de la Universidad Simón Bolívar.

Sánchez, Rafael. 2006. "Intimate Publicities: Retreating the Theologico-Political in the Chávez Regime?" In *Political Theologies: Public Religions in a Post-Secular World*, edited by Hent de Vries and Lawrence E. Sullivan, 401–26. New York: Fordham University Press.

Sánchez, Rafael. 2016. *Dancing Jacobins: A Venezuelan Genealogy of Latin American Populism*. New York: Fordham University Press.

Sánchez, Rafael. 2019. "Los ojos de Chávez: Post-verdad y populismo en Venezuela." *Theorein: Revista de Ciencias Sociales* 1, no. 4: 189–220.

Santner, Eric. 2011. *The Royal Remains: The People's Two Bodies and the Endgames of Sovereignty*. Chicago: University of Chicago Press.

Sarduy, Severo. 1994. "El estampido de la vacuidad." *Vuelta* 206:36–38.

Schiller, Naomi. 2018. *Channeling the State: Community Media and Popular Politics in Venezuela*. Durham, NC: Duke University Press.

Schneider, Rebecca. 1997. *The Explicit Body in Performance*. London: Routledge.

Schneider, Rebecca. 2011. *Performing Remains: Art and War in Times of Theatrical Reenactment*. Abingdon, UK: Routledge.

Schwartz, Margaret. 2015. *Dead Matter: The Meaning of Iconic Corpses*. Minneapolis: University of Minnesota Press.

Sedgwick, Eve Kosofsky. 2003. *Touching Feeling: Affect, Pedagogy, Performativity*. Durham, NC: Duke University Press.

Semana. 2013. "Descuartizó a su mamá para 'salvar' a Chávez." *Semana* (Bogotá), January 16. https://www.semana.com/descuartizo-su-mama-para-salvar-chavez/329885-3/.

Semana. 2021. "'Yo te creo': La era del #MeToo llegó a Venezuela." *Semana* (Bogotá), May 8. https://www.semana.com/mundo/articulo/yo-te-creo-la-era-del-metoo-llego-a-venezuela/202100/.

Shifman, Limor. 2014. *Memes in Digital Culture*. Cambridge, MA: MIT Press.

Sibilia, Paula. (2005) 2010. *El hombre postorgánico: Cuerpo, subjetividad y tecnologías digitales*. Mexico City: Fondo de Cultura Económica.

Silva-Ferrer, Manuel. 2014. *El cuerpo dócil de la cultura: Poder, cultura y comunicación en la Venezuela de Chávez*. Madrid: Iberoamericana Editorial Vervuert.

Smilde, David. 2021. "From Populist to Socialist to Authoritarian Chavismo: Obstacles and Opportunities for Democratic Change." Latin American Program, Wilson Center, Washington, DC, September. https://www.wilsoncenter.org/sites/default/files/media/uploads/documents/From%20Populist%20to%20Socialist%20to%20Authoritarian%20Chavismo_Obstacles%20and%20Opportunities%20for%20Democratic%20Change.pdf.

Smilde, David, Veronica Zubillaga, and Rebecca Hanson, eds. 2022. *The Paradox of Violence in Venezuela: Revolution, Crime, and Policing during Chavismo.* Pittsburgh, PA: University of Pittsburgh Press.

Smith Rumsey, Abby. 2016. *When We Are No More: How Digital Memory Is Shaping Our Future.* New York: Bloomsbury Press.

Smith, Mark. 2007. *Sensing the Past: Seeing, Hearing, Smelling, Tasting, and Touching in History.* Berkeley: University of California Press.

Sobchack, Vivian. 2004. *Carnal Thoughts: Embodiment and Moving Image Culture.* Berkeley: University of California Press.

Solanas, Fernando, and Octavio Getino, dirs. 1968. *La hora de los hornos.* Grupo Cine Liberación, 4 hr., 20 min.

Sontag, Susan. 2001. *"Illness as Metaphor" and "AIDS and Its Metaphors."* New York: Picador.

Spivak, Gayatri Chakravorty. 2013. "From *Ghostwriting.*" In *The Spectralities Reader: Ghosts and Haunting in Contemporary Cultural Theory,* edited by María del Pilar Blanco and Esther Peeren, 317–34. New York: Bloomsbury Academic.

Stefanoni, Pablo. 2020. "Los dilemas de la oposición venezolana: Entrevista a Luis Vicente León." *Nueva Sociedad* (Buenos Aires), September. https://nuso.org/articulo/venezuela-Maduro-Guaido/.

Stewart, Kathleen. 2007. *Ordinary Affects.* Durham, NC: Duke University Press.

Stewart, Susan. 1993. *On Longing: Narratives of the Miniature, the Gigantic, the Souvenir, the Collection.* Durham, NC: Duke University Press.

Stolk, Raul. 2016. "A Date with Chavela Frías." *Caracas Chronicles,* October 14. https://www.caracaschronicles.com/2016/10/14/date-chavela-frias/.

Straka, Tomás. 2013. "Lamiendo al Libertador." In *Acción y culto,* 6–7. Caracas: La Caja. Exhibition catalog.

Straka, Tomás. 2021. "The Political Life of Statues." *ReVista* 20, no. 3. https://revista.drclas.harvard.edu/the-political-life-of-statues/.

Strauss, David Levi, and Michael Taussig. 2005. "The Magic of the State: An Interview with Michael Taussig. Hierarchy, Stratification, and the Power of Spirit Possession." *Cabinet* 18. https://www.cabinetmagazine.org/issues/18/strauss_taussig.php.

Sturken, Marita. 2007. *Tourists of History: Memory, Kitsch, and Consumerism from Oklahoma City to Ground Zero.* Durham, NC: Duke University Press.

Superchief TV. 2016. "'We Are Violence': Sergio Barrios 'El Hase' Solo Exhibition." Vimeo video, 3:40. Accessed September 19, 2020. https://vimeo.com/159578516.

Taussig, Michael. 1993. *Mimesis and Alterity: A Particular History of the Senses.* New York: Routledge.

Taussig, Michael. 1997. *The Magic of the State.* New York: Routledge.

Taylor, Diana. 1997. *Disappearing Acts: Spectacles of Gender and Nationalism in Argentina's "Dirty War."* Durham, NC: Duke University Press.

Taylor, Diana. 2005. *The Archive and the Repertoire: Performing Cultural Memory in the Americas.* Durham, NC: Duke University Press.

Taylor, Diana. 2016. *Performance*. Durham, NC: Duke University Press.

Taylor, Diana, and Roselyn Costantino, eds. 2003. *Holy Terrors: Latin American Women Perform*. Durham, NC: Duke University Press.

TeBokkel, Nathan. 2017. "Falterity: The Toy as Otherwise than Hero." In *Toy Stories: The Toy as Hero in Literature, Comics and Film*, edited by Tanya Jones, 94–113. Jefferson, NC: McFarland and Company.

Theodore Roosevelt Association. n.d. "The Real Teddy Bear Story." https://theodoreroosevelt.org/content.aspx?page_id=22&club_id=991271&module _id=333084.

Thomas, Pamela Bilo, Emily Saldanha, and Svitlana Volkova. 2021. "Studying Information Recurrence, Gatekeeping, and the Role of Communities during Internet Outages in Venezuela." *Scientific Reports* 11, no. 1: 8137.

Tiniacos, Natasha, and Florencia Alvarado. 2013. "La lucidez es una condena: Entrevista a Deborah Castillo." *Backroom*, December 24. http://backroomcaracas.com/entrevista/la-lucidez-es-una-condena-entrevista-a -deborah-castillo/.

Todo Chávez. 2011. "Intervención del Comandante Presidente Hugo Chávez durante oración ecuménica de sanación y acción de gracias por su salud." Todo Chávez, August 21. www.todochavez.gob.ve/todochavez/520-intervencion -del-comandante-presidente-hugo-chavez-durante-oracion-ecumenica-de -sanacion-y-accion-de-gracias-por-su-salud.

Toothaker, Christopher. 2005. "Incluso opositores compran muñeco de Chávez para Navidad." *Laredo (TX) Morning Times*, November 17. https://www .lmtonline.com/lmtenespanol/article/Incluso-opositores-compran-mu-eco -de-Ch-vez-10343787.php.

Torres, Ana Teresa. 2009. *La herencia de la tribu: Del mito de la Independencia a la Revolución Bolivariana*. Caracas: Editorial Alfa.

Troconis, Irina R. 2022. "Unfinished Business: Visuality, Space, and the State in (Post)Socialist Venezuela." *Comparative Literature Studies* 59, no. 3: 527–48.

Troconis, Irina R. 2023a. "French Kissing the Idol: Erotic Iconoclash and Political Subversion in Deborah Castillo's *The Emancipatory Kiss*." *Journal of Latin American Cultural Studies* 32, no.4: 567–85.

Troconis, Irina R. 2023b. "Leaky, Dead, and Restless: Afterdeath in Contemporary Venezuelan Fiction." *Latin American Literary Review* 50, no. 100: 46–55.

20 Minutos. 2022. "Chávez, convertido en estampa junto al cristo Nazareno." *20 Minutos* (Madrid). Accessed February 25, 2022. https://www.20minutos.es /fotos/actualidad/las-mejores-fotos-de-la-semana-9389/19/.

Univision Noticias. 2013a. "¿Cómo luce Hugo Chávez en su féretro?" YouTube video, 2:32. Accessed June 6, 2022. https://www.youtube.com/watch?v =Me8lLnNTy9Y.

Univision Noticias. 2013b. "Venezuela crea un ministerio 'de la Felicidad.'" Univision Noticias, October 25. https://www.univision.com/noticias/noticias-de -latinoamerica/venezuela-crea-un-ministerio-de-la-felicidad.

Univision Noticias. 2014. "Una foto de una mujer que se parece a Hugo Chávez está causando gran revuelo." YouTube video, 2:27. Accessed January 30, 2021. https://www.youtube.com/watch?v=MTJbCYl1QnY.

Vásquez Lezama, Paula. 2012. "El Caracazo (1989) y la tragedia (1999): Economía moral e instrumentalización política del saqueo en Venezuela." *Cuadernos Unimetanos* 30:5–15.

Vásquez Lezama, Paula. 2019. "Somatic Power in the Bolivarian Revolution: Biopolitics and Sacrifice in the Case of Franklin Brito." In *The Politics of Culture in the Chávez Era*, edited by Lisa Blackmore, Rebecca Jarman, and Penélope Plaza, 94–108. Chichester, UK: Wiley.

Velasco, Alejandro. 2015. *Barrio Rising: Urban Popular Politics and the Making of Modern Venezuela*. Berkeley: University of California Press.

Velasco, Alejandro. 2022. "The Many Faces of Chavismo." NACLA *Report on the Americas* 54, no. 1: 20–73.

Velásquez Urribarrí, Jessica. 2023. "Resemiotisations across Time, Space, Materials and Modes: An Analysis of Political Signage in Venezuela." *Social Semiotics* 33, no. 1: 25–44.

Verdery, Katherine. 1999. *The Political Lives of Dead Bodies: Reburial and Postsocialist Change*. New York: Columbia University Press.

Vinogradoff, Ludmila. 2015. *El ocaso del comandante*. Caracas: Libros El Nacional.

ViVe. 2011. "Realizan ceremonia ecuménica de sanación por el presidente Chávez." YouTube video, 59:27. Accessed January 30, 2022. https://www.youtube.com/watch?v=vsKwoHI8xfk.

Voz de América. 2014. "Perfumes olor al 'Ché' y a Chávez." Voz de América, September 25. https://www.vozdeamerica.com/a/cuba-perfume-ernesto-hugo/2462779.html.

VTV (Venezolana de Televisión). 2012. "Hugo Chávez: 'Christ!!! Don't Take Me Away Yet.'" YouTube video, 7:21. Accessed June 4, 2024. https://www.youtube.com/watch?v=_NGCctvUKVo.

VTV. 2020. "Entregan 90 viviendas en el urbanismo 'La Gran Villa' en Aragua como parte del hito 3.300.000 de la GMVV." VTV, December 5. https://www.vtv.gob.ve/develan-hito-3-300-000-entrega-90-viviendas-aragua/vtv.gob.ve/develan-hito-3-300-000-entrega-90-viviendas-aragua/.

VTV. 2021a. "Entrevista al caricaturista Omar Cruz por exposición 'Campos de Libertad' en el Museo Cruz Diez." YouTube video, 21:44. Accessed January 30, 2022. https://www.youtube.com/watch?v=KccvoOPH-_Y&t=1077s.

VTV. 2021b. "Venezuela conmemora día de la lealtad y el amor al Comandante Chávez y a la patria." VTV, December 8. https://www.vtv.gob.ve/venezuela-conmemora-dia-lealtad-amor-comandante-chavez/.

VTVN (Ver TV Noticias). 2015. "Este es el comercial chileno que se burla de Maduro y su pajarito." YouTube video, 00:36. Accessed January 30, 2022. https://www.youtube.com/watch?v=P15pC-1s7YM.

Weber, Max. 1968. *On Charisma and Institution Building.* Edited by S. N. Eisenstadt. Chicago: University of Chicago Press.

Weisbrot, Mark, and Jeffrey Sachs. 2019. "Punishing Civilians: US Sanctions on Venezuela." *Challenge* 62, no. 5: 299–321.

Will, David. 1985. "Interview with Diego Rísquez." *Framework: The Journal of Cinema and Media*, nos. 26/27, 122–31.

Williams, Linda. 2008. *Screening Sex.* Durham, NC: Duke University Press.

Wilson Wetter, Yaneira. 2020. "Le logement social au XXIe siècle au Venezuela: l'État après la catastrophe." *Cahiers de la Recherche Architecturale Urbaine et Paysagère* 8. https://journals.openedition.org/craup/4903#text.

Wilson Wetter, Yaneira. 2021. "The Eyes of Chávez: Social Housing as Monument and Image." *ReVista* 20, no. 3. https://revista.drclas.harvard.edu/the-eyes-of -chavez/.

Wolfreys, Julian. 2013. "Preface: On Textual Hauntings." In *The Spectralities Reader: Ghosts and Haunting in Contemporary Cultural Theory*, edited by María del Pilar Blanco and Esther Peeren, 69–74. New York: Bloomsbury Academic.

Yurchak, Alexei. 2015. "Bodies of Lenin: The Hidden Science of Communist Sovereignty." *Representations* 129:116–57.

Zapata, Juan Carlos. 2021. *Chávez a la hora y en la hora de su muerte.* n.p.: Biblioteca Juan Carlos Zapata.

Zerpa, Carlos. 1979a. *Yo soy la patria.* Video performance. Universidad Central de Venezuela, Festival de Caracas, Venezuela.

Zerpa, Carlos. 1979b. "Carlos Zerpa: 'Señora Patria, sea usted bienvenida' (1979)." YouTube video, 5:11. Accessed January 30, 2022. https://www.youtube .com/watch?app=desktop&v=3yoHbhc5Da8&embeds_referring_euri =https%3A%2F%2Fcarloszerpa.blogspot.com%2F&feature=emb_imp_woyt.

INDEX

Page numbers followed by *f* refer to figures.

Chávez's signature, 16, 36, 40, 87, 124, 158,
160–61, 165, 221; on buildings, 20, 21f,
41, 125f, 129, 156, 161–63, 166, 169, 174;
intimacy and, 159; tattoos of, 41, 74–75,
156–57, 167–69, 171, 276n31. *See also*
Gran Misión Vivienda Venezuela

Chávez's specter, 4–6, 19–20, 24, 33–35,
37, 155, 220, 270n18; affective excess
and, 28; Chávez's eyes and, 116; death
and, 76; as hologram, 2, 4, 184, 188; as
meme, 193

Chávez-themed memorabilia, 36, 110,
122–24, 189, 194, 271n25

Chávez-themed objects, 16, 69, 122, 135–36,
138–39, 201

Chávez-themed toys, 16, 178, 202, 205, 209,
292n24. *See also* Chavecito; DIY Chávez

chavismo, 6, 62, 101, 116, 164, 179, 182,
267n3, 279n12, 289n10

chavistas, 14, 20, 31, 34–35, 50, 58, 63, 86, 256;
Chavecito and, 204; Chávez's eyes and,
109, 111, 113, 116; TC Chavez Pro and, 167

Chile, 24, 136

Ciccariello-Maher, George, 80, 194, 268n6,
277n5

citation, 126–27, 170, 284n4, 288n34

collection, 37, 123, 124f, 134, 141–42, 143f,
145–46, 148–55, 201; acts of, 41, 130, 141

Comando Carabobo, 95, 280n16

Coronil, Fernando, 79–80, 84, 87, 156, 177,
221; "Magical History," 85, 269n12,
277n5; *The Magical State*, 53–54, 56,
267n4, 269n13

corpse, 16, 58, 75, 224–28, 242, 251–53;
Chávez's, 64, 66, 105, 192, 198; materiality of, 241, 254; Perón's, 64–65

The Creation of Adam (Michelangelo), 87, 89

Cruz, Omar, 41, 133–35, 145, 285n14.
See also Chávez phone cards

Cuartel de la Montaña, 34, 66–71, 72f, 74,
111, 117, 276n29

Cuba, 96, 183, 219, 272n3, 275n24, 280n19;
government of, 285n13

cultural studies, 5, 15, 37

death, 7, 16, 18, 23, 44–46, 62–63, 70, 75,
142, 146, 155, 172, 198, 225–27; Bolívar's,
91, 196; in Castillo's work, 241–42, 253;

in Chávez's rhetoric, 273n8; children
and, 216; cult of, 292n2; materiality of,
225, 241; as obsolete, 186; Sarduy's, 90;
toys and, 205–6, 209. *See also* Chávez's
death

Debord, Guy, 79, 81

democracy, 25, 278n11

Derrida, Jacques, 4, 72, 105, 127, 129, 173,
281n27; signature and, 158, 161, 163,
168; specters and, 6, 18–19, 89, 102–3,
287n29; *Specters of Marx*, 19, 130.
See also citation; haunting; mourning;
spectral gaze; spectrality

dictatorships, 3, 24, 79, 156

Didi-Huberman, Georges, 242, 261, 294n1

digital media, 193–94, 198

DIY Chávez, 199–202, 210–11, 213, 216, 291n20

Dominican Republic, 51, 274n13

doubles, 126, 189; Chávez's, 41, 178, 188–94,
198, 215. *See also* Bazán, Alí

doubling, 22, 27, 71, 126, 181, 193, 197–98,
207, 271n25; Bazán and, 191; of the I, 166

Doyle, Jennifer, 224, 233, 236

Duno-Gottberg, Luis, 48–49, 53, 59, 268n7

Ejército Comunicacional de Liberación,
110, 282n31

El Caracazo, 83, 278–79n11, 291n19

elections, 58, 96, 102; democratic, 25, 219;
local, 196; parliamentary, 105; presidential, 27, 40, 46, 60, 76, 111, 145, 183,
217, 270n21, 271n24, 285n16

Elkins, James, 38, 95–96, 102, 105, 115, 281n26

erasure, 218–19, 233, 249, 258; social, 23

excess, 8, 41, 52, 125, 228; affective, 27–28,
30; bodily, 53, 246–47; Chávez and,
141; of Chávez's eyes, 98; of Chávez's
imagery, 88; of Chávez's political
performance, 55–56; haunting and,
130; mimetic, 13, 189; theatrical, 233

Facebook, 20, 30, 35, 178–80, 182, 291n21

Faddoul brothers, 48–49

family, the, 99–100, 128, 131–33, 141, 145,
147–51

FANtasmo (Romero García), 41, 78, 80,
82–93, 119, 128, 130, 210, 276n1, 279n13,
280n22

figurines, 110, 203–4, 210, 293n5; Bolívar, 244–45; Chávez, 22, 49, 80, 140*f*, 203*f*, 213

Flores, Cilia, 10, 176, 180

Foucault, Michel, 103–4, 106, 211, 281n23

futurity, 42, 140, 186, 212, 215, 226, 261; child-oriented, 90; of hope, 69

García Márquez, Gabriel, 86, 91

gaze, 4, 18–19, 47, 50, 78, 95–97, 105, 109, 115, 146, 177, 212, 282n28, 283n35; Bolívar's spectral, 240; Chávez's, 99–100, 102, 104, 112–13, 119, 122, 280n15; Chávez's spectral, 108, 113; of divine transcendence, 281n25; object of, 245; of the specter, 19, 23–24, 42, 103, 120, 150, 223, 229; of the state, 215; surveilling, 19, 23, 120, 149–50. *See also* spectral gaze

ghost h(a)unting, 5–6, 35–40, 128

ghost hunting, 33–35

ghostly, the, 3, 270n20

ghosts, 3–5, 12, 18, 23–24, 220; belief in, 3, 39; living with, 130, 173, 224; of the Spanish Civil War, 270n20

Gómez, Juan Vicente, 79, 156, 274n20

Gordon, Avery, 6, 23, 39, 91–92, 220, 224

graffiti, 23, 37, 48, 111, 115; Bolívar and, 244; Chávez and, 25, 35, 49, 80–81, 84–85, 94, 144, 147, 230, 280n21; of Chávez's eyes, 36, 110, 116–17, 271n24; of Chávez's signature, 164–65; culture, 112; Trinchera Creativa and, 284n6

Gran Misión Vivienda Venezuela (GMVV), 20, 41, 96, 124, 128–29, 155–56, 165–66, 280n17; buildings, 158, 163, 171, 287n25; constructions, 161

Gratch, Lyndsay Michalik, 192–93

Guaicaipuro, 8, 26, 234

Guaidó, Juan, 25, 196–97, 219, 221, 262, 270n21, 292n1

Guerrero, Javier, 48–49, 60, 291n20

Guevara, Ernesto "Che," 111, 134, 139, 150, 219, 287n32; eyes of, 99, 280n19

Guzmán Blanco, Antonio, 235, 289n6

habits, 17, 30, 106, 165

habituation, 41, 130

habitus, 30, 107

handwriting, 127, 158–60; Chávez's, 41, 126–27, 129–30, 166–67, 171. *See also* signature; TC Chavez Pro

Harris, Jonathan Gil, 21, 270n19

Harrison, Robert Pogue, 75, 225–28, 251, 254

haunting, 6–7, 11, 21–22, 33–35, 37, 39–40, 91, 121, 130, 220, 222, 251, 253, 270n19; Bolívar's, 250; Chávez's, 4, 17, 35, 90, 165, 193, 200, 220; Chávez's hologram and, 2–4; Chávez's pre-posthumous, 41, 81, 93; Chávez's posthumous, 272n2; social media and, 31; state and, 41, 129

Hernández, José Gregorio, 175, 288n2

Hirsch, Marianne, 38, 146–50

holograms, 2, 12, 22, 184–86, 215–16. *See also* Chávez's hologram

Huyssen, Andreas, 136

ideology, 30, 51, 63, 133, 137, 149, 172, 211, 255; Chávez's, 48, 179; interpellation and, 282n28; of modern family, 147

illness, 44, 48, 75, 273n7; Chávez's, 27, 44–45, 47, 49–51, 53, 59, 62–63, 75–76, 81, 90, 150, 183

imaginal, the, 88, 119

imagination, 16, 19, 34, 62, 109, 157, 178, 192, 221–22, 229; acts of, 36, 88, 90, 177–78, 219, 224, 259; acts of, 219, 224, 259; afterlife and, 65, 225; in Castillo's work, 257; Chávez dolls and, 207; Chávez's cancer and, 76; Chávez's spectral afterlife and, 37; childhood and, 208; children and, 216; collective, 235; crisis of, 120; desire and, 215; DIY Chávez and, 210, 212; emotion and, 279n13; haunting and, 220; holograms and, 186; memory and, 148, 174, 215; obligation and, 201; political, 5–6, 38, 42, 77, 82, 223, 289n7; spaces of, 265; spectral intimacy and, 41; spectral remains and, 23; the state and, 5, 81; toys and, 213–14, 292n24; whisper and, 200

imperialism, 150, 280n19

inhabitation, 41, 130

Instagram, 20, 30, 111, 291n21

interpellation, 111, 126, 246, 252, 282n28; affective, 100; multisensory, 80

ination and, 148, 174, 215; markets, 136, 140, 285n19; market and, 130, 135–36; narratives, 36, 41, 81, 101, 136, 141, 148, 219, 222–23; national, 182, 209, 253; pain and, 74–75; performance and, 38, 224; politics and, 34; politics of, 218, 294n3; practices, 12, 22, 36, 148, 219, 222–23, 246; quilts, 144; residential buildings as sites of, 163; of Ron, 283n3; studies, 5, 37; toys and, 211

Méndez Guédez, Juan Carlos, 113, 115, 283n35

Mercado, Walter, 49, 59

Merleau-Ponty, Maurice, 47, 115

Mexico, 24, 129, 136

Michelutti, Lucia, 26, 57, 281n24, 284n5

Miller, Daniel, 38, 195

mimesis, 22, 41, 191, 208, 240, 271n25; necromantic, 126; sensuous, 197, 244

miniaturization, 41, 130, 142, 207, 286n21

Misión Milagro, 133, 285n13

Misión Ribas, 188, 290n14

Mitchell, W. J. T., 95, 98, 119, 200, 281n28, 290n17

modernity, 55, 85, 274n17, 294n3; spectacular, 79, 277n22

monumentality, 80, 156, 172, 221, 290n11

mourning, 25, 40, 45, 64–65, 72, 74–76, 140, 222, 226, 230

murals, 284n6; Bolívar in, 13, 244, 280n21; Chávez in, 25, 84, 111, 202, 280n21; Chávez's eyes in, 100, 110, 117

Museo Bolivariano, 34, 244–45, 271n24

Navarrete, Rodrigo, 95, 99–101, 111, 280n21, 281n27

necromancy, 5–6, 15–17, 269n14

Neef, Sonja, 158–60, 287n29

new materialism, 37–38

Ngai, Sianne, 258–59

Nietzsche, Friedrich, 74, 272n2

nostalgia, 28, 129, 174, 192, 219, 258–59; childhood, 204; in contemporary Venezuelan fiction, 293n9; restorative, 29

Nye, David, 185, 290n12

oil, 15, 53–54, 86, 138, 177, 223, 263, 285n16; boom, 234; dependency, 263, 294n5;

economy, 137, 278n11; industry, 79; magical state and, 269n13; metaphors and, 274n16; prices, 135–36, 210; production, 267n2; refineries, 274n13, 278n7; reserves, 54, 156; spectacles funded by, 55, 80. See also Petróleos de Venezuela (PDVSA)

Olalquiaga, Celeste, 69, 285n19

Olavarría, Juan José, 234–35

Olivares, Francisco, 44–45, 272n3

opositores, 14, 31, 34–35, 50, 86, 167, 204, 256

Orwell, George, 19, 98

Paasonen, Susanna, 39, 247, 252, 255

Panteón Nacional, 2, 34, 66, 117, 184, 187, 198–99, 202; remodeling of, 276n28

Paz Dominicana, 51, 273n13

Pérez, Carlos Andrés, 79, 83, 156, 268n11, 278n11; coup against, 14, 44, 56, 127, 167, 170, 275n21, 283n4

Pérez, Óscar Alberto, 113, 115

Pérez Delgado, Pedro. See Maisanta

Pérez Jiménez, Marcos, 79, 156, 274n17, 277n3, 278n11

Pérez Pirela, Miguel, 231–33, 253, 293n1

performance, 16, 37–38, 42, 53, 192–93, 208, 213, 220, 234–36, 240, 243, 258, 295n7; of Chávez's doubles, 189–91, 194–95, 215; of family, 147; of remains, 198; studies, 5, 15, 37, 192. See also Bazán, Alí; Castillo, Deborah; Taylor, Diana

Perón, Eva, 64–65, 219

Peru, 24, 136

Petersen, Amanda L., 24, 270n20

Petróleos de Venezuela (PDVSA), 155, 271n23, 285n16

photography, 33, 146–47, 149, 234, 285n16

Pino Iturrieta, Elías, 6, 56–57, 137, 243, 274n19, 284n4

Placer, David, 44–45, 51, 57–59

plagiarism, 126–27, 170

playfulness, 41, 178, 192–93, 198, 204, 214, 216, 292n24

Plaza Lina Ron, 109, 122, 283n3

poetry, 32, 115

polarization, 29, 50, 92, 256, 279n12; political, 15, 48, 222, 259

magical, 6, 15, 53–54, 56, 79–80, 84–85, 156, 182, 269n13; oil and, 53–54, 79; people and, 87, 100, 179, 220–21, 289n7; personalization of, 277n5; popular movements and, 80–81; popular organizations and, 109; public and, 129; public space of, 55; rituals and, 101, 281n23; space and, 172–73; Venezuelan, 53–55, 109, 136, 182, 220, 267n4

stately, the, 20, 128, 164

state power, 6, 178, 215, 220, 281n23

Stewart, Kathleen, 4, 38, 171, 260, 266, 271n27

Stewart, Susan, 127–28, 141, 144, 151, 157, 205–7, 291n20

Sturken, Marita, 209, 292n24

sublime, the, 53, 185; technological, 185, 290n12

surveillance, 19, 130, 251; Chávez's eyes and, 101–4, 113; state, 286n23

tattooing, 158, 168–69. *See also* Chávez's signature: tattoos of

Taussig, Michael, 6, 12–15, 53–55, 63, 69, 97, 177, 187; *The Magic of the State*, 8, 13–14, 33, 53–54, 183, 267n4; *Mimesis and Alterity*, 191

Taylor, Diana, 17, 37–38, 190, 271n25, 293n4

TC Chavez Pro, 41, 126–27, 129, 166–67, 170–71, 173–74, 176, 284n6

technology, 11, 32, 127, 185–86, 247; digital, 88, 186; hologram, 2; of the self, 170

texture, 241, 247–50

time, 4, 11, 23–24, 29, 32–33, 62, 75, 83, 90, 133, 170, 174, 186–87, 206–7, 209; body and, 228; *cadenas* and, 277n6; Chávez's voice as unit of, 88; collection and, 141–42, 153; digital methods and contexts and, 192; in the erotic act, 233; habits and, 165; historical, 206; history and, 232; horizons of, 136; limits of, 111; linear, 186, 220; monopoly over, 102; out of joint, 270n19; physical properties and, 249; texture and, 248

Torres, Ana Teresa, 6, 10–11, 56, 244, 284n4, 292n2

Torres, Elizabeth, 70–71, 152

toys, 20, 22, 35, 40, 199, 204–9, 213–16, 221, 291nn22–23; DIY, 211. *See also* Chávez-themed toys

trauma, 33, 39, 197

Trinchera Creativa, 41, 110, 126, 166, 284n6. *See also* TC Chavez Pro

Trump, Donald, 77, 262

T-shirts, 22, 49, 140, 195; Chávez on, 139; Chávez's eyes on, 14, 20, 35, 95, 100, 102, 110, 194; red, 35, 50, 95, 100, 102, 230

Twitter, 2–3, 7, 59, 133, 180, 182–83, 267n1, 292n21; censorship and, 286n23; Chávez's account, 31, 61, 96, 287n28

Vásquez Lezama, Paula, 53, 59, 274n15, 279n11

Velasco, Alejandro, 179, 267n3, 268n6, 289n7, 289n10

Velásquez Urribarrí, Jessica, 111–12, 280n22

Venezuelan flag, 43, 50, 110, 131, 134, 152, 176, 284n8

Venezuelan people, the, 7–8, 35, 76, 82, 96, 100, 112, 183, 204, 265, 283n4; collective consciousness of, 81; needs of, 32; *nosotros* of, 122

Verdery, Katherine, 75, 240–41, 269n14

Villegas, Ernesto, 2–3, 183–84, 188

Vinogradoff, Ludmila, 44, 61, 284n12

violence, 48, 82, 112, 117, 157, 219, 267n2, 283n34, 291n19; Chávez's spectral gaze and, 119; drug-related, 24; of Maduro's regime, 111; state, 5, 12, 23, 136, 178, 215, 235

Virgin Mary, 71, 134

Volpe, Marcelo, 166–67, 171. *See also* TC Chavez Pro

VTV, 183–84

vulnerability, 39–40, 179, 224

WhatsApp, 20, 30–31, 35, 182, 197, 291n19

Wilson Wetter, Yaneira, 165, 280n17, 287n25, 287n30

Wolfreys, Julian, 18, 24

YouTube, 51, 66, 180; videos, 31, 61, 178, 275n25

Zamora, Ezequiel, 26, 203, 212–13, 234

Zapata, Juan Carlos, 44, 116, 272n3, 283n36

Zerpa, Carlos, 265, 293n3

www.ingramcontent.com/pod-product-compliance
Lightning Source LLC
Chambersburg PA
CBHW032343280326
41935CB00008B/428